Voices from the Peninsula

Eyewitness Accounts by Soldiers of
Wellington's Army, 1808–1814

Edited by Ian Fletcher

Greenhill Books, London
Stackpole Books, Pennsylvania

Greenhill Books

Voices from the Peninsula
first published 2001 by Greenhill Books, Lionel Leventhal Limited,
Park House, 1 Russell Gardens, London NW11 9NN
and
Stackpole Books, 5067 Ritter Road, Mechanicsburg, PA 17055, USA

British Library Cataloguing in Publication Data
Voices from the Peninsula : eyewitness accounts by soldiers of
Wellington's army, 1808–1814
1. Great Britain, Army - History - Peninsular War, 1807–1814
2. Peninsular War, 1807–1814 - Campaigns
3. Peninsular War, 1807–1814 - Personal narratives,
British I. Fletcher, Ian, 1957–
940.2'7

ISBN 1-85367-459-1.

Library of Congress Cataloging-in-Publication Data available

Designed and Edited by Madeleine Wood
Printed and bound in Great Britain by Creative Print and Design
(Wales),
Ebbw Vale

CONTENTS

LIST OF ILLUSTRATIONS

1. Guns of the Royal Horse Artillery.
2. The 1st Foot Guards embark at Ramsgate, 1808.
3. Piper George Clark at the Battle of Vimeiro, 1808.
4. Sir John Moore's army during the retreat of Corunna, 1809.
5. The 43rd Light Infantry during the retreat to Corunna, 1809.
6. The action at Sahagun, 1808.
7. Sir John Moore is carried mortally wounded from the battlefield of Corunna, 1809.
8. Robert Dalrymple, of the 3rd Foot Guards, at the Battle of Talavera, July 1809.
9. The 9th (East Norfolk) Regiment line up for inspection in the Peninsula.
10. Robert Craufurd's Light Division in action at the Battle of Busaco, 1810.
11. Norman Ramsey's guns in action at Fuentes de Oñoro, 1811.
12. The Battle of Albuera, 1811.
13. British infantry from Hoghton's and Abercrombie's brigades at Albuera, 1811.
14. The storm of Badajoz, 1812.
15. The classic image of the storming of Badajoz by Caton Woodville, 1812.
16. British infantry of Pakenham's 3rd Division at the Battle of Salamanca, 1812.
17. Charge of the 12th Light Dragoons at Salamanca, 1812.
18. King Joseph's coach is captured by the 18th Hussars at Vittoria, 1813.
19. British hussars at Vittoria on June 1813.
20. British troops halt on the roadside in the Peninsula.
21. Lieutenant Maguire, of the 4th (King's Own), at San Sebastian, 1813.
22. British infantry trying to storm the beaches of San Sebastian, 1813.
23. British guns at the siege of San Sebastian, 1813.
24. British troops cross the Bidassoa River, 1813.
25. Another view of the crossing of the Bidassoa, 1813.
26. The assault on the Calvinet Ridge during the Battle of Toulouse, 1814.
27. The sortie from Bayonne, 1814.

Maps

INTRODUCTION

The Spanish call it, 'la Guerra de Independencia', or War of Independence. The French call it, 'la Guerre d'Espagne', the War in Spain. In Britain, the war that was fought in Spain, Portugal and southern France between 1807 and 1814 is called the Peninsular War. Whatever one chooses to call it the war remains one of the most successful campaigns in the history of the British Army. Fought between the armies of France on one side and the Allied armies of Britain, Portugal and Spain on the other, it proved to be Britain's greatest military contribution to the downfall of Napoleon Bonaparte. Britain, of course, did not enter the fray until 1808 but by 1814 its army had fought its way from the Lisbon to Toulouse, where the war ended in April of that year.

There are, of course, no living survivors of the Peninsular War. Old soldiers from World War II and post-1945 conflicts are alive today, as are a dwindling band of men from the Great War of 1914–18, and it is from these old warriors that we continue to receive first-hand accounts of the fighting that took place, accounts that help lift the fog of war. Historians of more distant conflicts have no such luxury. Instead, they are forced to rely upon the published and unpublished letters and diaries of the participants, of official documents and other archival sources. The Peninsular War is no different, for no one alive today can really know what it was like to fight under Wellington in the Peninsula, and thus we are forced to turn to the men themselves, and their letters and diaries.

This book takes us back to August 1808, when the British Army first set foot on Portuguese soil. It was from here that they began a march that was to end hundreds of miles away in southern France. We will follow this march, stopping every now and then to listen to the men who fought under Wellington. We hear how they stormed mighty fortresses and won great victories, we hear of their hardships, of the retreats, and of the mile after endless mile that they marched back and forth across the Iberian Peninsula until they finally drove the French over the

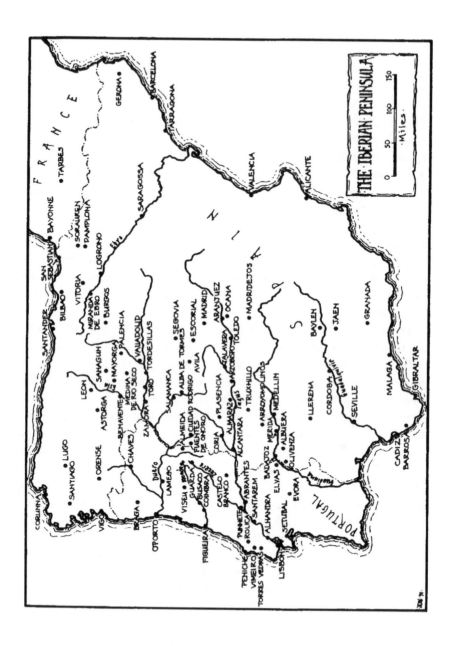

Pyrenees and back into France. We then hear about the final push for victory that came at Toulouse on 10 April 1814. We also hear about the infamous sortie from Bayonne, executed by the French four days after Toulouse, a needless sortie that resulted in over 1,500 French and Allied casualties.

The Peninsular War was not only a very successful campaign for the British Army but it was one that prompted a great flood of memoirs, written by Wellington's men. This was due to a combination of an increase in literacy amongst British soldiers coupled with the fact that after years of under-achievement they finally had something worth writing about. In fact, accounts of the war began to appear almost as soon as the war had begun. The Corunna campaign, with its tragic ending, naturally inspired more accounts, whilst Wellesley's return to Portugal in 1809 similarly prompted an increase. Accounts appeared regularly throughout the war and continued after it had ended. But it was, perhaps, the appearance in 1828 of the first volume of William Napier's *A History of the War in the Peninsula*, that really opened the floodgates. Napier, himself a veteran, proved a master with the pen and his dramatic descriptions of the battles and sieges captured the imagination not only of the British public but of veterans also. It has since become one of the great masterpieces of English literature. The 6-volume work inspired scores of other veterans to put pen to paper in order to recount the war as they saw it. Some of these accounts were, sadly, simply rehashes of Napier, whilst others drew heavily from his history. But there were many more accounts, written by veterans, which provided a hungry readership with gripping accounts of what happened between 1808 and 1814. Many of these remain equally vivid today, whilst others are merely rare and highly collectable, their contents being mundane and often dry.

Eye-witness accounts of the war are still published today, having lain undiscovered in family vaults or in dusty archives since they were deposited there by their authors. All of these tend to add to our knowledge of the Peninsular War, for no matter how boring they may seem there will always be one small phrase or sentence that unlocks a hitherto unknown secret. Some of the correspondents in this book are well known to students of the Peninsular War, whilst others remain relatively obscure. But all have been chosen with care in order to bring to life the great events that took place in the Peninsula. We ourselves will never really understand what it was like to fight beneath the broiling

Spanish sun, to endure the miseries of the Corunna and Burgos retreats, or to face the volcano at Badajoz. Nor can we ever begin to understand what it was like to share in the great triumphs at Vimeiro, Salamanca, and the Nivelle, or how it felt to have stumbled upon the great treasures found amongst the French baggage after Vittoria. We can, however, tap into a rich vein of literature, inspired by the Peninsular War and written by the men who did know. After all, these were the men that lived through it, that fought there and saw their comrades die there. These are the Voices from the Peninsula.

Many thanks go to Tim Edwards, for the loan of items from his extensive collection of Peninsular War literature, and to Brian Ambler, for the loan of other items.

Ian Fletcher, 2001

THE PENINSULAR WAR

Britain's involvement in the Peninsular War began in July 1808 when a small British force, no more than 9,000 men, sailed from Cork to the Iberian Peninsula. The force was commanded by 39-year-old Sir Arthur Wellesley, Under Secretary of State for Ireland. Wellesley, who had gained a fine reputation for himself following his campaigns in India, had been busy during the summer with many things, including a feasibility study on the possibility of resurrecting British ambitions in South America, ambitions that had been so shamefully terminated following John Whitelocke's disastrous attack on Buenos Aires the previous year. The quest for the new El Dorado would have to wait, however, for in June 1808 Wellesley received new orders. Instead he was to sail to Portugal, where events were moving on at a fast pace since the November the previous year when French troops under General Andoche Junot had invaded the country. They had marched through Spain on the pretext of enforcing Napoleon's so-called Continental System, whereby European nations were forbidden to trade with Britain, his hated nation of shopkeepers. Thus denied their valuable trade he hoped to starve and bankrupt them into submission but in order to accomplish this he needed to control every one of Europe's ports. The Portuguese, to their immense credit, refused to comply with Napoleon's wishes and so he despatched Junot with an army of 30,000 men with orders to seize the Portuguese royal family and implement the new system.

Fortunately, the Portuguese royal family eluded Junot's clutches, sailing to Brazil just a day before the French arrived. Nevertheless, Portugal was occupied and with it the last ports trading with Britain were effectively closed. In the meantime, the Spanish people watched with growing anxiety as a steady stream of French troops continued to pour across the Pyrenees and into their country. Naturally, this was put down to the fact that French troops, in order to reach Portugal, had to march through Spain. However, the Spanish people were deceived, for soon afterwards French troops occupied the fortresses of Pamplona and Barcelona, and soon afterwards Joachim Murat rode into Madrid with a French army to occupy the capital. The deception should not have come as a great surprise, however, for Napoleon had already arrested King Carlos IV and his quarrelsome son, Ferdinand, after the two men had gone to meet the French emperor at Bayonne. Thus, not only was the Spanish king being held by the French but the country was effectively under French occupation. Emissaries were despatched to Britain requesting assistance whilst in the meantime insurgencies sprang up all over the country, the most famous resulting in the infamous 'Dos de Mayo', a rising in Madrid on 2 May 1808 that was ruthlessly suppressed by Murat and his men.

Britain was encouraged by these revolts into drawing up plans for an expeditionary force that was to be despatched to Spain, the force being commanded by Sir Arthur Wellesley who sailed from Cork with an army of 9,000 men. The British Army had enjoyed scant success in recent years, with Maida, in July 1806, being the only real high point. Otherwise one had to go back to 1801, and Abercrombie's success in Egypt. Set against this were the recent bitter memories of Buenos Aires in 1806 and 1807 and the disaster at El Hamet, in Egypt, also in 1807. It was, therefore, with some trepidation that the British government despatched Wellesley to Portugal with a preciously small army of 9,000 men, a force that duly sailed on 20 July 1808. In fact, Wellesley's orders had him land at Corunna, in northern Spain, if he thought this a more useful place to land. Once he had arrived at Corunna, Wellesley duly went ashore but found to his dismay that the local Junta required nothing from him in the way of military assistance, but simply wanted gold, arms and ammunition. The Spaniards, proud people, were intent on fighting the French on their own and had little need of help from Wellesley and his men. Therefore, Wellesley returned to his ship, *HMS Crocodile*, and continued on his journey to Portugal, landing on 1 August at Figueiras, at the mouth of the Mondego river, after first having stopped at Oporto to consult with Portuguese authorities.

Wellesley was joined soon after by Brent Spencer who had sailed up from Andalucia with a further 5,000 men. It then became a question of strategy. Wellesley's movements were largely dictated by his lack of either cavalry or wheeled vehicles. With barely 240 cavalry of the 20th Light Dragoons at his disposal, he was unable to consider undertaking any lengthy marches inland, which would take him away from the

British fleet and his supplies. The lack of cavalry was more keenly felt when scores of troopers were taken for reconnaissance and staff duties. There was, in fact, a great deal of work to be done even before Wellesley could consider military operations. Transport had to be procured as well as horses, whilst the Portuguese authorities had to be consulted, for their co-operation was vital if the campaign was to succeed. One of Wellesley's – and later Wellington's – greatest achievements was the administration of his army. Indeed, it is not for nothing that we refer to the British Army in the Peninsula as being Wellington's Army, for he saw to every little detail and nothing seemed to escape his eagle eyes. It was during these early days of the campaign that he began to take the first steps on the road that would see his army turn from a relatively untried and inexperienced one into a superb fighting machine.

Wellesley decided to march south towards Lisbon, keeping contact with the fleet. The French had been busy plundering the countryside and had little trouble dealing with the many bands of guerrillas that sought to upset the French military machine. Perhaps their big mistake was in underestimating the British Army advancing towards them. After all, even the French officers were familiar with the poor fighting record of the British in recent years and not even the latter's recent victory at Maida gave them cause for anything other than optimism. The French had swept aside the Prussians, Austrians and Russians in recent years, and they considered this weak British force to be nothing more than an irritation. It was, therefore, with great optimism that some 4,500 French troops under General Delaborde casually threw themselves across the Lisbon road at Obidos on 12 August 1808.

CHAPTER ONE

ROLIÇA AND VIMEIRO

The first battle of the Peninsular War for the British Army was, by later standards, more of a skirmish. The action, fought on 17 August 1808, saw Wellesley's men flushing some 4,500 French troops, under General Delaborde, from the villages of Roliça and Columbeira where they had been barring the road to Lisbon. Having seen the French drawn up on a low ridge at Roliça, Wellesley divided his force into three, in order to launch an enveloping movement against Delaborde's centre and around his flanks. The wily French commander spotted the move long before it was completed and skilfully drew his men back to a much stronger position along the top of some steep hills to the south of Columbeira. Once again, Wellesley employed the pincer movement, but before he could complete it Colonel George Lake, commanding the 29th Regiment, mistook the sounds of skirmishing as the signal for the main attack in the centre to begin and led his men up a gully, straight into the heart of the French position. Lake was unfortunately killed, and his men badly mauled, but the rest of the British infantry stormed forward, driving Delaborde from his position and causing some loss as the French tried to pass through a defile to the rear. Wellesley's victory was achieved with the minimum of fuss, and with fairly light casualties, losing 485 men compared with 600 French killed and wounded.

Sergeant Stephen Morley fought at Roliça with the 5th (Northumberland) Fusiliers. He had previously seen service with the regiment during Whitelocke's disastrous attempt on Buenos Aires in 1807. His regiment had landed amidst heavy surf at the mouth of the river Mondego on 1 August 1808 and, sixteen days later, was taking part in the first action of the war. His memoirs, entitled *Memoirs of a Sergeant of the 5th Regiment of Foot*, were published in Ashford, Kent, in 1842. The book covered Morley's services in South America and the Peninsula. He was taken prisoner during the retreat to Corunna, but managed to escape, and was badly wounded at Salamanca. He was also slightly wounded at Roliça, as he later recalled:

On the 17th, marched, and soon after, heard firing again. The men's spirits were exhilarated and we passed through Obidos, the firing not only continuing, but getting nearer to us, while we, as we quickly marched on, were greeted with "viva les Ingleses!" nor did the young ladies forget to cheer us by waving white handkerchiefs from the windows; refreshments were also offered, but we could not then partake of them.

When we had got about a mile from the town, we saw the enemy, by their fires, posted to great advantage.

We rapidly approached the field of battle, and found a difficulty at first in getting within range. The hills on which the enemy was posted were high, and too perpendicular, to attempt a direct ascent.

Our staff officers, however, discovered certain chasms or openings, made, it should seem, by the rain, up which we were led. As soon as we began our ascent, Colonel McKenzie who was riding on a noble grey, dismounted, turned the animal adrift, and sword in hand, conducted us onwards until we gained the summit of the first hill; the enemy playing upon us all the time. Having gained the crest, we rushed on them in a charge; whoever opposed us fell by the ball or bayonet. We then proceeded towards another hill, where the enemy had formed again; but as one route lay through vineyards, we were annoyed by a destructive fire. Our Colonel, whom no impediment could intimidate, said, "charge" we did so, but I could go no further, having received a wound in my leg. It turned out be only a flesh wound, but it bled so profusely, that I became faint; a surgeon of the regiment tied it up, and I then followed and arrived just in time to see the enemy in full rout, after one of our regiments had received and repulsed a charge in the most gallant style by a reserved fire, when every shot seemed to tell.

One of the earliest and rarest accounts of Roliça was published in a very early biography of Wellington. In fact, the book, *The Most Noble Marquis of Wellington*, was published just after the retreat from Burgos. The account of Roliça featured here was written by an anonymous officer of the 29th Regiment. He was evidently in the thick of the action, and was actually taken prisoner during Lake's ill-fated attack on the gully:

The enemy occupied the village of Columbeira, situated on the principle road to Lisbon, and of course necessary for our further operations. After some skir-

14

mishing, and under a heavy fire from the surrounding heights, we drove the French from this point; but their principal position was on the heights of Roleia [sic], which overlook and overtop the village. These were our next objective; and, on comparison, Salisbury Craigs, (near Edinburgh,) will give you the nearest idea of them, with the exception of a few passages leading from the top. Our enterprising antagonist, you may be sure, had not neglected these; and, while climbing up through briars and brushwood, plied us successively with grape and musketry. I commanded the right centre company, the fifth from the right; each scrambled up the best way he could; and, on gaining the summit, I found several officers, and about 60 privates of the 29th, who were in front of me; only one of my own company reached the top with me, the rest following fast. Here we lost that distinguished ornament of his profession, my good friend Colonel Lake, and many other gallant officers, long my companions in the regiment. My poor private, the moment he stepped up, was also knocked down by my side; in the agonies of death, he asked leave to shake hands with me; he was a good soldier, and few knew their duty better. Upon advancing, we were immediately attacked by a French platoon of ninety men, whom we repeatedly repulsed; these were, however, joined by another of the same number, who charged us with the bayonet, with whom we sustained the unequal conflict; but our little band being now considerably advanced in front, and reduced to 25, Major Wray, Captain Ford, and myself, and our brave companions, were under the painful necessity of surrendering. Even this, however, did not satisfy the sanguinary enemy, who seemed bent on bayonetting us all. After many narrow escapes, General Brennier at last came up, and with difficulty put an end to the carnage, and to the distressing scene around the dead and dying. I have been oftener than once engaged with French troops, and my former opinion still remains unchanged; upon any thing like equal terms, they have no chance with the British bayonet; so it would have been the case now.

32 year-old Norbert Landsheit was born in Crefeldt, Germany, and had seen service with the Hompesch Hussars before enlisting in the 20th Light Dragoons. His memoirs appeared under the title *The Hussar*, edited by the Reverend George Gleig, the second edition of which, published in 1844, provides us with the following extract. Landsheit was one of the few cavalrymen serving with Wellesley in the summer of 1808, and although there was little employment for them at Roliça, they were, nevertheless, close enough to witness for themselves the first clash between the two sides, as Landsheit later wrote:

15

We had watched the progress of the battle for some time, without sustaining any injury, except from a single shell, which, bursting over our column, sent a fragment through the backbone of a troop-horse, and killed him on the spot — when a cry arose, 'The cavalry to the front!' and we pushed up a sort of hollowed road towards the top of the ridge before us. Though driven from their first position, the enemy, it appeared, had rallied, and showing a line both of horse and foot, were preparing to renew the fight. Now, our cavalry were altogether incapable of coping with that of the French; and the fact became abundantly manifest, so soon as our leading files gained the brow of the hill — for the slope of a rising ground opposite was covered with them in such numbers, as to render any attempt to charge, on our part, utterly ridiculous. Accordingly, we were directed to form up, file by file, as each emerged from the road — not in two ranks, as is usually done both on parade and in action — but in rank entire. Moreover, we were so placed, that the French officers could not possibly tell what was behind us; and thus made a show which appeared to startle them; for they soon began to change their dispositions, the infantry moving off first, the cavalry following, upon which we likewise broke again into column of threes, and rode slowly after them. But we had no desire to overtake them. They therefore pursued their march unmolested, except by a few discharges of cannon; and we, after seeing them fairly under weigh, halted on the field of battle.

Three days after the action at Roliça, Landsheit was ordered out on patrol to try and find the whereabouts of the approaching enemy force, marching up from Lisbon. His wonderfully descriptive piece conjures up the flavour of those early days in the Peninsula for a British cavalryman.

The patrol, consisting of twelve men and a corporal, besides myself, mounted and took the road as soon as I had received my instructions. These were, to move very slowly to the front, keeping every eye and ear on the alert, till we should reach the Red Chapel — not to engage an enemy's patrol, should we fall in with one — to hasten back to the piquet on the first appearance of danger — and on no account to trust ourselves beyond the limits which General Fane had marked out. Thus instructed, I ordered the men to march; and, as far as silence and an acute observation could go, we obeyed the officer's directions to the letter. Nor, indeed, would it have been easy, on such a night, and when so occupied, to indulge idle or ribald conversation. The moon shone full and bright, millions of stars were abroad, and the silence was so profound, that the very ripple of the stream could be heard as it wound its tortuous way along the base of the hill down the slope of which we were riding...The world seemed asleep; and we reached the Red Chapel, fully assured that no enemy was or could be within many miles of us. At the Red Chapel we halted, quitted our horses, and, holding the bridles over our arms, applied ourselves to the contents of our haversacks and canteens...My men again mounted, and taking every possible precaution, by sending forward a corporal and a file of troopers to feel the way, we pushed on. At the meeting of the roads the advanced file had pulled up, and once more we were all together; when I directed two men to pass to the right, two to the left, and, with the main body under my own command, I kept the centre. We were to meet in the square or open space round which the village was built, and to communicate each to the other the results of our investigations.

Everything was done with the most perfect regularity. My party, having the shortest distance to travel, was the first to reach the village square, though the detachments were not long after us; and we found, on comparing notes, that the same tranquillity had prevailed here which had prevailed elsewhere. Now then, what should we do? I recollected the innkeeper, and thinking it not impossible that he might have acquired more information since General Fane had examined him, I rode to his house, and asked whether all was quiet?

"I am glad you have come," replied the padrone; "for I have some important news to tell you. My young man came home from Lisbon an hour ago, and passed the whole of the French army on its march; and so close are they by this time, that I expect them in the village in less than half an hour." I questioned him very closely as to the degree of dependence that might be placed on his report, and he assured me that there could be no mistake in it; adding his advice that I would return to the English camp without delay, and put the General on his guard. I did not think that it would be prudent to neglect the recommendation, so I stated to my comrades how matters stood, and we evacuated the village.

It was not our policy, however, to return to the camp with a vague rumour. We were inclined to believe the innkeeper, certainly, yet we wished to have his tale confirmed; so I halted the patrol as soon as we regained the Red Chapel, and determined to wait the event. I knew that the advance of the enemy, if it did occur, would be made known to us clearly enough by the clatter of their horses' hoofs when crossing the wooden bridge, by which alone they would enter the village; and being now within my prescribed limits, and having a good half-mile start of all pursuers, the thought of danger never crossed my mind. Accordingly, after placing a couple of vedettes somewhat lower on the slope, in such a situation that they could not be surprised, I directed the remainder to alight, and to keep their ears open. For a while all was still. Not a breeze moved the branches; not a beast or bird uttered a cry; indeed, the only sound distinguishable was the running water, which came upon us most musically. But by and by 'a change came over the spirit of our dream'. Wheels began to rumble; there was a dead heavy noise, like the tread of many feet over a soft soil; and then, the wooden bridge rang again with the iron hoofs of horses. Immediately the vedettes fell back, according to my orders, to report what they had heard, and to learn from us that we had heard it also; and then, after waiting a sufficient time, to leave no doubt upon our minds as to the formidable extent of the column that was moving, we vaulted into our saddles, and returned at a brisk trot towards the piquet.

There was much challenging, of course, as we drew towards the vedettes, and demanding and giving the countersign; for we rode briskly; and whether we came as friends or foes, our people knew that there must be something in the wind.

There was indeed something in the wind, for another French force, under General Andoche Junot, was barring the way to Lisbon. The Battle of Vimeiro, fought four days after Roliça, was a much harder fought contest. The French, under Junot, numbered 13,000, with 24 guns, which was about 4,000 men fewer than Wellesley's own force. Once again, the French barred the way to Lisbon but on this occasion it was the British who found themselves on the defensive as Junot sent his men forward into battle. Wellesley's men were drawn up on two ridges, which lay behind the village of Vimeiro, whilst other British troops occupied the village itself. This lay on some rising ground, which enabled Wellesley to employ for the first time his classic reverse slope position, something which would become a feature of his battles against the French in the Peninsula.

The ensuing battle involved a succession of attacks by Junot's infantry, supported by cavalry and horse artillery, whose dense columnar formation came face to face with the British line for the first time in the Peninsula. The resulting contest was decided by a combination of a dense British skirmishing screen, combined with artillery fire, and, finally, a two-deep line of British infantry who were kept out of sight on the reverse slope until the final moment, at which they were ordered forward, presented arms and opened fire. Only one of the French infantry attacks seriously threatened Wellesley, and even this was defeated with loss to the French.

The 50th Regiment, commanded by Colonel George Townsend Walker, was one of the most famous British regiments in the Peninsula. Nicknamed 'The Dirty Half Hundred' or 'The Black Cuffs', on account of their black facings, the 50th put in one of the most memorable performances by a British regiment at Vimeiro. Barely a year earlier, a young subaltern, John Patterson, had joined the regiment and now found himself in the midst of his first real action, for although he had been present at Roliça it had been a mere skirmish compared with the fighting on 21 August. Twenty-nine years later, Patterson put pen to paper to record his experiences in the British Army, his memoirs being titled *The Adventures of Captain John Patterson*, published in 1837. His book follows his services throughout the entire Peninsular War, and is one of the most enjoyable of Peninsular War memoirs. His description of the Battle of Vimeiro remains one of the best:

At a very early hour, on the morning of the day already mentioned [21 August], some random shots were heard in front of our piquets, which gave us intimation that the French were on the move, and we doubted not that they were about to assist our toilet in the way of brushing; in plain English, it was clear enough that they had it in contemplation to try our metal, and ascertain whether it was a base kind or not. Under these circumstances it was quite natural that we should anticipate their wishes; and measures were accordingly taken to give them a warm welcome.

Very few of us were ever in action before, and as for the smell of gunpowder, all our young hands were perfect griffins in that way. It being our initiatory battle, our minds were under no small degree of excitement. The idea of engaging in deadly strife with the soldiers of Austerlitz and Jena inspired the ambitious hero, escaped from the apron-string, with feelings of emulation well calculated to keep alive the flame of military ardour; and each, screwing his courage to the sticking place, resolved that he would be famed for deeds of arms, and that his name would go down to posterity under an accumulated weight of laurels.

The 43rd, (2nd battalion) 50th, and 95th Rifle Corps were formed into a light brigade, under the command of General (now Sir Henry) Fane, and certainly I never beheld so fine a body of men; the 43rd, in particular, were a most shewy set of fellows, a healthy collection of John Bulls, hot from their own country, and equally hot for a slap at the Frenchmen. The 95th, (now the Rifle Brigade) was commanded by Major Robert Travers, an officer whose bravery, on all occasions, made him worthy of a place in that crack regiment. We were posted on an eminence, to the right of the village; the 50th, being the junior corps, was stationed in the centre, and consequently on the highest part of the hill. From hence, as the day was fine, and the atmosphere quite clear, we had a distinct view of all that was going forward in the front, also a tolerably good prospect in every other direction.

The country was overspread with vineyards, and, the vintage season being at hand, nothing could be more beautiful than the luxuriant foliage. Intermingled with the vines were chestnut and olive trees, while in the parts more distant, were rich and closely planted woods, forming a background in good keeping with the whole of the splendid landscape.

The plot began to thicken about 8 o'clock, when a brisk firing of musketry, among the troops in advance, announced that it was high time to reinforce the piquets, which were commanded by Captain Thomas Snowe, of the 60th Regiment. They were immediately strengthened by the 4th battalion company of that regiment, under Captain Coote. A sharp discharge of small arms was kept up by a cloud of French riflemen, who, gathering round under cover of the vines and cornfields, gave their fire with a degree of activity that certainly did them credit. Our men were at this time exposed in the open field, and scarcely knew from what direction the enemy were coming; but though they were nearly all young soldiers, unaccustomed to gunpowder, they behaved with a degree of steadiness worthy of their corps. Snowe in the meantime, with his party, which had extended to the right, was ordered to close on either flank, to support the centre, when the principal attack was made, and where the enemy, still pressing in, galled us with a peppering that was rapidly thinning the ranks, and made our situation by no means either cool or comfortable. With admirable presence of mind, Coote directed his men to take advantage of every means of cover the place afforded; and, encouraging them by his own example, they kept their ground under a galling and destructive fire, from an enemy whom they were unable to answer or even to see. At this trying moment, while in the act of cheering his little band, and urging them to behave with firmness and courage, a musket-ball struck him in the heart, and reeling back a few paces, he fell, and instantly expired. His fall did not, however, dispirit his followers, on the contrary it excited an indignant feeling, which prompted them to redouble their exertions in order to avenge his death.

Arthur Gethin Coote was a native of the south of Ireland, and had served

20

in the 50th regiment for some years. He was a military looking man, strong, and well built, having dark features, and sharp penetrating eyes. He was somewhat stately in deportment, but withal a daring soldier, steady and collected in the hour of danger.

The command devolving on Lieutenant Mark Rudkin, (Captain Snowe being detached to some woods on the right) he gave orders to retire. The piquets extending right and left immediately fell back, under a shower of bullets, from the enemy's light troops, who continued forcing on in spite of all opposition. We gave them in return the full benefit of our small shot, as we occasionally drew up, covered by the vine hedges and olive trees, that lay within our path; and in this manner, alternately firing and retreating, so as to keep the foe aloof, we gained our situation in the line.

Before twelve o'clock, the contending forces were hard at work. Dark and accumulating masses of the enemy were advancing on every side; for, resolving that this should be a decisive combat, and that he would drive us back by the road on which we came, and perhaps into the sea, Junot brought into the field every man that he could muster. Such being his determination, it is no wonder that he pushed his warriors into our very teeth. They, too, if we might judge from the coolness with which they travelled up to the muzzles of our guns, seemed to think that they had nothing whatever to do, but to cut us into mince-meat, and devour us all by way of an early dinner. To the left of Vimeiro was a chain of lofty hills, extending for a considerable way to the eastward. Upon these the main body of the British force was arrayed, and here the contest was fought with desperation. The enemy, at last, after many a hard struggle to gain the position, was completely routed, leaving a vast number of his killed and wounded on the sides of the precipice, as well as in the hollows and ravines at its base.

The 71st Highland Light Infantry was greatly distinguished on those heights, and, with the other corps of Sir Ronald Ferguson's Brigade, charged the assailants repeatedly from the ground. They were then commanded by Sir Dennis Pack, and fully maintained the high station which they had always held in the military records of their country.

Among their wounded was poor George Clarke, their piper, who was struck by a musket ball, while cheering up his comrades in the charge. Unable to proceed, the intrepid Clarke still continued to play in animated strains the favourite national music, and with a noble spirit remained upon the spot, under a heavy fire, until, having fully accomplished the object of their mission, his regiment came back victorious to the station on the hill.

The 50th regiment, commanded by Colonel George Townsend Walker, stood as firm as a rock, while a strong division under General Laborde continued to advance, at a rapid step, from the deep woods in our front, covered by a legion of tirailleurs, who quickened their pace as they neared our line. Walker now ordered his men to prepare for close attack, and he watched with eagle eye the favourable moment for pouncing on the enemy.

When the latter, in a compact mass, arrived sufficiently up the hill, now bristled with bayonets, the black cuffs poured in a well directed volley upon the dense array. Then, cheering loudly, and led on by its gallant chief, the whole regiment rushed forward to the charge, penetrated the formidable columns, and carried all before it. The confusion into which the panic-struck Frenchmen were thrown it would be difficult to express. No longer able to withstand the British steel, Laborde and his invincibles made a headlong retreat, and never looked behind them till they reached the forest and vineyards to the rear.

As far as the eye could reach over the well planted valley, and across the open country lying beyond the forest, the fugitives were running in wild disorder, their white sheep-skin knapsacks discernible among woods far distant. There were, however, many resolute fellows, who, in retiring, took cover behind the hedgerows, saluting us with parting volleys, which did considerable execution amongst our advancing troops. At length, even this remnant of the vanquished foe, dispersed and broken in piece-meal, betook themselves to flight in every quarter of the field. The ground was thickly strewed with muskets, side arms, bayonets, accoutrements, and well-filled knapsacks, all of which had been hastily flung away as dangerous encumbrances. Several of the packs contained various articles of plunder, including plate in many shapes and forms, which they had robbed from the unfortunate Portuguese. Books of songs, romances, and other commodities of a similar kind, were scattered about in all directions; and many a tender billet-doux lay open to the profane gaze and the laughing comments of the vulgar multitude. It was amusing, after all was over, to see the strange medley of curiosities, that had, doubtless with much pains, been collected by those who lately owned them; and it was with no very nice feelings that a general inspection of the rarities took place, as soon as the defeated army had left the field.

While we were pursuing our opponents, the 20th Light Dragoons, led on by Colonel Taylor, galloped furiously past us, in order to put a finishing stroke to the business, by completing any thing that the infantry might have left undone. The horsemen, unsupported, charging the enemy with impetuosity, and rashly going too far, were involved in a difficulty of which, in their eagerness to overtake the stragglers, they had never thought; for, getting entangled among the trees and vineyards, they could do but little service, and suffered a loss of nearly half their number; their brave commander being also one of those who fell in that desperate onset.

The 43rd regiment was very much cut up, being, while employed in skirmishing, considerably exposed. I noticed at least a subdivision of their men lying killed in a deep gulley or trench, as they fell over each other, from a raking discharge of round or grape shot.

The 50th lost a great proportion of rank and file, which chiefly arose from the fire of the French light troops, while covering their column, and during their retreat. Major Charles Hill was wounded, and Captain A. G. Coote and Lieutenant I. N. Wilson were among the slain.

Upon the bleak surface of the hill, from which the regiment had charged Laborde, we bivouacked that night, and reposed our weary limbs. Although the air was cold, and our situation comfortless, yet, from extreme fatigue, we rested perhaps more soundly than the pampered alderman on his downy couch. A windmill on the summit afforded excellent quarters for the Colonel and his personal staff, while the other officers, less fortunate, crouched together, shivering outside its base.

The 50th took a standard pole and box, which were borne by a sergeant between the colours, as a trophy, during the succeeding campaigns. The French, instead of colours, display a small brass eagle, screwed to a square box of the same metal, both of which are attached to a pole or staff. This eagle is seldom exhibited in the heat of action, the staff being carried as a rallying point, in the same way, and for the same object as our banners.

If the Battle of Vimeiro was notable for the first use of Wellesley's linear tactics, coupled with his use of the reverse slope position, it also saw the first of a series of mishaps to his cavalry. With the French having been repulsed, the 20th Light Dragoons were launched in pursuit, but after cutting down scores of fleeing French infantry they were in turn severely mauled by French cavalry, losing their commanding officer Colonel Taylor. It was an incident that would have a great effect on Wellesley's relationship with his cavalry throughout the war. Once again, Norbert Landsheit takes up the story:

The regiments which occupied the hill near us, seemed, indeed, to be very hard pressed; for the shot came every instant more thick in that quarter; and if they advanced one moment a few paces, the next they fell back again.

Colonel Taylor, who commanded us, repeatedly asked leave to charge, but on each occasion was held back, by the assurance that the proper moment was not yet come; till at last General Fane rode up and exclaimed, "Now, Twentieth! Now we want you. At them, my lads, and let them see what you are made of." Then came the word, "threes about and forward", and with the rapidity of thought we swept round the elbow of the hill, and the battle lay before us.

As we emerged up this slope, we were directed to form in half-squadrons, the 20th in the centre, the Portuguese cavalry on the flanks, and the brief space of time that was necessary to complete the formation enabled me to see over a wide extent of the field. The French were coming on in great force, and with the utmost show of confidence. A brigade of cavalry was in front, followed by a line of infantry, in rear of which again were some heavy columns and guns. On our side there were some infantry who had long and gallantly maintained the hill, but who were so overmatched, that our advance was ordered up for the purpose more effectually served. 'Now, Twentieth! Now!' shouted Sir Arthur, while his staff clapped their hands and gave us a cheer; the sound of which was still in our ears, when we put our horses to their speed. The Portuguese likewise pushed forward, but through the dust which entirely enveloped us, the enemy threw in a fire, which seemed to have the effect of paralysing altogether our handsome allies. Right and left they pulled up, as if by word of command, and we never saw more of them till the battle was over. But we went very differently to work. In an instant we were in the heart of the French cavalry, cutting and hacking, and upsetting men and horses in the most extraordinary manner possible, till they broke and fled in every direction, and then we fell upon the infantry. It was here that our gallant Colonel met his fate. He rode that day a horse, which was so hot that not all his exertions would suffice to control it, and he was carried headlong upon the bayonets of the French infantry, a corporal of whom shot him through the heart. The corporal took, of course, his plunder, including the Colonel's watch, seals, and a ring set with Mrs Taylor's hair, as well as his horse; and though he sold the animal afterwards, he refused to part with the watch and its appendages, even when offered for them, as I have understood, more than their value.

We were entirely ignorant of the fall of our commanding officer, and had the case been otherwise, we were too eager in following up the advantages which we had gained, to regard it at the moment. Though scattered, as always happens, by the shock of a charge, we still kept laying about us, till our white leather breeches, our hands, arms, and swords, were all besmeared with blood. Moreover, as the enemy gave way we continued to advance, amid a cloud of dust so thick, that to see beyond the distance of those immediately about yourself, was impossible. Thus it was till we reached a low fence, through which several gaps had been made by the French to facilitate the movements of their cavalry; and we instantly leapt it. The operation cost some valuable lives, for about twenty or thirty of the French grenadiers had laid themselves on their bellies beneath it, and now received us as well as they could upon their bayonets. Several of our men and horses were stabbed, but of the enemy not a soul survived to speak of his exploit — we literally slew them all — and then, while in pursuit of the horse, rushed into an enclosure, where to a man we had well nigh perished. For the fold in which we were caught was fenced round to a great height, and had but a single aperture — the door of which, the enemy, who hastened to take advantage of our blunder, immediately closed. Then was our situation trying enough, for we could neither escape nor resist; while looking over the wall we beheld that the French had halted, and were returning in something like order to the front.

While we were thus situated, vainly looking for an aperture through which to make a bolt, one of our men, the same Corporal Marshall, of whom I have elsewhere spoken, was maintaining a most unequal combat outside the close, with four French dragoons that beset him together. An active and powerful man himself, he was particularly fortunate in the charger which he bestrode — a noble stallion which did his part in the mêlée, not less effectually than his master. The animal bit, kicked, lashed out with his fore-feet, and wheeled about and about like a piece of machinery, screaming all the time; while the rider, now catching a blow, now parrying a thrust, seemed invulnerable. At last he clove one of the enemy to the teeth, and with a back stroke took another across the face, and sent him forth from his saddle. The other two hung back, and made signs to some of their comrades, but these had no time to help them, for a hearty British cheer sounded above the battle, and the 50th Regiment advanced in line with fixed bayonets. The consequence was, an immediate flight by the enemy, who had calculated on making every man of the 20th prisoners; and our release from a situation, of all others the most annoying to men who, like ourselves, had no taste for laying down their arms. Moreover, to that charge, supported as it was by the simultaneous advance of other portions of the line, the enemy did not venture to show a front. They were beaten on all sides, and retreated in great disorder, leaving the field covered with their dead.

The Battle of Vimeiro was Wellesley's second success of the war. Seven-hundred-and-twenty British troops had been either killed or wounded whereas the French had suffered three times that number including 450 killed. It was also a victory that caused some comment in Paris and throughout the French Army generally. Wellesley, the hitherto relatively unknown British commander, who had achieved his only successes to date in far off India, suddenly became a name to be reckoned with. Indeed, General Maximilien Foy was moved to comment that Wellesley's victory at Vimeiro raised his reputation to that of Marlborough. At the time it was almost certainly an exaggeration, but in a few short years it would indeed become true.

For the time being, however, Wellesley had other matters to concern him. Immediately prior to the battle, General Harry Burrard had arrived to supersede him, and soon after General Hew Dalrymple arrived also. These two gentlemen decided that there was no need for any further action and thus the French were allowed to draw off without being molested further, which it was certainly in Wellesley's power to do. Presently, yet another British general arrived. It was Sir John Moore. With three officers senior to him now with the army in Portugal, Wellesley had little reason to believe that there would be any further useful employment for him. However, one great controversial act was to change all that. It was the infamous Convention of Cintra.

With the French penned in against the Atlantic, with no prospect whatsoever of fighting their way out, they decided to sue for peace. The British held all of the trump cards but Burrard and Dalrymple fumbled the chance to play them correctly and thus, by some skilful dealing, the French were allowed to get away. The agreement allowed for the evacuation by the French of all of the fortresses that they occupied in Portugal as well as leaving the country altogether. The controversies that blew up afterwards concerned the manner of their evacuation, for not only were they to hitch a lift home in the ships of the Royal Navy but they were allowed to take with them all their arms and plunder. When the news reached England the country rose as one in a state of outcry. Politicians were outraged and immediately recalled to England Wellesley, Burrard and Dalrymple to face a court of inquiry.

In the meantime, command of the British Army in Portugal passed into the hands of the more than able Sir John Moore, who was about to embark upon the ill-fated campaign that would forever be associated with his name: Corunna.

CHAPTER TWO

THE CORUNNA CAMPAIGN

With all three signatories of the Convention of Cintra having been recalled to England, the British Army in Portugal was left under the command of Sir John Moore. His force numbered around 30,000 and on 6 October 1808 he received orders from London to march north from Lisbon to join up with a further 10,000 troops who were on their way to Portugal under the command of Sir David Baird. Once united with Baird, Moore was to act in conjunction with the Spaniards who were holding positions on the Ebro river, although the British government had not stipulated how this was to be done. And so in mid-October Moore, having left 10,000 British troops behind to defend Portugal, began his march north towards Salamanca.

As his army marched north, Moore was assured by the Spaniards that all Spain was ready to rise against Napoleon – who had come in person to enforce his brother's authority and drive the British into the sea – provided substantial British help was to be had. Unfortunately, Moore was about to discover what Wellesley himself would throughout the war, that working with their Spanish allies was an extremely difficult business. Promises of supplies and transport frequently failed to materialise, whilst the Spanish commanders themselves had their own thoughts on how the war should be prosecuted. They were certainly in no mood to take orders from English heretics and simply got on with the war regardless of their allies.

The tired and weary British troops began to trundle into Salamanca on 13 November but fifteen days later came the news that Napoleon, at the head of 200,000 troops, had smashed the Spanish armies. Moore, waiting at Salamanca and still not having been joined by Baird, had to decide whether to retreat, which would leave a hopeless situation, or to advance right across Napoleon's lines of communication, his objective being to relieve the pressure on the Spanish capital Madrid, which he still thought lay in Spanish hands. This might force Napoleon to move against him and thus allow the Spaniards to reorganise their revolts against the French. Moore chose this second course and so began his bold march across Napoleon's front. However, unbeknown to him, the capital had already fallen. Napoleon duly moved against the British but the promised Spanish insurgencies either did not occur or were easily suppressed and Moore, in the depths of winter, was forced into a fighting retreat to Corunna, where transports were to assemble to bring away the British army.

The retreat to Corunna conjures up harrowing images of snow, mountains, undisciplined British soldiers and a heroic final action. The retreat was indeed one of great epics in British military action and is one that remains a great punctuation mark in the history of the British campaign in the Peninsula. It was the one great campaign that did not feature Wellington and is one that, for many British people, is the most famous. This early nineteenth century 'Dunkirk' was marked by a series of small rearguard actions and by three very significant cavalry actions at Sahagun, Mayorga and Benavente. Sahagun, in fact, was actually an episode during Moore's advance against Marshal Soult, an advance that was brought abruptly to a halt following the receipt of accurate information as to the exact dispositions and strengths of the French Army. All three cavalry actions, despite being small-scale affairs, demonstrated the superiority of the British cavalry over their French counterparts, and confirmed Henry, Lord Paget's status as the finest cavalry commander in the army. Unfortunately, his showing in the Peninsula was all-too brief, as he eloped with Wellesley's sister-in-law when he returned to England and was thus *persona non grata* with the army when the latter returned to Portugal in April 1809.

The cavalry action at Sahagun took place on 21 December 1808, on a grey, freezing cold morning. Paget's men surprised the numerically superior French force under Debelle close to the town and defeated it after a fine charge, which saw Debelle's men scattered in all directions. One of the officers of the 15th Hussars who had taken part in the action was Captain Alexander Gordon. In 1913 his account of the retreat to Corunna was published under the title *A Cavalry Officer in the Corunna Campaign, 1808–1809*. His account of the action at Sahagun is one of the highlights of the book, with a vivid description of that cold, icy morning of 21 December.

The officers commanding troops and squadrons were summoned to Colonel Grant's quarters at ten o'clock in the evening, when he acquainted us that

28

Lord Paget had directed the regiment to be formed in readiness to march on a particular service precisely at midnight, and that we should probably be engaged with the enemy before daylight.

The Colonel ordered the troops to be assembled as silently as possible at eleven o'clock, and cautioned us to keep the Spaniards in ignorance of the intended march, that they might not have it in their power to give information to the enemy. The regiment was formed at the hour appointed, but owing to the irregular manner in which we had been obliged to take up our quarters, and the bugles not being allowed to sound, several men were left behind whom the non-commissioned officers had not informed of the order to turn out. Lieutenant Buckley, who had joined us in the evening with a number of men and horses that had been left in Galicia, remained in the village to follow with the baggage and ineffectives in the morning.

Whilst we were drawn up at the alarm-post, waiting for the arrival of Lord Paget, a fire broke out in the village, occasioned, probably, by the carelessness of some of our dragoons. The glare of the flames partially illuminated the ground where we stood, and contrasted finely with the dark mass of our column; whilst the melancholy sound of the church bell, which was struck to rouse the sleeping inhabitants, broke the silence of the night, and, combined with the object and probable consequences of our expedition, made the whole scene peculiarly awful and interesting.

Captain Thornhill, of the Seventh, who attended Lord Paget, with ten or twelve orderlies of his regiment, rode beside me during part of the night, and told me the object of our movement was to surprise a body of cavalry and artillery posted in a convent at Sahagun, a large town on the Cea, five leagues from Melgar de Abaxo. I afterwards learnt that General Slade was directed to attack the convent with the Tenth and Horse Artillery, whilst the Fifteenth was to make a circuit and form on the opposite side of the town, in order to intercept their retreat. This plan, however, was rendered abortive by the bad state of the roads and the dilatory proceedings of the Brigadier, who on this occasion is reported to have made a long speech to the troops, which he concluded with the energetic peroration of "Blood and slaughter — march!"

Our march was disagreeable, and even dangerous, owing to the slippery state of the roads; there was seldom an interval of many minutes without two or three horses falling, but fortunately few of their riders were hurt by these falls. The snow was drifted in many places to a considerable depth, and the frost was extremely keen. We left Melgar in the midst of a heavy fall of snow, and when that ceased I observed several vivid flashes of lightning.

We passed through two small towns or villages; in one of these, about two leagues from Sahagun, is a noble castle, which appeared to great advantage "by the pale moonlight". Near this place our advanced guard came upon the enemy's picquet, which they immediately charged; the Frenchmen ran away, and in the pursuit both parties fell into a deep ditch filled with snow. Two of the enemy were killed, and six or eight made prisoners; the remainder escaped and gave the alarm to the troops at Sahagun. Just at this period, when despatch was particularly required, our progress was very much impeded by two long narrow bridges, without parapets, and covered with ice, which we were obliged to cross in single file.

On our arrival at Sahagun we made a detour, to avoid passing through the streets, and discovered the enemy formed in a close column of squadrons near the road to Carrion de los Condes; but, owing to the darkness of the morning and a thin mist, we could neither distinguish the number nor the description of the force opposed to us, further than to ascertain it consisted of cavalry.

Lord Paget immediately ordered us to form open column of divisions and trot, as the French, upon our coming in sight, made a flank movement, apparently with the intention of getting away; but the rapidity of our advance soon convinced them of the futility of such an attempt. They therefore halted, deployed from column of squadrons, and formed a close column of regiments, which, as it is their custom to tell off in three ranks, made their formation six deep. During the time the two corps were moving in a parallel direction, the enemy's flankers, who came within twenty or thirty yards of our column, repeatedly challenged, "Qui vive?" but did not fire, although they received no answer. As soon as the enemy's order of battle was formed, they cheered in a very gallant manner, and immediately began firing. The Fifteenth then halted, wheeled into line, huzzaed, and advanced. The interval betwixt us was perhaps 400 yards, but it was so quickly passed that they had only time to fire a few shots before we came upon them, shouting: "Emsdorff and victory!" The shock was terrible; horses and men were overthrown, and a shriek of terror, intermixed with oaths, groans, and prayers for mercy, issued from the whole extent of their front

Our men, although surprised at the depth of the ranks, pressed forward until they had cut their way quite through the column. In many places the bodies of the fallen formed a complete mound of men and horses, but very few of our people were hurt. Colonel Grant, who led the right centre squadron, and the Adjutant who attended him, were amongst the foremost who penetrated the enemy's mass; they were both wounded — the former slightly on the forehead, the latter severely in the face. It is probable neither of them would have been hurt if our fur caps had been looped with iron like those of the French chasseurs, instead of being stiffened with pasteboard.

It was allowed, by everyone who witnessed the advance of the Fifteenth, that more correct movements, both in column and in line, were never performed at a review; every interval was accurately kept, and the dressing admirably preserved, notwithstanding the disadvantages under which we laboured. The attack was made just before daybreak, when our hands were so benumbed with the intense cold that we could scarcely feel the reins or hold our swords. The ground was laid out in vineyards intersected by deep ditches and covered with snow. Our horses, which had suffered from confinement on shipboard, change of forage, and the fatigues of incessant marches in inclement weather, were not in their usual condition; and, as the commanding officer had neglected to halt the regiment during the march for the purpose of tightening their girths, they had become so slack that when we began to gallop several of the blankets slipped from under the saddles.

The French were well posted, having a ditch in their front, which they expected to check the impetus of our charge; in this, however, they were deceived. Lord Paget misjudged the distance or halted the Fifteenth too soon, by which means our right was considerably outflanked, and we outflanked their's by a squadron's length. It was said afterwards that he intended the left squadron should have remained in reserve to support the charge, but no explicit order to that effect reached us. After the horses had begun to gallop, indeed, the word of command, "Left squadron to support!" was passed from the centre, but so indistinctly that Major Leitch did not feel authorised to act upon it, and at that moment we were so near the enemy that it would have been difficult to restrain either the men or horses.

My post being on the left of the line, I found nothing opposed to my troop, and therefore ordered, "Left shoulders forward!" with the intention of taking the French column in flank; but when we reached the ground they had occupied, we found them broken and flying in all directions, and so intermixed with our hussars that, in the uncertain twilight of a misty morning, it was difficult to distinguish friend from foe. Notwithstanding this there was a smart firing of pistols, and our lads were making good use of their sabres. Upon reaching the spot where the French column had stood, I observed an officer withdrawn from the mêlée. I followed, and, having overtaken him, was in the act of making a cut at him which must have cleft the skull, when I thought I distinguished the features of Lieutenant Hancox; and, as I then remarked that he wore a black fur cap and cloak which, in the dim light of the morning, looked like blue, I was confirmed in the idea that he belonged to our regiment. Under this impression, although his conduct in quitting the field at such a period struck me as very extraordinary, I sloped my sword, and merely exclaiming, "What, Hancox! Is it you? I took you for a Frenchman!" turned my horse and galloped back to the scene of the action. The shock I felt from the idea that I had been on the point of destroying a brother officer instead of an enemy deprived me of all inclination to use my sword except in defence of my own life; and the hostility I had cherished against the French only a few minutes before was converted into pity for them. When I met Hancox after the action, I found that he wore an oilskin cover on his cap, and was not the person I had followed, who, I conclude, was an officer of the *grenadiers à cheval* or *compagne d'élite*, which is attached to each regiment of dragoons in the French service, and doubtless was much astonished at my sudden appearance and abrupt departure. For my own part, I shall always consider it a most fortunate circumstance that I was thus deceived, since I have escaped the feeling of remorse to which I should have been exposed had I taken that man's life.

Many mistakes of the same kind must have occurred in the confusion after the charge. One of our men told me that I had a narrow escape myself, for that during the mêlée he had his sword raised to cut me down, but luckily recognised his officer in time to withhold the stroke.

At this time I witnessed an occurrence which afforded a good deal of amusement to those who were near the place. Hearing the report of a pistol close behind me, I looked round and saw one of the Fifteenth fall. I concluded the man was killed, but was quickly undeceived by a burst of laughter from his comrades, who exclaimed that the awkward fellow had shot his own horse, and many good jokes passed at his expense.

The mêlée lasted about ten minutes, the enemy always endeavouring to gain the Carrion road. The appearance of their heavy dragoons was extremely martial and imposing; they wore brass helmets of the ancient Roman form, and the long black horsehair streaming from their crests as they galloped had a very fine effect.

Having rode together nearly a mile, pell-mell, cutting and slashing at each other, it appeared to me indispensable that order should be re-established, as the men were quite wild and the horses almost blown; therefore; seeing no superior officer near me, I pressed through the throng until I overtook and halted those who were farthest in pursuit. As soon as I had accomplished this object, the bugles sounded the "rally". Whilst we were re-forming our squadrons, the enemy also rallied and continued their flight by different routes. Our left and left centre squadrons were detached in pursuit of the *chasseurs à cheval*, who took the road to Carrion; the other two squadrons followed the dragoons, who retired in the direction of Saldana.

Lord Paget accompanied the left centre squadron, and allowed the body he pursued to escape by sending an officer, with a white handkerchief as a flag of truce, to propose to them to surrender. The French took advantage of the delay this occasioned, and gained so great a start as to render further pursuit hopeless. The left squadron was more successful, and made about seventy prisoners, amongst whom were a Lieutenant-Colonel and three other officers; but we could not prevent the escape of the main body, which although more than double our number, never attempted to face us. Soon after our left squadron was put in motion in pursuit of the *chasseurs à cheval*, Baron Tripp came up to us and said that Lord Paget had sent him to desire the commanding officer to ride forward with a flag of truce and propose to them to surrender. Major Leitch made no answer, but, as if he had misunderstood the order, immediately gave the word of command to "Gallop!" upon which the squadron rushed on, leaving the Aide-de-Camp petrified with astonishment. It was entirely owing to Major Leitch's judicious conduct, in declining to act upon the flag of truce system, that his squadron was enabled to secure so many prisoners.

Whilst we were engaged in the pursuit of this division, my mare fell with me in leaping a very wide ditch, and floundered in a snow-wreath on the farther side; my foot hung in the stirrup, and, being encumbered with my cloak, it was some time before I could extricate myself. The mare in the meantime ran away, leaving me in no very enviable situation.

Whilst I was following the squadron on foot, after having been dismounted by the fall of my horse, I was greatly shocked at witnessing an act of wanton cruelty which it was not in my power to prevent. A man of Griffith's troop rode up to a French dragoon who was lying wounded on the ground, and at his approach raise himself with difficulty to beg for mercy, stripping off his cross-belts at the same time to show that he surrendered. I hallooed to the fellow to spare him, but before I could reach the spot the villain had split the Frenchman's skull with a blow of his sabre, and galloped away. It was fortunate for him that he got out of my reach, for, in the indignation I felt at his conduct, I should certainly have treated him in the same manner. I heard afterwards that the excuse he offered for this dastardly conduct, when twitted by his comrades, was that he did not like "to let the day pass without cutting down a Frenchman, and could not suffer such a favourable opportunity to slip!"

It was also reported that several of the French who were wounded and had received quarter, fired at our men as soon as their backs were turned, and of course paid the forfeit of this treachery with their lives.

After running three or four hundred yards, I met some men of my troop leading captured French horses, from which I selected one to replace my lost charger. Several straggling Frenchmen passed close beside me, whilst I was on foot, without offering me the slightest molestation; they probably took me for one of their own people, or were too intent on providing for their own safety to think of any other object. The animal I selected was a bad goer and very ill-broke; it had belonged to a quartermaster or subaltern officer, and was handsomely caparisoned, but the saddle was far from comfortable, and the stirrups so long that I could scarcely reach them with the point of my toe. This horse was such a headstrong beast that he was near placing me in an awkward predicament. In the act of leading the men I had collected against the squadron of Chasseurs which had escaped from Lord Paget, I leaped over a ditch which lay between the two bodies; and when the attack was counter-manded, I suppose my steed recognised his old companions, as the enemy was then passing at the distance of little more than a hundred yards, and I had the greatest difficulty in forcing him to recross the ditch, and for some time expected to be carried into the midst of the French squadron in spite of all my exertions to the contrary.

When I was remounted, I saw that the squadron was so far advanced I had no chance of overtaking it. I therefore employed myself in collecting the prisoners we had taken, whom I sent to the rear under an escort. They seemed very much terrified, having, as I understood, been taught to expect no quarter would be given them; and when I assured them they had no cause for apprehension of that sort, they kissed my hands, embraced my knees, and committed all manner of extravagancies. Many of these men were Germans and remarkably fine-looking fellows.

I had now collected about thirty hussars — including those who had been sent back with the prisoners, and whose horses had been unable to keep up with the rest — when the Tenth appeared on an eminence near the scene of the action, and were supposed to belong to the enemy. As soon as I noticed this fresh body of cavalry, I looked anxiously round the plain in hopes of discovering a rallying point; but the regiment was so completely scattered in pursuit that I could not perceive a single squadron formed on the field, and our situation appeared so desperate that I considered the only thing that remained for us to do was to sell our lives as dearly as possible. I therefore determined to lead my small division against the body of Chasseurs which had escaped from Lord Paget; but I had scarcely given the word to advance, when his lordship, who as well as every other officer had been deceived by the appearance of the Tenth in a quarter where they were not expected, ordered the "rally" to be sounded, and Colonel Grant, who had just arrived at the spot and approved of my design, said the signal must be immediately obeyed. I was thus reluctantly obliged to abandon the meditated attack, which, from our relative positions, would in all probability have been attended with complete success, as we had an opportunity of charging on the enemy's flank.

I was happy to exchange the French horse for my own mare, which was brought to me soon after the regiment had reassembled, having been found in the custody of some men of the Tenth, but I was not so fortunate as to recover the valise with my baggage, which was strapped to the saddle at the time I lost her.

We learned from the prisoners that their force consisted of the 8th Regiment of Dragoons and a provisional regiment of *chasseurs à cheval*, commanded by General of Brigade, Debelle, whose horses and baggage fell into our hands. It appeared by the returns found in his portfolio that the French had about eight hundred men mounted in the field, whilst we only mustered betwixt three and four hundred, as, independent of various small detachments, above a hundred men and horses were left at Melgar de Abaxo. Although but few of the enemy were killed on the spot, a great proportion of the prisoners were severely wounded, chiefly by the sabre; their total loss exceeded 300 men, for a number of their wounded who, after escaping from the field had been left on the road from inability to proceed, were secured and brought to headquarters by our infantry, who afterwards occupied the villages where they had taken shelter.

Colonel Dud'huit and twelve officers of the 8th Dragoons were taken. This regiment, which was in the front, bore the brunt of the attack, and suffered most severely. Colonel Dugens, three officers, and about a hundred of the Chasseurs, were made prisoners. We understood that the Eighth was a favourite corps; it had served in all the late campaigns, and gained great credit at Marengo, Austerlitz, Jena, Eylau, and Friedland; several of the officers wore the Cross of the Legion of Honour; and several of the sergeants and privates bore honorary badges. The clothing and appointments, both of men and horses, were strong and serviceable; and the brass helmets, in point of utility and martial appearance, might be substituted with advantage in our Service for the cocked hat of the heavy dragoon. The French officers expressed surprise at our temerity in attacking them, and at their own defeat. At first they took us for Spaniards, and expected an easy victory. It is but doing them justice to remark that they received our charge with the most determined firmness, but after their ranks were once broken they made no effort to retrieve the day, but appeared panic-struck, and only intent on making their escape.

Colonel Tashcer, nephew to the Empress Josephine, commanded the Chasseurs, but we could not ascertain whether he was present in the action. The French were better mounted than we had been led to expect from the report of some of our officers who had been on service with the regiment in the campaigns of 1794 and 1799. None of their horses were under fourteen hands and a half, and several were taken into our brigade to replace such as had become unfit for service. They were in pretty good condition, but most of their backs were galled; this was not surprising, as they had only arrived at Sahagun a few days before, having made almost daily marches since the beginning of October, when they left Hanover; and the French dragoons take very little care of their horses.

There was not a single man of the Fifteenth killed in the field; we had about thirty wounded, five or six severely, two of whom died the next day; most of the others were so slightly hurt that they returned to their duty within a week. I expected the French would have displayed more skill in the use of the sabre than our men, but the fact proved quite the reverse, for notwithstanding their swords were considerably longer, they had no chance with us. Our hussars obtained a good deal of plunder, as the prisoners were well supplied with many trinkets and ingots of silver, the produce of plate stolen from the churches and houses of the Spaniards, and melted to render it more portable. Many of their valises contained fans and parasols — rather extraordinary articles of equipment for a winter campaign. General Debelle lost his baggage and horses; we also got possession of the papers belonging to the staff of the brigade, and the seals of the 8th Regiment, besides a great number of private letters which were scattered about the fields by the captors without any regard to the tender nature of the contents.

Although the success of the action was rendered incomplete, owing to the very extraordinary conduct of General Slade and some mistakes by Lord Paget, it nevertheless impressed such an idea of the superiority of our cavalry on the mind of the enemy as induced them to avoid as much as possible coming in contact with us. Indeed, I can only attribute the want of enterprise displayed by them on many subsequent occasion, when, owing to their immense superiority in point of numbers and the inefficient state of our horses, they had favourable opportunities of destroying the regiment, to the lessons they had received at Sahagun, Rueda, Valencia, etc.

Eight days later Paget repeated the feat at Benavente on the banks of the Esla river. On this occasion the fight was watched by none other than Napoleon himself who arrived just in time to see his favourite cavalry commander, Lefevre-Desnouettes, captured by a private of the 15th Hussars, Levi Grisdale, although other claimants include a private of the King's German Legion Hussars.

Napoleon himself gave up the pursuit at Astorga and left the chase to Marshal Soult, the 'Duke of Damnation', as he was known to the British. Soult harried and hustled the British through the bleak Galician mountains, his vanguard taking hundreds of prisoners, whilst hundreds more perished in the cold mountainous wastes. It was a terrible experience for both pursued and pursuer, although morale was, of course, much higher with the French. One of the pursued was Augustus Schaumann, a German commissary officer in the British Army. His *On the Road with Wellington* is one of the most enjoyable of Peninsular War memoirs, recalling his experiences in the Peninsula between 1808 and 1814. The first German edition was published in 1922 and was published in English two years later. Born in Hanover, Schaumann was thirty years old when the retreat to Corunna commenced, and his account of the epic is a real gem, as is his book generally. We pick up his story in the first week of 1809, with Schaumann picking his way along the bleak, icy road to Corunna.

As far as Heresias, where one enjoys an extensive view of the surrounding country, the wild chaos of the mountain scenery is somewhat modified, and there are also signs of human habitation and cultivation. In the valleys, and on the hills between the rocks, small enclosures can be descried, and here and there a hut with a slate roof; while there is not a square yard of earth, however unprofitable, that has not been used by the industrious and hardy natives. From this point onwards the mountains rise ever higher and higher.

Many of the soldiers, worn out with hunger and fatigue, had fallen out of the ranks during this rapid march, and had flung themselves in despair in the midst of the mud and filth on the side of the road. Insubordination was noticeable everywhere. The men regarded the retreat as an indignity, and many bitter remarks were made, all of which usually ended with the following prayer: "Give us something to eat; let us just take a little rest, then lead us against the enemy, and we shall beat him!" As for any order on the march, or regular halts — such things were not even thought of! He who could go no further, stood still; he who still had something to eat, that ate he in secret, and then continued marching onwards; the misery of the whole thing was appalling — huge mountains, intense cold, no houses, no shelter or cover of any kind, no inhabitants, no bread. Every minute a horse would collapse beneath its rider, and be shot dead. The road was strewn with dead horses, bloodstained snow, broken carts, scrapped ammunition, boxes, cases, spiked guns, dead mules, donkeys and dogs, starved and frozen soldiers, women and children — in short, the sight of it all was terrible and heartrending to behold. In addition, the road frequently followed a zigzag course along the very edge of a precipice. We often reached small villages completely deserted by their inhabitants, and anybody who at night succeeded, by dint of many appeals to the soldiers, in being given a tiny bit of space either in a stable or a sty, in which to lie down and rest, together with a small fragment of bread, considered himself lucky.

On the 6th January we were climbing the mountains again. The army was now retreating along a road which had been very much deteriorated by the bad weather, and through mountainous country, intersected in all directions by swollen mountain streams, and utterly devoid of all human food. It was, moreover, constantly exposed to rain and stormy weather, and its progress was incessantly hindered and arrested owing to the many wounded and sick, and the wretched women and still more wretched children. Discipline became ever more and more relaxed, and horrible deeds of every description shed a black stain upon the fair fame of the British soldier. Every hour the misery of the troops increased. We were working our way through open, naked mountain country, covered all over with snow, but wonderfully sublime in aspect. Unfortunately, sublimity is not nourishing! Our road, which wound round the mountains, was often bounded by the most forbidding precipices, or else flooded by torrential forest streams. Many, who were too weary to resist, were flung down the former by the powerful and violent gusts of wind that would blow up quite suddenly; while others were constantly being washed by the current into the mountain torrents. Much time was spent in climbing the steep mountain slopes, and in travelling over the increasingly bad roads; and then night would fall — pitch black night! At every step we took, we waded through snow and mud over the bodies of dead men and horses. The howling wind, as it whistled past the ledges of rock and through the bare trees, sounded to the ear like the groaning of the damned; and while the darkness certainly concealed all the horrors of our plight, it only made us the more attentive to the moans of the dying and the execrations of the hungry.

Having reached Puerto, we soon got as far as Cabrera, whence we ascended to the summit of the snow mountains, where the army again suffered the most terrible hardships. Everybody was so drunk with lack of sleep that again and again one of the throng would stop, and in spite of all appeals and warnings, drop down and fall asleep and freeze, and never wake again. Many wounded and sick men, whom we had brought all the way with us, met with their end now. Beasts of draught and beasts of burden gradually sank in ever greater numbers beneath their load and died of hunger, after they had devoured the snow in the hope of slaking their thirst. I saw one bullock cart, belonging to the Paymaster-general's department, loaded with six barrels full of Spanish dollars, standing on the side of the road, with its back resting against a rock. The bullocks were lying on the ground under their yokes, utterly exhausted. A soldier with a bayonet fixed stood guard over the treasure, and with a desperate air implored every officer that passed by to relieve him of his duty. But of course no one dared to do so! If only those dollars had been bread! Now, however, nobody paid any heed; the most confirmed thief passed by unmoved. Further on a Portuguese bullock driver lay dead beside his fallen bullocks. A soldier's wife had sought shelter beneath his cart, but she, too, was lying lifeless; and the tragic part of it was that her child, who was still alive, was whimpering and trying to find nourishment at her frozen breasts! One or two officers had the child taken from her, and wrapping it in a blanket, carried it away.

Among the disasters that befell us while ascending this dreadful mountain, was the fact that we found ourselves compelled to rid our wagons of the load of Spanish dollars which constituted our war treasure. Most of the mules and bullocks that were drawing it had fallen down dead, and we had no fodder for those that remained. The speed with which the French were pursuing us, moreover, left us no time in which to take any measures to save this money. A hussar regiment had, indeed, been furnished with bags, in order that they might carry some of it on their saddles; but as the men could not endure the load, they put as much of it as they could in their pockets and flung the rest away. As, therefore, it was impossible to conceal the stuff, the barrels containing it were rolled over the side of the precipice, where they smashed to pieces, and hurled their bright silver contents ringing into the abyss. And there, when the snow melted, many a poor shepherd or peasant must have found his fortune. For much the same reasons we had been obliged, when two miles beyond Villafranca, to abandon seventy to eighty wagonloads of arms and equipment intended for the Spanish army, which were either plundered by the body of a hundred Spanish patriots escorting and protecting them, or, what is more likely, taken by the French advanced guard.

The road now became more terrible than ever. It was so stormy that we could hardly stand against the wind and snow, and it was horribly cold. A division which had been unable to continue on its way had evidently bivouacked here on the previous night, and had left melancholy traces of its sojourn. To the right, at the summit of the peak, we saw by the wayside, under the shelter of a ledge of rock, an overturned cart with the mules lying dead beside it. Under the cart lay a soldier's wife with two babies in her arms, evidently twins, which could not have been more than a day or two old. She and a man, who was probably a canteen attendant, lay frozen to death, but the children were still alive. I halted for a moment to contemplate the wretched group. A blanket was thrown over the bodies, and I had the pleasure of witnessing the rescue of the infants, who were handed over to a woman who came along in a bullock cart, to whom a few officers offered a substantial reward for taking care of them. It was a most harrowing spectacle. The enemy did not need to inquire the way we had gone; our remains marked out his route. From the eminence on which I stood I saw our army, winding its way along the serpentine road, and the motionless blotches of red, left and right, upon the white snow, indicated the bodies of those whom hunger and cold had accounted for.

The retreat to Corunna came to a climax on 16 January 1809 when Moore's army turned to face their pursuers. In the ensuing battle the French were completely defeated, which allowed the exhausted British troops to board the waiting ships of the Royal Navy who transported them back to the safety of England. Sadly, Sir John Moore himself was not amongst them. Towards the end of the battle on 16 January he was struck by a French cannon ball and thrown from his horse with a terrible wound. He was borne from the battlefield to a house in the Canton Grande in Corunna itself, where he lingered in some pain until the early morning of 17 January. Then, as his men sailed home to old Albion, his faithful followers buried him on the ramparts of the castle overlooking the harbour, before they too sailed away, leaving him, 'alone with his glory'.

CHAPTER THREE

OPORTO AND TALAVERA

The British Army may have been driven out of Spain by Soult, but there still remained some 10,000 British troops left behind by Moore at Lisbon, under the command of Sir John Craddock. On 22 April 1809, however, Sir Arthur Wellesley, having been cleared of all charges arising from the Convention of Cintra, arrived at Lisbon aboard the frigate *Surveillante* to resume command of the army. Two weeks later he was ready to resume the offensive, with a campaign that would see the French driven from Portugal for a second time.

Wellesley's plan involved an advance upon Oporto in order to deal with the French force under Soult before returning south to confront the forces of Victor and Lapisse, at the time concentrated around Ciudad Rodrigo and Talavera, respectively. The rugged nature of the terrain meant that these latter two French commanders would not be able to unite with Soult before Wellesley came up with him. In any case he had devised a plan to deal with that eventuality, but, in the event, it was not required.

On the morning of 12 May Wellesley's troops, numbering 16,000 British and 2,400 Portuguese, began to filter into the suburb of Villa Nova, on the south bank of the Douro. Shortly afterwards, he himself arrived and, taking post at the monastery of Serra do Pilar, a commanding viewpoint high above the river, he took out his telescope and began scanning the north bank of the river where Oporto sprawled before him. The mouth of the river Douro lay away to the west, at the Atlantic, and it was from this direction that Soult expected any British attack. Thus, he had taken no precautions to guard against an attack from any other direction. Wellesley watched as a few French troops bathed in the Douro. Others whiled away their time idling on the quayside away to the west. Meanwhile, Wellesley watched from above at the Serra do Pilar. The problem was, how to cross the river, as there was no bridge. But even as Wellesley was surveying the scene before him a Portuguese barber was hastily rowing across the river to inform the

British that four wine barges lay unguarded on the northern bank of the river, a fact brought to Wellesley's immediate attention by Colonel John Waters, commanding Wellesley's scouts. Waters was immediately ordered to cross the river and bring the barges back, a feat accomplished with the aid of four local peasants and a priest. Once the barges had been secured Wellesley said simply, "Well, let the men cross", and so the crossing of the Douro began. This short account of the crossing of the Douro was written by Assistant Surgeon Good, of the 3rd Foot Guards. It was printed in Volume 1 of *The History of the Scots Guards*, by Major General Sir F. Maurice, in 1934.

The brigade of Guards crossed the Douro from Villa Nova with General Sherbrooke in boats timely procured and forming on the quay of Oporto, loaded and advanced up the town, but the devil a Gaul would wait for us, they were all out, except some few dead and wounded lying in the streets at the upper end of the City. Indeed they went away in such a hurry that they left the streets blocked up with artillery, ammunition wagons, etc. Some of these had broken down and the horses of others had been shot. We pursued the fugitives through the town, but they would not stop for us, however we should soon have got up to them, had we not been ordered to halt; so that we could not get one shot at them. The brigade which crossed the river first had a good deal to do and indeed were the only part of the army except the Dragoons and the artillery that were engaged; they killed a vast number of the enemy and the prisoners came in by dozens. Although we had a march of over 20 miles over a difficult road, yet now we did not feel the want of rest indeed our only anxiety was to push forward. Whilst we remained on the road waiting for orders we were inspired, if inspiration was necessary, by the passing of the 14th Light Dragoons by us at full speed, all eager for the combat and waving in their hands handkerchiefs which had been thrown to them by the females of the town. Indeed that compliment was paid to us too, for we went through the town amidst shouts of "Viva", a shower of roses, and a hail of handkerchiefs. Even the nuns protruded their heads through the railings of the convent to welcome our arrival.

The crossing of the Douro was one of the most daring feats of the war, one which helps nail the myth that Wellesley was simply a defensive-minded general. His men crossed without opposition, establishing themselves on the northern bank of the river at the site of the old bridge, which had been destroyed, and at the Bishop's Seminary, a high walled building situated high above the river. Once this building was taken and held by the 3rd Foot (The Buffs), there was little prospect of Soult remaining in Oporto. Hundreds more British troops came gliding across the river, driving the French through the streets and throwing them out of the city to bring about an end to the second French invasion of Portugal.

Wellesley's daring crossing of the Douro had been a masterstroke, which had been with the loss of just 23 killed and 98 wounded as opposed to French casualties of 300 killed and wounded as well as 1,500 prisoners. The victory was followed up a few days later at Salamonde where units of the British Army came up with and scattered Soult's rearguard. Eventually, Soult was forced to burn his baggage and throw his 58 guns down the mountainside in order to facilitate his retreat, which ended only when he had recrossed the border into Spain. Wellesley, meanwhile, called a halt to the pursuit and returned to Oporto before considering his next move, a move that would result in one of the bloodiest battles of the war: Talavera.

Having driven Soult from Portugal Wellesley looked to the south, towards Victor whose force was concentrated in and around the Spanish town of Talavera, situated on the river Tagus. Wellesley's 20,000 troops were to link up with 35,000 Spanish troops under the 73-year-old General Cuesta, a proud, dilatory Spaniard with whom it was virtually impossible for Wellesley to co-operate. On 20 July the two armies forged their uneasy link at Oropesa before advancing towards Talavera and Victor's 20,000 men. The problem was that Victor had to be attacked before he could join up with the 46,000-strong army under King Joseph, which was making its way to Talavera from Madrid, and a further 15,000 troops under Sébastiani.

Three days later the Allies had a perfect opportunity to attack Victor who had yet to meet either Sebastiani or Joseph and who was outnumbered by just over two to one. Unfortunately, Cuesta refused to move, and the opportunity of attacking Victor on advantageous terms went begging, the French retiring before the Allied host. Wellesley's annoyance is understandable, and his exasperation increased on 25 July when Cuesta, against Wellesley's advice, pursued the French, only to be savaged by Victor's veterans. The Spaniards duly returned, chastised, and with Victor having been reinforced the scene was set for the bloody showdown on 27 July 1809.

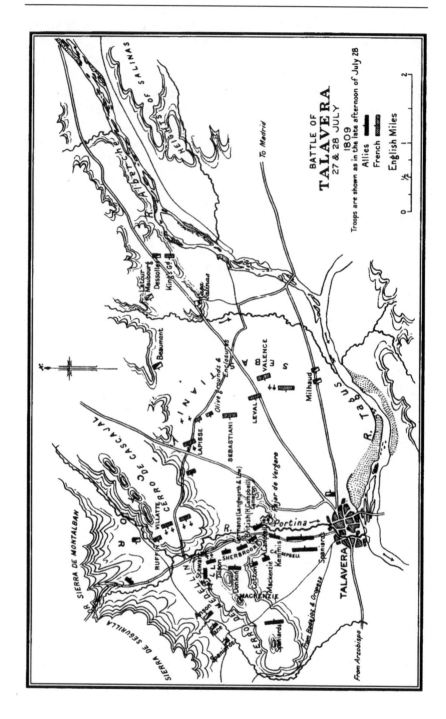

After Albuera, Talavera was the bloodiest battle of the Peninsular War involving the British Army. It was fought over two extremely hot days, during which countless wounded men died of thirst whilst lying out in the middle of the battlefield. The French began their attack on the night of the 27th, when three strong columns blundered their way into the British positions, overrunning the forward posts and establishing themselves on a hill called the Medellin, which dominated the British position. It was only the intervention of Rowland Hill that cleared them from it, bringing forward the 29th Regiment to drive the French off in a blaze of musketry. It was an act which almost cost him his life, for, in the dark, he had ridden straight into the midst of the French troops before he realised what was happening. The position thus being restored, the French columns returned to their own lines and both sides settled down for the night.

The fighting began at dawn on the 28th, with a great French artillery barrage which heralded the start of a series of attacks by Victor's infantry on Wellesley's position. As at Vimeiro, the French were driven back by the steady, controlled musketry of the British line, although the day did not pass off without incident. Indeed, at one point, the two battalions of Foot Guards, the 1/Coldstream and 1/3rd Foot Guards, carried away with their success, pursued the French too far and suffered over six hundred casualties before they withdrew to their own lines.

The battle culminated in the second great mishap to the British cavalry, when the 23rd Light Dragoons, after badly negotiating a dry watercourse, rode straight into the midst of the much stronger French cavalry, suffering severe casualties. Indeed, so badly mauled was the regiment that it was forced to return home to England, never to return to the Peninsula. Commanding the 2/53rd Regiment at Talavera, and in fact throughout the Peninsular War was Lieutenant Colonel Sir George Ridout Bingham KCB. He wrote several detailed letters to friends and family, one of which was written just four days after the battle:

As I know that you will expect that I should attempt to describe the sanguinary action that took place on the spot from which I am now writing; and having in some measure recovered the fatigue, collected my scattered ideas, and having gone over the ground once or twice, I sit down to use my best endeavours. You will see at Wycombe a great many accounts, and this may serve to add a little to the stock of general information.

The Whole Army having assembled at Plasencia, moved from that on the

45

17th and on the 22nd, having joined Cuesta's Army, came to this place. The French who were not in strength, retired on our approach behind the Alberche. The 23rd, for some reason or other yet unknown on the part of the Spaniards, we remained idle. On the 24th we intended to have made our attack, but on our arrival on the ground, we found the enemy gone. We were unable to follow for want of provisions, in the mean time the French who had retired in the direction of Toledo, having received reinforcements and being honoured with the presence of their King Joseph Napoleon, returned on the Spaniards who had followed them singly, and drove them before them like sheep. On the 27th, they made their appearance on the Alberche, the Dragoons of General McKenzie's division were sent to cover the retreat of the Spaniards, which they did, closely followed by the French, who advanced so rapidly, that we had hardly time to occupy the position, which was as follows. Our right was on the town of Talavera and the Tagus, a perfect flat for about three quarters of a mile, much intersected with ditches, vineyards and covered with olive trees. This space was occupied by the Spaniards in two lines three deep, and with reserves. Just on the left of their line was a small eminence that commanded the plain. On this a battery was established and a work hardly more traced out, having been interrupted by the unlooked for rapid advance of the enemy. In front of this, were two small enclosures, and beyond that, all the enemy's movements were obscured by olive trees. On the left of the battery a small plain began to extend itself with olive groves on each side, and with a dry watercourse running through it. As you went on to the left, the plain widened and the olive groves ceased, where the ground began to rise which it did suddenly, and terminated in a high conical hill; beyond this was a deep narrow valley with bold rocky mountains on the other side. The round hill was our extreme left, and the extent we had to occupy, was so great that the Army was in some places in two, and in others only in one line. I before observed that the French followed our troops very close. About 7 o'clock they appeared in force on our left, and after a cannonade that lasted till sunset, as soon as it was dark brought up their columns to charge. They had succeeded in getting possession of the hill, but the 2nd division coming up, drove them from it. This hill was of the utmost consequence to us. It commanded, and was in fact the key of the position, and we retained it against several attacks the enemy made on it. About 10 o'clock the firing ceased for the night, which we passed under arms, occasionally entertained by a heavy fire from the Spanish line, which they kept up on being disturbed by the enemy's patrols. At day break the Army appeared in nearly the same position as the night before, except that our line a little to the left of our centre, was rather further advanced and stood on the edge of a ravine, that there separated the two armies, and was very much exposed to the fire of the French batteries, which had not yet opened. There was nearly an hour of suspense after daylight, before the least movement was to be seen on either side. About the expiration of that time the French filed a strong body of chasseurs into a wood in front of our centre, and on the advanced part of our line falling back, opened a tremendous cannonade on them, which was soon directed to the whole left of the line, and did great execution. Some guns we had on the circular hill commanded theirs and dismounted several of their guns, and there were frequent explosions of ammunition waggons, but they had so many guns in the field that they maintained the superiority of fire, and under cover of which they made another unsuccessful attempt to possess themselves of the hill on the left. About 12 o'clock the fire ceased and the French cooked their dinners. At 2 o'clock they had completed their arrangements for a general attack along the whole front of the British line; they moved down under a plunging cannonade from our batteries on the left, they drove in our light companies in front, and coming on the flank of the Fusiliers drove them back also; some of them penetrated nearly to the work in front. They were immediately repulsed by a charge made by the Fusiliers, who had instantly rallied, aided by the 2nd, right company of the 53rd, supported by the remaining seven companies of that Battalion. In this charge, we passed at first the outermost of the two enclosures in front of the work, and in retreat of the enemy they left a brigade of ten guns and some tumbrels of musket ammunition. The brigade then lined the ditches of the enclosures, and thus formed a flanking fire on the column that attacked our line more to the left, by which means the Nassau regiment suffered severely. We were aided in our charge by the Spanish Regiment of Cavalry Princessa, who charging down the road in our front, just came on the French as they were retiring before us, and took several prisoners. The attack of the enemy on the centre was more favourable to them. The Brigade of Guards moved forward to the charge about the same time as we did; the French columns had not entered on the plain they lined an enclosure on their side, and as the Guards were broken in crossing the dry water course, gave them a most tremendous volley and then quitting the enclosure charged in their turn. This crisis might have been fatal; the enemy were near or rather beyond the centre of our position, when the 48th Regiment further to the left was thrown forward and brought on their flank, which movement was decisive. They retired with loss and the attacks were not repeated; on the left of the whole, they tried to pass a strong body along the valley on the left of the position, their force was charged in the most gal-

47

lant manner by the 23rd Light Dragoons and the 1st Hussars of the German Legion. Although these regiments made no impression on the squares which the enemy promptly formed, and suffered (especially the former) a very serious loss, yet it effectually stopped the advance of the enemy.

Failing in all these attacks they retired to their original position and kept up a cannonade directed more towards our part of the line, till sunset, when all was quiet, and during the night they crossed the Alberche unmolested. It was intimated to the Spaniards that not having been engaged, and the French Army being much crippled it afforded them a good opportunity of achieving something; Cuesta flatly refused to move, and the want of supplies prevented our profiting by our success. Thus ended an action, which perhaps not so useful, has been brilliant and as glorious as any we have ever (in these late wars) been engaged in, when it is considered the numbers with whom we had to contend; which from the accounts of the wounded amounted to 40,000. We had not in the field more than 18,000. The Brigade of Light infantry did not arrive till the day after the action (29th). Of what service to the cause this victory may prove, I cannot venture to say. The Spanish Army is in so disorganised state, the under officers such poltroons, the superior such traitors, I am afraid one day or other they will lead us into a scrape, from which it will be difficult to extricate ourselves. We are now without a day's provision in advance, without magazines and (notwithstanding what you may hear in England) with a population very lukewarm in our behalf. The whole day of the action our people were without provisions, and we have been detained here ever since for want of it. Our loss has been considerable, which considering the length of time we were engaged is not to be wondered at; two generals killed and three wounded. Your regiment the 23rd has suffered much, as have the Guards, 24th, 48th, 61st, and 83rd, regiments. The total numbers is said to be 5,100; the loss of the enemy is variously stated. About 1,000 prisoners mostly wounded have been brought in; these fell in the last attack only, for those who were wounded on the evening of the 27th, and in the first attacks on the morning of the 28th, had been removed.

John Spencer Cooper, of the 7th (Royal) Fusiliers, was another combatant at Talavera. He was 21 years old at the time and it was his first real experience of battle. The first edition of his classic memoir, *Rough Notes of Seven Campaigns*, was published in Carlisle in 1869. In it, Cooper left a wonderful account of the major actions in which he took part, as well as leaving details of his equipment and uniform, of the army system and his rations, amongst other things. Cooper was awarded nine clasps to his General Service Medal, for Talavera, Busaco, Albuera, Ciudad Rodrigo, Badajoz, Vittoria, Pyrenees, Orthes and Toulouse. His account of the Battle of Talavera ran as follows:

On the 27th there was much firing in front, and the enemy strongly reinforced, came on rapidly. To receive them the Anglo-Spanish army took up position about two or three p.m. in the following order: Nearly all the Spanish troops were posted on the right of the British; their right resting on the river Tagus, and their left touching an unfinished breastwork thrown up on our right flank. They also occupied the town of Talavera, and were snugly ensconced in hollow ways and behind walls and hedges, with a thick wood and vineyards in their front. Thus they were screened from the view of the enemy.

The right of the British line covered the unfinished breastwork above mentioned; the centre extended over a partly exposed plain and broken ground; and the left touched a rocky mountainous ridge which ran at nearly a right angle with the whole line. On the left of the centre was a hill occupied by General Hill's division and several guns. This might be considered the key of our position, as the enemy struggled hard for its possession in the battle. Along the front ran a small rivulet, dry in many places, but where there were pools, black, ugly-looking snakes were plentiful. Of this water we had to drink. I may here remark that our brigade stood on the right of the British line.

About 6 p.m. the enemy driving in our advanced picquets, debouched in large masses between the rocky heights and the vineyards in front of the English right wing. The appearance of their black columns was very imposing, and as they moved forward rapidly, we expected an immediate attack. But seeing our line steady and ready, they suddenly halted and contented themselves with cannonading till dark. Our artillery though few in number replying briskly.

After sunset our company and a company of Brunswick riflemen, called "Death and Glory Boys", were sent forward as a piquet into a vineyard, where we laid down silently among the bushes. Though the day had been hot yet the night was very cold; notwithstanding this the order was "No great coats to be put on."

At 10 p.m. the enemy made a furious attack on the hill where General Hill's division was posted, and they succeeded in gaining the summit. For some time our men and the enemy were mixed and the contest was dubious, but ultimately they were driven down and over the snake pools again with great

49

loss. Soon after they stole through the vineyards in front, and opened a sharp fire upon us and the Spanish left, but repulse was their portion. Finding themselves foiled they made no more attempts during the night; so ended the 27th.

The dawn of July 28th saw more than 100,000 men standing ready to slay one another. None but those who have been in similar circumstances can even guess what is felt. Just as the sun shot his first beams over the mountains on our left, bang went the first gun from the enemy, and bang was the answer from our battery on the hill. Battery after battery now opened, that on our right joining in the fray, and firing over our heads. Who the gunners were in our battery I don't know, but an unlucky shot from it killed a Brunswick rifleman by tearing out his bowels.

By and by the cannonading nearly ceased, but it was only a prelude to more serious work. The enemy were massing for attack. The death cloud was gathering blackness, and soon burst with fury. Several columns were set in motion, and directed towards different points of our line.

One of these, after threading its way among the trees and grape vines, came up directly in our front, and while deploying, called out Espanholas, wishing us to believe they were Spaniards. Our captain thought they were Spaniards, and ordered us not to fire. But they soon convinced us who they were by a rattling volley. We instantly retired upon our regiment, which sprung up and met the enemy on the rising ground, but our men being all raw soldiers, staggered for a moment under such a rolling fire. Our colonel Sir William Myers seeing this, sprang from his horse and snatching one of the colours, cried "Come on Fusiliers", 'Twas enough. On rushed the Fusiliers and 53rd regiment and delivered such a fire, that in a few minutes the enemy melted away, leaving 6 pieces of cannon behind, which they had not had time to discharge. The 6 pieces were immediately rendered unfit for use, as our balls were too large for their bore.

While charging the enemy, a Frenchman fell in his hurry, and was collared by a brutal sergeant of ours, who exclaimed "I'll kill a Frenchman for once," and then deliberately shot the poor fellow dead This sergeant whose name was Oliver, was wounded in three places while ascending the hill at Albuera, of which he died.

The enemy having failed on the right, hurled a stronger force over the open ground against the centre. Here the battle raged with great fury, and the struggle was continued on nearly the same ground, with the utmost fierceness on both aides. For a considerable time the combatants were enveloped in a mighty cloud of smoke.

This, with the thunder of artillery, the roll of musketry, and the huzzas of our men as they pushed back the masses of the foe, constituted one vast continuous uproar. At this time the British guards were brought up, who charged the enemy and swept them back instantly, but pursuing them too far, they suffered heavily before support came up. This was seen by Wellington, who immediately sent forward a body of fresh men into the fray. These, in turn, charged so roughly, that the enemy retired precipitately leaving heaps of dead and wounded.

A few minutes after one of the guards came for water to one of the pools. I said "You have had warm work, how many may your brigade have lost?" He very dryly answered, "About 600 I think."

Another lull in the storm and fresh formations. "Here they come again," said many voices; so they did, but we were ready, and gave them such a warm reception that they speedily went to the right about. As in their first attack, they now left several pieces of cannon, which we secured as before. After these two attacks and smart repulses, we were not troubled with their company any more during the battle.

In the course of the day the 26th Dragoons [actually the 23rd Light Dragoons] who were posted on the left of the line, and out of our view, made a dashing charge at the French cavalry, but not being aware of a deep ravine between them and the enemy, they went headlong down into it, which caused great confusion. Not disheartened the unhurt men galloped up the opposite bank, and charged through the enemy's ranks, then wheeling about they gallantly cut their way back. This was not done without great loss both of men and horses.

The battle now languished, both armies were weary, notwithstanding the light troops on both sides kept up a brisk fire, on the rocky side of the mountain on the left, long after sunset. About 11 p.m. all was still. Not a voice was heard, but the cry of agony and distress from the wounded and dying. Both armies rested on the same ground they had occupied the preceding night except our brigade, which had advanced about 200 yards.

Long before daylight next morning, we were startled by drums being beaten in the enemy's lines. Of course we expected another brush, but when morning dawned no enemy was to be seen. It was ascertained that they had in their retreat crossed a branch of the Tagus and carried away 70 or 80 cars laden with their wounded. Surely the French did not fight well in this battle, when it is considered that they threw nearly the whole force of about 50,000 upon our small army of 19,000. They had been well supplied with provisions previously. We had been half starved. They had dined on the field of battle,

51

and liquor had been served out to them before they attacked us. This was proved by what was found in the possession of the dead. On the contrary, nothing was served out to us from 2 or 3 p.m. on the 27th, until about 10 a.m. on the 29th.

The British in this engagement lost nearly 5,000 and the enemy by their own account about 9,000. The morning after the battle, the Light Brigade consisting of the 43rd, 52nd, and 95th Regiment, joined us on the bloody field, having made a forced march of 60 miles in 24 hours. We received them with loud cheers though they arrived too late.

The first work to be done, was to remove nine or ten thousand English and French wounded into Talavera; and to bury four or five thousand dead bodies. What a task for 16 or 17,000 hungry worn out men to undertake! 'Twas impossible! We had but few tools, and the ground was hard and rocky, therefore the dead were either thrown into the dry beds of winter torrents, &c., and scantily covered with earth; or, together with dead horses, gathered into heaps and burned. The smell was intolerable. As for the wounded, they perished in great numbers while lying in the blazing sun, in want of water, dressing, and shelter.

The excitement of battle being over, we all severely felt stomach complaints. I had not tasted food for 43 hours. This was not Wellington's fault, for previous to the battle much flour had been collected, and made into bread by bakers belonging the army; but during the battle, the Spaniards had broken open our stores and left very little for us. In the heat of the fight, many of these boasting Spaniards deserted, and spread the news that the English were defeated.

About 10 a.m. on the 29th, we were served with 4 ounces of bread, which was for the next 24 hours. This might make 6 or 8 decent mouthfuls.

Early in the morning of the 30th, twenty-five Spanish soldiers, dressed in white and attended by several popish priests, were marched up to the front of our regiment and shot. One a young lad of 19 or 20 years of age, dropped before the party fired. But it was of no use, for after a volley at 10 paces distance had been given by about 50 men, the whole party ran forward, and firing through heads, necks, breasts, &c., completed their horrid work. The executioners having tools with them, the bodies were hidden in shallow graves in a few minutes. These unfortunates belonged to a regiment that had given way in the late battle.

We were now in a trap: the enemy we had beaten were still more than double our number and not far off in front: another army under General Soult, perhaps nearly as numerous as that before us, had come through a mountain pass in our rear, and taken possession of the large stores of bread that we had left at Placentia.

These two French armies, probably numbered about 70,000, well supplied with provisions, &c.; while ours only amounted to 17,000 in want of nearly every necessary. We were actually reduced to a starvation point, besides being encumbered by numerous wounded. Those who were seriously crippled were left at Talavera, to whom the French behaved well.

Talavera cost the British some 5,365 casualties, whilst the French themselves lost 7,268. Cuesta's Spaniards, meanwhile, had not been involved in much of the fighting, having held the right flank of the Allied position throughout the day. The battle here was nowhere as intense as that to the north where Wellesley's men had fought. Thus, their loss was trifling.

The Battle of Talavera was a victory for the British only in as much as the French had left them in possession of the battlefield. Apart from that, there was little advantage gained. Indeed, with Victor having received even more reinforcements, and with the French having cut Wellesley's communications to the north, he was forced to retreat across the Tagus and make for the relative safety of the Portuguese border. Oh, yes, and there was one other reward for Arthur Wellesley for his victory at Talavera. He was given the title Baron Douro and Viscount Wellington.

CHAPTER FOUR

ON THE BORDER

Wellington's victory at Talavera had brought him few rewards, save for a new name, and left him pondering his next move. Following the battle he had retired to the vicinity of Badajoz, the massive fortress town on the Spanish–Portuguese border. The British Armys sojourn here was not a happy one. The people were distinctly unfriendly, whilst many of the population were considered to be Afrancecados, or pro-French.

The unhealthy region along the banks of the Guadiana, upon which Badajoz was situated, caused Wellington's army a great number of sick. 'Guadiana sickness,' the men called it. And so, with the French advancing in great numbers and with his men wilting in the valley of the sickly Guadiana, Wellington marched north in order to hold the line of the Coa and Agueda rivers, which flowed through the border area around Ciudad Rodrigo and Almeida, the twin fortresses that controlled the northern corridor between Spain and Portugal.

With the army having marched north, Wellington took himself off to Lisbon for an examination of the ground to the north of the city. He had spent some time here during the Cintra negotiations the previous summer and noted how the hills to the north of the capital leant themselves to a strong defensive position. His visit in September and October 1809 was for the purpose of putting the finishing touches to his instructions for the famous Lines of Torres Vedras, lines that would prove to be one of the major factors in the defeat of the French in the Peninsula.

Meanwhile, his men took up their positions on the Spanish–Portuguese border. The winter and early spring of 1809–10 saw little action, save for the odd skirmish, but in late March 1810, things began to change. Wellington knew that the French, under Marshal Andre Massena, were preparing for a third invasion of Portugal, and knew also that the invasion must come through Ciudad Rodrigo and Almeida. It came as no surprise, therefore, that the French began to probe his lines along the Agueda and Coa rivers, trying to discover British dispositions and troop numbers. The incursions involved

Wellington's men in a series of sharp little actions, mainly involving the Light Division, under Robert 'Black Bob' Craufurd, whose job it was to ensure the safety of Wellington's main field army. The division covered an area forty miles from north to south, and ten miles deep, thus making an incredible four hundred square miles. And yet, such was the effectiveness of Craufurd's outposts that if the French attempted to probe any part of the line, it 'quivered at the slightest touch'. One of the earliest attempts by the French on Craufurd's line came on the night of 19 March 1810, when 600 grenadiers attacked the British troops holding the bridge over the Agueda at Barba del Puerco. One of the defenders was 24 year-old Yorkshireman, Lieutenant George Simmons, of the 95th Rifles. In his classic, *A British Rifle Man*, published in 1899, he described the night's fighting:

On the 11th, with four companies of Rifle Men, we again occupied this post, having our company posted on piquet near the most formidable passes I ever beheld. The French were also posted opposite us. The river Agueda, which rises in the great Spanish mountains named Sierra de Gata, and runs furiously in the bottom of this deep chasm over rugged rocks, causing a continued noise, separated us. At the bottom of the zig-zag pass is the bridge over the river, 100 yards long and 5 yards wide. San Felices, in which the advance of the French army were lodged under the command of General Baron de Ferey, is about half a league from the pass. We remained quietly here until the night of the 19th inst., being upon outlying piquet with Captain O'Hare's Company. Early in the evening I crossed the bridge to find a paper left there (in the piquet house) for me to fetch from the French side, and had just returned from visiting the advanced double sentry and made my report to Lieutenant Mercer, when a tremendous firing commenced. Mercer immediately ordered the men to fall in and move forward to our alarm post, which was on the edge of the rocky chasm. The night being dark and stormy, with rain occasionally, caused the river to make more noise in its passage over the rocky bed than usual, and completely prevented our advanced sentinels hearing the approach of the enemy. Also from the obscurity of the night, it was not possible to see any object, so that the enemy passed the bridge so rapidly that only one sentinel fired before they were both knocked down. Two men, Maher and McCan, were taken at the bridge. However, this gave the alarm, and a small party stationed amongst the rocks kept up a fire. The sergeant being shot through the mouth and the enemy being so numerous, they could not impede their progress. In a moment, after the arrival of the main body of the piquet, the French were literally scrambling up the rocky ground within ten yards of us. We commenced firing at each other very spiritedly. Their drums beat a charge, and the French attempted to dislodge us without effect. My friend, Lieutenant Mercer, who was putting on his spectacles, received a musket ball through his head, and fell dead close to my feet. Several were now falling, and the moon for a few minutes shone brightly, then disappeared, and again at intervals let us see each other. We profited by this circumstance, as their belts were white and over their greatcoats, so that where they crossed upon the breast, combined with the glare of the breast-plate, gave a grand mark for our rifles. Our men being in dark dresses, and, from their small number, obliged to keep close together, the ground also being exceedingly rugged, were all favourable circumstances. We fought in this way for at least half an hour against fearful odds, when Lieutenant-Colonel Beckwith brought up the three reserve companies from the village, who soon decided the affair. The enemy was driven in the greatest confusion back over frightful precipices, leaving two officers killed and a number of men wounded. About 9 o'clock in the evening, Captain O'Hare had been taken unwell, and as there was no idea of an attack, he went home to bed. Lieutenant Cowan was sent for him when the firing commenced. They arrived after poor Mercer was killed, so the command of the piquet devolved upon me for a quarter of an hour. Thus I had the honour to command for some time after poor Mercer was killed and until O'Hare returned. I merely mention this circumstance as it was the first time I had been in a fight, but the gallantry displayed by the varmint fellows that were with me left no doubt on my mind that we should have resisted all these attempts to dislodge us until the reserves came up. A young Frenchman that was taken, fired into Colonel Beckwith's face. A Rifle Man was just going to blow his brains out, when the Colonel stopped him, saying, "Let him alone; I daresay the boy has a mother. Knock the thing out of his hand, that he may do no more mischief with it, and give him a kick on the bottom and send him to the rear." The next morning the boy was given a hearty breakfast at the Colonel's house. On being questioned about firing so wantonly, he said he was in such agitation that he was not aware his finger was upon the trigger of his gun. The ball went through the Colonel's cap peak, which, being turned up, made it take a slanting direction; it passed through and grazed the top of his head. Six hundred volunteers were chosen by the French general to attempt the annihila-tion of our party, and fifteen hundred more were formed to support the attack in case of success. A number of men kept up a fire from the enemy's side of the river during the time the soldiers were passing the ravine. A body of

Spaniards under a captain was stationed on our right. We had a corporal and file with them, merely to give us intelligence if necessary. When the firing commenced the Spaniards became very uneasy; the officer wished our corporal to leave his post; he said he was determined to wait until the enemy overpowered him, so the noble Castilian and his forces started off. Two French officers, a Light Infantry captain and a subaltern, and seventeen men lay stretched upon the rough ground. We afterwards heard from a deserter that the colonel who led the attack was shot through the mouth and his jaw broken. He was making a great noise before, but this circumstance made him so quiet that a child might have played with him. Several other officers were wounded and a number of men who were carried off during the affray, Lieutenant Mercer killed, seventeen of our men killed and wounded. Fairfoot was of the party taken; Betts, the sergeant, wounded in the jaw; O'Gallagher wounded and died; William David, his skull blown off and his *dura mater* exposed. A French sergeant was wounded through the knee, and afterwards I assisted Surgeon Burke to remove his leg.

The French were thrown back but continued to probe Craufurd's lines. Ciudad Rodrigo fell in July 1810, at which the Light Division fell back upon Almeida. Robert Craufurd and his men were in their element, constantly keeping a vigil on the frontier, scanning the horizon for enemy movements, and encouraging the Portuguese garrison of Almeida by their presence. The period was, however, one of the most controversial for Craufurd, who embroiled himself in one or two scrapes that he should and could have avoided, none more so than the infamous fight on the river Coa, on 24 July 1810. Wellington had ordered Craufurd not to dally on the right bank of the river longer than was necessary, but left it to his own discretion. Sadly, Craufurd delayed too long, and when the French attacked on 24 July he was found wanting as the French, under Marshal Ney, came on in vastly superior numbers. In fact, had it not been for his superb battalion commanders, the Light Division may well have been lost. As it was, they fought a fighting retreat down the rocky gorge of the Coa, down to the one bridge behind them, all the time falling back with the French at their heels. Once across the bridge they formed up in the hills above it and kept up such a tremendous fire that not a single French soldier crossed and lived to tell the tale. The combat of the Coa cost Wellington over 350 men of the Light Division, although French apologists would have us believe the number was three times as high. As it was, the fight was bad enough, but although Wellington was annoyed at Craufurd he refused to condemn him publicly, claiming his error was one of judgement and not intent.

George Simmons was once again in the thick of the action, and was, in fact, badly wounded, as he recalled in his journal.

I was on outlying piquet. I fully expected to be attacked this morning, as several peasantry told us that large bodies of men were concentrating close to us, and all the villages were filled with what was now called the Army of Portugal, amounting at least to 100,000 men, many of whom had been in a number of Napoleon's great battles.

Lieutenant Uniacke and Lieutenant McCullock relieved us this morning. Spent a jovial evening with Lieutenants Pratt and Beckwith in Almeida. About eight o'clock an officer told us that he had orders to clear the town of every person that was not to be employed in the siege, and regretted that we could not be allowed to remain longer within its walls. We drank success to their defence of the fortress, and that many Frenchmen might bite the dust before the place, shook him by the hand, and departed. We had scarcely left the town when the rain began to fall in torrents; the thunder and lightning of that night was the most tremendously grand I ever beheld either before or since. The Division, officers and men, had no shelter from this inclement night; as to lying down, it was nearly impossible, for the water ran in gutters amongst the rocks. I sat upon a stone like a drowned rat, looking at the heavens and amusing myself with their brilliancy and longing for the morning, which came at last, and the rain ceased. Our next consideration was to set the men to work to clean their arms and look after their ammunition. Our cavalry outposts since the fall of Fort Conception had been on the Turon.

A little after daybreak the enemy advanced against our piquets and drove them in. The Division was put into position, the left upon Almeida and the right in rugged ground upon the Coa, which river was running furiously in its course; several companies of Rifle Men and the 43rd Light Infantry were placed behind stone walls. The enemy now advanced in vast bodies. The whole plain in our front was covered with horse and foot advancing towards us. The enemy's infantry formed line and, with an innumerable multitude of skirmishers, attacked us fiercely; we repulsed them; they came on again, yelling, with drums beating, frequently the drummers leading, often in front of the line, French officers like mountebanks running forward and placing their hats upon their swords, and capering about like madmen, saying, as they turned to their men, "Come on, children of our country. The first that

59

advances, Napoleon will recompense him." Numbers returned to the attack. We kept up a very brisk fire. Several guns began to play upon us, and as the force kept increasing every moment in our front, and columns of infantry were also moving upon our right flank, we were ordered to retire half the company. Captain O'Hare's retired, and the remainder, under Lieutenant Johnston, still remained fighting for a few moments longer. I was with this party. We moved from the field into the road, our men falling all round us, when a body of Hussars in bearskin caps and light-coloured pelisses got amongst the few remaining Rifle Men and began to sabre them. Several attempted to cut me down, but I avoided their kind intentions by stepping on one side. I had a large cloak rolled up and strapped across my body; my haversack was filled with little necessary articles for immediate use; thus I got clear off. A volley was now fired by a party of the 43rd under Captain Wells, which brought several of the Hussars to the ground. In the scuffle I took to my heels and ran to the 43rd, Wells calling out, "Mind the Rifle Man! Do not hit him, for heaven's sake." As I was compelled to run into their fire to escape, he seized me by the hand and was delighted beyond measure at my escape. The road to a small bridge across the Coa, which the Division would have to retire over, was very bad and rocky. Our gallant fellows disputed manfully every inch of ground and retired towards the river. Every place we left was covered with the enemy's Light Infantry in ten times our number. As we got near the river the enemy made several attempts to cut us off. General Craufurd ordered a number of Rifle Men who had occupied a place that prevented the French from stopping our retreat over the bridge to evacuate it before half the 5nd, who were on the right, had filed over. The enemy directly brought up their infantry to this hill, which commanded the bridge, and kept up a terrible fire. Colonel Beckwith, a most gallant and clever soldier, saw this frightful mistake and ordered us to retake the wall and hill instantly, which we did in good style, but suffered severely in men and officers. Lieutenant Harry Smith, Lieutenant Thomas Smith, and Lieutenant Pratt were wounded, and I was shot through the thigh close to the wall, which caused me to fall with great force. Being wounded in this way was quite a new thing to me. For a few moments I could not collect my ideas, and was feeling about my arms and body for a wound, until my eye caught the stream of blood rushing through the hole in my trousers, and my leg and thigh appeared so heavy that I could not move it. Captain Napier took off his neckerchief and gave it to a sergeant, who put it round my thigh and twisted it tight with a ramrod, to stop the bleeding. The firing was so severe that the sergeant, on finishing the job for me, fell with a shot through the head.

Captain Napier was also about the same time wounded in the side. The Division had now nearly got over the bridge; some men put me into a blanket and carried me off. Our General had placed himself some distance from the fight to observe the enemy's movements. I passed him in the blanket. The General had still in his remembrance the loss of his light cart. He told the men this was no time to be taking away wounded officers, and ordered them back. They observed, "This is an officer of ours, and we must see him in safety before we leave him." The last party of our men retired over the bridge and occupied it. The ground was very rugged and rocky close to the bridge, so that Rifle Men were placed behind every stone, and two companies of the 43rd hid themselves and were ready to support our men. Several Frenchmen held up calabashes as much as to say, "Let us get some water to drink." Our men allowed some of the enemy to get water, and did not fire upon them, but the cunning rogues made lodgements between the stones, and when their party was ready to storm the bridge, they commenced firing upon our men.

A number of French officers and some drummers headed the storming party. Our fellows allowed them to come close to the bridge. Some officers got over before they fell, but few went back to tell the tale, either men or officers. They attempted to force the bridge several times before the evening, and finding it impossible to effect their purpose, they made a signal to cease firing. An officer came forward waving a white handkerchief and requested to be allowed to remove their wounded, as the bridge and its vicinity were covered with their killed and wounded. This request was granted. The officer said he had heard of the English fighting well, but he could not have supposed men would have fought against such fearful odds. He complimented our men much upon their gallantry, and observed what a pity it was we were enemies. During this day it rained occasionally, and towards evening more so, which made the arms frequently miss fire. After dark the Light Division marched to Carvalha.

A party of the 1st Hussars, under Colonel Arentschildt, was upon the road. He paid me the most kind attention and ordered an Hussar to dismount. I was placed upon the horse, and was taken on it to the church of Alverca, where I found a number of poor fellows as bad, and some worse wounded, laid in every direction upon the stone floors. A poor fellow, who died some time after I entered, begged of me to lie upon a paillasse beside him, as I was upon the bare stones; he divided it with me. In the evening I was put upon a car drawn by bullocks — the most clumsy machine possible. Here now commenced my misfortunes. The car proceeded, with me upon it, to Pinhel, suffering the most severe torture from the jolting motion to my poor limb, sustained at almost every movement. I was lodged in the Bishop's house, and Colonel Pakenham behaved very kindly to me. I now became anxious to know the nature of my wounds. My trousers and drawers were cut up the side; the latter article of dress was literally glued to my thigh; in fact, I had bled so profusely that it had steeped my shirt, which stuck to my skin most unpleasantly. I found the ball had passed through the sartorius muscle and close to the main artery, directly through my thigh, partially injuring the bone. The surgeon who visited me shook his head and looked serious, recommending a tourniquet to be put round my thigh, and in case of a sudden effusion of blood to stop it by tightening the ligature until assistance was procured. A spent ball had also hit the calf of my leg, but the skin was not broken.

Put into an English spring waggon with Lieutenants Reilly, Pratt, and Smith. The springs of this machine were very strong, and the rough ground we passed over made them dance us up and down in an awful manner. Bad as the movement of the bullock car was, this was ten times worse, if possible. I felt happy when I was put under cover for the night upon the ground floor of a dilapidated house at Baraca with a little straw and my blanket. My thigh and leg were frightfully swollen, and also the lower part of my body. My ration bread I directed my faithful servant, Henry Short, to make into a large poultice, which was soon done. I then dressed the wound of Lieutenant Coane, who was shot in the side; he was in the same company as myself.

Poor Reilly this morning told me it was useless tormenting himself by taking another day's journey, as he felt he could not live many hours (the ball had gone directly through the lower part of his body); he shook me by the hand and regretted our parting. As the wounded were obliged to proceed daily to the rear or fall into the hands of the enemy, I was obliged to leave him in this unfortunate manner.

At daylight we proceeded to Celorico, which place we reached, after suffering indescribable torture, in the evening. Here I learned our loss more particularly, a sergeant having come to take charge of us. Captain Creagh, shot through the lower part of his body, died the night of the action; Lieutenant McLeod shot through the heart, eight officers wounded, and Lieutenant McCullock taken prisoner.

This morning we found the Portuguese muleteers had disappeared and left the spring waggon without the mules, so we were all put upon bullock cars once again. These were easier to ride upon, so I was pleased with the change. I had the intelligence that Reilly breathed his last towards evening yesterday. Several of our poor fellows died from the rough usage they suffered, and several soldiers who had neglected to cover their wounds now became one frightful mass of maggots all over the surface, which really made me tremble to see them dressed. The flies and mosquitoes followed us in myriads. We had no means of keeping off the swarms of insects, and the slow pace that the bullocks went, made us feel the vertical rays of the sun with redoubled force. We had some salt meat as rations, which, in the feverish state of our existence, we turned from with disgust; we very seldom got bread, generally biscuit, and that full of worms or mouldy; we were hurried away daily to the rear as fast as possible in order that our army, if pressed by the enemy, should not have us on the line of its march to impede its progress to the rear. Halted for the night at Villa Cortez.

Simmons endured a painful journey to Lisbon, where he recovered from his wound, returning to join his battalion later on. Fighting on the same broken hillside was an anonymous sergeant of the 43rd Light Infantry, another of Craufurd's superb regiments. In 1835 the sergeant published his memoir of the war under the rather long-winded title, *Memoirs of a Sergeant late in the Forty-Third Light Infantry Regiment, previously to and during the Peninsular War; including an account of his conversion from Popery to the Protestant Religion.* His account of the combat on the Coa ran as follows:

The most dangerous crisis had now arrived; this was on the evening of the 24th of July, which was stormy, and proved to be a memorable period. Our whole force under arms consisted of four thousand infantry, eleven hundred cavalry, and six guns; and the position occupied was about one mile and a half in length, extending in an oblique line towards the Coa. The cavalry picquets were upon the plain in front, the right on some broken ground, and the left resting on an unfinished tower eight hundred yards from Almeida: the rear was on the edge of the ravine forming the channel of the Coa, and the bridge was more than a mile distant in the bottom of the chasm. The lightning towards midnight became unusually vivid. Having been under arms for several hours, we were drenched with rain: as the day dawned a few pistol-shots in front, followed by an order for the cavalry reserve and the guns to advance, gave notice of the enemy's approach; and as the morning cleared, twenty-four thousand French infantry, five thousand cavalry, and thirty pieces of artillery were observed marching from Turones. Our line was immediately contracted, and brought under the edge of the ravine: in an instant four thousand hostile cavalry swept the plain, and our regiment was unaccountably placed within an enclosure of solid masonry at least ten feet high, situated on the left of the road, with but one narrow outlet about half musket-shot down the ravine. While thus shut up the firing in front redoubled, the cavalry, the artillery, and the cacadores successively passed by in retreat, and the sharp clang of the 95th Rifle was heard along the edge of the plain above. A few moments later and we should have been surrounded; but here, as in every other part of the field, the quickness and knowledge of the battalion officer remedied the faults of the General. In little more than a minute, by united effort, we contrived to loosen some large stones, when, by a powerful exertion we burst the enclosure, and the regiment, reformed in column of companies, was the next instant up with the riflemen. There was no room to array the line, no time for any thing but battle; every Captain carried off his company as an independent body, the whole presenting a mass of skirmishers, acting in small parties and under no regular command, yet each confident in the courage and discipline of those on his right and left, and all regulating their movements by a common discretion. Having the advantage of ground and number, the enemy broke over the edge of the ravine; their guns, ranged along the summit, played hotly with grape; and their hussars, galloping over the glacis of Almeida, poured down the road, sabring every thing in their way. The British regiments, however, extricated themselves from their perilous situation. Falling back slowly, and yet stopping and fighting whenever opportunity offered, they made their way through a rugged country, tangled with vineyards, in despite of the enemy, who was so fierce and eager, that even the horsemen rode in among the enclosures, striking at us, as we mounted the walls, or scrambled over the rocks. Just then, I found myself within pistol-shot of the enemy, while my passage was checked by a deep chasm or ravine: as not a moment was to be lost, I contrived to mount to the edge, and, having gained the opposite side, put myself in a crouching position, and managed to slide down the steep and slippery descent without injury. On approaching the river, a more open space presented itself; but the left wing being harder pressed, and having the shortest distance, the bridge was so crowded as to be impassable: here therefore we made a stand. The post was maintained until the enemy, gathering in great numbers, made a second burst, when the companies fell back. At this moment the right wing of the 52nd was seen marching towards the bridge, which was still crowded with the passing troops, when McLeod, a very young man, immediately turned his horse round, called to the troops to follow, and, taking off his cap, rode with a shout towards the enemy. The suddenness of the thing, and the distinguished action of the man, produced the effect he designed: we all rushed after him, cheering and charging as if a whole army were behind to sustain us; the enemy's skirmishers, amazed at this unexpected movement, were directly checked. The conflict was tremendous: thrice we repulsed the enemy at the point of the bayonet. McLeod was in the hottest of the battle, and a ball passed through the collar of his coat; still he was to be seen with a pistol in his right hand, among the last to retire. At length the bugle sounded for re-treat: just then, my left-hand man, one of the stoutest in the regiment, was hit by a musket shot, — he threw his head back, and was instantly dead. I fired at the fellow who shot my comrade, and before I could re-load, my pay-sergeant, Thomas, received a ball in the thigh, and earnestly implored me to carry him away. As the enemy was not far off, such a load was by no means desirable : but he was my friend desirable; I therefore took him up; and though several shots were directed to us, they all missed, and I was able, though encumbered with such weight, to carry him safely over the bridge. At length the assistance of another soldier was procured; we then carried the wounded man between us, when he was placed on a car. He returned me sincere thanks, and, what was just then much better, gave me his canteen, out of which I was permitted to take a draught of rum: how refreshing it was, can be fully known only to myself. As the regiments passed the bridge, they planted themselves in loose order on the side of the mountain; the artillery drew up on the summit, and the cavalry were disposed in parties on the roads to the right, because two miles higher up the stream there were fords, and beyond them the bridge of Castello Bom. The French skirmishers, swarming on the right bank, opened a biting fire, which was returned as bitterly; the artillery on both sides played across the ravine, the sounds were repeated by numberless echoes; and the smoke, rising slowly, resolved itself into an immense arch, sparkling with the whirling phases of the flying shells. The enemy despatched a dragoon to try the depth of the stream above; but two shots from the 52nd killed man and horse, and the carcasses floating down the river discovered that it was impassable. The monotonous tones of a French drum were then heard; and in another second the head of a column was at the long narrow bridge. A drummer and an officer in splendid uniform, leaped forward together, and the whole rushed on with loud cries. The depth of the ravine at first deceived the soldier's aim on our side, and two-thirds of the passage were won before an English shot had brought down an enemy. A few paces onward the line of death was traced, and the whole of the leading French section fell as one man. Still the gallant column pressed forward, but no foot could pass that terrible line: the killed and wounded rolled together, until the heap rose nearly to a level with the parapet. Our shouts now rose loudly, but they were confidently answered; and in half an hour a second column, more numerous than the first, again crowded the bridge. This time the range was better judged, and ere half the distance was passed, the multitude was again torn, shattered, dispersed, and slain: ten or twelve men only succeeded in crossing, and took shelter under the rocks at the brink of the river. The skirmishing was renewed, and a French surgeon, coming down to the very foot of the bridge, waved his handkerchief, and commenced dressing the wounded under the hottest fire: the appeal was heard; every musket turned from him, although his still undaunted countrymen were preparing for a third attempt. This last effort was comparatively feeble, and soon failed. The combat was nevertheless continued by the French, as a point of honour to cover the escape of those who had passed the bridge, and by the English from ignorance of their object. One of the enemy's guns was dismantled; a powder magazine blew up; and many continued to fall on both sides till four o'clock, when a heavy rain caused a momentary cessation of fire: the men among the rocks returned unmolested to their own party, the fight ceased, and we retired behind the Pinhel river. On our side upwards of three hundred were killed or wounded. The French lost more than a thousand men.

A month after the fight at the Coa bridge, Ney's guns opened fire on the fortress of Almeida. It was a strong fortress and was one that Wellington hoped would buy him valuable time as he began his retreat to the Lines of Torres Vedras. In the event, one of the first shots fired by the French ignited a leaky powder keg, which led back to the main magazine. The ensuing blast killed over 500 Portuguese soldiers and led to the surrender of the town the following morning. Thus, Wellington was denied the valuable miles that he had hoped to put between himself and the pursuing French. Needless to say, he had taken precautions to guard against such an event. For, even as Massena and his army embarked upon their pursuit of Wellington, the latter had arranged a nasty little surprise for them in the shape of one of the best kept secrets of the war.

CHAPTER FIVE

BUSACO AND THE RETREAT
TO TORRES VEDRAS

When Wellington ordered his army to retreat towards Lisbon, he did so in the knowledge that the Lines of Torres Vedras were waiting for him. What he was not sure about, however, was whether they would be completed when he arrived there. He needed to put some distance between himself and the French and so he determined to fight a delaying action. Wellington retreated deeper into Portugal until on 26 September his army reached the commanding position upon the great ridge at Busaco, overlooking the Mondego river.

The great ridge towered some eighteen hundred feet above sea level and was covered by a vast expanse of gorse and heathland strewn with rocks and boulders. Any army wishing to dislodge a defending force would, therefore, have to be at their very best. Unfortunately for Massena, the French were not. Indeed, it was only when the French discovered a road round Wellington's left flank, the day after the battle of Busaco, that they succeeded in forcing Wellington to shift from his ridge. By that time, however, they had suffered more heavy casualties in yet another of Wellington's classic defensive battles.

Wellington's army at Busaco numbered about 50,000 men with 60 guns. Opposed to him were Massena's three corps, Ney's Junot's and Reynier's, which together numbered 66,000 men with 114 guns. The 27 September dawned grey and misty, a thick grey fog completely blanketing the valley below the ridge. But by 5.30 a.m. the noise from below signalled the advance of Massena's attacking columns. The French attack ended in the same sorry state as their efforts at Vimeiro and Talavera. By mid-morning all but four of the twenty-seven battalions that had struggled and striven to reach the top of the ridge had been sent reeling to the bottom after having sustained heavy casualties.

Some of the most intense and desperate fighting took place at the pass of San Antonio and in the rocks either side of it. Here, Picton's 3rd Division and Leith's 5th Division engaged the French in close combat, with the French coming close to forcing the British position. One of the

3rd Division's officers was Ensign William Grattan, of the 88th. Grattan's *Adventures with the Connaught Rangers*, published in 1847, is one of the most famous and enjoyable Peninsular memoirs. The 3rd Division saw more than its fair share of action in the Peninsula, where it was known as the 'Fighting' division. Busaco was no exception, as Grattan later wrote.

On the morning of the 27th the haze was so thick that little could be seen at any great distance, but the fire of the light troops along the face of the hill put it beyond doubt that a battle would take place. Lord Wellington was close to the brigade of Lightburne, and from the bustle amongst his staff, it was manifest that the point held by Picton's division was about to be attacked. Two guns belonging to Captain Lane's troop of artillery were ordered upon the left of the 88th Regiment, and immediately opened their fire, while the Portuguese battery, under the German Major Arentschildt, passed at a trot towards the Saint Antonio Pass, in front of the 74th British.

A rolling fire of musketry, and some discharges of cannon, in the direction of Saint Antonio, announced what was taking place in that quarter, and the face of the hill immediately in front of the brigade of Lightburne, and to the left of the 88th Regiment, was beginning to show that the efforts of the enemy were about to be directed against this portion of the ground held by the 3rd Division.

The fog cleared away, and a bright sun enabled us to see what was passing before us. A vast crowd of tirailleurs were pressing onward with great ardour, and their fire, as well as their numbers, was so superior to that of our advance, that some men of the brigade of Lightburne, as also a few of the 88th Regiment, were killed while standing in line; a colour sergeant named Macnamara was shot through the head close beside myself and Ensign Owgan. Colonel King, commanding the 5th Regiment, which was one of those belonging to Lightburne's brigade, oppressed by a desultory fire he was unable to reply to without disturbing the formation of his battalion, brought his regiment a little out of its range, while Colonel Alexander Wallace, of the 88th, took a file of men from each company of his regiment, and placing them under the command of Captain George Bury and Lieutenant William Mackie, ordered them to advance to the aid of our people, who were overmatched and roughly handled at the moment. Our artillery still continued to discharge showers of grape and cannister at half range, but the French light troops, fighting at open distance, heeded it not, and continued to multiply in great force. Nevertheless, in place of coming up direct in front of the 88th, they edged off to their left, out of sight of that corps, and far away from Lightburne's brigade, and from the nature of the ground they could be neither seen nor their exact object defined; as they went to their left, our advance inclined to the right, making a corresponding movement; but though nothing certain could be known, as we soon lost sight of both parties, the roll of musketry never ceased, and many of Bury's and Mackie's men returned wounded. Those two officers greatly distinguished themselves, and Bury, though badly wounded, refused to quit the field. A soldier of Bury's company, of the name of Pollard, was shot through the shoulder; but seeing his captain, though wounded, continue at the head of his men, he threw off his knapsack, and fought beside his officer; but this brave fellow's career of glory was short, a bullet penetrated the plate of his cup, passed through his brain, and he fell dead at Bury's feet. These were the sort of materials the 88th were formed of, and these were the sort of men that were unnoticed by their General! Lord Wellington was no longer to be seen, and Wallace and his regiment, standing alone without orders, had to act for themselves. The Colonel sent his captain of Grenadiers (Dunne) to the right, where the rocks were highest, to ascertain how matters stood, for he did not wish, at his own peril, to quit the ground he had been ordered to occupy without some strong reason for so doing. All this time the brigade of Lightburne, as also the 88th, were standing at ordered arms.

In a few moments Dunne returned almost breathless; he said the rocks were filling fast with Frenchmen, that a heavy column was coming up the hill beyond the rocks, and that the four companies of the 45th were about to be attacked. Wallace asked if he thought half the 88th would be able to do the business. "You will want every man," was the reply.

Wallace, with a steady but cheerful countenance, turned to his men, and looking them full in the face, said, "Now, Connaught Rangers, mind what you are going to do; pay attention to what I have so often told you, and when I bring you face to face with those French rascals, drive them down the hill — don't give the false touch, but push home to the muzzle! I have nothing more to say, and if I had it would be of no use, for in a minute or two there'll be such an infernal noise about your ears that you won't be able to hear yourselves."

This address went home to the hearts of us all, but there was no cheering; a steady but determined calm had taken the place of any lighter feeling, and it seemed as if the men had made up their minds to go to their work unruffled and not too much excited.

Wallace then threw the battalion from line into column, right in front, and moved on our side of the rocky point at a quick pace; on reaching the rocks, he soon found it manifest that Dunne's report was not exaggerated; a number of Frenchmen were in possession of this cluster, and so soon as we approached within range we were made to appreciate the effects of their fire, for our column was raked from front to rear. The moment was critical, but Wallace, without being in the least taken aback, filed out the Grenadiers and the first battalion-company, commanded by Captains Dunne and Dansey, and ordered them to storm the rocks, while he took the fifth battalion-company, commanded by Captain Oates, also out of the column, and ordered that officer to attack the rocks at the opposite side to that assailed by Dunne and Dansey. This done, Wallace placed himself at the head of the remainder of the 88th, and pressed on to meet the French column.

At this moment the four companies of the 45th, commanded by Major Gwynne, a little to the left of the 88th, and in front of that regiment, commenced their fire, but it in no way arrested the advance of the French column, as it, with much order and regularity, mounted the hill, which at this point is rather flat. But here, again, another awkward circumstance occurred. A battalion of the 8th Portuguese Infantry, under Colonel Douglas, posted on a rising ground on our right, and a little in our rear, in place of advancing with us, opened a distant and ill-directed fire, and one which would exactly cross the path of the 88th, as that corps was moving onward to meet the French column, which consisted of three splendid regiments, viz. the 2nd Light Infantry, the 36th, and the 70th of the line. Wallace, seeing the loss and confusion that would infallibly ensue, sent Lieutenant John Fitzpatrick, an officer of tried gallantry, with orders to point out to this regiment the error into which it had fallen; but Fitzpatrick had only time to take off his hat, and call out *"Vamos commarades,"* when he received two bullets — one from the Portuguese, which passed through his back, and the other in his left leg from the French, which broke the bone, and caused a severe fracture; yet this regiment continued to fire away, regardless of the consequences, and a battalion of militia, which was immediately in rear of the 8th Portuguese, took to their heels the moment the first volley was discharged by their own countrymen!

Wallace threw himself from his horse, and placing himself at the head of the 45th and 88th, with Gwynne of the 45th on the one side of him, and Captain Seton of the 88th on the other, ran forward at a charging pace into the midst of the terrible flame in his front. All was now confusion and uproar, smoke, fire and bullets, officers and soldiers, French drummers and French drums knocked down in every direction; British, French, and Portuguese mixed together; while in the midst of all was to be seen Wallace, fighting —

like his ancestor of old — at the head of his devoted followers, and calling out to his soldiers to "press forward!" Never was defeat more complete, and it was a proud moment for Wallace and Gwynne when they saw their gallant comrades breaking down and trampling under their feet this splendid division composed of some of the best troops the world could boast of. The leading regiment, the 86th, one of Napoleon's favourite battalions, was nearly destroyed; upwards of two hundred soldiers and their old colonel, covered with orders, lay dead in a small space, and the face of the hill was strewed with dead and wounded, which showed evident marks of the rapid execution done at this point; for Wallace never slackened his fire while a Frenchman was within his reach. He followed them down the edge of the hill, and then he formed his men in line, waiting for any orders he might receive, or for any fresh body that might attack him. Our gallant companions, the 45th, had an equal share in the glory of this short but murderous fight — they suffered severely; and the 88th lost nine officers and one hundred and thirty-five men. The 8th Portuguese also suffered, but in a less degree than the other two regiments, because their advance was not so rapid, but that regiment never gave way nor was it ever broken; indeed there was nothing to break it, because the French were all in front of the 45th and 88th, and if they had broken the Portuguese they must have first broken the two British regiments, which it is well known they did not! The regiment of militia in their rear ran away most manfully; and if they were able to continue for any length of time the pace at which they commenced their flight, they might, I should say, have nearly reached Coimbra before all matters had been finally settled between us and the French. Two of their officers stood firm and reported themselves in person to Wallace on the field of battle; so there could be no mistake about them, no more than there was about the rest of their regiment.

Meanwhile, Captains Dunne, Dansey, and Oates had a severe struggle with the French troops that occupied the rocks. Dunne's sergeant (Brazil) killed a Frenchman by a push of his halberd, who had nearly overpowered his captain. Dansey was slightly wounded in four places, but it was said at the time that he killed three Frenchmen — for he used a firelock. Oates suffered less, as the men opposed to him were chiefly composed of those that fled from Dunne and Dansey. Dunne's company of Grenadiers, which at the onset counted about sixty, lost either two or three-and-thirty, and Dansey's and Oates's companies also suffered, but not to the same amount. The French troops that defended those rocks were composed of the 4th Regiment and the Irish Brigade; several of the latter were left wounded in the rocks, but we could not discover one Irishman amongst them.

71

Lord Wellington, surrounded by his staff and some general officers, was a close observer of this attack. He was standing on a rising ground in rear of the 88th Regiment, and so close to that corps that Colonel Napier of the 50th — who was on leave of absence — was wounded in the face by a musket shot quite close to Lord Wellington. His Lordship passed the warmest encomiums on the troops engaged, and noticed the conduct of Captain Dansey in his despatch. It has been said, and I believe truly, that Marshal Beresford, who was colonel of the 88th, expressed some uneasiness when he saw his regiment about to plunge into this unequal contest; but when they were mixed with Reynier's men and pushing them down the hill, Lord Wellington, tapping him on the shoulder, said, "Well, Beresford, look at them now!"

While these events which I have described were taking place, Picton in person took the command against the other division of Reynier's corps and had a sharp dispute with it at the pass of Saint Antonio; but General Mackinnon, who led on the troops, never allowed it to make any head. A shower of balls from Arentschildt's battery deranged its deployment, and a few volleys from the 74th British and the Portuguese brigade of Champlemond totally routed this column before it reached the top of the ridge. This attack was feeble in comparison with the one directed against Wallace, and, besides, Picton's force was vastly superior to that commanded by Wallace, while the troops opposed to him were little, if anything, more numerous. Picton had at this point five companies of the 45th under Major Smyth, all the light companies of the 3rd Division, one company of the 60th Rifles, the 74th British and the Portuguese brigade of Champlemond, besides Arentschildt's battery of guns. It is not, therefore, to be wondered at that Reynier made little or no impression on Picton's right.

The 5th Division, commanded by General Leith, was in movement towards the contested point, and reached it in time either to take the fugitives in flank or to drive back any fresh body destined to support their defeated comrades. It made great efforts to join Picton when he was attacked, but the advance was so rapid, the defeat so signal, and the distance — two miles across a rugged mountain — so great, that Leith and his gallant division could only effect in part what they intended. The arrival of this force was, however, fully appreciated; for although the brigade of Lightburne, belonging to Picton's division, had not fired a shot or been at all molested, and although the 74th Regiment was nearly at liberty, still, had another attack with fresh troops been made, Leith might have stood in Picton's shoes on the extreme right, while the latter could in a short time concentrate all his battalions, and either tight beside Leith or turn with vigour against any effort that might be made against his centre or left. But it would seem that no reserve was in hand — at all events none was thrown into the fight; and Massena gave up without a second trial that in which he lost many men and much glory!

While Picton, Mackinnon, Wallace and Champlemond, and Leith's division, were occupied as I have described, the Light Division, under the gallant Robert Craufurd, maintained a severe struggle against a large proportion of Ney's corps. Those French troops were driven down the hill with great loss, and the general of brigade, Simon, who headed and led the attack, was taken prisoner by the 52nd Regiment, and between two and three hundred unwounded men shared the fate of their general. The leading brigade of Leith's division put to flight some of the enemy who kept a hold of a rocky point on Picton's right, and had Picton been aware of their being there he might have cut off their retreat, while Leith attacked them in front and flank; but their number, were scanty, and they might not have been aware of the fate of their companions, otherwise they would in all probability have got out of Leith's clutches before his arrival for their remaining in the rocks could be of no possible avail, and their force was too weak to hazard any serious attack on Picton's right. Indeed, they were routed by a battalion or two of Leith's division; and the entire British loss at this point did not count above forty or fifty. And thus ended a battle of which so many accounts have been given: all at variance with each other — and none more so than what I have, just written.

It has been said that Picton directed the attack of the 45th under Major Gwynne, the 88th under Wallace, and the 8th Portuguese under Douglas. Not one syllable of this is true. The conception of this attack, its brilliant execution, which ended in the total overthrow of Reynier's column, all belong to Colonel Alexander Wallace of the 88th Regiment. At the time it was made Generals Picton and Mackinnon had their hands full at the pass of Saint Antonio, and were, in effect, as distant from Wallace as if they had been on the Rock of Lisbon; neither was General Lightburne to be seen. The nearest officer of rank to Wallace was Lord Wellington, who saw all that was passing and never interfered *pro* or *con*, which is a tolerably strong proof that his lordship thought no alteration for the better could be made; and Wallace had scarcely reformed his line, a little in front and below the contested ground, when Lord Wellington, accompanied by Marshal Beresford and a number of other officers, galloped up, and passing round the left of our line, rode up to Wallace, and seizing him warmly by the hand, said, "Wallace, I never witnessed a more gallant charge than that made just now by your regiment!"

Wallace took off his hat — but his heart was too full to speak. It was a proud moment for him; his fondest hopes had been realised, and the trouble he had taken to bring the 88th to the splendid state of perfection in which that corps then was, has been repaid in the space of a few minutes by his gallant soldiers, many of whom shed tears of joy. Marshal Beresford addressed several of the soldiers by name who had served under him when he commanded the regiment; and Picton, who at this time came up, expressed his satisfaction. Lord Wellington then took leave of us; and Beresford, shaking the officers by the hand, rode away with his lordship, accompanied by the officers about him. We were once more left to ourselves; the arms were piled, the wounded of all nations collected and carried to the rear, and in a short time the dead were left without a stitch of clothes to cover their bodies. All firing had ceased, except a few shots low down the hill on our right; and shortly after the picquets were placed in front, a double allowance of spirits was served out to Wallace's men.

We had now leisure to walk about and talk to each other on the events of the morning, and look at the French soldiers in our front. They appeared as leisurely employed cooking their rations as if nothing serious had occurred to them, which caused much amusement to our men, some of whom remarked that they left a few behind them that had got a "bellyful" already. The rocks which had been forced by the three companies of the 88th presented a curious and melancholy sight; one side of their base strewed with our brave fellows, almost all of them shot through the head, while in many of the niches were to be seen dead Frenchmen, in the position they had fought; while on the other side, and on the projecting crags, lay numbers who, in an effort to escape the fury of our men, were dashed to pieces in their fall!

Day at length began to close, and night found the two armies occupying the ground they held on the preceding evening; our army, as then, in utter darkness, that of the enemy more brilliant than the preceding night, which brought to our recollection the remark of a celebrated general when he saw bonfires through France after a signal defeat which the troops of that nation had sustained. "Gad!" said the general, "those Frenchmen are like flintstones — the more you beat them the more fire they make!"

Captain Seton, Ensign Owgan, and myself, with one hundred of the Connaught Rangers, formed the picquet in advance of that regiment, and immediately facing the outposts of the enemy in our front. The sentries of each, as is customary in civilised armies, although within half shot range of each other, never fired except upon occasions of necessity. Towards midnight Seton, a good and steady officer, went in front, for the third time, to see that the sentinels which he himself had posted were on the alert. He found all right; but upon his return to the main body he missed his way, and happening in the dark to get too close to a French sharpshooter, he was immediately challenged, but not thinking it prudent to make any noise, in the shape of reply or otherwise, he held his peace. Not so with the Frenchman, who uttered a loud cry to alarm his companions, and discharged the contents of his musket at Seton; the ball passed through his hat, but did no other injury, and he might have rejoiced at this escape had the matter ended here; but the cry of the sentinel and the discharge of his musket alarmed the other, and one general volley from the line of outposts of both armies warned Seton that his best and safest evolution would be to sprawl flat on his face amongst the heath with which the hill was copiously garnished. He did so, and us soon as the tumult had in a great degree abated, he got up on his hands and knees and essayed to gain the ground which no doubt he regretted he had ever quit. He was nearing the picquet fast, when the rustling in the heath, increased by the awkward position in which he moved, put us on the *qui vive*. Owgan, who was a dead shot with a rifle, and who on this day carried one, called out, in a low but clear tone, "I see you, and if you don't answer you'll be a dead man in a second"; and he cocked his rifle, showing he meant to make good his promise.

Whether it was that Seton knew the temperament of the last speaker, or was flurried by the recollection of what he was near receiving from his obstinate taciturnity with the French soldier, is uncertain. But in this instance he completely changed his plan of tactics, and replied in a low and scarcely audible tone, "Owgan! don't fire — it's me." So soon as he recovered his natural and more comfortable position — for he was still "all-fours" — we congratulated him on his lucky escape, and I placed my canteen of brandy to his mouth; it did not require much pressing to prevail upon him to take a hearty swig, which indeed he stood much in need of.

The night passed over without further adventure or annoyance, and in the morning the picquets on both sides were relieved. The dead were buried without much ceremony, and the soldiers occupied themselves cleaning their arms, arranging their accoutrements, and cooking their rations. The enemy showed no great disposition to renew his attack, and a few of us obtained leave to go down to the village of Busaco, in order to visit some of our officers, who were so badly wounded as to forbid their being removed further to the rear. Amongst the number was the gallant Major Silver of the 88th. He had been shot through the body, and though he did not think himself in danger, as he suffered no pain, it was manifest to the medical men he could not live many hours. He gave orders to his servant to leave him for a short time,

75

and attend to his horses; the man did so, but on his return in about a quarter of an hour he found poor Silver lying on his right side as if he was asleep — but he was dead! Silver was one of the best soldiers in the army, and was thanked by Colonel Donkin, who commanded the brigade at the battle of Talavera, for his distinguished bravery in that action. He was laid in a deep grave in the uniform he had fought and died in.

One of the most disastrous attacks began at around 8.30 a.m., when Massena sent forward Loison's division to attack the part of the ridge held by the Light Division. Loison's men succeeded initially in driving back Craufurd's skirmishers and, in fact, they reached the top of the ridge. When they arrived there they found the British position deserted, save for a solitary figure in a great coat and cocked hat. It was Robert Craufurd. Behind him, lying in a sunken lane, lay nearly two thousand of the finest infantry in the British Army. As the French reached the summit of the ridge, Craufurd took off his hat and waved it in the air, crying, "Now 52nd! Avenge the death of Sir John Moore!" and then, in the words of William Napier, "eighteen hundred British bayonets went sparkling over the hill." Loison's men were driven helter-skelter down the hillside, pursued all the way by enthusiastic British bayonet-wielding infantry. The attack was a total disaster. Of the 6,500 men used by Loison 1,200 had become casualties including 21 officers who were killed and 47 wounded including an enraged General Simon who was taken prisoner by privates Hopkins and Harris of the 52nd. The 43rd and 52nd between them lost just three men killed and two officers and eighteen men wounded, which reflects the outstanding success achieved by the Light Division.

One of the Light Division's officers was George Napier, of the 52nd Light Infantry. In his memoir, *Passages in the Early Military Life of General Sir George T Napier*, published in London in 1884, he described the battle and, in particular, the defeat of Loison's division.

In the course of a short time the army retreated towards Busaco. As our brigade formed the rearguard we were continually in conflict with the enemy's advance, but as we generally kept at a respectable distance from each other, but few men were killed and wounded, and two or three officers at most. Every night I suffered from fever or ague during this retreat; but what is very curious, as showing the effect the mind has upon the body, the moment we engaged with the enemy the ague left me, and I was quite strong and able to do my duty, and go through my day's work as well as any officer in the regiment, without the least feeling of illness or weakness; but when we halted at night I lost all energy, and was as suffering and miserable a wretch as can well be conceived. At length we arrived at the heights of Busaco, a range of mountains very high, and in parts very steep and difficult of access. There was a convent of the order of La Trappe on the top, but some distance in the rear of the position. At this convent Lord Wellington took up his quarters, and disposed his army in position to fight a battle if the enemy had the boldness — indeed I might say the temerity — to attack him. Lord Hill's (then General Hill) corps was on our right, the 3rd (General Picton's) division and the lst division were in the centre, the Light Brigade on their left, and General Cole, with the 4th division, quite on the left flank of the whole. The Portuguese regular troops were mixed with our divisions, and a second line was formed of the Militia and armed peasantry. I should suppose the whole force under the Duke of Wellington was about sixty-five or seventy thousand men, and the position itself was by nature as strong as possible, so that it appeared to all of us that Marshal Massena would never attempt to carry it; and if he did make the attempt, we were perfectly certain he would be driven back and repulsed with great slaughter. We remained in position one day, during which time the various divisions and brigades were employed in getting everything in order, so that when the enemy did come on he should have enough of it. The morning of the second day we perceived a movement in the enemy's camp, which was on the heights opposite us, a small stream running through the valley which divided the armies. We judged their force to be nearly equal to ours — certainly Massena could not have had less than sixty thousand men in his camp — so that about one hundred and thirty thousand men were going to have a fierce and bloody struggle with each other; the forces of the two armies nearly equal in point of numbers, but not so in composition, as the enemy's was composed of the finest soldiers of France, none of whom that could not count many years of hard-fought campaigns, and had gained numerous victories and in various countries; in short, a finer army or better appointed could not be well conceived, and at its head was Marshal Massena, then looked upon as next to Napoleon himself in military fame. Our army was, on the contrary, composed of bad and inexperienced troops as well as good and experienced ones, for Lord Wellington had not above thirty thousand real soldiers, the rest were raw and undisciplined Militia, who had never seen a shot fired or an enemy in battle array before; so that upon the British soldiers he depended for the successful issue of the fight, and gloriously did they prove themselves worthy of his confidence. The French had now formed their columns and were moving steadily and gallantly down to the valley below in three bodies, meaning to attack and penetrate our line at three different points — viz. the right, centre, and left, where our division (for we had been formed into two brigades, having had two Portuguese regiments incorporated with us, under the command of Colonels Beckwith, Rifle Corps, and Barclay, 52nd Regiment) was stationed on the steepest part of the mountain. We were retired a few yards from the brow of the hill, so that our line was concealed from the view of the enemy as they advanced up the heights, and our skirmishers retired, keeping up a constant and well-directed running fire upon them; and the brigade of horse artillery under Captain Hugh Ross threw such a heavy fire of shrapnel-shells, and so quick, that their column, which consisted of about eight thousand men, was put into a good deal of confusion and lost great numbers before it arrived at a ledge of ground just under the brow of the hill, where they halted a few moments to take breath, the head of the column being exactly fronting my company, which was the right company of our brigade, and joining the left company of the 43rd, where my brother William was with his company. General Craufurd himself stood on the brow of the hill watching every movement of the attacking column, and when all our skirmishers had passed by and joined their respective corps, and the head of the enemy's column was within a very few yards of him, he turned round, came up to the 52nd, and called out, "Now, 52nd, revenge the death of Sir John Moore! Charge, charge! Huzza!" and waving his hat in the air he was answered by a shout that appalled the enemy, and in one instant the brow of the hill bristled with two thousand British bayonets wielded by steady English hands, which soon buried them in the bodies of the fiery Gaul! My company met the head of the French column, and immediately calling to my men to form column of sections in order to give more force to our rush, we dashed forward; and as I was by this movement in front of my men a yard or two, a French soldier made a plunge at me with his bayonet, and at the same time his musket going off I received the contents just under my hip and fell. At the same instant the French fired upon my front section, consisting of about nine men in the front rank, all of whom fell, four of them dead, the rest wounded, so that most probably by my being a little advanced in front my life was saved, as the men killed were exactly those nearest to me. Poor Colonel Barclay also received a severe wound (of which he afterwards died in England). I got upon my legs immediately again and pursued the enemy down the hill, for by this time they had been completely repulsed, and were running away as fast as their legs could carry them. William and his friend Captain Lloyd, who were upon my right, seeing that the French were still in column and in great confusion from the unexpected suddenness of the charge and the shout which accompanied it, had wheeled up their companies by the left, and thus flanked the French column and poured a well-directed fire right into them. Major Arbuthnott, who was on my left, did the same with the remaining companies of the 52nd, so that the enemy was beset on both flanks of his column, and, as you may suppose, the slaughter was great. We kept firing and bayoneting till we reached the bottom, and the enemy passed the brook and fell back upon their main body, which moved down to support them and cover their retreat. All this was done in a very short time — that is, it was not above twenty minutes from the charge till the French were driven from the top to the bottom of the mountain like a parcel of sheep. I really did not think it was possible for such a column to be so completely destroyed in a few minutes as that was, particularly after witnessing how gallantly they moved up under a destructive fire from the artillery and a constant galling one from our sharp-shooters.

We took some prisoners, and among them General Simon, a gallant officer, but a bad and a dishonourable man, who afterwards broke his parole of honour. He was horribly wounded in the face, his jaw being broken and almost hanging down on his chest. Just as myself and another officer came to him, a soldier was going to put his bayonet into him, which we prevented, and sent him a prisoner to the general. As I went down the hill following the enemy, I saw seven or eight French officers lying wounded. One of them as I passed caught hold of my little silver canteen and implored me to stop and give him a drink, but, much as it pained me to refuse, I could not do it, being in full pursuit of the enemy, and it was impossible to stop for an instant. This may be thought hard-hearted, but in war we often do and must do many harsh and unfeeling things. Had I stopped to give him a drink I must have done so for the others, and then I should have been the last at the bottom of the hill instead of one of the first in pursuit of the enemy and recollect, my boys, that an officer should always be first in advancing against the enemy and last in retreating from him. When we got to the bottom, where a small stream ran between us and the enemy's position, by general consent we all mingled together searching for the wounded. During this cessation of fighting we spoke to each other as though we were the greatest friends and without the least animosity or angry, feeling! One poor German officer in the French army came to make inquiries respecting his brother, who was in our service in the 60th Regiment, which was at that time composed principally of foreigners, and upon looking about he found him dead, the poor fellow having been killed. Very soon Lord Wellington, finding we remained as he thought too long below, ordered the bugles to sound the retreat, and the French general having done the same, off scampered the soldiers of each army and returned to their several positions like a parcel of schoolboys called in from play by their master.

I was so stiff by this time that I had difficulty in walking up the hill again and was obliged to get Mr. Winterbottom, the adjutant of the regiment, to help me up. When I arrived at the top, I understood that my brother Charles was severely wounded in the face while attending Lord Wellington during the battle, and that he was gone, or rather carried, to the rear, attended by our cousin Captain Charles Napier of the navy, who had been with us for some weeks as an amateur, not having a ship at that time and being too active and enterprising a fellow to remain at home idle waiting for one. He had gone out with me the evening before the battle to skirmish a little with the French pickets, as General Craufurd thought they had advanced rather closer to the foot of our position than was right, so I was ordered to move down and push them a little farther off. Charles Napier our cousin would take a little white pony I had to ride with us, notwithstanding I told him it was very foolish for most certainly he would get hit, being the only person on horseback. But he chose to go his own way and in less than half an hour he got shot in the calf of the leg, but very slightly; and I was delighted at it; the obstinate dog, he deserved it well! However, he was very good-humoured and laughed as much as anyone at his own folly. William had escaped being wounded in the battle and he and I were very glad to find ourselves side by side again. In about half an hour after we returned to our position the whole army was under arms and Lord Wellington rode along the line receiving a cheer from every regiment as he passed. While in the act of doing this I am sorry to say the French general did a most unhandsome thing, and that was to make one of his batteries fire at Lord Wellington as he rode along accompanied by his staff! This was shameful and cowardly, because Marshal Massena knew (the thing was too evident for him not to know) that he was only reviewing and thanking his troops for their bravery, and he should have prevented any such act. Had Marshal Soult or Marshal Ney been the general in command of the French army they would have scorned such an act. We remained the rest of that day and the one following in the position, expecting a fresh attack from the enemy; but Marshal Massena had enough of it, and the second day after the action our army silently moved off before daybreak on the road to Coimbra, leaving our fires and pickets, the latter retreating also as soon as daylight came. Our division as usual formed the rear-guard and as we were passing by the Convent of La Trappe General Craufurd ordered me to post myself in the garden of it, which overlooked the late position of the army and commanded the road by which the troops were retiring, and there to remain and defend it as long as I had a man left! This I should have done, for I was determined to keep my post if I lived as long as I had a cartridge left to load with; but as no enemy appeared I had no opportunity of showing what good stuff an English company of light infantry was made of. It was ascertained in about an hour that the enemy had moved off also and were marching by another road to Coimbra, which they expected to reach before us and so cut off the British army, or at least a large portion of it, from the retreat to the Lines.

By midday, all French attacks had been bloodily repulsed and, although there was some skirmishing throughout the afternoon, the battle of Busaco was as good as over. Wellington had again triumphed at the cost of 1,252 casualties. Massena, on the other hand, had seen 4,600 of his men killed, wounded or taken prisoners including 234 officers. Busaco was a yet another success for Wellington, although the gloss was undeniably taken off the victory the following day when the French discovered the road round Wellington's left flank. Nevertheless, Wellington had already determined upon continuing his retreat, and so he and his men continued towards Lisbon. As he did so, Wellington could, no doubt, afford him a little smile, for he knew exactly what awaited the French when they arrived before Lisbon; the Lines of Torres Vedras. Before he reached the Lines, however, there remained the business of driving the Portuguese people south to the Lines, after ordering them to destroy their crops and burn anything that may be of use to the French. Naturally, there was a good deal of reluctance on the part of the population, although their sacrifice was not in vain. Indeed, Wellington's sojourn behind the Lines of Torres Vedras marked a significant and crucial phase of the war.

Sergeant William Lawrence, of the 40th Foot, was a veteran of the ill-fated campaign in the Rio de la Plata, and had already seen action in the Peninsula. His memoir, *The Autobiography of Sergeant William Lawrence*, was published in London in 1886, and contains a good description of the retreat towards Lisbon and the accompanying chaos on the road.

From Coimbra we proceeded farther south, having again to cross the Mondego, which we did in the latter end of September, reaching Leiria on the 2nd of October.

On the march we passed a nunnery, where we halted for about a quarter of an hour. A great many of the nuns were crowding the balconies to watch us, and as the French were following us up pretty close, the colonel ordered the doors to be broken open by a body of grenadiers, which was soon done, myself being among the number told off for the purpose. This was not carried out, however, without an accident, for one of the women meanwhile fell from a balcony, owing to the crowded state in which they were packed on it. The poor women seemed very glad to get their liberty, for they came out as thick as a flock of sheep, and a great many of them soon passed us bound for Lisbon, being fearful of consequences if they took any other direction: as the French were after us so near as to skirmish with our rear-guard, which chiefly consisted of cavalry.

Lord Wellington had indeed issued a proclamation ordering all the inhabitants to fall back on the approach of the enemy, and destroy any articles that they might possess and were not able to carry with them, that were at all likely to be of any use to the enemy; and so thousands of the population of the country that seemed about to fall within the bounds of the enemy's marches were to be seen flying from their dwellings, and our army during its retreat was accompanied by crowds of miserable men, women, and children, all eager to reach the capital, as they knew that if they fell in with the French, they would be treated as some had been before, with all the barbarities of an atrocious enemy. I have often heard talk of "moving" in England and have seen a cart or wagon with a man driving a load of furniture, at the rate of three miles an hour, with a woman and perhaps several children sitting on the top, or at the back; but I never before or since saw such a wholesale move as this was, for every one seemed anxious to carry as many of his effects as he could find room for. The farther we proceeded the more confused our retreat appeared, for multitudes were obliged to rest weary and exhausted by the roadside, and often, though made eager in their endeavours as they heard of the enemy's approach to again renew their tedious journey, were found dying or even dead from their hard exertions, and the road was everywhere strewn with pieces of all kinds of furniture, which the poor fugitives had vainly attempted to get forward.

From Leiria we went on further to Torres Vedras, which we gained after a long, tedious, and impressive march; and there we took up our position at some fine breastworks which Lord Wellington had for some time previous ordered to be thrown up by the Portuguese peasantry in case of the retreat of our army. Now we found how much we needed them, for on the 10th of October the French came in sight of our strong position, where we had drawn up, determined that they should not proceed one step farther towards Lisbon.

Massena was rather surprised at our strength, which was quite unexpected by him. He had thought of driving the English into the sea, but he now found his mistake, so encamped about a mile and a half from our position.

On the 14th, however, he attacked our lines near Sobral, but was repulsed; and on another occasion a slight skirmish took place on the right of the line, in which the French general, St. Croix, was killed by the fire from our gun-boats; but on account of our strong position, the French did not come to a general engagement.

The cold and rainy weather having now set in, Lord Wellington had provided as well as possible for the best reception of his troops, who were mostly now in cantonments, whilst those of Massena's army were subject to hardships of the worst description, owing to the cold, wet, and above all insufficient food and raiment, for they were far away from all supplies from their own country, and there were guerrillas or mountain rebels always on the watch to intercept such as were sent, while our army was so near Lisbon that it could always get abundance. Our regiment was situated in a village called Patamara, in the front of our works, where we lay as comfortably as if we had been living in peaceful times; though we were so near the enemy that we very often wandered into the same vineyards, and exchanged compliments by shaking hands.

We were cantoned in a large cellar, but it was unfortunately empty, or at least there was no wine in it, and though there was a quantity of wheat in a vat, we had no need of that, as we had plenty of our own supplies. The owner of our cellar generally visited us every day, and we could not help thinking after a time that he seemed to take particular notice of a large box or bin that two of our men were using to sleep in, so we moved it one morning, and found that the ground underneath had been disturbed. Of course we thought that there must be some treasure concealed there, so we went to work with our bayonets, having no other tools at hand, and soon we came across a large jar, which we found contained bags of dollars, about two hundred and fifty in each bag; which treasure we distributed privately among the cellar company, carefully breaking the jar and returning the earth to its proper place, with the chest on the top of it, so that a minute eye could not have told that it had been disturbed.

Next morning as usual the owner came, bringing with him two labourers, who set to work filling the chest with wheat from the vat, evidently with the intention of making it weighty, he little suspecting that his treasure, which he supposed was underneath, had been divided amongst his tenants. After that we thought we were pretty right from detection, but we were mistaken, for in the morning our restless owner again made his appearance with the two labourers. I should think that that night he must have dreamt of our manoeuvre, for he now shifted the wheat back again into its place, moved the chest, and raised the earth and the broken jar, but found the bird had flown. I shall never forget the rage the man was in. I thought he would have torn the hair off his head; in fact, he did tear some up by the roots, but he must have found that a poor way of showing his spite. He cried, "Ladrone! Ladrone!"which was his way of expressing "Thief! Thief!" but finding that we did not take much notice of him, he reported his loss to the colonel, or rather went off to him with that intention; but as the colonel did not understand his language, I was sent for, as by that time I was pretty well acquainted with it; and on my replying to the question as to what the Portuguese wanted, that he required a corporal and three privates to guard a stack of wood, the colonel told me to let him know that he had nothing to do with it. I told the Portuguese that it was no use his making a noise about the money, as it must have been only a little change that he could not conveniently recover, unless he could bring proper witnesses to prove he had put the money there.

That only appeased him for the night, however, for he came bothering the colonel again next morning. The colonel again sent for me and asked me what on earth this man wanted now, so I was then obliged to admit the truth. I asked him if he would forgive me for telling him an untruth overnight, and on his consenting, I told him the Portuguese had lost a quantity of money, which he put down at seven thousand dollars. The Portuguese's answer to the question who had placed the money there was that he had himself, but he could bring no witnesses to show that he had really done it, so the colonel said he could have nothing to do with the affair. However, the following morning the plague again appeared, so the colonel to quiet him told him that the grenadiers had some prize money which was expected in a few days, and which he should receive in lieu of what he had lost, which sent the old man off seemingly as satisfied as if he had already got the money in his possession, shaking hands with us all round, and bowing and scraping as if we had been so many kings.

There were, no doubt, hundreds of similar incidents as a result of thousands of British soldiers living cheek by jowl with the Portuguese people. The French, meanwhile, made no offensive moves for the next month. Indeed, Massena was totally baffled by the Lines and was unable to conjure up any effective strategy to pass them. Wellington, on the other hand, simply sat back and enjoyed the services of the Royal Navy, which kept his army well supplied, while Massena's men continued to waste away through disease and starvation.

CHAPTER SIX

MASSENA'S RETREAT, SABUGAL AND FUENTES DE OÑORO

The Lines of Torres Vedras proved to be one of the best kept secrets of the Peninsular War. In fact, many regard their secrecy as one of the best secrets in military history generally. They were also a very cheap and very effective weapon, upon which Wellington could call if he ever had need to use them in future campaigns. In the event, they were used only once, in the winter of 1810–11.

Wellington's army entered the Lines almost a year to the day after he had issued Sir Richard Fletcher, his head engineer, with orders to begin their construction. The French were following close behind but reeled back when they saw the numerous redoubts and forts that had been erected upon the many hillsides in front of them. So strong was the position, in fact, that Massena's army came grinding to a halt in front of them, and after a brief attempt at storming them, at Sobral on 14 October 1810, they pulled back and waited while their commander tried to work out how he was to deal with them.

It seems strange today, that such an extensive set of earthworks, forts, dams, walls and other obstacles, had been constructed in secrecy. Well, this is true to a point, but it was impossible for Wellington to keep them a total secret. Indeed, many of Wellington's officers wrote in their journals of the construction of forts along the hilltops. What they did not grasp, however, was the manner in which they linked up with each other to form three sets of lines, which extended from the Atlantic in the west to the Tagus in the east. This was the beauty of Wellington's secret. The Lines of Torres Vedras proved impassable to Massena, and in November 1810 he pulled his army back to Santarem, where forage and supplies were more easily gathered. In the event, this proved somewhat difficult, as Wellington had ordered a 'scorched earth' policy to be enforced as his men pulled back within the lines.

On 5 March, with his army starving, and with thousands of French troops dead through sickness and starvation, Massena retreated altogether and began marching north towards the Mondego river. A delighted Wellington ordered the immediate pursuit of the French and so his army, fresh from their sojourn inside the lines, where they had been well supplied by the Royal Navy and by British merchants, emerged to begin the pursuit and to drive the French from Portugal once and for all.

The French retreat was one of the most harrowing episodes of the war, marked by a series of small actions at Pombal, Redinha, Condeixa, Cazal Nova, Foz d'Arouce and Sabugal, this latter action being the sharpest of the fights. The retreat was marked also by unsurpassed brutality on the part of the French, whose route was clearly discernible by the sight of burning villages, the bodies of dead and tortured Portuguese peasants, and by the discarded baggage and equipment of the French Army. It was also littered with the sad spectacle of hundreds of hamstrung animals which the French had left, floundering by the wayside.

Twenty-three-year-old Edward Costello, of the 95th Rifles, arrived in the Peninsula in May 1809, and had seen action in several skirmishes, although he had yet to fight in a major battle. At the action on the river Coa, on 24 July 1810, he was wounded by a musket ball that remained lodged in his leg until the day he died. His reminiscences were first published in 1841 under the title *Autobiography of a Soldier* and then again in a series of articles in *The United Service Journal*, from 1838 to 1840. Costello was at the forefront of the pursuit of Massena's army as it retreated.

> The French got under arms before the dawn of the morning, and we as usual followed, keeping them well on before us.
>
> In the course of the noon we passed through the pretty little town of Condeixa, which the enemy had fired in several places. The main street was completely blocked by the flames darting across the road from the opposite houses. To enable the troops to pass, we were obliged to 'break' a way through some dry walls. This caused a temporary halt, during which the chief part of the division gallantly employed themselves extricating the unfortunate inhabitants from the burning houses. Tom Crawley (forgetful of the coach) made use of his great strength to some purpose, and chucked some five or six old people, whom he had brought forth on his shoulders, over a wall as he supposed, out of immediate danger. Tom, however, who should have 'looked' before he made the old ones 'leap', was not aware that close to their descent was a large well, into which, to their great terror, he had very

nearly dropped the terrified and screeching sufferers.

Having cleared the houses 'a way', we proceeded to Casal Nova, where we came up with the incendiaries, whom we found perfectly prepared to receive us. The country all about was greatly intercepted by old walls, and afforded excellent facilities for skirmishing. In a few seconds some of our division was observed moving upon our right, and we were ordered instantly to extend, and at it we went. After several hours' hard fighting, kept up with great spirit on both sides, we compelled the enemy to retire, but not before we had lost an excellent officer in the person of Major Stewart, who received a shot through the body. He was led by two buglers to the rear, where he died shortly after. The death of this officer gave a step to my old Captain O'Hare, who obtained the majority.

In this skirmish Lieutenant Strode also received a severe (mortal) wound. This officer in action always carried a rifle, for the skilful use of which he was celebrated. A man of our company named Pat Mahon received three balls on the hip at the same instant, and so close together that a dollar might have covered the three holes they made.

The enemy still continued the retreat, their skirmishers, at times, making short stands to keep our rifles in check, and a few of their rear sections occasionally pouring a running fire into us. We drove them, however, through the village of Casal Nova. Some of the French for a few minutes here availed themselves of pieces of dilapidated walls, but as soon as we commenced outflanking them, they all retreated, with the exception of one man, who, to our surprise, remained loading and firing as if he had a whole division to back him. I scarcely know what could have induced me to fire at this poor fellow alone, and exposed as he was to at least twenty other shots; but my blood was up, through his having once aimed at me, his ball whizzing close by as I approached. Be that as it may, I had got within fifty yards when I fired. In an instant I was beside him, the shot had entered his head, and he had fallen in the act of loading, the fusil tightly grasped in his left hand, while his right clutched the ramrod. A few quick turns of the eye as it rolled its dying glances on mine turned my whole blood within me, and I reproached myself as his destroyer. An indescribable uneasiness came over me, I felt almost like a criminal. I knelt to give him a little wine from a small calabash, which hung at my side, and was wiping the foam from his lips, when a heavy groan drew my attention aside, and turning round my head I beheld, stretched near him and close to the wall, another wounded Frenchman, a sergeant. 'Helas,' exclaimed the wounded man, the big tears suddenly gushing down his sunburnt countenance, as he pointed with his finger to my victim, 'vous avez tue

89

mon pauvre frere' (you have killed my poor brother), and indeed such was the melancholy fact.

The sergeant, a stout heavy man, had fallen, his thigh broken by a shot. The younger brother, unable to carry him off the field, had remained, apparently with the intention of perishing by his side. We halted for the night on an adjacent hill, about a mile in advance. The French also took up their position opposite us. The picquets of both armies occupied a beautiful ravine, that sloped between us. I took advantage of the few moments' leisure our position afforded to return to the French sergeant. But I found him and his brother both as naked as they were born, perforated with innumerable wounds, no doubt administered by the Portuguese. I turned back to the camp, but in a very poor humour with myself, though I could not well close my eyes to the magnificent scene around me. The sun had set, its light had been supplanted by burning villages, and fires that on vale and mountain correctly pointed out where the hostile divisions were extended.

The following morning, the French continued their march of havoc, and we closed after them, village after village giving flaming proofs of their continued atrocities. Passing through one which had been fired by reason, as we were informed, of its having been the quarters of Marshal Ney and staff an appalling instance of vengeance here occurred. The parents of one of our Cacadores had lived in this village, and immediately we entered, he rushed to the house where they resided. On reaching the doorway, the soldier hesitated a few seconds, but the door was open, and stretched across the threshold he beheld the mangled bodies of his father and mother, the blood still warm and reeking through the bayonet stabs, while an only sister lay breathing her last, and exhibiting dreadful proofs of the brutality with which she had been violated. The unhappy man staggered, frenzied with grief, and stared wildly around him; till suddenly burying all other feelings in the maddening passion of revenge, he rushed forth from what had probably been once a happy home. His first act was to dash at some French prisoners that unfortunately were near the spot, guarded by some of our dragoons. These he attacked with the fury of a madman. One he shot and another he wounded, and he would have sacrificed a third, had not the guard made him prisoner. On the circumstances being made known to the General, he was liberated.

Commissary Auguste Schaumann was another who was horrified by the scenes along the route of the French retreat, and wrote of the episode in his *On the Road with Wellington*.

On the 17th March a thick mist prevented us from marching before midday, as it was impossible to discover the road the enemy had taken. We marched across the battlefield [Foz d'Arouce] to the narrow pass through which the enemy had been forced across the small bridge of the Ceira. We found the bridge blown up, and the river, a foaming forest stream, roaring along and swollen with the rain, its bed so full of large, smooth flints, that it was dangerous to ride through it. Here we began to see evidences of the appalling consequences of a too hasty flight. Prisoners assured us that the crowd on the bridge was so thick at the time it was blown up that a number of men had been flung into the air, and about 500 had been drowned in crossing the river. The banks were still covered with dead bodies. A number of exhausted donkeys, horses and mules, which had not been able to wade across the large smooth stones of the roaring stream, and which the barbarians had made unfit for use by either hamstringing them or twisting their necks, were still writhing in the mud, half dead. Among them lay commissariat carts, dead soldiers, women and children, who had died either from want and cold, or through the explosion. Over the whole of this ghastly confusion of bodies, our cavalry and artillery now proceeded to march without mercy, until the whole was churned into a mess of blood and slush. Never during the whole of the war did I again see such a horrible sight.

Our hussars came back with a number of prisoners, and in a chapel we found a poor Portuguese peasant, probably a guide, who for some reason or other had been cruelly cut to pieces. After following the enemy for two leagues, we camped out in a pine wood close to the road. Death and destruction, murder and fire, robbery and rape, lay everywhere in the tracks of the enemy. Every morning at dawn when we started out the burning villages, hamlets and woods, which illuminated the sky, told of the progress of the French. Murdered peasants lay in all directions. At one place, which contained some fine buildings, I halted at a door to beg water of a man who was sitting on the threshold of the house staring fixedly before him. He proved to be dead, and had only been placed there, as if he were still alive, for a joke. The inside of the house was ghastly to behold. All its inmates lay murdered in their beds, but their faces were so peaceful that they looked as if they were sleeping, and some were even smiling. They had probably been surprised at night by the French advanced guard and murdered. The corpse of another Portuguese peasant had been placed in a ludicrous position in a hole in a garden wall, through which the infantry had broken. It had probably been put there in order to make fun of us when we came along.

As on the 19th March we thought the enemy were still occupying their strong position on the Ponte de Murcella, our baggage was sent to the rear, and we marched to the attack at dawn. But we had made a mistake. The enemy had gone and the bridge had been destroyed. The sappers were already engaged in building a light wooden bridge for the passage of our infantry. The cavalry and artillery had to go through the roaring stream, on the stony bed of which many a horse fell. We halted on the opposite bank and waited until a portion of our infantry had crossed, and then continued our pursuit, and found the plain covered with stragglers, dead Frenchmen, arms and baggage. Gradually they were compelled to abandon upon the high road all the silver, gold, valuables, silks and velvets, costly ecclesiastical vestments, monstrances and crucifixes, which they had plundered from the churches, convents and private houses; and as the Portuguese peasants cut the throats of all the Frenchmen they encountered, the Light Division became the heirs to all their abandoned treasure. The villages through which we marched were nothing but heaps of debris. We followed the enemy over five leagues, and Captain Aly, who commanded the advanced guard, made 600 prisoners. In the afternoon we caught sight of some French cavalry, but they vanished again. Late in the evening we camped close to a swamp in which several enemy soldiers and animals had sunk and perished. A few that were still alive were rescued. Among other things our booty consisted of 1,000 bullocks, cows, goats and sheep, which were handed over to me. The rest of the plunder was either sold by auction that night, or else bartered away. In addition to other things, I bought two very sharp amputating knives out of the instrument case of a French surgeon, who was a prisoner; and for a long time I used them as carving knives at table.

Having been thwarted in his attempts to cross the Mondego river at Coimbra, the local Portuguese militia having barred the river crossing, Massena turned east towards Spain, with Wellington's army getting ever closer. On 3 April 1811, the French reached Sabugal, on the river Coa, where Reynier's corps drew up and turned to face the pursuing Anglo–Portuguese army. Wellington now had a chance to drive the French south into the bleak wilderness of the Sierra de Gata, but only if he could turn their right flank. Unfortunately, Wellington's plans went awry in a dense fog, which rendered control of the battle impossible. The battle is remembered mainly for the heroics of the Light Division, which crossed the river Coa and blundered into the left flank of Reynier's corps, rather than pass around it, as had originally been planned. In fact, it was just one brigade, Beckwith's, that did the initial fighting, taking on an entire French division until Drummond arrived in support. At the same time the fog lifted, allowing the 3rd and 5th Divisions to cross the Coa, and when Reynier saw the entire Anglo–Portuguese Army drawn up on the opposite hillside he wisely disengaged and continued off towards Spain.

Lieutenant John Hopkins, of the 43rd Light Infantry, played a major part in the battle at Sabugal, when he brought his company up to support Beckwith and the 95th. His account of the action was published in 1868 in the *Historical Records of the 43rd Light Infantry*.

Early on the morning of the 3rd of April, during heavy rains, the 43rd Regiment was formed in column of companies at their alarm post, close to the miserable Portuguese village in which they had passed the night. They were kept a considerable time under arms, awaiting orders for crossing the river Coa. At last an officer of the Staff rode up, and in a hasty, petulant manner asked Colonel Beckwith, who commanded the Brigade, why he had not marched to the ford. The Colonel replied that he had not received any instructions from the General, Sir William Erskine, for that movement. On this, however, the Colonel marched us rapidly towards, the ford. We advanced right in front; four companies of the 95th led. We all crossed the Coa, which from incessant rains had become so swollen as to render the passage difficult and dangerous. The bank on the further side of the river was steep in ascent, covered with thick underwood. We soon gained its summit, halting in front of the brow of the hill to avoid the torrents of rain, fast pouring down, with the wind at our backs. The officers sat themselves, with their backs against a low stone wall. The enemy in position at Sabugal discovered us, and fired several shot. Colonel Beckwith laughingly said, "Gentlemen, you have an extraordinary taste, to prefer shot to rain." He ordered the 95th to advance to the town, which was some distance to our left front. They advanced in skirmishing order, under a sharp fire from the enemy, many of the shot reaching us. The atmosphere was greatly darkened by the bad weather.

The firing on the Rifles became incessant, but they gained their ground up to the French position. Colonel Beckwith sent the 43rd forward in support of the Rifles; they descended towards the river, into a sort of plain, interspersed with trees and underwood. As we approached, the heavy fire of the French marked their line of battle; and the riflemen retired upon us in good order. Colonel Beckwith having gone some distance towards the left, in order to reconnoitre the position of the enemy, Colonel Patrickson was left in the entire command, and close upon the enemy. He gave orders for an instant advance and charge against the line in our front, which was on an eminence. At this moment a slight clearance from the rain enabled me, who was in command of the company on the extreme right of our line, to perceive that at some distance, towards our right rear, a strong detachment of the French from Rovena were directing their march to the ford. I saw all the danger of our being so turned, and immediately requested Captain Duffy, commanding the next company, to allow me to take mine to oppose the attempt of the enemy, who were gaining fast upon our rear. He replied that he could not take upon himself such a responsibility as allowing the separation of my company from the regiment. I said no time should be lost, and that I would take the responsibility at such a moment on myself; and instantly I marched off the company, by bringing up their left shoulders, advancing rapidly to the right towards an eminence at some distance, on which I placed the company in position, fronting the enemy, who were marching round the right flank: I was now quite separated from the Regiment, which was fiercely engaged with the French. I had above 100 men in the company; as several of Duffy's men had followed. The two subalterns with the company were William Freer and Henry Oglander, both most excellent officers.

The body of French, who were marching towards the Coa, halted on seeing us, and despatched a body of infantry against us. I reserved my fire until they neared the summit of the hill, when I opened upon them, causing them to retire in some disorder to the plain. They again formed, and advanced as before, but were checked, retreating to a greater distance. At this time Colonel Beckwith rode up; I reported all that had occurred, and that the French had brought up two guns in rear. I requested his instructions. He spoke most handsomely to me, approving and thanking me for what I had done, and said that he should give me no orders, but leave me to act entirely on my own judgement, in which he had perfect confidence; that he would not forget me, and that he would bring me to the notice of Lord Wellington. On his leaving, Sir John Elley, who commanded the cavalry came up, when I begged that some dragoons might reinforce me. He made no reply, but rode off, shaking his head as if unable to comply. During this time the enemy were forming in greater strength; they advanced with the drummer beating the *pas de charge;* the officer in command; some paces to the front; leading his people to the hill. William Freer asked permission to go forward and personally engage him; this I of course refused, as his presence with the company was more important.

The French bravely stood our fire, and their two guns were brought to bear upon us. I ordered a charge, which was done with great spirit, driving the enemy to some distance. Whilst these attacks were made, the Regiment was constantly engaged at Sabugal. The firing was severe and continuous, never receding nor slackening, thus affording me the utmost confidence; for had not the French left been so severely attacked, they would have been able to detach a body against my rear or on my left flank, which would have compelled me to retreat upon the troops now advancing to our support.

It was at this time the captured howitzer was left under command of the fire of the 43rd and Rifles, as every attempt of the French to carry it off was ineffectual, causing severe loss both in cavalry and infantry.

The enemy were still at some distance, and appeared to be reinforced, and intending another attack; and I perceived the 2nd Battalion of the 52nd advancing rapidly. I went to the commanding officer, pointing out the enemy near, and we agreed it would be best for him to form his regiment on the right of my company, and make an immediate advance upon the French, which we did. As we advanced they retired, forming themselves into the line perpendicular to our left, and in continuation of their line to Sabugal, where their chief body was posted. I therefore brought up my right shoulders to front them, extending all my men as skirmishers; the 52nd doing the same to my right, we all commenced skirmishing amid the trees in unabated rain.

The French showed fight, in their new line, mingling several dragoons with their skirmishers; their sudden debouch from behind the trees at first shook ours and severely wounded several. One man, close to me, was cut in the face, but he would not leave the field. A marksman, of the name of Cassan, was taking his aim at a dragoon riding towards him, when another horseman appearing suddenly on his right, he turned his firelock and shot him dead, the other dragoon instantly galloping away. Colonel Mellish, of the Staff, rode along the line; he was to be seen in every pest of danger, loudly and gallantly cheering the men. Colonel Beckwith, also with the blood streaming down his face, encouraged the men to stand fast against the enemy. Our whole line preserved their ground for some time, until a few of the horsemen getting amongst the skirmishers on the right, a sudden cry, "The cavalry! The cavalry is in the midst of us!" caused the 52nd to retreat in confusion.

I was with the skirmishers on the left, and did not retire my men, seeing that the horsemen who had got into the line were so few. Some men of the 52nd remained on the left with my company. It was fortunate that we remained skirmishing, as it prevented one of the colours of the 52nd falling into the hands of the French, owing to the firmness of the men. The officer bearing the colour came up to thank me, at the same time highly praising the gallantry of my men.

The enemy, perceiving strong reinforcements marching up, commenced a hurried retreat. Seeing that the 52nd were now in line, with an opening between the wings, we forming in the centre, I directed William Freer to wheel the company into sections, as I intended to rejoin the Regiment. He was struck down by a shot in his face, but persevered in marching.

The French, though fast retreating, were not pursued by the divisions of the army which had joined us; instead of which, the staff officers employed their time in complimenting the regiment for their conduct in the combat, and the pursuit was given up.

I marched to my regiment along the line leading straight to Sabugal, on which we had last engaged, and came upon the howitzer, at the point where it had been posted by the enemy and where it had been compelled to remain.

The Battle of Sabugal was the culmination of Wellington's campaign to throw the French out of Portugal. It was the third time he had done it, and it would be the last. However, there still remained Almeida to be dealt with, the frontier fortress that had been taken by the French in August the previous year. Wellington could not consider advancing deeper into Spain whilst the fortress remained garrisoned by the French. Massena knew this too, and his attempts to relieve the place led to the closest battle fought by Wellington in the Peninsula, Fuentes de Oñoro.

Fought over three days, between 3 and 5 May 1811, Fuentes de Oñoro prompted Wellington to say that he would have been beaten if Bonaparte had been there himself. It was indeed a close fought contest, between 38,000 Anglo–Portuguese troops and 48,000 French troops. The battlefield was one of the largest in the Peninsula, extending from Fort Conception in the north, which effectively covered Almeida, and the village of Nave de Haver in the south, a distance of around twelve miles. However, the fighting occupied only the southern half of the battlefield, from Nave de Haver to Fuentes de Oñoro itself, a small village of alleyways, small streets, and hovels made from rough stone.

The fighting centred upon the village of Fuentes de Oñoro, which marked the centre of Wellington's line. Battalion after battalion of French troops was sent into the village, only to be thrown out at bayonet point by the British and Portuguese defenders. The first day ended in stalemate, with little progress being made by the French. The 4 May saw no fighting at all, save for the popping of muskets at the piquet lines. Instead, the French paraded and their bands played, whilst the

Guns of the Royal Horse Artillery in action against French infantry somewhere in the Peninsula.

The 1st Foot Guards embark at Ramsgate for the Peninsula in September 1808.

Piper George Clark, of the 71st Highland Light Infantry, continues to play on despite being wounded at the Battle of Vimeiro, 21 August 1808.

Robert Craufurd and the rearguard of Sir John Moore's army make a roadside stop in the snow during the retreat to Corunna.

Sergeant Newman, of the 43rd Light Infantry, gathers a group of stragglers around him in order to fight off French cavalry during the retreat to Corunna.

The action at Sahagun, 21 December 1808. The charge by Lord Paget's hussars during the Corunna campaign was one of the finest cavalry actions of the war.

Sir John Moore is carried mortally wounded from the battlefield of Corunna, 16 January 1809. He died the following day after learning of his army's victory over Marshal Soult which enabled it to sail away to England.

Robert Dalrymple, of the 3rd Foot Guards, is the central figure in this painting by Charles Stadden of the Battle of Talavera, 27–28 July 1809. Dalrymple was one of the many casualties suffered by the British during this, the bloodiest battle of the war.

The 9th (East Norfolk) Regiment line up for inspection in the Peninsula. Their regimental badge, Britannia, was mistaken by the Spaniards for the Virgin Mary. Thus, they became known as, 'The Holy Boys.'

Robert Craufurd's Light Division in action at the Battle of Busaco, 27 September 1810. The attacking French troops were repulsed here with complete success by Craufurd at little cost to his own division.

Norman Ramsay's guns in action at Fuentes de Oñoro. Ramsay became cut off during the retreat of the Light Division, forcing him to cut his way through the surrounding French cavalry to make his escape.

The Battle of Albuera, 16 May 1811. Polish lancers set about the 3rd (East Kent) Regiment. Caught in line, the British battalion suffered an appalling 83% casualties during the attack.

Albuera. British infantry from Hoghton's and Abercrombie's brigades are seen here engaged in a close quarter musket duel with Soult's 5th Corps.

The storm of Badajoz. British infantry are seen here scaling the walls of Badajoz under a hail of missiles from the French defenders. Where ladders were too short, men clambered on each other's shoulders.

The classic image of the storming of Badajoz by Caton Woodville shows Henry Ridge, of the 5th Foot, standing upon the walls of the castle after having finally managed to fight his way to the top. He was killed shortly afterwards.

British infantry of Pakenham's 3rd Division smash into Thomieres's division at the Battle of Salamanca, 22 July 1812. Wellington's great victory at Salamanca opened the way to the Spanish capital, Madrid.

Charge of the 12th Light Dragoons at Salamanca.

King Joseph's coach is captured by the 18th Hussars at Vittoria. The king only just managed to make his escape before the British cavalrymen came upon the scene.

British hussars crash into the fleeing rearguard of the French army, shortly after its collapse at Vittoria on 21 June 1813. During the subsequent looting of the French baggage train, almost five millions francs disappeared into the pockets of Wellington's men.

British troops halt on the roadside in the Peninsula. Scenes like this were frequent during the terrible retreat from Burgos, regarded by many as being worse than the retreat to Corunna.

Lieutenant Maguire, of the 4th (King's Own), leads the forlorn hope into the breach at San Sebastian. Maguire, who wore a large white plume in his cap to distinguish himself, was killed during the assault.

British infantry trying to storm the breaches of San Sebastian, 31 August 1813. Heavy casualties were sustained during the attack which took place in full daylight.

British guns in action, firing at extreme range during the siege of San Sebastian, July to August 1813.

(Above and Below) British troops cross the Bidassoa river on 7 October 1813 to begin the invasion of France. The crossing was a complete success, with Marshal Soult deceived into thinking that Wellington would invade further inland.

The assault on the Calvinet Ridge by Wellington's 6th Division during the Battle of Toulouse. The French redoubts here were cleared only after extremely bloody fighting.

The sortie from Bayonne, 14 April 1814. This last, unnecessary action of the war cost both sides a total of 1,500 casualties. The war had, in fact, ended some four days earlier.

British played football and cricket. The following day, however, was in marked contrast. Massena decided to put pressure on Wellington's left flank in order to try and induce him into moving men south, away from Fort Conception. This, in theory, would uncover Almeida and would allow the waiting convoy through to revictual the place. The plan nearly worked.

Thousands of French infantry, supported by cavalry and horse artillery, attacked the village of Nave de Haver, driving out the defenders who scurried away to the north, covered by British cavalry. At Poço Velho, the next village, even greater pressure was brought to bear. Here, the newly-formed 7th Division, was soon in trouble, prompting Wellington to send Robert Craufurd and his Light Division to its relief. While the 7th Division retreated to the safety of the main Allied position, Craufurd formed his division into seven squares and slowly and steadily began to fall back, three miles across the undulating plain that separated Poço Velho from Fuentes de Oñoro. It was, as William Napier wrote, "England's most dangerous hour," as the Light Division retreated, all the time surrounded by the swirling eddies of French cavalry, that watched, ready to pounce at the first signs of any disorder. But the Light Division would have none of it, and retreated majestically, all the while supported by British cavalry and by horse artillery, until they regained the main British position. It was a tremendous achievement.

Private William Wheeler was with the 51st Light Infantry, which made up part of the 7th Division. His diary, *The Letters of Private Wheeler*, published in 1951, is one of the most famous of all Peninsular War journals. He described his experiences at Fuentes de Oñoro in a letter written on 21 May 1811.

We remained at Villa Mayor until the 2nd inst. then marched on Fuentes d'onor. The enemy had assembled all his force, intending to relieve the Garrison of Almeida. On the 3rd about mid day we went into position on a height in front of the village of Fuentes. The 71st Light Infantry Regt. with other troops was warmly engaged at the village until night, various was the success of each party, the place was many times lost and won, at last the British succeeded in possessing the place and held it until the 5th when the battle was fought.

On the 4th both armies were occupied in manoeuvring. The morning of the 5th showed us the enemy in columns waiting for the word to attack us, as they did not seem in much hurry we began boiling some rice for breakfast, but they soon spoiled our cooking by sending some round shot amongst us. We soon took up our position — it was on the right of the line and at some distance from the main body. The enemy came down on our right in an immense body of cavalry, we had to throw back our right wing to oppose them. We had only two Portuguese Guns, one of these the enemy dismounted the first round they gave us, and the Portuguese very prudently scampered off with the other for fear it would share the same fate.

Our position after throwing back our Right wing was about twenty paces under the brow of a gentle descent, beyond which was a large plain covered with the enemy. A little distance in our rear the ground began to rise rather abruptly, it was covered with cork trees, rocks and straggling bushes, there was also a long wall behind us. On the high ground this was occupied by the Chasseurs Britanniques Regt. and the Portuguese Brigade. We had some men in our front skirmishing but they were soon driven in and formed with us, thus situated we anxiously waited the attack.

An officer of Hussars soon showed himself on the brow, he viewed us with much attention then coolly turned round in his saddle and waved his sword. In an instant the brow was covered with Cavalry. This was a critical moment, the least unsteadiness would have caused confusion. This would have been followed with defeat and disgrace. The enemy had walked to the brow, and their trumpeter was sounding the Charge, when Colonel M gave the words 'Ready, Present, Fire.' For a moment the smoke hindered us from seeing the effect of our fire, but we soon saw plenty of horses and men stretched not many yards from us.

The C.B. Regt now opened a fire, as did the Portuguese over our heads. It was a dangerous but necessary expedient, for our fire was not sufficient to stop the cavalry, so we were obliged to lay down and load. The confusion amongst the enemy was great, and as soon as the fire could be stopped a squadron of the 1st Royal and of the 14th Light Dragoons gallantly dashed in amongst the enemy and performed wonders, but they were soon obliged to fall back — for the enemy out-numbered them twenty to one or more; we now sorely felt the want of artillery and cavalry.

The enemy had formed again and was ready for another attack, our force was not sufficient to repel such a mass, so the order was given to retire independently by regiments. We retired through the broken ground in our rear, crossed the wall, and was pretty safe from their cavalry, but they had brought up their guns to the brow and was serving out the shot with a liberal hand. We continued retiring and soon came to a narrow rapid stream, this we waded up to our armpits and from the steepness of the opposite bank we found much difficulty in getting out. This caused some delay so the Regiment waited until all had crossed, then formed line and continued our retreat in quick time; it was now the division was suffering much from, the enemy's fire, the Portuguese in particular, the C.B. regiment came in for their share.

Thanks to Colonel M. we came off safe, although the shot was flying pretty thick, yet his superior skill baffled all the efforts of the enemy, he took advantage of the ground and led us out of a scrape without loss. I shall never forget him, he dismounted off his horse, faced us and frequently called the time "right, left" as he was accustomed to when drilling the regiment. His eccentricity did not leave him, he would now and then call out 'That fellow is out of step, keep step and they cannot hurt us.' Another time he would observe such a one, calling him by name, 'cannot march, mark him for drill, Sergeant Major.' 'I tell you again they cannot hurt us if you are steady, if you get out of time, you will be knocked down.' He was leading his horse and a shot passed under the horses belly which made him rear up. 'You are a coward' he said 'I will stop your corn three days.'

At length we came to Alamadela. Here the Division went into a strong position behind the village, our Regt. was posted in the Vineyards in front of the village, this put a stop to the further progress of the enemy. The 85th joined us here, they had been employed on out duty, unfortunately the cavalry came upon them when they were extended. They had lost upwards of three parts of the Regiment, I believe mostly prisoners. The battle lasted until night but the enemy could make nothing of us, indeed with some skirmishing against a few parties they sent to reconnoitre is all we had to do after.

On the 7th at night the garrison of Almeida blew up some works and managed to get away, the reports in circulation do not reflect much credit on the troops employed before the town. The object of the enemy being to relieve the Garrison, and as the works was now in our possession, they retired across the Agueda.

The 3rd and 7th Divisions marched to Villa Velha, here we crossed the Tagus and proceeded to Portalegre where we have halted for a few days, having received the intelligence of the defeat of Soult at Albuera. Soult was aware of our approach, he therefore tried his luck before we could arrive. It was well for him he did, if we had joined the army we should have overwhelmed him. My letter is almost full, I have many anecdotes to you that came under my notice. One of our men shot a horse, the dragoon made an attack on him with his sword but Maxwell, for that is his name, ran him through his body with such force that he could not extricate his bayonet without placing his foot to the fellow's ribs. General Houston was separated from us by the enemy;

when our Cavalry charged, his orderly Dragoon (1st Royal) cut a lane through the enemy and they both escaped. One of the 14th Lt. Dragoons behaved gallantly, he was attacked by five at once, he managed to kill and wound the whole and rejoined his comrades in handsome style.

Meanwhile, Massena intensified his efforts to take the village itself. Thousands of French troops were thrown into the streets of Fuentes de Oñoro, and gradually the British and Portuguese troops were driven back to the church which stood on some rising ground above the village. But this was as far as they got. Wellington ordered the 3rd Division into the fray, charging down the slopes from in front of the church and driving the French back into the village where they set about them with their bayonets. No quarter was given and none asked for as units became trapped in the alleyways, which were soon awash in blood. William Grattan, of the 88th (Connaught Rangers) described the bloody fighting at Fuentes de Oñoro in his book, *Adventures with the Connaught Rangers.*

Day had scarcely dawned when the roar of artillery and musketry announced the attack of Fuentes d'Onoro and Pozo Bello. Five thousand men filled the latter village, and after a desperate conflict carried it with the bayonet. General Montbrun, at the head of the French cavalry, vigorously attacked the right of our army; but he was received with much steadiness by our 7th Division, which, though it fought in line, repulsed the efforts made to break it, and drove back the cavalry in confusion. The light troops, immediately in front of the 1st and 3rd Divisions, were in like manner charged by bodies of the enemy's horse, but by manoeuvres well executed, in proper time, these attacks were rendered as fruitless as the main one against the right of our army. The officer who commanded this advanced either too much elated with his success, or holding the efforts of the enemy in too light a point of view, unfor-tunately extended his men once more to the distance at which light troops usually fight; the consequence was fatal.

The enemy, though defeated in his principal attack, was still powerful as a minor antagonist; and seeing the impossibility of success against the main body, redoubled his efforts against those which were detached; accordingly he charged with impetuosity the troops most exposed, amongst whom were those I have been describing. The bugle sounded to close, but whether to the centre, right, or left, I know not; certain it is, however, that the men attempted

100

to close to the right, when to the centre would have been more desirable, and before they could complete their movement the French cavalry were mixed with them.

Our division was posted on the high ground just above this plain; a small rugged ravine separated us from our comrades; but although the distance between us was short, we were, in effect, as far from them as if we were placed upon the Rock of Lisbon. We felt much for their situation, but could not afford them the least assistance, and we saw them rode down and cut to pieces without being able to rescue them, or even discharge one musket in their defence.

Our heavy horse and the 16th Light Dragoons executed some brilliant charges, in each of which they overthrew the French cavalry. An officer of our staff, who led on one of those attacks, unhorsed and made prisoner Colonel La Motte of the 15th French Chasseurs; but Don Julian Sanchez, the Guerrilla chief, impelled more by valour than prudence, attacked with his Guerrillas a first-rate French regiment; the consequence was the total overthrow of the Spanish hero; and as I believe this was the first attempt this species of troops ever made at a regular charge against a French regiment, so I hope, for their own sakes, it was their last.

All the avenues leading to the town of Fuentes d'Onoro were in a moment filled with French troops; it was occupied by our 71st and 79th Highlanders, the 83rd, the light companies of the 1st and 3rd Divisions, and some German and Portuguese battalions, supported by the 24th, 45th, 74th, and 88th British Regiments, and the 9th and 21st Portuguese.

The sixth corps, which formed the centre of the French army, advanced with the characteristic impetuosity of their nation, and forcing down the barriers, which we had hastily constructed as a temporary defence, came rushing on, and, torrent-like, threatened to overwhelm all that opposed them. Every street, and every angle of a street, were the different theatres for the combatants; inch by inch was gained and lost in turn. Wherever the enemy were forced back, fresh troops, and fresh energy on the part of their officers, impelled them on again, and towards mid-day the town presented a shocking sight; our Highlanders lay dead in heaps, while the other regiments, though less remarkable in dress, were scarcely so in the numbers of their slain. The French Grenadiers, with their immense caps and gaudy plumes, in piles of twenty and thirty together — some dead, others wounded, with barely strength sufficient to move; their exhausted state, and the weight of their cumbrous appointments, making it impossible for them to crawl out of the range of the dreadful fire of grape and round shot which the enemy poured into the town. Great numbers perished in this way, and many were pressed to death in the streets.

It was now half past twelve o'clock, and although the French troops which formed this attack had been several times reinforced, ours never had; nevertheless the town was still in dispute. Massena, aware of its importance, and mortified at the pertinacity with which it was defended, ordered a fresh column of the ninth corps to reinforce those already engaged. Such a series of attacks, constantly supported by fresh troops, required exertions more than human to withstand; every effort was made to sustain the post, but efforts, no matter how great, must have their limits. Our soldiers had been engaged in this unequal contest for upwards of eight hours; the heat was moreover excessive, and their ammunition was nearly expended. The Highlanders were driven to the churchyard at the top of the village, and were fighting with the French Grenadiers across the tomb-stones and graves; while the ninth French Light Infantry had penetrated as far as the chapel, distant but a few yards from our line, and were preparing to *debouche* upon our centre. Wallace with his regiment, the 88th, was in reserve on the high ground which overlooked the churchyard, and he was attentively looking on at the combat which raged below, when Sir Edward Pakenham galloped up to him, and said, "Do you see that, Wallace?" — "I do," replied the Colonel, "and I would rather drive the French out of the town than cover a retreat across the Coa" — "Perhaps," said Sir Edward, "his lordship don't think it tenable:" Wallace answering said, "I shall take it with my regiment, and keep it too." "Will you?" was the reply; "I'll go and tell Lord Wellington so; see here he comes." In a moment or two, Pakenham returned at a gallop, and, waving his hat, called out, "He says you may go — come along, Wallace."

At this moment General Mackinnon came up, and placing himself beside Wallace and Pakenham, led the attack of the 88th Regiment, which soon changed the state of affairs. This battalion advanced with fixed bayonets in column of sections, left in front, in double quick time, their firelocks at the trail. As it passed down the road leading to the chapel, it was warmly cheered by the troops that lay at each side of the wall, but the soldiers made no reply to this greeting. They were placed in a situation of great distinction, and they felt it; they were going to fight, not only under the eye of their own army and general, but also in the view of every soldier in the French army; but although their feelings were wrought up to the highest pitch of enthusiasm, not one hurrah responded to the shouts that welcomed their advance. There was no noise or talking in the ranks; the men stepped together at a smart trot, as if on a parade, headed by their brave colonel.

102

It so happened that the command of the company which led this attack devolved upon me. When we came within sight of the French 9th Regiment, which were drawn up at the corner of the chapel, waiting for us, I turned round to look at the men of my company; they gave me a cheer that a lapse of many years has not made me forget, and I thought that that moment was the proudest of my life. The soldiers did not look as men usually do going into close fight — pale; the trot down the road had heightened their complexions, and they were the picture of everything that a chosen body of troops ought to be.

The enemy were not idle spectators of this movement; they witnessed its commencement, and the regularity with which the advance was conducted made them fearful of the result. A battery of eight-pounders advanced at a gallop to an olive-grove on the opposite bank of the river, hoping by the effects of its fire to annihilate the 88th Regiment, or, at all events, embarrass its movements as much as possible; but this battalion continued to press on, joined by its exhausted comrades, and the battery did little execution.

On reaching the head of the village, the 88th Regiment was vigorously opposed by the French 9th Regiment, supported by some hundred of the Imperial Guard, but it soon closed in with them, and, aided by the brave fellows that had so gallantly fought in the town all the morning, drove the enemy through the different streets at the point of the bayonet, and at length forced them into the river that separated the two armies. Several of our men fell on the French side of the water. About one hundred and fifty of the grenadiers of the Guard, in their flight, ran down a street that had been barricaded by us the day before, and which was one of the few that escaped the fury of the morning's assault; but their disappointment was great, upon arriving at the bottom, to find themselves shut in. Mistakes of this kind will sometimes occur, and when they do, the result is easily imagined; troops advancing to assault a town, uncertain of success, or flushed with victory, have no great time to deliberate as to what they will do; the thing is generally done in half the time the deliberation would occupy. In the present instance, every man was put to death; but our soldiers, as soon as they had leisure, paid the enemy that respect which is due to brave men. This part of the attack was led by Lieutenant George Johnston, of the 88th Regiment.

By the afternoon of 5 May the fighting had died down, with Massena having been beaten back on all fronts, but only after some severe and desperate fighting. The French marshal had failed in his attempt to relieve Almeida and, while the battle had not been an entirely satisfactory one for Wellington, it had, nevertheless, resulted in another victory at a cost of 1,545 men killed and wounded, Massena's army suffering 2,192 casualties. He did not know it at the time, but Massena, 'the fox', had fought his last battle in Spain, for he was relieved shortly afterwards by Marshal Auguste Marmont. As we shall see, however, Marmont would fare little better than any of his predecessors.

CHAPTER SEVEN

ALBUERA

Eleven days after the Battle of Fuentes de Oñoro, and 130 miles to the south, the bloodiest battle of the Peninsular War was fought on the undulating slopes south of the village of Albuera. With Wellington occupied in the north, William Carr Beresford was sent south with an Anglo–Portuguese force to besiege the mighty fortress of Badajoz, which commanded the southern corridor between Portugal and Spain. It had fallen to the French in March 1811 and, like Ciudad Rodrigo in the north, was one of the so-called, 'keys to Spain,' for without posses- sion of it no commander could consider advancing into Spain.

Beresford had one or two minor clashes with the French, notably at Campo Mayor, even before he had arrived at Badajoz, but by the second week in May he was ready to begin laying siege to the place. Unfortunately, he had barely begun opening up trenches before the walls of the place when he received news that Marshal Soult was advancing north from Seville with 25,000 men, with the intention of relieving Badajoz. Thus, on 13 May Beresford, after abandoning the siege, marched south with 32,000 British, Portuguese and Spanish troops, the British contingent numbering about 7,000. Two days later he reached the small town of Albuera where he was destined to fight one of the bloodiest and most desperate battles of the war.

Beresford's force was drawn up facing east on a series of low heights that ran south from the village of Albuera itself, which marked the cen- tre of Beresford's line. At about 8 a.m. 4,000 French infantry marched forward to attack the village, whilst 6,000 more manoeuvred away to their left, although their attack was never pressed home. The fighting at the village and around the bridge in front of it was not particularly fierce but, unbeknown to Beresford, it was all part of a French decep- tion, designed to draw the Allies in towards the centre whilst the real French attack unfolded away to the south.

Unlike successive French commanders in the Peninsula who simply launched frontal attacks and hoped for the best, Soult was attempting to outflank the Allied right, which was held by Spanish troops, with the object of rolling up the entire Allied line. It was an attack that almost succeeded had it not been for the stubbornness of Zayas' Spanish infantry and, in particular, the British infantry brigades of Hoghton and Abercrombie.

Whilst Beresford was concentrating on his centre two French divisions suddenly appeared away to the south, prompting Beresford to issue orders to Blake, the Spanish commander, to pull back his right flank to face the oncoming threat. Blake, however, refused, believing that it was only a feint and that the frontal attack was the real attack. Thus, it was left to four battalions of Spanish infantry under Zayas, to stem the French tide long enough for Colborne's British brigade to get forward. Zayas, in fact, did a fine job in holding back the French until the red-jacketed British arrived on their right flank to join them. Colborne's men had joined in the fight as the skies darkened above them, and soon the clouds opened to send millions of hailstones lashing into their faces, blinding them and rendering their muskets ineffective. Unfortunately, the French picked this very same moment to send forward the Polish Lancers of the Vistula, who caught Colborne in line and unprepared to receive cavalry. The resulting attack left 1,300 of Colborne's 1,600 men dead, wounded or taken prisoner. It was a devastating charge.

Soon afterwards, the brigades of Hoghton and Abercrombie arrived, and together they took on the might of the French 5th Corps until their ranks were whittled away by point-blank musketry. Hundreds of British troops were killed or wounded in this, the most intense musket duel of the entire war. 'Die hard, 57th!' cried William Inglis, commanding the 57th, and so they did, earning for themselves a nickname that has remained with the regiment ever since. So incredible was the fight that other senior British officers, among them Lowry Cole and Henry Hardinge, could hardly watch the slaughter, and with Beresford paralysed by the situation, took it upon themselves to move the Fusilier Brigade into action to save the day.

The combination of the great advance by the Fusiliers and by the heroics of Hoghton, who was killed, and by Abercrombie, saved Beresford and won the day for the Allies. It prompted Soult to say, 'the day was mine, but the British did not know it and would not run'. The price of glory was terrible, nearly 6,000 Allied dead, most of them British, whilst the French suffered 7,000 casualties. One of the better eye-witness accounts of the Battle of Albuera was written by Moyle Sherer, an officer with the 34th Regiment. Sherer's regiment formed part of Abercrombie's brigade, which took part in the vicious firefight with Gazan and Girard and thus he was ideally situated to recall the horror of that terrible morning's fighting. Twenty-two-year-old Sherer, who had been promoted to the rank of captain barely six weeks before the battle, published his memoirs in 1823 under the title *Recollections of the Peninsula*, his account of Albuera running as follows:

Our cavalry had already retired upon this post, the enemy's horse, who were vastly superior in number, having pushed them from Santa Martha in the morning. Albuera, the scene of a most murderous and sanguinary conflict, it may not be amiss to describe. It is a small inconsiderable village, uninhabited, and in ruins: it is situated on a stream from which it takes its name, and over which there are two bridges; one about two hundred yards to the right of the village, large, handsome, and built of hewn stone; the other, close to the left of it, small, narrow, and incommodious. This brook is not above knee-deep: its banks, to the left of the small bridge, are abrupt and uneven; and, on that side, both artillery and cavalry would find it difficult to pass, if not impossible; but, to the right of the main bridge, it is accessible to any description of force. The enemy occupied a very large extensive wood, about three quarters of a mile distant, on the other side of the stream, and posted their picquets close to us. The space between the wood and the brook was a level plain; but on our side the ground rose considerably, though there was nothing which could be called a height, as from Albuera to Valverde every inch of ground is favourable to the operations of cavalry — not a tree, not a ravine, to interrupt their movements.

I shall here interrupt my private Recollections, to give a rapid and general sketch of the battle, which took place on the morrow. On the morning of the l6th our people were disposed as follows: The Spanish army, under the orders of General Blake, was on the right, in two lines; its left rested on the Valverde road, on which, just at the ridge of an ascent, rising from the main bridge, the right of our division (the second) was posted, the left of it extending to the Badajos road, on ground elevated above the village, which was occupied by two battalions of German riflemen, General Hamilton's Portuguese division being on the left of the whole. General Cole, with two brigades of the fourth division (the fusilier brigade and one of Portuguese), arrived a very short time before the action, and formed, with them; our second line. These dispositions the enemy soon compelled us to alter. At eight o'clock he began to move; and menacing, with two columns, the village and bridges, under cover of his cavalry, he filed the main body of his infantry over the rivulet, beyond our right, and attacked that flank with very superior numbers and with great impetuosity. The greater part of the Spaniards hastily formed front to the right to meet the attack; and, after a short and gallant resistance, were overpowered and driven from their ground. The enemy now commanded and raked our whole position: the fire of his artillery was heavy, but, fortunately for us, not very well directed. It became now imperiously necessary to retake, at any price, the important post, unfortunately, not blameably, lost by the Spaniards. The three brigades of the division Stewart marched on it in double quick time, led by that General. The first, or right brigade, commanded by Colonel Colborne, was precipitated into action under circumstances the most unfavourable: it deployed by corps as it arrived near the enemy, fired, and was in the act of gallantly charging with the bayonet a heavy column of their infantry, when a body of Polish lancers, having galloped round upon its rear in this most unfortunate moment, (for a charge is often a movement of exulting confusion), overthrew it with a great and cruel slaughter. The 3lst regiment, not having deployed, escaped this misfortune; and the third brigade, under General Houghton, and second, under Colonel Abercromby, successively arriving, re-established the battle, and, with the assistance of the fusilier brigade under Sir William Myers, the fortunes of this bloody day were retrieved, and the French driven in every direction from the field. I should not omit to mention that, during the whole of the day, there was very heavy skirmishing near the village, which was occupied and held, throughout the contest, by the German light infantry, under the orders of Major-General Alten. General Lumley, who commanded the allied cavalry, displayed great ability, and foiled every attempt of the enemy's horse to turn our right, who were in that arm very superior, and who directed their efforts repeatedly to that object. The Portuguese troops, with the exception of one brigade, were very little engaged in this affair, and numbers of the Spanish troops never came into action. The brunt of the battle fell on the British, who lost 4,103 killed and wounded, including in this number 120 of the German legion. The Portuguese lost about 400; the Spaniards 1,800: making a total of about 6,000. The French lost, at the lowest calculation, 9,000. Soult had about 24,000; and we were, perhaps, in point of numbers, a little superior to him altogether, but had only 7,000 English. The two British brigades, who more particularly distinguished themselves on this glorious day, were the Fusilier brigade, commanded and led by Sir William Myers, and the third brigade of the second division, headed by General Houghton. The first of these, composed of two battalions of the 7th regiment and one of the 23rd, lost upwards of 1,000 men; and the other; composed of the 29th, first 48th, and 57th regiments, lost 1,050 men killed and wounded, having entered the field about 1,400 strong. This last brigade went into action led by a major-general, and with its due proportion of field officers and captains. I saw it at three in the afternoon: a captain commanded the brigade; the 57th and 48th regiments were commanded by lieutenants; and the junior captain of the 29th regiment was the senior effective officer of his corps. Not one of these six regiments lost a man by the sabre or the lance; they were never driven, never thrown into confusion; they fought in line, sustaining and replying to a heavy fire, and often charging; and when the enemy at length fled, the standards of these heroic battalions flew in proud, though mournful triumph, in the centre of their weakened but victorious lines. I have read the annals of modern warfare with some attention, and I know of' little, which can compare with, nothing, which has surpassed, the enthusiastic and unyielding bravery, displayed by these corps on the field of Albuera. Yet this dear-bought, and, let me add, not useless victory, won by unaided courage, graced with no trophies, and followed by no proportionate result, has almost sunk into oblivion, or is remembered only, and spoken of, as a day of doubtful success, if not of positive disaster. It was certainly not useless, because the object of Marshal Soult, which was the relief of Badajos, and the expulsion of our troops from Spanish Estremadura, was wholly defeated; but it had yet a higher, a nobler, a more undying use, it added one to the many bright examples of British heroism; it gave a terrible and long-remembered lesson to the haughty legions of France; and, when Soult rode by the side of his Imperial Master on the field of Waterloo, as the cheering at the English soldiery struck upon his ear, Albuera was not forgotten, and he could have whispered him, that they were men, who could only be defeated, by being utterly destroyed. So much for the battle, generally con-sidered: I would now relate what fell under my own observation, and describe, if it be possible, my feelings on that day. We stood to our arms an hour before break of day: it was a brilliant sight at sun-rise; to see the whole of the French cavalry moving on the plain; but in a short time they retired into the wood, leaving their picquets as before. The battalion being dismissed, I breakfasted, and immediately afterwards set out to walk towards the Spanish troops, little dreaming, that day, of a general action. But the sound of a few shots caused me to return; and I found our line getting hastily under arms, and saw the enemy in motion. The prelude of skirmishing lasted about an hour and a half; and our division lost a few men by random gun-shot; all this time we were standing at ease, and part of it exposed to a heavy, chilling, and comfortless rain. Sounds, however, which breathed all the fierceness of battle; soon reached us; the continued rolling of musketry, accompanied by loud and repeated discharges of cannon on our extreme right, told us, convincingly, that the real attack was in that quarter. The brigades of our division were successively called to support it. We formed in open column of companies at half distance, and moved in rapid double quick to the scene of action. I remember well, as we moved down in column, shot and shell flew over and through it in quick succession; we sustained little injury from either, but a captain of the twenty-ninth had been dreadfully lacerated by a ball, and lay directly in our path. We passed close to him, and he knew us all; and the heart-rending tone in which he called to us for water, or to kill him, I shall never forget. He lay alone, and we were in motion, and could give him no succour; for on this trying day, such of the wounded as could not walk lay unattended where they fell: all was hurry and struggle; every arm was wanted in the field. When we arrived near the discomfited and retiring Spaniards, and formed our line to advance through them towards the enemy, a very noble-looking young Spanish officer rode up to me, and begged me, with a sort of proud and brave anxiety, to explain to the English, that his countrymen were ordered to retire, but were not flying. Just as our line had entirely cleared the Spaniards, the smoky shroud of battle was, by the slackening of the fire, for one minute blown aside, and gave to our view the French grenadier caps, their arms, and the whole aspect of their frowning masses. It was a momentary, but a grand sight; a heavy atmosphere of smoke again enveloped us, and few objects could be discerned at all, none distinctly. The coolest and bravest soldier, if he be in the heat of it, can make no calculation of time during an engagement. Interested and animated, he marks not the flight of the hours, but he feels that,

"Come what come may,

Time and the hour run through the roughest day."

This murderous contest of musketry lasted long. We were the whole time progressively advancing upon and shaking the enemy. At the distance of about twenty yards from them, we received orders to charge; we had ceased firing, cheered, and had our bayonets in the charging position; when a body of the enemy's horse was discovered under the shoulder of a rising ground, ready to take advantage of our impetuosity. Already, however, had the French infantry, alarmed by our preparatory cheers, which always indicate the charge, broken and fled, abandoning some guns and howitzers about sixty yards from us. The presence of their cavalry not permitting us to pursue, we halted and recommenced firing on them. The slaughter was now, for a few minutes, dreadful; every shot told; their officers in vain attempted to rally them; they would make no effort. Some of their artillery, indeed, took up a distant position which much annoyed our line; but we did not move, until we had expended every round of our ammunition, and then retired, in the most perfect order, to a spot sheltered from their guns, and lay down in line, ready to repulse any fresh attack with the bayonet. To describe my feelings throughout this wild scene with fidelity, would be impossible: at intervals, a shriek or groan told that men were falling around me; but it was not always that the tumult of the contest suffered me to catch these sounds. A constant feeling to the centre of the line, and the gradual diminution of our front, more truly bespoke the havoc of death. As we moved, though slowly, yet ever a little in advance, our own killed and wounded lay behind us; but we arrived among those of the enemy, and those of the Spaniards who had fallen in the first onset: we trod among the dead and dying, all reckless of them. But how shall I picture the British soldier going into action? He is neither heated by brandy, stimulated by the hope of plunder, or inflamed by the deadly feelings of revenge; he does not even indulge in expressions of animosity against his foes; he moves forward, confident of victory, never dreams of the possibility of defeat, and braves death with all the accompanying horrors of laceration and torture, with the most cheerful intrepidity. Enough of joy and triumph. The roar of the battle is hushed; the hurry of action is over; let us walk over the corpse-encumbered field. Look around, behold thousands of slain, thousands of wounded, writhing with anguish, and groaning with agony and despair. Move a little this way, here lie four officers of the French hundredth, all corpses. Why, that boy cannot have numbered eighteen years? How beautiful, how serene a countenance! Perhaps on the banks of the murmuring and peaceful Loire, some mother thinks anxiously of this her darling child. Here fought the third brigade; here the fusiliers: how thick these heroes lie! Most of the bodies are already stripped; rank is no longer distinguished. Yes: this must have been an officer; look at the delicate whiteness of his hands, and observe on his finger the mark of his ring. What manly beauty; what a smile still plays upon his lip! He fell, perhaps, beneath his colours; died easily; he is to be envied. Here charged the Polish lancers; not long ago; the trampling of horses, the shout, the cry, the prayer, the deathstroke, all mingled their wild sounds on this spot; it is now, but for a few fitful and stifled groans, as silent as the grave. What is this? A battered trumpet; the breath which filled, this morning, its haughty tone, has fled, perhaps, forever. And here again, a broken lance: Is this the muscular arm that wielded it? 'Twas vigorous, and slew, perhaps, a victim on this field; it is now unnerved by death. Look at the contraction of this body, and the anguish of these features; eight times has some lance pierced this frame. Here again lie headless trunks, and bodies torn and struck down by cannon shot; such a death is sudden, horrid, but 'tis merciful. Who are these, that catch every moment of our coats, and cling to our feet, in such a humble attitude? The wounded soldiers of the enemy, who are imploring British protection from the exasperated and revengeful Spaniards. What a proud compliment to our country!

One of the British soldiers who played a part in the decisive advance of the Fusilier Brigade was John Spencer Cooper, whom we met at Talavera. In his *Rough Notes of Seven Campaigns*, Cooper gives a vivid description of the battle and of his own brigade's part in particular.

To prevent us taking this fortress, a large army under General Soult was assembled, and marched to relieve it. Therefore General Sir William Beresford sent off the guns, stores, etc., to Elvas, and prepared to meet the enemy near the village of Albuera. Of the enemy's approach we had no idea or appraisal. But about midnight on the 15th, we were suddenly ordered to march, weary and jaded as we were with being on piquet duty near the city walls for thirty-six hours.

After marching till daylight appeared, we halted and put off our great coats. Every one was complaining of want of rest and sleep. Having marched a few miles further up a valley we heard distant sounds, and though they grew more frequent, yet we did not think that they were the noises of a battle field, as we were quite ignorant of any enemy being near. But so they proved, for in a few minutes the words, "Light Infantry to front," "trail arms," "double quick," were given. We then knew what was astir. Being tired, we made a poor run up a steep hill in front; but on reaching its summit we saw the two armies engaged below, on a plain about three quarters of a mile distant.

The French army consisted of 22,000 infantry and 4,000 cavalry. Our army was composed of about 7,000 English, 2,000 Portuguese and 16,000 Spaniards; but on these we did not place any confidence. Of cavalry we had perhaps 1,200 or 1,400. I do not know the number of our guns, but I do remember that the French had more than double the number of ours.

We were now quite awake and roused in earnest. Towards the centre of the line we moved rapidly; then formed close column, and lay down in a storm of hail and rain waiting for orders.

112

During the blinding shower of hail, etc., the French, having crossed the river which ran between the two armies, made a furious onset on the Spanish right wing which was posted on a hill, and drove it in great confusion into a hollow.

In moving to the right, to regain the ground thus lost by the Spaniards, General Hill's right brigade suffered dreadfully. The carnage was awful on both sides, and the dead lay in rows where they had stood. What greatly contributed to the slaughter of our men, was an attack made by a body of Polish lancers on Hill's right, before it got solidly formed. The day was now apparently lost, for large masses of the enemy had gained the highest part of the battle field, and were compactly ranged in three heavy columns, with numerous cavalry and artillery ready to roll up our whole line. The aspect of that hill covered with troops directly on our flank was no jest, as we had no reserve to bring up.

At this crisis, the words, "Fall in Fusiliers," roused us; and we formed line. Six nine pounders, supported by two or three squadrons of the 4th Dragoons, took the right. The 11th and 23rd Portuguese regiments, supported by three light companies, occupied the centre. The Fusilier brigade with some small detachments of the brigade left at Badajoz, stood on the left: just in front of the centre were some squadrons of Spanish cavalry. The line in this order approached at quick step the steep position of the enemy; under a storm of shot, shell, and grape, which came crashing through our ranks.

At the same time the French cavalry made a charge at the Spanish horse in our front. Immediately a volley from us was poured into the mixed mass of French and Spaniards. This checked the French; but the Spanish heroes galloped round our left flank and we saw them no more.

Having arrived at the foot of the hill, we began to climb its slope with panting breath, while the roll and thunder of furious battle increased. Under the tremendous fire of the enemy our thin line staggers, men are knocked about like skittles; but not a step backward is taken. Here our Colonel and all the field-officers of the brigade fell killed or wounded, but no confusion ensued. The orders were, "Close up;" "Close in;" "fire away;" "forward." This is done. We are close to the enemy's columns; they break and rush down the other side of the hill in the greatest mob-like confusion.

In a minute or two, our nine-pounders and light infantry gain the summit, and join in sending a shower of iron and lead into the broken mass. We followed down the slope firing and huzzaing, till recalled by the bugle. The enemy passed over the river in great disorder, and attacked us no more, but cannonading and skirmishing in the centre continued till night.

Thus ended the bloody struggle at Albuera, 16th of May 1811. The enemy ought not to have been beaten, for they were greatly superior in all arms, besides having an advantageous position. To allow a line two deep without reserve, with few guns and cavalry, to drive them from a hill was positively shameful. Had those columns been deployed into line and; properly led, they might have swept us from the hill side like chaff. But they did not.

Having returned to the top of the ridge we piled arms and looked about. What a scene! The dead and wounded lying all around. In some places the dead were in heaps. One of these was nearly three feet high, but I did not count the number in it.

When our regiment was mustered after the battle it numbered about eighty. As we went into fire 435 strong, we lost 355. The first battalion some hundreds stronger than ours lost 353. All the three colonels of our brigade fell on that hillside; viz: Colonel Sir William Myers, killed; Colonels Edward Blakeney and Ellis, wounded.

What was now to be done with the wounded that were so thickly strewed on every side? The town of Albuera had been totally unroofed and unfloored for firewood by the enemy, and there was no other town within several miles; besides the rain was pouring down, and the poor sufferers were as numerous as the unhurt. To be short, the wounded that could not walk were carried in blankets to the bottom of the bloody hill and laid among the wet grass. Whether they had any orderlies to wait on them, or how many lived or died, I can't tell.

But if they were ill off our case was not enviable. We were wet, weary and dirty; without food or shelter. Respecting the wounded, General Blake, the Spanish Commander, was asked to help us with them, but he refused to send any men to carry them off.

We lay down at night among the mire and dead men. I selected a tuft of rushes and coiled myself up like a dog, but sleep I could not, on account of hunger and cold. Once I looked up out of my wet blanket, and saw a poor wounded man stark naked, crawling about I suppose for shelter. Who had stripped him or whether he lived till morning I know not.

Before daylight we were under arms shivering with cold, and our teeth very unsteady; but the sun rose and began to warm us. Half a mile distant were the French, but neither they nor we showed any desire of renewing hostilities. A little rum was now served out, and our blood began to circulate a little quicker. We then rubbed up our arms and prepared for another brush; but nothing serious took place, except cavalry skirmishes on the plain before us. Towards evening the enemy retreated into a wood two mile off, and next day disappeared. In this action the English and Portuguese lost between 4,000 and 5,000 in killed, wounded, and missing. The Spaniards suffered little. The enemy's loss was very great. Wellington arrived from the north of Portugal a few hours after the battle. Had he come sooner we should have had more confidence of victory. This may appear from the brief dialogue which took place between one Horsefall and myself, when marching to attack the dark columns on the hill. Turning to me Horsefall dryly said, "Whore's ar Arthur?" meaning Wellington. I said, "I don't know, I don't see him." He rejoined, "Aw wish he wor here." So did I.

The bulk of the 500 or so British prisoners captured at Albuera were taken during the cavalry charge on Colborne's brigade. One of them was Major William Brooke, of the 2/48th Regiment. Brooke was marched away from the battlefield to Seville after being taken, but managed to escape from there, rejoining the British Army in August the same year. His account of his capture and of his subsequent escape was published under the title 'A Prisoner of Albuera', in Sir Charles Oman's *Studies in the Napoleonic Wars*, first published in 1929.

On the morning of May 16, 1811, our whole army, English and Spanish, was drawn up in two lines along the heights of Albuera. We of the 2nd Division were in the right centre. The enemy commenced their attack by a lively advance against the bridge and village in front of us. The 2/48th and its neighbours in Colborne's brigade suffered very considerably from the cannonade, losing several men killed and wounded by random cannon shot that came over the hill in our front. But this was an evil that did not long continue. The fire becoming extremely warm at the village and bridge, Sir William Beresford ordered forward our brigade to support the fatigued battalions of the German Legion, who were gallantly defending those posts. But before we had reached the village the attack there slackened, and the most tremendous fire commenced on the extreme right of our line, at the hill on which Blake's Spaniards were posted. It obliged them to retire, and to take shelter in good order under cover of the slope. In consequence of the retreat of the Spaniards our brigade (1st Brigade of the 2nd Division, consisting of the 3rd or Buffs, 3Ist, 66th, and 2/48th received orders to mount the hill and dislodge the enemy. On gaining the summit of the hill we discovered several very heavy columns of French troops ready to receive us. The British line deployed, halted, and fired two rounds: the heads of the French columns returned the fire three deep, the front rank kneeling.

Finding these columns were not to be shaken by fire, the three leading battalions of the brigade prepared to charge with the bayonet, by order of Major-General the Hon. William Stewart, who led them on in person to the attack in the most gallant manner. The charge being delivered, the French 28th Leger gave way, as did also the front ranks of their Grenadiers. In the latter we could see the officers trying to beat back the men with the flats of their swords.

During this contest a body of French cavalry, that had been judiciously posted on the left rear of their heavy column, took advantage of our brigade's being unsupported, galloped round the hill, some 2,500 strong, and coming into the rear of our unfortunate battalions, cut them off. Two squadrons of our 4th Dragoons were dispatched by General Lumley for the purpose of giving us assistance: but they only shared the same fate as our infantry, and their commanding officers, Captains Phillips and Spedding, were both of them made prisoners. The 31st Regiment, the left battalion of our brigade, alone escaped: it was still at the foot of the hill in solid column, not having had time to deploy along with the 3rd, 66th, and 48th.

Part of the victorious French cavalry were Polish Lancers: from the conduct of this regiment on the field of action I believe many of them to have been intoxicated, as they rode over the wounded, barbarously darting their lances into them. Several unfortunate prisoners were killed in this manner, while being led from the field to the rear of the enemy's lines. I was an instance of their inhumanity: after having been most severely wounded in the head, and plundered of everything that I had about me, I was being led as a prisoner between two French infantry soldiers, when one of these Lancers rode up, and deliberately cut me down. Then, taking the skirts of my regimental coat, he endeavoured to pull it over my head. Not satisfied with this brutality, the wretch tried by every means in his power to make his horse trample on me, by dragging me along the ground and wheeling his horse over my body. But the beast, more merciful than the rider, absolutely refused to comply with his master's wishes, and carefully avoided putting his foot on me!

From this miserable situation I was rescued by two French infantry soldiers, who with a dragoon guarded me to the rear. This last man had the kindness to carry me on his horse over the river Albuera, which from my exhausted state I could not have forded on foot. The cause of my being so carefully looked after was that my captors would not believe that I was of no higher rank than a major. I was led to some rising ground on the left rear of the French army, from which the remaining part of the action was clearly to be seen. I was a prisoner, dreadfully wounded, and loss of blood had made me faint and weak, yet, notwithstanding all my misfortunes, my whole heart was with my countrymen, and from the brisk fire they kept up I augured a successful end to the battle. About two o'clock I had the happiness of seeing the French run, and the English mounting the hill and giving three cheers. At this moment I was sent to the rear.

When I arrived at the French hospital, one of their surgeons, seeing me so badly wounded, left his own people and examined my head. He cut off much of my hair, and, having put some lint on my two wounds, tied up my head so tightly, to keep the skull together, that I could not open my mouth for three days, except to take a little to drink. He told me that at the expiration of that time I might venture to loosen the bandage a little. This surgeon spoke English tolerably well: having been a prisoner in our country, and well treated, he had a respect for us. Of my final recovery he gave me little hope, as my skull had received fractures of whose consequences he was fearful. The French soldiers abused him for attending to me before them: he left, promising to see me again, but I never met with him after.

Weak as I was, I reconnoitred the French guard over the prisoners in the evening: it had been reinforced, and their sentries being posted three deep, I found it impossible to get past them, although on the other side of the river I could see my friends resting on their arms after their victory. The night was extremely cold and damp; we had but few clothes left, and no blankets. We made a fire by gathering boughs from the trees near us, but could get no sleep from the pain of our wounds, the loss of blood, and our distressing circumstances.

The Battle of Albuera was the bloodiest of the war and proved the most controversial, with Beresford drawing much criticism for his handling of the battle and for his choice of position. When Wellington arrived he was horrified by the casualty returns and, fearing a hostile reaction from the British public, told Beresford to, 'write me down a victory,' after reading the despondent tone of the original despatch. But at least Soult had suffered too, and he was forced to retreat south leaving Beresford to resume his siege of Badajoz.

The siege went badly from the start. Wellington decided to direct his efforts against Fort San Christobal, a fort that lay on the northern bank of the Guadiana. If this fell, the fortress itself would surely follow. But it was not to be. Two assaults on the fort were bloodily repulsed and with French forces marching to the relief of the place Wellington was forced to abandon the siege, marching north once again and taking up positions on the river Caia. Badajoz had denied him on this occasion. He would not let it elude him next time.

CHAPTER EIGHT

THE BLOODY SIEGES: CIUDAD RODRIGO AND BADAJOZ

The battles of Albuera and Fuentes de Oñoro were the two major actions in 1811, although there were several other notable events in the Peninsula. On 5 March 1811, Sir Thomas Graham had led a small British force to victory at Barrosa, during which Sergeant Patrick Masterson achieved the notable distinction of becoming the first British soldier to capture a French Imperial Eagle in the Peninsula. Elsewhere, Sir Rowland Hill had fought several small actions, not least of which was the surprise, in October, of a French force at Arroyo dos Molinos. Other notable actions included El Bodon, Aldea da Ponte, and Los Santos, although when compared with the two great battles already named they were very small affairs.

The year of 1811 petered out with much manoeuvring by both sides as they jostled for positions, looking to establish themselves in suitable positions in which to end the year, when they went into cantonments. But as the year drew to a close Wellington was far from shutting up shop for the winter. In fact, he was considering a move against Ciudad Rodrigo, the frontier fortress town that had fallen to the French in July 1810. Possession of the town would give him complete control of the northern corridor between Portugal and Spain, as he already held Almeida. The question was, when to strike? He had the means, being a sufficient siege train, but needed to wait for a suitable time to move. That particular moment came when thousands of French troops, under Dorsenne, were removed from the area around Ciudad Rodrigo, in order to march east to join Suchet, currently engaged in operations of Spain's east coast.

With the window of opportunity suddenly open, Wellington ordered an advance and on 8 January 1812 his troops began laying siege to Ciudad Rodrigo. The siege operations in the Peninsula proved an unhappy time for Wellington and his men. They lacked proper tools, were woefully short of trained engineer officers, and were deficient in the science of siegecraft. Whereas the French had a dedicated corps of sappers and miners to dig their own trenches, or parallels as they were called, and construct gun batteries, Wellington had to rely upon the brawn of the ordinary line infantry who positively loathed the job. When a man volunteered for service in the British Army he joined up to fight the French, not dig holes in the ground. But such was the case in the Peninsula. The task of digging parallels was a dangerous one also, with the men being constantly under fire from the garrison. Conditions were not good either, with the siege at Ciudad Rodrigo taking place in extremely cold weather, the ground being covered with snow and ice.

Notwithstanding the problems, the siege of Ciudad Rodrigo proved the shortest of Wellington's sieges in the Peninsula, and on the night of 19 January the 3rd and Light Divisions stormed the two breaches to take the town from a less than aggressive garrison. The storming of the town was followed by a brief period of disorder, during which houses were set on fire and some of the local population roughly handled. The scenes, however nasty, were nothing compared with those that would follow the storming of Badajoz three months later.

Twenty-one-year-old John Cooke was a lieutenant in the 43rd Light Infantry, one of the regiments that formed the famous Light Division. Cooke had arrived in the Peninsula in July 1811 and thus had yet to see any fighting on the grand scale. After being printed in 'Colburn's United Service Journal' in 1829, Cooke's memoirs were published in book form in 1831 under the title *Memoirs of the Late War, Comprising the Narrative of Captain Cooke*. The book is one of the most entertaining Peninsular memoirs and is full of wonderful, picturesque vignettes, which bring the British Army, its battles and billets, to life again. Ciudad Rodrigo was Cooke's first major action, and thus he devoted many words to this crucial operation.

On the 8th of January, 1812, the light division crossed the Agueda, *sans culotte*, (a cooler!) at a ford about four miles above Ciudad Rodrigo. The day was fine, and, indeed, during the operations of the siege, the atmosphere was mild for the season of the year, although sometimes frosty of a morning.

The division bivouacked for some hours two miles from the town. When the darkness had set in, three hundred soldiers drawn from the 43rd, 52nd, and the rifle corps, moved under the command of Colonel Colborne, to assault the fort of Francisco. The enemy fired about two rounds; our good troops did not allow more time, and the fort was taken. It was situated on a rising, ground, six hundred yards from the town, was of a square form, with two small howitzers, "en barbette," and had a garrison of two officers and forty soldiers, who were made prisoners. Six or eight others either were killed or escaped into the town, where the drums began to beat to arms, and a furious fire of shot and shell opened on us, while digging a parallel close to the captured fort; the earth being thrown up on the town side. The land is arable, and bestrewn with loose stones, which were flying on all sides from the impulse given by the cannon balls, and the bursting of shells, which were exploding on every side, killing and maiming many soldiers.

The great convent of Saint Francisco, in the suburb, was carried a few days before the storming of the town, and also the ruined convent of Santa Cruz. On the morning of the 14th, about five hundred French soldiers made a sortie from the city, and before they retired were very nearly succeeding in entering the batteries, where the battering cannon had been placed the night before. The twenty-four pounders were of iron, mounted like field guns, on handsome carriages, painted lead colour.

An hour before dark on this day, the batteries opened within six hundred yards of the ramparts for the purpose of battering in breach. The first, third, fourth, and light divisions, employed in the siege moved by turns from their cantonments, each taking a twenty-four hours' spell.

On the 19th of January, the light division was ordered to the assault out of its turn. During the greater part of the day we remained cooking behind the convent of the Norbortins, a most splendid ruin, with very extensive cloisters, situated close on the right bank of the Agueda, three miles S. E. of the town. Soon after three o'clock we moved towards the ground occupied by the foot guards, who were halted one mile and a half from the suburbs of Ciudad Rodrigo. These troops came forward to wish us success; and our band struck up the *Fall of Paris*. The third division occupied the trenches, and the garrison must have observed the march of the light division from the ramparts, — extra troops! The governor should have pondered on it! If he had kept a sharp look-out, he must have been expecting the assault.

There were two breaches effected in the walls of this town. By the small breach the large one was taken in reverse.

At half-past six o'clock the light division was formed behind the convent of Saint Francisco, near the suburb, and almost exactly opposite to the small breach, and about four hundred yards from it. The third division, under General Sir Thomas Picton, was also formed behind the ruins of Santa Cruz, and in the trenches opposite the large breach. All was silent, four or five shells excepted, which were thrown by the enemy into our left battery, and fell not a great distance from our column. Now, if the governor thought that the assault was preparing, he ought not to have fired at all from the ramparts, as it prevented the approach of the troops from being discovered by the ear.

I heard the town-clock strike seven, and at the same time saw a match lighted in one of the embrasures — (very awful!) at that moment the "forlorn hope," headed by Lieut. Gurwood, of the 52nd, and the storming party (composed of three hundred soldiers, with a proportion of officers) moved on, carrying a number of bags, filled with dried grass, to lessen the depth of the fausse braie and the ditch. In a few minutes they were on the brink of the ditch, and the fire of the town opened briskly on them. There was a sort of check, but no longer than might be expected, as they had to scramble in and out of the fausse braie, and then to jump into the dry ditch; but having gone too far to the left, the advance got on the wrong side of the tower, which was not breached, and the soldiers, for a few seconds, were knocking with the butt-ends of their fire locks against the wall, crying out "Where's the breach?" for although the enemy were firing rapidly from the top of the wall, still the troops, on first descending to the bottom of the ditch, were in total darkness. This state of suspense lasted, however, a very short time, for two soldiers, stumbling on the loose rubbish called out "Here's the breach," and Lieut. Gurwood led up it; but the French swore they should not enter, and fought most desperately on the crest of the breach, throwing down large stones and missiles, and keeping up a most deadly fire. Here many brave officers and soldiers fell. General Craufurd received a mortal wound, and fell into his aide-de-camp's arms on the glacis, while cheering on the main body of the division. Major-General Vandeleur and Colonel Colborne were wounded. How the troops contrived to force the breach I know not: I can only say that it was well done. The breach was exceedingly steep: about five yards wide at the top, having a cannon, of heavy calibre, placed sideways, to block up the passage; however, there was a clear yard from the muzzle of the gun to the wall, a sufficient space for one or two soldiers to enter at a time, besides those who could pass underneath the muzzle of the gun, or over the wheels of the carriage.

The moment the division entered, a number of soldiers rushed to the right, along the ramparts, to the large breach (one hundred and fifty yards), and then engaging those of the French who were still firing on the third division, absolutely drove them over the breast-work, on to the large breach. At this time a wooden spare magazine, placed on the rampart, exploded, and blew up some French grenadiers, and many of the light division. Lieutenant Patterson, of the 43rd, and Lieut. Uniacke, of the rifle corps, were of the number. This occurred just behind the traverse, which, on the enemy's right, confined and guarded the great breach.

On ascending the small breach, directly after it was carried, I found myself with the crowd. Lieut. Colonel McLeod managed to collect, with the assistance of some other officers, on the rampart about two hundred soldiers of our regiment, and was exhorting them to keep together. At this time there was not any firing on us, with the exception of a few stray shots from the opposite buildings; but there was sharp musketry still at the great breach.

I ran towards the large breach, and met an officer slowly walking between two soldiers of the rifle corps. I asked who it was, when he faintly replied, "Uniacke," and walked on. One of his eyes was blown out, and the flesh was torn off his arms and legs. He had taken chocolate, with our mess, an hour and a half before!

The regiment was now formed, and Colonel McLeod immediately detached officers with guards, to take possession of all the stores they could find, and to preserve order. These parties ultimately dissolved themselves. If they had not done so, they would have been engaged in the streets with our own troops.

Colonel McLeod caused Lieutenant Madden, of the 43rd, to descend the small breach with twenty-five men, ordering him to continue at the foot of it during the night, and to prevent soldiers leaving the town with plunder. At eleven o'clock I went to see him; he had no sinecure, and had very judiciously made a large fire, which, of course, showed the delinquents to perfection, who were attempting to quit the town with plunder, in the garb of friars, nuns, or enveloped in silk counterpanes, or loaded with silver forks, spoons, and church plate, all of which was of course taken from them, and was piled up, to hand over to the proper authorities on the following day. He told me that no masquerade could, in point of costume and grotesque figures, rival the characters he stripped that night.

The fire was large, and surrounded by the dead bodies of those who fell in the first onset at the foot of the breach. The troops must have rushed up and taken the latter without hesitation: had the governor of the town only placed a few obstacles on the crest of the breach, he must have stopped the entrance of the light division altogether. He had time, as the firing from our batteries ceased two hours before the assault, and then from the rampart there was a gentle slope into the town, leading into a narrow lane, which was blocked up with a cart only, leaving a sufficient space for one person to pass at a time. The Governor was most culpable! There was no musketry from any part of the ramparts until the head of the light division column was close to the small breach. Amongst others lay Captain Dobbs, of the 52nd, on his back, at the foot of the breach, and stripped of his uniform. An officer at first thought he was a Frenchman, who had tumbled headlong during the strife from the top of the breach; but, while he was holding a piece of lighted wood, to contemplate, with admiration, his extremely placid and handsome countenance, even in death, a captain of the 52nd knew it to be the body of poor Dobbs. On lifting him up, the blood flowed copiously from his back, a musket ball having entered at the breast, and passed through his body. A soldier of the third division came up to me and said, "Captain Hardyman, of the 45th, is killed!" for although three generals and seventy other officers had fallen, yet the soldiers fresh from the strife talked of him; and if a soldier's praise can add to a man's fame, certainly no one had a greater share than Hardyman; he was the real type of a soldier, and kind to every one.

When the troops had sipped the wine and the Cognac brandy in the stores, the extreme disorders commenced. To restore order was impossible; a whole division could not have done it. Three or four large houses were on fire, two of them were in the market-place and the town was illuminated by the flames. The soldiers were drunk, and many of them for amusement were firing from the windows into the streets. I was talking to the regimental barber, private Evans, in the square, when a ball passed through his head. This was at one o'clock in the morning. He fell at my feet dead, and his brains lay on the pavement. I then sought shelter, and found Colonel McLeod with a few officers in a large house, where we remained until daylight. I did not enter any other house in Ciudad Rodrigo; and if I had not seen, I never could have supposed that British soldiers would become so wild and furious. It was quite alarming to meet groups of them in the streets, flushed as they were with drink, and desperate in mischief.

On the morning of the 20th the scene was dreary; the fires just going out; and about the streets were lying the corpses of many men who had met their death hours after the town had been taken. At eleven o'clock, I went to look at the great breach. The ascent was not so steep as that of the small one, but there was a traverse thrown up at each side of it on the rampart; hence there was no way into the town, as the wall was quite perpendicular behind the breach. When the third division had gained the top of the rampart, they were in a manner enclosed and hemmed in; and had no where to go, while the enemy continued to fire upon them from some old ruined houses, only twenty yards distant.

I counted more than sixty-three soldiers of the third division lying dead on the *terre-plein* of the rampart exactly between the traverses I have already described. I did not see one dead soldier of that division on the French side of those traverses; but I saw some of the light division.

I saw General Mackinnon lying dead on his back, just under the rampart, on the inside, that is, the town side. He was stripped of every thing except his shirt and blue pantaloons; even his boots were taken off. He was a tall thin man. There were no others dead near him, and he was not on the French side of the traverse either; nor was there any possibility of getting at the General without a ladder, or traversing a considerable distance along the ramparts to descend into the town, and then passing through several narrow lanes, ruined houses, and over broken stone walls being a distance of at least a quarter of a mile, and what no human being could have accomplished during the night. It is said that he was blown up. I should say not. There was no appearance indicating that such had been his fate. Neither the state of his skin nor the posture in which he was lying, led me to think it. When a man is blown up, his hands and, face, I should think, could not escape. I never saw any whose face was not scorched. Mackinnon's was pale, and free from the marks of fire. How strange, that with the exception of the General, I did not see a soldier of the third division who had been stripped! Neither was there any officer among the dead, or else they had been carried away. I should not wonder, (if it is not uncharitable,) that the General had been killed with all the others between the traverses, and that some tender-hearted follower of the army had taken his clothes off, and then just given him a hand over the wall, and so placed him in the position described.

The two divisions attacked without knapsacks. The greater portion of the light division lay at the foot of the small breach in the ditch; hence it was that they fought on the slope, and rolled down in succession as they were killed; but, on gaining the ramparts (there being no interior defences) they followed the French right and left, who retreated, panic-struck, into the interior of the city, keeping up; however, a running fire from the different streets, or the massive stone buildings.

The third division, at the first onset, were fired on from the parapets of the ramparts, and assailed by missiles and live shells, which were rolled from the summit of the wall: but the enemy did not stand on the crest of the great breach to oppose their ascent; for, if they had, it would have been impossible to escape behind their traverses. The enemy had left a space for one man to pass at a time, on the left of the right traverse, but expecting the attack, they had previously blocked it up with barrels filled with earth, having placed others behind to stand on for the purpose of firing over them. Before the morning, all these barrels, except one, were thrown down the scarped wall. The fact is, that the third division mounted to the *terre-plein* with facility; but when on the rampart, they were fired on in front and both flanks, as before described, and in this small space, they suffered a tremendous loss of nearly five hundred heroic officers and soldiers. During the fighting, their dead and wounded were piled one on the top of the other; crying out in agony as they were trampled upon, and impeding the progress of others, who exerted themselves in vain amongst such havoc to carry the traverses.

The moment the wooden magazine blew up, all firing nearly ceased; for the enemy literally jumped over the right entrenchment on to the *terre-plein* of the great breach, to save themselves from the bayonets of the light division. A young Italian officer there seized Captain Hopkins, of the 43rd; round the neck, and implored his life.

At about eleven o'clock in the morning (of the 20th) the great explosion took place a few yards to the right of the small breach, blowing up the *terre-plein* of the rampart, four yards in breadth and ten in length. This fatal explosion (which was accidental, owing to some sparks of fire igniting some barrels of gunpowder in a casement,) happened while the French garrison were marching out of the city by the small breach, which had become so hard, owing to such numbers of soldiers walking up and down it, as to make the ascent nearly impracticable. The French, as well as the British soldiers, were carried up into the air, or jammed amongst the rubbish; some with heads, arms, or legs sticking out of the earth. I saw one of the unfortunate soldiers in a blanket; with his face, head, and body, as black as a coal, and cased in a black substance like a shell; his features were no longer distinguishable, and all the hair was singed from off his head, but still the unfortunate man was alive. How long he lived in this horrible situation I cannot say.

A tall athletic soldier of the 52nd lay amongst the dead at the foot of the breach, on his back; his arms and legs being at their full extent. The top of his head, from the forehead to the back part of his skull, was split in twain, and the cavity of the head entirely emptied of the brains, as if a hand-grenade had exploded within, and expanded the skull, till it had forced it into a separation with the parts ragged like a saw, leaving a gaping aperture nine inches in length, and four in breadth. For a considerable time I looked on this horrible fracture; to define, if possible, by what missile or instrument so wonderful a wound could have been inflicted; but without being able to come to any conclusion as to the probable cause.

From this place I walked to the convent of Saint Francisco to see a wounded friend. The interior was crowded with wounded soldiers lying on the hard pavement. A soldier of the third division was sitting against a pillar, his head bent forward, and his chin resting on his breast, his eyes open, and an agreeable smile on his countenance. For half a minute I stopped with surprise to observe him sitting in so contented a posture; surrounded by the groans of his companions. At length, I addressed him, but, no answer being returned; I called a doctor, under the impression that the man was delirious. On the contrary, we found he was quite dead.

In the afternoon we returned to our quarters by regiments across the stone bridge, having been relieved by the fifth division, which came from the rear, and took charge of the city.

A few days after the assault, most of the officers of the light division attended General Craufurd's funeral. He was buried under the wall near the small breach.

In a few days we moved from La Encina to El Bodon, where our principal amusement consisted in playing at rackets with wooden bats, against the side of the church, or riding about the country.

One day we visited the heights about half a league from this place, where, on the previous September, a brigade of the third division had been engaged. Many skeletons of the French horses lay in deep ravines, or on the shelvings of rocks, to the very summit of the ridge, on the crest of which some of the Portuguese gunners were cut down; and where for a short time the cannon remained in the hands of the enemy. It must have been at this moment that the second battalion of the fifth regiment retook them by charging in line, before the enemy's cavalry had time to form. I rode up the ragged ground myself with the utmost difficulty; the ground near the summit was so steep that the Portuguese, while throwing balls into the valley, could not see the advance of the French cavalry until quite upon them. Not that I wish to detract from the deserts of the Portuguese; but, as it has been stated that they stood to their guns to the last, I only wish to demonstrate how it happened. The very print of the wheels of the cannon were still indented in the ground, and showed, to an inch, where they had stood.

The whole of the dead French soldiers lying in the valley were stripped, and in a perfect state of preservation, blanched like parchment by the alternate rain and sunshine; and their skins had become so hard, that the bodies on being touched sounded like a drum. The vultures had picked the bones of the horses perfectly clean, but had left the soldiers untouched; and, although four months had elapsed since they had fallen, their features were as perfect as on the day they were killed. Some of these soldiers were gracefully proportioned, and extended in every possible attitude.

The rubbish of the breaches at Ciudad Rodrigo having been cleared away, the parapets built up with gabions and fascines, all the trenches filled up, and a garrison of Spanish soldiers left for its defence — at the latter end of February we marched towards Badajoz, for the purpose of laying siege to that fortress, a distance of one hundred and sixty miles, the road more than half way lying through the rocky provinces of Portugal, where the villages are generally built on the tops of the highest mountains, with the remains of Moorish castles, or towers, studding the wildest rocks and the most tremendous precipices.

We remained a week at Castello de Vida, then resumed our march, and, on the 16th of March, entered Elvas, the principal fortress on the frontier of the Alentejo, three leagues distant from Badajoz. It is situated on a hill, flanked on the right by a fort or citadel, half a mile without its walls, and on the left by the fort La Lippe, which stands on a scarped hill, a mile from the town.

While quartering off the soldiers, I observed a very pretty young lady looking out of a casement, which occasioned her house to be selected for our quarter. In the evening, myself and messmate were invited to take chocolate and sweetmeats with the family; and, before retiring, the good old Senhora remarked our youthful appearance, and begged that, should either of us be wounded, we would come to her house. My companion was subsequently shot through the body, and, being conveyed back to Elvas, the mother and daughter kindly watched over him until he was perfectly recovered.

The siege and storming of Ciudad Rodrigo cost Wellington nine officers killed and 70 wounded whilst 186 men were killed and 846 wounded. Of these, 59 officers and 503 men became casualties during the actual storming. The most notable of the British casualties was, of course, Robert Craufurd, commander of the Light Division. He was struck down by a musket ball which lodged in his spine and he lingered in some agony before finally passing away on 23 January. Henry Mackinnon, who led the 3rd Division into the breach, was killed also. The French garrison, meanwhile, numbered 2,000 at the beginning of the siege of which 60 officers and 1,300 men were taken prisoner. Eight officers were killed and 21 wounded and about 500 men were either killed or wounded.

With Ciudad Rodrigo in his hands Wellington turned his attention to the south, and to Badajoz, the mighty fortress that had denied him in June 1811. Whilst Wellington, his staff, and much of his cavalry remained behind, in order to keep up the pretence of their staying in the north, his infantry marched south, concentrating around Elvas, Badajoz's Portuguese neighbour, during the second week in March.

Then, on 16 March, the great siege of Badajoz began.

The fortress of Badajoz consisted of around 5,000 French troops under the command of Baron Armand Phillipon, a wily old fox who knew exactly how to defend a beleaguered fortress, and defend it well. He had denied Wellington in 1811 and was determined to repeat the feat again. He was the epitome of an aggressive defender, launching sorties, encouraging his men, clearing away debris from the ditches at the foot of the walls, and generally doing everything in his power to prevent Wellington's men from taking the place before help arrived. Phillipon was assisted by the bad weather, that caused Wellington's men no end of problems. At Ciudad Rodrigo the weather had been intensely cold but here it was a case of heavy rain that fell in torrents during the first two weeks of the siege.

At length, the 18- and 24-pounder guns of the Royal Artillery opened up on the walls of the town, concentrating their fire on the Trinidad bastion and the Santa Maria bastion. By 5 April, after a prolonged bombardment, and after endless days of misery in the trenches, Wellington's men were able to look out at the walls of the town and see two huge breaches that had been made. Given enough time, Wellington would have preferred to have starved the garrison into submission but he knew French forces were on their way to relieve the place and thus was left with little option but to storm it. He knew he would be throwing his men against fire and stone but he was left with little option. Nevertheless, in order to try and make the attack less of a trial he postponed the assault in order for a third breach to be made in the curtain wall between the Trinidad and Santa Maria bastions. The guns blasted away throughout the 6th until a large breach had been created, whereupon Wellington gave positive orders that the place was to be carried that same night.

The storming of Badajoz took place on the night of 6 April, when the 4th and Light Divisions attacked the three breaches, whilst the 3rd Division escalated the walls of the castle. On the other side of the town Leith's 5th Division escaladed the walls of the San Vicente bastion. It was one of the most momentous nights of the war, as thousands of British and Portuguese troops attacked their designated targets, largely without success. Indeed, it is said that over forty separate attacks were made on the breaches, not one of which succeeded. However, the two diversionary attacks by the 3rd and 5th Divisions were successful, and thus the town, after a great deal of bloodshed, was taken.

One of the stormers of Badajoz was Lieutenant Robert Blakeney, of the 36th Regiment. Blakeney had joined the army in 1804 at the tender age of 15. He served in the 28th Regiment in the Peninsula until he was given a company in the 36th, with whom he served at Badajoz. His memoir, entitled *A Boy in the Peninsular War: The Services, Adventures and Experiences of Robert Blakeney,* was edited by Julian Sturgis and published in London in 1899. His account of the storming of Badajoz is one of the book's highlights.

The dreadful strife now commenced. The thundering cheer of the British soldiers as they rushed forward through the outer ditch, together with the appalling roar of all arms sent forth in defiance from within, was tremendous. Whenever an instant pause occurred it was filled by the heartrending shrieks of the trodden-down wounded and by the lengthened groans of the dying. Three times were the breaches cleared of Frenchmen, driven off at the point of the bayonet by gallant British soldiers to the very summit, when they were by the no less gallant foe each time driven back, leaving their bravest officers and foremost soldiers behind, who, whether killed or wounded, were tossed down headlong to the foot of the breaches. Throughout this dreadful conflict our bugles were continually sounding the advance. The cry of "Bravo! bravo!" resounded through the ditches and along the foot of the breaches; but no British cry was heard from within the walls of Badajoz save that of despair, uttered by the bravest, who despite of all obstacles forced their way into the body of the place, and there through dire necessity abandoned, groaned forth their last stabbed by unnumbered wounds. Again and again were the breaches attacked with redoubled fury and defended with equal pertinacity and stern resolution, seconded by every resource which science could adopt or ingenuity suggest. Bags and barrels of gunpowder with short fuses were rolled down, which, bursting at the bottom or along the face of the breaches, destroyed all who advanced. Thousands of live shells, hand-grenades, fire-balls and every species of destructive combustible were thrown down the breaches and over the walls into the ditches, which, lighting and exploding at the same instant, rivalled the lightning and thunder of heaven. This at intervals was succeeded by an impenetrable darkness as of the infernal regions. Gallant foes laughing at death met, fought, bled and rolled upon earth; and from the very earth destruction burst, for the exploding mines cast up friends and foes together, who in burning torture clashed and shrieked in the air. Partly burned they fell back into the inundating water, continually lighted by the incessant bursting of shells. Thus assailed by opposing elements, they made the horrid scene yet more horrid by shrieks uttered in wild despair, vainly struggling against a watery grave with limbs convulsed and quivering from the consuming fire. The roaring of cannon, the bursting of shells, the rattle of musketry, the awful explosion of mines and the flaring sickly blaze of fireballs seemed not of human invention, but rather as if all the elements of nature had greedily combined in the general havoc, and heaven, earth and hell had united for the destruction alike of devoted Badajoz and of its furious assailants.

In consequence of untoward disasters, which occurred at the very onset by the troops being falsely led, their numbers were seriously diminished and their compact formation disorganised. The third or last opening in the curtain was never attempted, although this breach was the most practicable, as it had been made only a few hours before, and thus there had been no time to strengthen its defences. Owing to this ruinous mistake, the harassed and depressed troops failed in their repeated attacks.

At length the bugles of the 4th and light divisions sounded the recall. At this moment General Bowes, whom I accompanied in the early part of the fight, being severely wounded, and his aide-de-camp, my old comrade and brother officer Captain Johnson, 28th Regiment, being killed, as I had no duty to perform (my regiment not being present), I attended the general as he was borne to his tent. He enquired anxiously about poor Johnson, his relative, not being aware that this gallant officer received his death-shot while he was being carried to the rear in consequence of a wound which he had received when cheering on a column to one of the breaches.

Having seen the general safely lodged, I galloped off to where Lord Wellington had taken his station. This was easily discerned by means of two fireballs shot out from the fortress at the commencement of the attack, which continued to burn brilliantly along the water-cut which divided the 3rd from the other divisions. Near the end of this channel, behind a rising mound, were Lord Wellington and his personal staff, screened from the enemy's direct fire, but within range of shells. One of his staff sat down by his side with a candle to enable the general to read and write all his communications and orders relative to the passing events. I stood not far from his lordship. But due respect prevented any of us bystanders from approaching so near as to enable as to ascertain the import of the reports which he was continually receiving; yet it was very evident that the information which they conveyed was far from flattering; and the recall on the bugles was again and again repeated. But about half past eleven o'clock an officer rode up at full speed on a horse covered with foam, and announced the joyful tidings that General

Picton had made a lodgement within the castle by escalade, and had withdrawn the troops from the trenches to enable him to maintain his dearly purchased hold. Lord Wellington was evidently delighted, but exclaimed, "What! abandon the trenches?" and ordered two regiments of the 5th Division instantly to replace those withdrawn. I waited to hear no more, but, admiring the prompt genius which immediately provided for every contingency, I mounted my horse. I was immediately surrounded by a host of Spaniards, thousands of whom, of all ages and sexes, had been collecting at this point for some time from the neighbouring towns and villages to witness the storming and enjoy the brilliant spectacle, wherein thousands of men, women and children, including those of their own country, were to be shot, bayoneted or blown to atoms. Notwithstanding the hundreds of beautiful females who closely pressed round and even clung to me for information, I merely exclaimed in a loud voice that Badajoz was taken and then made the best of my way to the walls of the castle; their height was rather forbidding, and an enfilading fire still continued. The ladders were warm and slippery with blood and brains of many a gallant soldier, who but a few moments previously mounted them with undaunted pride, to be dashed down from their top and lie broken in death at their foot.

As soon as General Picton had arrived at the walls he instantly ordered them to be escaladed, frightful as was their height. Ladder after ladder failed to be placed against the walls, their determined bearers being killed. But Picton, who never did anything by halves or hesitatingly, instead of parsimoniously sending small parties forward and waiting to hear of their extinction before fresh support was furnished, boldly marched his whole division to the foot of the walls; and thus, without loss of time, by immediately supplying the place of the fallen, he at length succeeded in rearing one ladder. Then having his reserves close at hand, scarcely was a man shot off when an equally brave successor filled his place; and in this manner those who mounted that one ladder at length made a lodgement. This being firmly established, the fire from within slackened; many ladders were soon reared and the whole of the 3rd Division entered the castle. The Connaught Rangers were said to be the first within the wall. In consequence of some misconduct, General Picton had changed the name "Rangers" to "Robbers". After the storming of the castle a private of the corps called out half drunken to the general, "Are we the Connaught Robbers now?" "No," answered Picton; "you are the Connaught Heroes." The confusion in the castle was awful all night long. All the gates had been built up but one, and that narrowed to the width of two men. On this straight gate a terrible fire was directed from outside and in. The 3rd Division first fired on the French and, when they had gone, continued to fire on their own comrades of the 5th Division, who had entered the town on the opposite side by escalading the bastion of San Vincente. This capture was opposed as fiercely and made as bravely as that of the castle. The 3rd Division having taken the castle about half past eleven, Picton received orders to maintain it until break of day, when he was to sally forth with two thousand men and fall on the rear of the breaches, which it was intended should again be attacked by the 4th and light Divisions. The party who carried the ladders of the 5th Division lost their way and did not come up until after eleven o'clock, which necessarily made General Leith an hour late in his attack on the bastion of San Vincente, so that before he entered the town the castle was in possession of the 3rd Division. The enemy who defended the breaches being no longer attacked in front, turned all their force against the 5th Division as they advanced from their captured bastion along the ramparts. As soon as General Walker's brigade of this division gained the interior of the fortress, they moved forward along the ramparts, driving everything before them until they arrived not far from the breach in the Santa Maria bastion; here the enemy had a gun placed, and as the British troops advanced a French gunner lit a port fire. Startled at the sudden and unexpected light, some of foremost British soldiers cried out, "A mine, a mine!" These words passing to the rear, the whole of the troops fell into disorder, and such was the panic caused by this ridiculous mistake that the brave example and utmost exertions of the officers could not prevail upon the men to advance. The enemy, perceiving the hesitation, pushed boldly forward to the charge, and drove the British back to the bastion of San Vincente, where they had entered. Here a battalion in reserve had been formed, who, in their turn rushing forward to the charge; bayoneted or made prisoner every Frenchman they met, pursuing those who turned as far as the breaches. The 3rd and 5th Divisions interchanged many shots, each ignorant of the other's success and consequent position; and both divisions continued to fire at the breaches, so that had the 4th and light divisions made another attack many must have fallen by the fire of both divisions of their comrades.

From both within and without, as has been said, a constant fire was kept up at the narrow and only entrance to the castle. This entrance was defended by a massive door, nearly two feet thick, which was riddled throughout; and had the 3rd Division sallied forth during the confusion and darkness, they must have come in contact with the 5th Division, when no doubt many more lives would have been lost before they recognised each other. This was fortunately prevented by Picton being ordered to remain in the castle until morning.

The scenes in the castle that night were of a most deplorable and terrific nature: murders, robberies and every species of debauchery and obscenity were seen, notwithstanding the exertions of the officers to prevent them. Phillipon expecting that, even though he should lose the town, he would be able to retain the castle at least for some days, had had all the live cattle of the garrison driven in there. The howling of dogs, the crowing of cocks, the penetrating cackle of thousands of geese, the mournful bleating of sheep, the furious bellowing of wounded oxen maddened by being continually goaded and shot at and ferociously charging through the streets, were mixed with accompani-ments loudly trumpeted forth by mules and donkeys and always by the deep and hollow baying of the large Spanish half wolves, half bloodhounds which guarded the whole. Add to this the shrill screaming of affrighted children, the piercing shrieks of frantic women, the groans of the wounded, the savage and discordant yells of drunkards firing at everything and in all directions, and the continued roll of musketry kept up in error on the shattered gateway; and you may imagine an uproar such as one would think could issue only from the regions of Pluto; and this din was maintained throughout the night.

Towards morning the firing ceased; and the 4th and light divisions passed through the breaches over the broken limbs and dead bodies of their gallant comrades. A great part of the garrison were made prisoners during the night by the 5th Division; but Phillipon, with most of the officers and a portion of the men, retreated across the Guadiana into Fort Cristoval. He demanded terms of capitulation next morning; but Lord Wellington gave him ten minutes to consider and straightway prepared the guns to batter the place. However, that was prevented by Phillipon surrendering at discretion.

As soon as light served and communication between the castle and the town opened, I bent my way along the ramparts towards the main opening in the Trinidad bastion. The glorious dawn of day, contrasted with the horrible scenes which I had witnessed, filled the mind with joy. The sun rose in majesty and splendour, as usual in the blooming month of April, which in that climate is as our May. The country around was clothed in luxuriant verdure, refreshed by recent dew, which still clinging to each green leaf and blade in diamond drops reflected the verdant hue of the foliage upon which it hung till diamonds seemed emeralds. A thousand nameless flowers, displaying as many lovely colours, were on all the earth. Proudly and silently the Guadiana flowed, exhibiting its white surface to the majestically rising orb which gave to the ample and gently heaving breast of the noble stream the appearance of an undulating plain of burnished silver. On its fertile banks the forward harvest already promised abundance and contentment even to the most avaricious husbandman. The fruit trees opened their rich and perfumed blossoms; the burnished orange borrowing colour of the sun glowed in contrast with the more delicate gold of lemon; and everywhere grey olive trees spread ample boughs — but here, alas! they were not the emblems of peace. Every creeping bramble and humble shrub made a fair show that morning; birds sang in heaven; all sensitive and animated nature appeared gay and seemed with grateful acknowledgements to welcome the glorious father of light and heat. The lord of creation alone, "sensible and refined man," turned his back on the celestial scene to gloat in the savage murders and degrading obscenity that wantoned in devoted Badajoz.

When I arrived at the great breach the inundation presented an awful contrast to the silvery Guadiana; it was fairly stained with gore, which through the vivid reflection of the brilliant sun, whose glowing heat already drew the watery vapours from its surface, gave it the appearance of a fiery lake of smoking blood, in which were seen the bodies of many a gallant British soldier. The ditches were strewn with killed and wounded; but the approach to the bottom of the main breach was fairly choked with dead. A row of chevaux-de-frise, armed with sword-blades, barred the entrance at the top of the breach and so firmly fixed that when the 4th and light Divisions marched through, the greatest exertion was required to make a sufficient opening for their admittance. Boards fastened with ropes to plugs driven into the ground within the ramparts were let down, and covered nearly the whole surface of the breach; these boards were so thickly studded with sharp pointed spikes that one could not introduce a hand between them; they did not stick out at right angles to the board, but were all slanting upwards. In rear of the chevaux-de-frise the ramparts had deep cuts in all directions, like a tanyard, so that it required light to enable one to move safely through them, even where there no opposing enemy. From the number of muskets found close behind the breach, all the men who could possibly be brought together in so small a place must have had at least twenty firelocks each, no doubt kept continually loaded by persons in the rear. Two British soldiers only entered the main breach during the assault; I saw both their bodies. If any others entered they must have been thrown back over the walls, for certain it is that at dawn of the 7th no more than two British bodies were within the walls near the main breach. In the Santa Maria breach not one had entered. At the foot of this breach the same sickening sight appeared as at that of Trinidad: numberless dead strewed the place. On looking down these breaches I recognised many old friends, whose society I had enjoyed a few hours before, now lying stiff in death.

Oppressed by the sight which the dead and dying presented at the breaches, I turned away and re-entered the town; but oh! What scenes of horror did I witness there! They can never be effaced from my memory. There was no safety for women even in the churches; and any who interfered or offered resistance were sure to get shot. Every house presented a scene of plunder, debauchery and bloodshed, committed with wanton cruelty on the persons of the defenceless inhabitants by our soldiery; and in many instances I beheld the savages tear the rings from the ears of beautiful women who were their victims, and when the rings could not be immediately removed from their fingers with the hand, they tore them off with their teeth. Firing through the streets and at the windows was incessant, which made it excessively dangerous to move out. When the savages came to a door which had been locked or barricaded, they applied what they called the patent key: this consisted of the muzzles of a dozen firelocks placed close together against that part of the door where the lock was fastened, and the whole fired off together into the house and rooms, regardless of those inside; these salvos were repeated until the doors were shattered, and in this way too several inhabitants were killed. Men, women and children were shot in the streets for no other apparent reason than pastime; every species of outrage was publicly committed in the houses, churches and streets, and in a manner so brutal that a faithful recital would be too indecent and too shocking to humanity. Not the slightest shadow of order or discipline was maintained; the officers durst not interfere. The infuriated soldiery resembled rather a pack of hell-hounds vomited up from the infernal regions for the extirpation of mankind than what they were but twelve short hours previously — a well-organised, brave, disciplined and obedient British army, and burning only with impatience for what is called glory.

But whatever accounts may be given of the horrors which attended and immediately followed the storming of Badajoz, they must fall far short of the truth; and it is impossible for any who were not present to imagine them. I have already mentioned that neither the regiment to which I was just appointed nor that which I had just left was at the siege. I therefore could have had but little influence in controlling the frenzied military mob who were ferociously employed in indiscriminate carnage, universal plunder and devastation of every kind. Three times I narrowly escaped with life for endeavouring to protect some women by conveying them to St. John's Church, where a guard was mounted. On one occasion, as Huddleston and I accompanied two ladies and the brother of one of them to the church mentioned, we were crossed by three drunken soldiers, one of whom, passing to our rear, struck the Spanish gentleman with the butt-end of his firelock on the back of his head, which nearly knocked him down. On my censoring the fellow's daring insolence in striking a person in company with two English officers, another of the men was bringing his firelock to the present, when I holloaed out loudly, "Come on quick with that guard." There was no guard near, but the ruse luckily succeeded, and so quickly did the soldiers run away that I felt convinced that their apparent intoxication was feigned. On another occasion a sergeant struck me with his pike for refusing to join in plundering a family; I certainly snapped my pistol in his face, but fortunately it missed fire or he would have been killed. However the danger which he so narrowly escaped brought him to his senses; he made an awkward apology and I considered it prudent to retire. By such means as these, by the risk and humanity of officers, many women were saved. We did not interfere with the plundering; it would have been useless.

One circumstance, being of a very peculiar nature, I shall relate. During the morning of the 7th, while the excesses, of which I have given but a faint idea, were at their height, Huddleston came running to me and requested that I would accompany him to a house whence he had just fled. The owner was an old acquaintance of all the officers of the 28th Regiment, when a few months previously we were quartered at Albuquergue, where he lived at the time. Huddleston conducted me to the bedroom of this man's wife. When we entered, a woman who lay upon a bed uttered a wild cry, which might be considered as caused either by hope or despair. Here were two British soldiers stretched on the floor, and so intoxicated that when Huddleston and I drew them out of the room by the heels they appeared insensible of the motion. The master of the house sat in a corner of the room in seeming apathy; upon recognising me he exclaimed, with a vacant stare, "And why this, Don Roberto?" Having somewhat recovered from his stupor, he told me that the woman on the bed was his wife, who was in momentary expectation of her accouchement. In my life I never saw horror and despair so strongly depicted as upon the countenances of this unfortunate couple. Several soldiers came in while we remained; and our only hope of saving the unfortunate lady's life was by apparently joining in the plunder of the apartments, for any attempt at resistance would have been useless and would perhaps have brought on fatal consequences. I stood as a kind of warning sentry near the bedroom door, which was designedly left open; and whenever any of the men approached it, I pointed out the female, representing her as a person dying of a violent fever; and thus we succeeded in preserving her life. Huddleston and I then set to work most actively to break tables and chairs, which we strewed about the rooms and down the stairs. I remained for some hours, when I considered that all was safe; for although many marauding parties had entered, yet on perceiving the ruinous appearance of the house, and considering that it must have already been well visited, they went off immediately in search of better prey. We even scattered a hopeful of stationery and books all over the apartments, and some of the articles we held in our hands as if plunder, for the purpose of deceiving the visitors. I recollect taking up some coloured prints of Paul and Virginia; these I afterwards presented as a trophy of war to an old friend, Mrs. Blakeney, of Abbert, Co. Galway, as the sole tangible remembrance of the storming of Badajoz. I frequently called at the house during the two following days and was happy to find that no further injuries were suffered. Huddleston's servant and mine slept in the house. We ourselves retired to the camp as darkness approached, for to remain in Badajoz during the night would have been attended with certain danger, neither of our regiments being in the place. The sack continued for three days 'without intermission'; each day I witnessed its horrid and abominable effects. But I shrink from further description.

To the account by Robert Blakeney, quoted above, we must add this account by an anonymous British officer, serving in Picton's 3rd Division, which appeared in a very early book, *Life of Wellington*, which was published in London shortly after the retreat from Burgos. His account is extremely interesting, not least for the fact that he wore a soldier's jacket and armed himself with a musket.

At eight o'clock at night, on Monday the 5th of April, we were formed without knapsacks, and in half an hour marched in an indirect line towards the town under strict orders *"that not a whisper should be heard."* Part of the 5th division were to attack the town on the south side, while the third division, to which I was attached, with their ladders were to scale the citadel, and the rest were to assault the grand breach.

I procured a soldier's jacket, a firelock, sixty round of ball cartridges, and was on the right of my company.

But before I proceed, I will give you some information which I have since obtained, to shew you where, and to what we were going! The governor is allowed to be one of the best engineers in the French service, and he has so proved himself; though our fire was continued at the breach, he had pieces of wood fastened into the ground, with sword blades and bayonets fixed in them standing outwards; behind this a chevaux de frise was chained at both ends across the breach; the beam of it is about a foot square, with points on all sides projecting about a yard from the centre, and behind that was a trench four feet wide and four deep. Covering all these, soldiers were planted eight deep, the first two ranks to fire as fast as they could, and those behind to load for them. Thus prepared he told the men, 'if they stuck to their posts, all the troops in the world could not enter:'

Trenches were also dug about fifty yards round the breach in case we did get in! In short, the oldest officers say, that no place has been defended with so much science and resolution in our times.

On the march all was silent, except that our cannon kept up the fire at the trenches till we got within a quarter of a mile of the town when there were two or three fire balls thrown from it in different directions, one of which falling close to us, we silently whispered to each other, "Now it will begin."

As the first division of our troops approached the place, the whole town appeared as if it were one mine, every yard throwing out bullets, cannon balls, etc., grape shot flying in every direction. On the fire balls striking near us, we moved out of the road to the green sward, but the cannon balls hissed by us along the grass, and the musket balls flew like hail about our heads; we immediately began; therefore, to run forward, till we were within about a hundred yards of the bridge across the first ditch, and then the balls came on so thick, that, as near as I can judge, twenty must have passed in the space of a minute, within a yard of my head.

While we were running on the grass, one or two men dropped every minute and were left behind; but now they fell faster; when we came to the bridge, which was about two yards wide, and twelve yards long, the balls came so thick that I had no expectation of getting across alive. We then began to ascend the hill, and were as crowded as people in a fair. We had to creep upon our hands and knees, the ascent being so steep and rocky; and, while creeping, my brother officer received a ball in the brain and fell dead.

Having got up this rock, we came to some palisades, within about twenty yards of the wall; those we broke down: but behind them was a ditch three feet deep, and just behind that a flat space about six yards broad, and then a hill thrown up, eight feet high, These passed, we approached a second ditch, and then the wall which was twenty-six feet high, against which we planted six or seven ladders.

The hill is much like that at Greenwich; about as steep and as high. Just as

I passed the palisaded ditch, there came a discharge of grape shot from a twenty-four pounder, directly into that flat space, and about twelve fine fellows sunk upon the ground, uttering a groan that shook the oldest soldier to the soul. Ten of them never rose again, and the nearest of them was within a foot of me; and the farthest not four yards distant. It swept away all within its range. The next three or four steps I took was upon this heap of dead! You read of the horrors of war, yet little understand what they mean.

When I got over this hill, (or escarpment,) into the ditch, under the wall, the dead and wounded lay so thick, that I was continually treading upon them. A momentary pause took place about the time we reached the ladders, occasioned I apprehend by the grape shot, and by the numbers killed from off the ladders; but all were soon up, and formed again in the road just over the wall. We now cheered four or five times! When we had entered the citadel, which was directly after we had scaled the wall, no shot came among us; the batteries there had been silenced before we were over, and we formed opposite the two gateways, with orders to 'let no force break through us.' I was in the front rank!

As soon as Philippon heard that we were in the citadel, he ordered two thousand men to retake it at all events; but when he was told that the whole of the third division had got in, 'Then,' said he, 'give up the town.'

One battery fired about two hours after we were in, but those near the breach were quiet in half an hour, part of the 5th division, which got in on the south, having silenced them. The attack upon the breach failed; it was renewed a second time; and again a third time; with equally bad fortune, which made Lord Wellington say, 'The third division has saved my honour, and gained the town!'

We continued under arms all night. About fifty prisoners were made in the citadel. Philippon withdrew into Fort St Cristoval, and most of the cavalry escaped by the sally port. By the laws of war we were allowed to kill all we found, and our soldiers declared they would do so; but an Englishman cannot kill in cool blood! Our regiment did not fire a gun the whole time. I saw one instance of bravery on the part of the French, just before the grape shot came; eight or ten Frenchmen were standing on the battery, No. 32: one of our regiments fired and killed one or two of them, but the rest stood like statues; they kept on firing till there were but two left; when, one of them being shot, the other jumped down.

The town is about the size of Northampton; all the houses near the breach were completely battered down, and most of the others damaged.

In the morning, I returned to the camp, and by daylight retraced my steps of the night before. In every place I passed a great many wounded; I saw eight or ten shot through the face, and their heads a mass of clotted blood, many with limbs shattered, many shot through the body, and groaning most piteously! I found the body of my brother officer on the hill, his pantaloons, sword, epaulet, and hat, taken away; the dead lay stretched out in every form; some had been dashed to pieces by bombs, many had been stripped naked, and others had been rolled in the dust, with blood and dirt sticking all over them.

When I came to the spot where the grape shot first struck us, the bodies lay very thick; but even there they bore no comparison to the heaps in the breach, where they lay one upon another, two or three deep; and many in the ditch were half in and half out the water! I shall give you my feelings through the whole affair, and I have no doubt when you read this you will feel similarly. I marched towards the town in good spirits; and when the balls began to come thick about me, I expected every one would strike me; as they increased I regarded them less; at the bottom of the hill I was quite inured to danger, and could have marched to the cannon's mouth. When the grape shot came, I suffered more for those who fell than for myself, and when I first trod upon the dead heaps, it was horrible. In the next twenty or thirty steps I trod upon many more dead, but each impression became less terrible. You see then that I have literally been within a few inches of death — upon the very verge of eternity! With you, when two or three of your acquaintance die, you say, 'These are awful times, death has been very busy.' Here he was busy indeed. Of three officers with whom I dined that day, one was killed, and another severely wounded, yet not a hair of my head has been hurt!

Of course, Badajoz is equally well known for the shocking scenes that followed the storming of the town, when the successful stormers embarked upon an orgy of rape, pillage, destruction and debauchery, that lasted a full seventy-two hours. The men were completely out of control and only gave up their orgy when they were exhausted. As furious as he was Wellington also understood his men, and refused to condemn them. Indeed, his own tribute to his men's prowess remains one of the most powerful and poignant of all: 'The storming of Badajoz affords as strong an instance of the gallantry of the British troops as has ever been displayed, but I anxiously hope I shall never again be the instrument of putting them to such a test as that to which they were put last night.'

Badajoz was won, and thus Wellington found himself in possession of the 'keys to Spain'. The price had been heavy, however. The capture of Badajoz cost Wellington some 5,000 men of which 3,000 had become casualties during the assault including five generals, Picton, Kempt, Bowes, Harvey and Colville who were wounded. The 4th and Light Divisions suffered 1,000 casualties, all of whom were struck down in a small area just one hundred yards long in front of the breaches. Little wonder, therefore, that Wellington broke down and wept when he saw the shattered remnants of his army lying dead in the breaches.

CHAPTER NINE

SALAMANCA

With both northern and southern corridors between Spain and Portugal in his hands, Wellington could finally consider an advance deeper into Spain. The logical route lay directly east from Badajoz, along the valley of the Tagus towards Madrid. However, while Wellington was in the south, Marmont made a move towards Ciudad Rodrigo, prompting Wellington to march north once more to head off the threat. Marmont duly fell back towards the great university town of Salamanca, thereby starting a series of movements that would lead to one of Wellington's greatest victories of the war.

On 13 June 1812 Wellington began his advance from Ciudad Rodrigo with 48,000 men and 54 guns. Four days later he entered Salamanca, although he found to his dismay that Marmont had left garrisons behind in three small, but strong forts. Wellington had been led to believe that it would take only a short time for him to take the forts but it took him ten days to do it, the last of the forts capitulating on 27 June.

Marmont, meanwhile, had taken himself and his army off to the Douro, which flowed through Tordesillas, about fifty miles north of Salamanca. On 16 July, Marmont marched west and crossed the Douro at Toro, at which Wellington duly shifted his forces to counter the move. The French move was, however, just a feint, for they quickly recrossed the river and marched back to Tordesillas where they crossed unopposed. In order to block the French move, Wellington hastily marched back again, which in turn prompted a shift further east by Marmont who was trying to get around Wellington's right flank. And so began the four days of marching south by both armies, the French trying to get around Wellington's flank, and he himself shifting across each time to block them. Finally, on 20 July, Wellington broke off contact and returned to Salamanca, passing through the town and taking up a position on the south side of the river Tormes.

Marmont, meanwhile, crossed to the south of the river by a ford away to the east of the town and immediately began marching south-west with the intention of trying to cut off Wellington's communications with Portugal. If he could get across Wellington's front he would pin the Allies against the great bend of the river Tormes. The night of 21 July was marked by a tremendous storm, the dark sky being illuminated by violent flashes of lightning. Similar storms on the eve of battle would soon become an omen of victory for Wellington's men.

On 22 July Marmont continued his march south-west, passing behind a large, square-shaped hill called the Greater Arapile, to the north of which stood a smaller, more rounded hill called, naturally, the Lesser Arapile. This latter hill marked the right flank of Wellington's position, but when Marmont occupied the Greater Arapile and used it as a hinge, behind which his columns began to march west, Wellington was forced to realign his troops, extending them west also, his line thus forming an inverted 'L' shape. As Marmont gazed out to the west he saw large clouds of dust rising in the air. It must be Wellington's baggage, he thought. Little did he know that it was Wellington's 3rd Division, which had marched to the village of Aldea Tejada, out of sight of the French. Marmont quickly ordered his leading divisions, under Thomieres and Maucune, to continue marching west in order to cut Wellington off from the road to Portugal. However, the French over-extended themselves and soon a large gap appeared between Thomieres and Maucune, something which Wellington was quick to exploit. He rode three miles to Edward Pakenham, commanding the 3rd Division, and ordered him to attack Thomieres, and then followed this with a series of orders to his other divisional commanders, bidding them attack the French in their front.

There followed a massive attack by Wellington's divisions on Marmont's strung-out troops, an attack which virtually destroyed the French Army. No sooner had Leith's 5th Division struck home than Le Marchant's heavy cavalry smashed into first Maucune and then Brennier's divisions, destroying eight infantry battalions at a stroke. By now Marmont himself was severely wounded and as he was carried from the field he could only watch as his world collapsed around him. Wellington did not have it all his own way, however, for Clausel mounted a spirited counter-attack, but even this was thwarted by Wellington's 6th Division, which plugged the gap in the nick of time. The battle ended late at night, with British musketry lighting up the sky as Clinton's 6th Division slowly drove the French from the field.

John Green was a private in the 68th Light Infantry. He was five weeks short of his 22nd birthday when he fought at Salamanca. In fact, his regiment was the first to engage the French, when it skirmished with some French at the chapel of Nuestra Senhora de la Pena, in front of Wellington's left flank. His account of Salamanca features in his book *The Vicissitudes of a Soldier's Life*, which was published in Louth in 1827.

Early on the morning of the 22nd July, we heard the firing of the advanced guard, and in less than ten minutes our regiment, being light infantry, was ordered forward: having reached the front, we saw the French piquets advancing on ours, and both were sharply engaged. In a moment the left wing was ordered to the front: no sooner did our advanced piquets perceive that they were supported by such a number of light troops, than they advanced on the French piquets, and drove them in confusion to the summit of a high hill; but the enemy receiving strong reinforcements, bore down on my brave comrades, who contested every inch with them. At this period a General came to the front, to see how things were going on: in a fit of passion he enquired, "Who commands here?" The answer was, "General Hope." He said, "Where is he? The whole of the advanced piquets will be taken prisoners." General Hope came up at the time, but did not appear at all afraid that the men would be taken: he sent one of his aide-de-camps with directions for a squadron of light dragoons to support the skirmishers immediately: they came forward, and had only just taken their stand, when one of them, a youth of about twenty-one years of age, was killed. The enemy now retired to the top of the hill, and brought six pieces of cannon to play on us. About this time the watering parties of the 7th division came to the valley for a supply of water: the French guns began to play on these unarmed and defenceless men; but not one of them was hurt, although shot and shell fell thickly amongst them. After this the enemy continued firing on us for some hours. In this skirmish Major Miller and several privates were wounded, and one of the latter had to undergo amputation.

We remained in this position until afternoon, but were not allowed to take off our accoutrements. About three o'clock the 95th rifle corps arriving, took our places, and we immediately marched off to join the division. About this time the cannonading commenced: the French had nearly one hundred pieces of cannon firing on our army, which was forming for the attack: we had about sixty pieces; and the thunder of these one hundred and sixty guns was terrible, and beggars description.

Having joined the division, and taken our place on the left of the first brigade; we halted a few minutes, and then advanced to the spot where our

145

artillery were stationed. We now came into an open plain, and were completely exposed to the fire of the enemy's artillery. Along this plain a division of the army was stationed: I think it was the 4th division: the men laid down in order to escape the shot and shells, the army not yet being ready to advance. As our regiment was marching along the rear of this division, I saw a shell fall on one of the men, which killed him on the spot; a part of the shell tore his knapsack to pieces, and I saw it flying in the air after the shell had burst.

The shot of the foe now began to take effect on us. As we were marching in open column to take our position, one of the supernumerary sergeants, whose name was Dunn, had both his legs shot from under him, and died in a few minutes. Shortly after, a shot came and took away the leg and thigh, with part of the body, of a young officer named Finukin: to have seen him, and heard the screams of his servant, would have almost rended a heart of stone: he was a good master, an excellent officer, and was lamented by all who knew him. The next thing I have to relate is of the company which was directly in our front, commanded by Captain Gough: a cannon-ball came, and striking the right of the company, made the arms jingle and fly in pieces like broken glass. One of the bayonets was broken off, and sent through a man's neck with as much force as though it had been done by a strong and powerful hand. I saw the man pull it out, and singular to relate, he recovered: three others were also wounded. About this time I had a narrow escape from a cannon-ball, which passed within a few inches of me: although it was nearly spent, yet, had it struck me, I should have been either killed or wounded by it.

After this, we formed column of quarter distance; and several shells fell into our column, and did execution: one shell I shall ever remember: we were in the act of lying down, that it might burst, and do no mischief: the colonel cried out, "It is a shot!" and we stood up immediately; but, while in the act of rising, the shell burst in the midst of the regimental column, and, astonishing to relate, not a man received an injury by it! We now took our position, and waited the signal to advance. About half past four o'clock Lord Wellington came into the front of our division, and pulled off his hat; our army gave three cheers, and advanced on the French, who were ready to receive us: we continued to advance some time without firing a shot; at length the firing of both armies commenced in such a way as I had never heard before; it was like the long roll of a hundred drums without an interval. Both armies fought with courage and determination; and it was doubtful for some time which would gain the day: at last the enemy gave way in all directions, and we com-

146

pletely beat them out of the field with dreadful carnage. Their loss in this memorable battle was eleven pieces of cannon, several ammunition waggons, two eagles, and six colours. The French commander in chief lost his arm; it was astonishing how soon we heard of his being wounded. We took one general officer, three colonels, three lieutenant-colonels, one hundred and thirty officers, and about seven thousand privates. Their loss in killed and wounded must have been very great indeed. The total loss of the allied armies in this desperate action was six hundred and ninety-four men killed, four thousand two hundred and seventy wounded, and two hundred and thirty-six missing; making a grand total of five thousand two hundred, beside what were lost in pursuit of the enemy; and to which may be added the loss of the 6th division at the forts in the city. Major-General Le Marchant was killed; Lieutenant-Generals Cole, Leith, Cotton, and Major-General Alten, were wounded. I think it was the 61st regiment that had only three officers left, and the command devolved upon the adjutant, who had been the sergeant-major. The loss sustained by our regiment was one subaltern and one sergeant killed, one major, two captains, and forty privates killed and wounded, making our total loss near this place ninety-three out of our small regiment, which was not more than three hundred strong in the field.

After the battle, we encamped on that part of the field where the carnage had been the most dreadful, and actually piled our arms amongst the dead and dying. We immediately sent six men from each company to collect the wounded, and carry them to a small village, where doctors were in attendance to dress their wounds. It really was distressing to hear the cries and moans of the wounded and dying, whose sufferings were augmented by the Portuguese plunderers stripping several of them naked. We took a poor Frenchman, who had been stripped by an unfeeling Portuguese: the adjutant gave him a shirt, an old jacket and trousers, and sent him to the village hospital.

In a short time the baggage and women arrived, and amongst them the wife of Sergeant Dunn, who was killed at the commencement of the action: the poor woman was nearly frantic when she heard her husband was no more. Her loss certainly was great; but in less than a week she took up with a sergeant of the same company, whose name was Gilbert Hinds, with whom she has lived ever since. This poor woman was unlucky, for she had lost five husbands: Hinds is her sixth!

William Grattan, of the 88th, left one of the most gripping accounts of Salamanca in his *Adventures With the Connaught Rangers*. His regiment was part of the 3rd Division, which began Wellington's great offensive on 22 July 1812. Indeed, the onslaught by Pakenham's division totally crushed Thomieres' division, and opened the way for Wellington's other divisions further east. Grattan is particularly hard on Pack's Portuguese brigade whose failed attempt to take the Greater Arapile led to Clausel's counter-attack, which almost snatched victory for the French.

At half-past one o'clock the two armies were within gunshot of each other. The British, placed as follows, awaited with calmness the orders of their General. We of the 3rd Division, under Pakenham, were on the right of the line, but hid by the heights in our front, and unseen by Marmont; two squadrons of the 16th Light Dragoons and a brigade of Portuguese horse, commanded by General D'Urban, supported us. Next to the 3rd Division stood the 5th, led on by Leith; next to the 5th, and at the head of the village of Arapiles, were placed the 4th and 7th Divisions; beyond them, and a little in the rear, was the 6th Division, under General Clinton; and to the left of all was the Light Division, commanded by Colonel Barnard. The 1st Division, composed of the Guards and Germans, was in reserve; and the cavalry, under Sir Stapleton Cotton, was behind the 3rd and 5th Divisions, ready to act as circumstances might require. The guns attached to each brigade were up with the infantry; the park in reserve was behind the cavalry of Cotton, while in the rear of all, and nearly *hors de combat*, might be seen the Spanish army, commanded by Don Carlos D'España. Thus stood affairs, on the side of the British, at half-past one o'clock.

The French army, composed of eight divisions of infantry, amounting to forty-two thousand bayonets, four thousand cavalry, and seventy pieces of artillery, occupied a fine line of battle behind a ridge whose right, supported by the Arapiles height held by them, overlooked the one upon which the left of our army rested. Their 5th Division occupied this point the 122nd Regiment, belonging to Bonnet's division, with a brigade of guns, crowned the Arapiles; the 7th Division supported the 122nd Regiment; the 2nd Division was in reserve behind the 7th; the 6th were at the head of the wood, protected by twenty pieces of artillery; and Boyer's dragoons occupied the open space in front of the wood to the left of all.

There was some irregularity in the arrangement of these troops, and the Duke of Ragusa essayed in person to remedy the evil. He marched with the 3rd and 4th Divisions to the head of the wood occupied by Boyer, and it was then he conceived the idea of extending his left, which afterwards proved so fatal to him. On our side all was arranged for defence; the bustle which was evident in the ranks of the enemy caused no change in our dispositions. Lord Wellington, having surveyed what was passing, and judging that something was meant by it, gave his glass to one of his aide-de-camps, while he himself sat down to eat a few mouthfuls of cold beef. He had scarcely commenced when his aide-de-camp said, "The enemy are in motion, my lord!" "Very well; observe what they are doing," was the reply. A minute or so elapsed, when the aide-de-camp said, "I think they are extending to their left." "The devil they are!" said his lordship, springing upon his feet, "give me the glass quickly." He took it, and for a short space continued observing the motions of the enemy with earnest attention. "Come!" he exclaimed, "I think this will do at last; ride off instantly, and tell Clinton and Leith to return as rapidly as possible to their former ground."

In a moment afterwards Lord Wellington was on horseback, and all his staff in motion. The soldiers stood to their arms — the colours were uncased — bayonets fixed — the order to prime and load passed, and in five minutes after the false movement of Marmont was discovered, our army, which so short a time before stood on the defensive, was arrayed for the attack! It was twenty minutes past four when these dispositions were completed; and here it may not be amiss to tell the reader the nature of the movement made by the French General, which so materially altered his position, as likewise that of his antagonist — and in doing so I shall be as brief as I can.

It has been already seen that both armies were so circumstanced as to almost preclude the possibility of a battle not taking place. Marmont coveted it — Wellington did not seek to decline it — both had the confidence of their soldiers — and both, as to numbers, might be said to be on an equality. When I speak of "numbers" I include the Portuguese troops. Military men know what was the real value of these soldiers! At two o'clock in the afternoon Marmont was the aggressor; he held the higher hand; yet at four, in two short hours afterwards, the relative situation of both was altogether changed. The natural question will be — How was this? It occurred just as I am about to describe.

The two armies took their ground under the impression that the French would attack, the British defend. All this was plain; but Marmont had no sooner mounted his horse and taken a survey of the field of battle than he conceived the idea — like Melas at Marengo — of extending his line; by marching his 7th Division to his left he might cause an alarm in the breast of the British General for the safety of his communication with the Rodrigo road, and in a manner circumvent his position. Lord Wellington, at a glance,

149

saw all that was passing in the mind of his antagonist — he saw the error he had committed; and calculating that his 3rd Division (distant but three-quarters of a league from the French 4th) would reach them before the 7th French Division could retrace their steps and be in a position fitted for fighting, he decided upon attacking the left, before this division, commanded by Thomieres, could regain its ground, or at all events be in an efficient state to resist the attack of his invincible Old Third. The result proved the soundness of the calculation, because, although Thomieres got into his place in the fight, he did so before his men had foreseen or expected it, and their total over-throw was in itself sufficient to cause the loss of this great battle.

The 3rd Division had but just resumed their arms when Lord Wellington, at the head of his staff, appeared amongst them. The officers had not taken their places in the column, but were in a group together in front of it. As Lord Wellington rode up to Pakenham every eye was turned towards him. He looked paler than usual, but notwithstanding the sudden change he had just made in the disposition of his army, he was quite unruffled in his manner, and as calm as if the battle about to be fought was nothing more than an ordinary assemblage of the troops for a field day. His words were few and his orders brief. Tapping Pakenham on the shoulder, he said, "Edward, move on with the 3rd Division — take the heights in your front — and drive everything before you." "I will, my lord," was the laconic reply of the gallant Sir Edward. Lord Wellington galloped on to the next division, gave, I suppose, orders to the same effect, and in less than half an hour the battle commenced.

The British divisions were scarcely in line when fifty pieces of artillery crowned the ridge occupied by the French. A heavy fire was soon opened from this park at Half range, and as the 4th and 5th Divisions advanced they were assailed by a very formidable fire; but as yet the French infantry, posted behind the ridge, were not visible. Cole's troops advanced to the left of the Arapiles height, while Pack, with his brigade of Portuguese, two thousand strong, pressed onward to attain it. The 5th Division, under Leith, advanced by the right of Cole's troops; and at this moment the French 7th Division were seen hurrying back to occupy the ground they had so short a time before quitted, while the 3rd and 4th French Divisions were arranging themselves to receive the attack of Cole and Leith.

When all was in readiness Pakenham departed at the head of ten battalions and two brigades of guns, to force the left of the enemy. Three battalions, the 45th, 74th, and 88th, under Colonel Alexander Wallace of the 88th, composed the first line; the 9th and 21st Portuguese of the line, under the Portuguese colonel, De Champlemond, formed the second line; while two battalions of the 5th, the 77th, 83rd, and 94th British, under the command of Colonel Campbell, were in reserve. Such was the disposition of the 3rd Division. In addition, General D'Urban, with six Portuguese squadrons, had orders to make head against Boyer's dragoons; and that the 3rd Division might not be molested in its operation, Le Marchant's three regiments of heavy cavalry were placed in reserve in the rear of it. It now only remains to relate what actually happened.

No sooner was Pakenham in motion towards the heights than the ridge he was about to assail was crowned with twenty pieces of cannon, while in the rear of this battery was seen Thomieres' division endeavouring to regain its place in the combat. A flat space, one thousand yards in breadth, was to be crossed before Pakenham could reach the heights. The French batteries opened a heavy fire, while our two brigades of artillery, commanded by Captain Douglas, posted on a rising ground behind the 3rd Division, replied to them with much warmth. Pakenham's men might thus be said to be within two fires — that of their own guns firing over their heads, while the French balls passed through their ranks, ploughing up the ground in every direction; but the veteran troops which composed the 3rd Divsion were not to be shaken even by this.

Wallace's three regiments advanced in open column until within two hundred and fifty yards of the ridge held by the French infantry. Thomieres' column, five thousand strong, had by this time reached their ground, while in their front the face of the hill had been hastily garnished with *tirailleurs*. All were impatient to engage, and the calm but stern advance of Wallace's brigade was received with beating of drums and loud cheers from the French, whose light troops, hoping to take advantage of the time which the deploying from column into line would take, ran down the face of the hill in a state of great excitement; but Pakenham, who was naturally of a boiling spirit and hasty temper, was on this day perfectly cool. He told Wallace to form line from open column without halting, and thus the different companies, by throwing forward their right shoulders, were in line without the slow manoeuvre of a deployment. Astonished at the rapidity of the movement, the French riflemen commenced an irregular and hurried fire, and even at this early stage of the battle a looker-on could, from the difference in the demeanour of the troops of the two nations, form a tolerably correct opinion of what would be the result.

Regardless of the tire of the *tirailleurs*, and the showers of grape and canister, Pakenham, at the head of Wallace's brigade, continued to press onward; his centre suffered, but still advanced; his left and right being less oppressed by the weight of the fire, continued to advance at a more rapid pace, and as his wings inclined forward and outstripped the centre, the brigade assumed the form of a crescent. The manoeuvre was a bold, as well as a novel one, and the appearance of the brigade imposing and unique, because it so happened that all the British officers were in front of their men — a rare occurrence. The French officers were also in front; but their relative duties were widely different: the latter, encouraging their men into the heat of the battle; the former keeping their devoted soldiers back! – what a splendid national contrast! Amongst the mounted officers were Sir Edward Pakenham and his staff; Wallace of the 88th, commanding the brigade, and his gallant aide-de-camp, Mackie (at last a Captain — in his regular turn!), Majors Murphy and Seton of the 88th, Colonels Forbes and Greenwell of the 45th, Colonel Trench of the 74th, and several others whose names I cannot now remember.

In spite of the fire of Thomieres' *tirailleurs*, they continued at the head of the right brigade, while the soldiers, with their firelocks on the rest, followed close upon the heels of their officers, like troops accustomed to conquer. They speedily got footing upon the brow of the hill, but before they had time to take breath, the entire French division, with drums beating and uttering loud shouts, ran forward to meet them, and belching forth a torrent of bullets from five thousand muskets, brought down almost the entire of Wallace's first rank, and more than half of his officers. The brigade staggered back from the force of the shock, but before the smoke had altogether cleared away, Wallace, looking full in the faces of his soldiers, pointed to the French column, and leading the shattered brigade up the hill, without a moment's hesitation, brought them face to face before the French had time to witness the terrible effect of their murderous fire.

Astounded by the unshaken determination of Wallace's soldiers, Thomieres' division wavered; nevertheless they opened a heavy discharge of musketry, but it was unlike the former; it was irregular and ill-directed, the men acted without concert or method, and many fired in the air. At length their fire ceased altogether, and the three regiments, for the first time, cheered! The effect was electric; Thomieres' troops were seized with a panic, and as Wallace closed upon them, his men could distinctly remark their bearing. Their moustachioed faces, one and all, presented the same ghastly hue, a horrid family likeness throughout; and as they stood to receive the shock they were about to be assailed with, they reeled to and fro like men intoxicated.

The French officers did all that was possible, by voice, gesture, and example, to rouse their men to a proper sense of their situation, but in vain. One, the colonel of the leading regiment (the 22nd), seizing a firelock, and beckoning to his men to follow, ran forward a few paces and shot Major Murphy dead in front of the 88th. However, his career soon closed: a bullet, the first that had been fired from our ranks, pierced his head; he flung up his arms, fell forward, and expired.

The brigade, which till this time cheerfully bore up against the heavy fire they had been exposed to without returning a shot, were now impatient, and the 88th greatly excited; for Murphy, dead and bleeding, with one foot hanging in the stirrup-iron, was dragged by his affrighted horse along the front of his regiment. The soldiers became exasperated, and asked to be let forward. Pakenham, seeing that the proper moment had arrived, called out to Wallace "to let them loose." The three regiments ran onward, and the mighty phalanx, which but a moment before was so formidable, loosened and fell in pieces before fifteen hundred invincible British soldiers fighting in a line two deep.

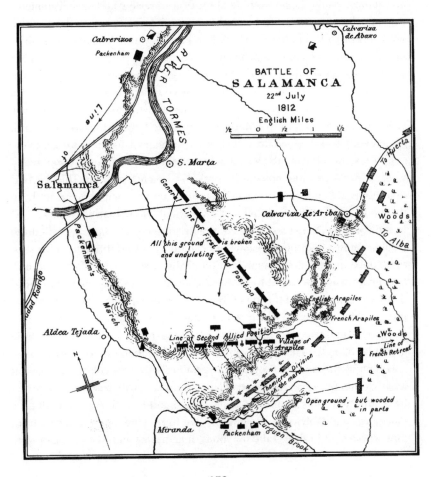

Wallace, seeing the terrible confusion that prevailed in the enemy's column, pressed on with his brigade, calling to his soldiers "to push on to the muzzle." A vast number were killed in this charge of bayonets, but the men, wearied by their exertions, the intolerable heat of the weather, and famishing from thirst, were nearly run to a standstill.

Immediately on our left, the 5th Division were discharging volleys against the French 4th; and Pack's brigade could be seen mounting the Arapiles height. But disregarding everything except the complete destruction of the column before him, Pakenham followed it with the brigade of Wallace, supported by the reserves of his division. The battle at this point would have been decided on the moment, had the heavy horse, under Le Marchant, been near enough to sustain him. The confusion of the enemy was so great, that they were mixed pell-mell together without any regard to order or regularity; and it was manifest that nothing short of a miracle could save Thomieres from total destruction. Sir Edward continued to press on at the head of Wallace's brigade, but the French outran him. Had Le Marchant been aware of this state of the combat, or been near enough to profit by it, Pakenham would have settled the business by six o'clock instead of seven. An hour at any time, during a battle, is a serious lapse of time; but in this action every minute was of vital import. Day was rapidly drawing to a close; the Tormes was close behind the army of Marmont; ruin stared him in the face; in a word, his left wing was doubled up — lost; and Pakenham could have turned to the support of the 4th and 5th Divisions had our cavalry been on the spot ready to back Wallace at the moment he broke Thomieres' column. This, beyond doubt, was the moment by which to profit, that the enemy might not have time to recollect himself; but while Le Marchant was preparing to take a part in the combat, Thomieres, with admirable presence of mind, remedied the terrible confusion of his division, and calling up a fresh brigade to his support, once more led his men into the fight, assumed the offensive, and Pakenham was now about to be assailed in turn. This was the most critical moment of the battle at this point. Boyer's horsemen stood before us, inclining towards our right, which was flanked by two squadrons of the 14th Dragoons and two regiments of Portuguese cavalry; but we had little dependence on the Portuguese, and it behoved us to look to ourselves.

Led on by the ardour of conquest, we had followed the column until we at length found ourselves in an open plain, intersected with cork-trees, opposed by a multitude who, reinforced, again rallied and turned upon us with fury. Pakenham and Wallace rode along the line from wing to wing, almost from rank to rank, and fulfilled the functions of adjutants, in assisting the officers to reorganise the tellings-off of their men for square. Meanwhile the first battalion of the 5th drove back some squadrons of Boyer's dragoons; the other six regiments were fast approaching the point held by Wallace, but the attitude of the French cavalry in our front and upon our right flank caused some uneasiness.

The peals of musketry along the centre still continued without intermission; the smoke was so thick that nothing to our left was distinguishable; some men of the 5th Division got intermingled with ours; the dry grass was set on fire by the numerous cartridge-papers that strewed the field of battle; the air was scorching; and the smoke, rolling onward in huge volumes, nearly suffocated us. A loud cheering was heard in our rear; the brigade half turned round, supposing themselves about to be attacked by the French cavalry. Wallace called out to his men to mind the tellings-off for square. A few seconds passed, the trampling of horses was heard, the smoke cleared away, and the heavy brigade of Le Marchant was seen coming forward in line at a canter. "Open right and left," was an order quickly obeyed; the line opened, the cavalry passed through the intervals, and, forming rapidly in our front, prepared for their work.

The French column, which a moment before held so imposing an attitude, became startled at this unexpected sight. A victorious and highly-excited infantry pressing close upon them, a splendid brigade of three regiments of cavalry ready to burst through their ill-arranged and beaten column, while no appearance of succour was at hand to protect them, was enough to appal the boldest intrepidity. The plain was filled with the vast multitude; retreat was impossible; and the troopers came still pouring in to join their comrades, already prepared for the attack. Hastily, yet with much regularity, all things considered, they attempted to get into square; but Le Marchant's brigade galloped forward before the evolution was half completed. The column hesitated, wavered, tottered, and then stood still! The motion of the countless bayonets as they clashed together might be likened to a forest about to be assailed by a tempest, whose first warnings announce the ravage it is about to inflict. Thomieres' division vomited forth a dreadful volley of fire as the horsemen thundered across the flat! Le Marchant was killed, and fell downright in the midst of the French bayonets; but his brigade pierced through the vast mass, killing or trampling, down all before them. The conflict was severe, and the troopers fell thick and fast; but their long heavy swords cut through bone as well as flesh. The groans of the dying, the cries of the wounded, the roar of the cannon, and the piteous moans of the mangled horses, as they ran away affrighted from the terrible scene, or lay with shat-

155

tered limbs, unable to move, in the midst of the burning grass, was enough to unman men not placed as we were; but upon us it had a different effect, and our cheers were heard far from the spot where this fearful scene was acting.

Such as got away from the sabres of the horsemen sought safety amongst the ranks of our infantry, and scrambling under the horses, ran to us for protection — like men who, having escaped the first shock of a wreck, will cling to any broken spar, no matter how little to be depended upon. Hundreds of beings, frightfully disfigured, in whom the human face and form were almost obliterated — black with dust, worn down with fatigue, and covered with sabre-cuts and blood — threw themselves amongst us for safety. Not a man was bayoneted — not one even molested or plundered; and the invincible old 3rd Division on this day surpassed themselves, for they not only defeated their terrible enemies in a fair stand-up fight, but actually covered their retreat, and protected them at a moment when, without such aid, their total annihilation was certain. Under similar circumstances would the French have acted so? I fear not. The men who murdered Ponsonby at Waterloo, when he was alone and unprotected, would have shown but little courtesy to the 3rd Division, placed in a similar way.

Nine pieces of artillery, two eagles, and five thousand prisoners were captured at this point; still the battle raged with unabated fury on our left, immediately in front of the 5th Division. Leith fell wounded as he led on his men, but his division carried the point in dispute, and drove the enemy before them up the hill.

While those events were taking place on the right, the 4th Division, which formed the centre of the army, met with a serious opposition. The more distant Arapiles, occupied by the French 122nd, whose numbers did not count more than four hundred, supported by a few pieces of cannon, was left to the Portuguese brigade of General Pack, amounting to two thousand bayonets. With fatal, though well-founded reliance — their former conduct taken into the scale — Cole's division advanced into the plain, confident that all was right with Pack's troops, and a terrible struggle between them and Bonnet's corps took place. It was, however, but of short duration. Bonnet's soldiers were driven back in confusion, and up to this moment all had gone on well. The three British divisions engaged overthrew every obstacle, and the battle might be said to be won, had Pack's formidable brigade — formidable in numbers at least — fulfilled their part; but these men totally failed in their effort to take the height occupied only by a few hundred Frenchmen, and thus gave the park of artillery that was posted with them full liberty to turn its efforts against the rear and flank of Cole's soldiers. Nothing could be worse than the state in which the 4th Division was now placed and the battle, which ought to have been, and had been in a manner, won, was still in doubt.

Bonnet, seeing the turn which Pack's failure had wrought in his favour, reformed his men, and advanced against Cole, while the fire from the battery and small arms on the Arapiles height completed the confusion. Cole fell wounded; half of his division were cut off, the remainder in full retreat; and Bonnet's troops, pressing on in a compact body, made it manifest that a material change had taken place in the battle, and that ere it was gained some ugly uphill work was yet to be done.

Marshal Beresford, who arrived at the moment, galloped up at the head of a brigade of the 5th Division, which he took out of the second line, and for a moment covered the retreat of Cole's troops; but this force — composed of Portuguese — was insufficient to arrest the progress of the enemy, who advanced in the full confidence of an assured victory; and at this critical moment Beresford was carried off the field wounded. Bonnet's troops advanced, loudly cheering, while the entire of Cole's division and Spry's brigade of Portuguese were routed. Our centre was thus endangered. Boyer's dragoons, after the overthrow of the French left, countermarched and moved rapidly to the support of Bonnet; they were close in the track of his infantry; and the fate of the battle was still uncertain. The fugitives of the 7th and 4th French Divisions ran to the succour of Bonnet, and by the time they had joined him his force had indeed assumed a formidable aspect; and thus reinforced, it stood in an attitude far different from what it would have done had Pack's brigade succeeded in its attack.

Lord Wellington, who saw what had taken place by the failure of Pack's troops, ordered up the 6th division to the support of the 4th; and the battle, although it was half-past eight o'clock at night, recommenced with the same fury as at the onset.

Clinton's division, consisting of six thousand bayonets, rapidly advanced to assert its place in the combat, and to relieve the 4th from the awkward predicament in which it was placed; they essayed to gain what was lost by the failure of Pack's troops in their feeble effort to wrest the Arapiles height from a few brave Frenchmen; but they were received by Bonnet's troops at the point of the bayonet, and the fire opened against them seemed to be threefold more heavy than that sustained by the 3rd and 5th Divisions. It was nearly dark; and the great glare of light caused by the thunder of the artillery, the continued blaze of the musketry, and the burning grass, gave to the face of the hill a novel and terrific appearance: it was one vast sheet of flame, and Clinton's men looked as if they were attacking a burning mountain, the crater of which was defended by a barrier of shining steel. But nothing could stop the intrepid valour of the 6th Division, as they advanced with a desperate resolution to carry the hill. The troops posted on the face of it to arrest their advance were trampled down and destroyed at the first charge, and each reserve sent forward to extricate them met with the same fate. Still Bonnet's reserves, having attained their place in the fight, and the fugitives from Thomieres' division, joining them at the moment, prolonged the battle until dark. Those men, besmeared with blood, dust, and clay, half-naked, and some carrying only broken weapons, fought with a fury not to be surpassed; but their impetuosity was at length calmed by the bayonets of Clinton's troops, and they no longer fought for victory but for safety. After a frightful struggle, they were driven from their last hold in confusion; and a general and overwhelming charge, which the nature of the ground enabled Clinton to make, carried this ill-formed mass of desperate soldiers before him, as a shattered wreck borne along by the force of some mighty current.

The mingled mass of fugitives fled to the woods and to the river for safety, and under cover of the night succeeded in gaining the pass of Alba over the Tormes. It was now ten o'clock at night: the battle was ended. At this point it had been confined to a small space, and the ground, trampled and stained deep, gave ample evidence of the havoc that had taken place. Lord Wellington, overcome as he was with fatigue, placed himself at the head of the lst and Light Divisions and a brigade of cavalry, and following closely the retreating footsteps of the enemy, with those troops who had not fired a shot during the conflict, left the remnant of his victorious army to sleep upon the field of battle they had so hardly won.

Robert Eadie served in the 79th (Cameron) Highlanders in the Peninsula. His account of his experiences in the British Army was published in Kincardine in 1829 under the title *Recollections of Robert Eadie* and is one of the rarer Peninsular War memoirs. Remarkably, Eadie was born in 1764, and thus was 48 years old when he fought at Salamanca, far older than the majority of officers and men in Wellington's army. The 79th Highlanders formed part of Wheatley's brigade of the 1st Division, which was engaged only briefly at Salamanca, being positioned to the east so that they could watch Foy's division, which hovered menacingly on Wellington's left flank. Nevertheless, his account is a detailed and highly personal narrative, in which the cooking of his meal seems to be almost as important to him and his comrades as the outcome of the battle itself!

For several days both armies continued thus manoeuvring in the face of each other down the country, until they arrived on that spot where they were to join in memorable conflict. Upon the day preceding the glorious encounter; we entered a wood; within a few miles of Salamanca, in which we halted. Here, under the verdant boughs of this sylvan retreat, we tarried for about four hours. We then got orders for the march; which we obeyed without sound of bugle, or beat of drum; and continued to advance in silence, until we reached the banks of the still rolling Tormes. Haying forded this river without much difficulty; the day, which a little before had begun to decline, now bade farewell to us forever. Though darkness was coming on apace, yet we pressed forward till we attained the heights of Las Arapiles. In close column we formed, piled our, arms, and sat down upon our knapsacks. We had not remained long in this position, when peals of distant thunder began to break upon our ears. The gloom of the atmosphere, though now awful, was rendered still more so by the flashes of lightning, and the nearer approach of the thunder. The sky, surcharged with dark watery clouds, poured down upon us torrents of, rain. Never was the morning light more anxiously longed for than at this time. My clothes were completely drenched. To stand erect was what I could not do, and in this uneasy state I was compelled to sit still. In consequence of this, I was seized with a violent ague. Thoughts, mournful and depressing, filled my mind, such as have been often experienced by soldiers on the eve of battle. Vivid recollections of our early years will, on such occasions, flit across the imagination with an enervating intensity, strangely at variance with that pitch of valorous determination which should then brace the mind:—

"No fond regrets must Norman know,
"When bursts Clan-Alpin on the foe,
"His heart must be the bended bow,
"His arm the arrow free, Mary!"

Dropping a tear therefore to "*auld lang syne*," I sighed as I reminded the sunny days, when I pressed the green sward, or climbed the steeps of the mountains of home; and ,the presentiment that I felt of my inability to perform my duty, on the imminent eventful morn, was painful and distressing. But the shades of night fled away, and with them was dispersed such a train of reflections.

No sooner had the dappled east announced the morn, than the shivering of my frame began to subside gradually. I suddenly felt the delightful influence of this happy change; grateful for which, I thanked the Father of Mercies for the never failing support of his invisible hand. The sun now burst from his Eastern couch and darted upon us his glorious beams. As he continued to advance in his course, all around was lighted up like a vast theatre, and portended the coming tragedy which was about to stalk forth in blood; the beating of drums; the snorting and prancing of steeds, and the warlike notes of the Pibroch.

When both armies had occupied the ground in battle-array, the division to which I belonged, stood in reserve, on the right of the line, near the deserted village of Arapiles.

It was about 2 o'clock, p.m. when the enemy extended his line to the left; under cover of his artillery, the roaring of which was like one continued peal of thunder. This was the time at which the dreadful conflict began. On the left, the onset was fearfully grand; there nothing could withstand the bravery of the troops. A short time before the enemy turned out from the woods, our division, being in reserve; received general orders to cook, which we set about with all dispatch. It being my turn for this duty, I had just commenced kindling a fire; while one of my comrades was preparing the kettle; when my attention was irresistibly called off, by the striking sight which unfolded itself: The French columns appeared covering all the opposite ground, and our lines being formed, marched gallantly forward to meet them in the attack. The grand charge of the cavalry on the right, was perfectly splendid; the glancing of the sabres, which burst like lightning from amid the clouds of dust, raised by the horses' feet — the noble bearing of the rival ranks, whose compact marshalling seemed incapable of discomfiture; the awful result of the next ten minutes to many of these proud, and noble hearts, — all formed a climax of moving excitement, from the very rapidity which they were whirling as a vision to be part of "a tale that is told!" During, this scene however, we were in great danger at the camp kettles, as both shells and shot were coming thickly and rapidly from the enemy, amongst us, occasionally exciting a smile at the ludicrous confusion which they caused, by striking a kettle, and upsetting its contents; the men scampering around to avoid being scalded, as they cursed the loss of the precious broth. Two of the cooks were killed before we left the ground; but as a precaution against what, might equally have been my fate, I took care always to lie down flat on the ground, whenever I could perceive a shell coming in my direction, and which I had time enough to do. The whole of the lines were closely engaged ere we had accomplished the business of cooking: but whenever that was effected, and the measures of beef boiled; the soup was emptied out; and the beef put into our haversacks; and we marched off the hill with the officer to join our division, which we found still lying in close column as a reserve. Just at the moment of our arrival at the regiment, a shell was thrown by the enemy that unpiled a whole company's arms, but luckily enough, no one received any hurt. Shortly afterwards the beef was divided into messes and each man received his welcome share; and as the most agreeable of all possible *desserts* to a party in our situation, an aide-de-camp came galloping up to our rear; crying out that the French were flying in every direction! — as he passed the place where I stood, a cannon shot struck his horse, and the poor animal fell under his rider, but he was instantly provided with a led horse, by a light dragoon who rode after him. By this time general Marmont was wounded. He was struck by a shell near the right shoulder, and so severely, that he had to be carried off the field in a litter, by six grenadiers; at Penarando his arm was amputated. The French had been successively dislodged from their advantageous positions, and lost all the artillery which they had placed there. After seven hours continued fighting, in which it is but justice to say, that the infantry, as well as the cavalry and artillery, of both nations, performed prodigies of valour, the enemy gave way on all sides. Our division was immediately ordered to join the light division, which we did at double quick time, and then the dreadful work of death began. Before us the crowding and disordered enemy was in full flight, while we sent volleys of shot with deadly effect after them. We thus continued the galling pursuit, at double quick time; during the remainder of that day, all night, and till 12 o'clock on the morrow, before we got a halt: I declare that never before, or since, have I felt so perfectly tired. We had so many large fields, covered with white stones, to pass, that our feet were much hurt; a great many prisoners, however, fell into our hands, but I confess I thought the best thing to be taken alive, would be a sheep from the many flocks we passed on our way. Wearied as I was, I succeeded in catching a pretty fat one; which I got upon my back, and carried along in the march for nearly four miles till we halted. The captain of the company repeatedly called to me to let go my prize, but his mind was changed, when the savoury smell of the mutton curled up from the cooking fire. I could then almost have refused him a mess, for which he anxiously asked, but he partook along with some of my comrades.

The total loss of the enemy was at first estimated at 10 or 12,000, but after wards, much more, when the immense number of prisoners had been taken. Many Eagles, — almost all the baggage, and an immense quantity of military stores, also fell into our hands. The loss of the Allies, in killed, wounded and missing, was, by the return afterwards made, 5879.

I had scarcely recovered from the fatigue of pursuit, when I was attacked by severe dysentery — I was reduced so weak that it was with difficulty that I could keep my seat upon a mule, upon which I was sent to Salamanca. Here, all the Convents, and Colleges, which had been nearly reduced to ruin by the French, were put into a state of repair, and fitted up in the best way possible as Hospitals. These were, unfortunately, but too well filled by the sick and wounded, of whom, numbers died every day.

The victory at Salamanca cost Wellington 5,214 casualties of whom 3,176 were British. The exact French casualty figure is hard to determine although it is fairly certain to have been around 14,000. Twenty guns were taken also. The battle came as a crushing blow to the French, and to Marmont in particular, whose arrogance in thinking he could simply waltz across Wellington's front without any danger to himself cost him the best part of his army. Salamanca also nailed the French belief that Wellington was just an over-cautious and defensive-minded commander and when news of the victory spread throughout Europe his reputation as one of the great commanders was assured. Indeed, referring to Wellington's performance at Salamanca, General Foy, no mean judge of character, claimed that the victory raised Wellington's reputation to that of Marlborough. Well, Wellington had some way to go yet to rise to that great height but within two years he would do so. For now, however, he could cast his eye over yet another satisfying victory, one that opened the way to the Spanish capital, Madrid.

CHAPTER TEN

BURGOS AND RETREAT

With Marmont's army having been smashed at Salamanca, the road to Madrid was now open. It was, however, not the logical route for Wellington to take. The most advantageous route lay towards Valladolid, Burgos and then Vittoria. From here, the road led directly to France via San Sebastian. However, the political implications of marching upon the Spanish capital far outweighed the military, and so Wellington marched to Madrid, which he entered in triumph on 12 August 1812.

When Wellington entered the capital he was received as a hero by the population who could finally look forward to an end to the four-year occupation of their country by the French. Their optimism, however, was to be ill founded. Less than three months later, Wellington and his army would be back in Portugal, unceremoniously pursued there by the French after having failed in his next military objective, the capture of Burgos.

Burgos, in fact, was the only blot on an otherwise whiter-than-white Wellington copybook. It was, he later remarked, 'the worst scrape I ever was in.' When Wellington made this remark he was not only referring to the abortive siege at Burgos but also to the retreat to Portugal that followed. For those who had experienced both the retreats to Corunna and from Burgos, the latter had been by far the worse of the two. The weather during the Corunna retreat had been bad enough, with snow, ice and cold biting winds. But, as the men commented, at least there was some shelter to be had along the way, unlike the retreat from Burgos which took place across barren open countryside, in pouring rain, and with no shelter whatsoever.

The siege of Burgos in September and October 1812 was unlike any of Wellington's other sieges in the Peninsula as it was directed against an old castle, which dominated the town, and not against the town itself, which Wellington's men occupied with ease, it having no fortifications or walls. The importance of the town lay in the fact that it commanded the main road between France and Madrid and thus threatened the communications of any hostile force moving one way or the other along the road.

The siege began on 19 September, and was essentially a 1st Division operation, whilst the men who had stormed Ciudad Rodrigo and Badajoz remained at Madrid. Crucially, Wellington took with him only three heavy guns, and these were only 18-pounders, the immensely powerful 24-pounders being left behind. One feels, in fact, that Wellington overstretched himself at Burgos with a lack of engineers, tools, heavy guns and ammunition. Even the decision to attack Burgos was, perhaps, a questionable one. Having decided upon this course of action he would have been far better off in taking with him the greater part, if not all, of his army, rather than take just a single division. The phrase, 'all or nothing,' certainly springs to mind.

In the event, a series of assaults went in against the castle, but all failed. The garrison, some 2,000 French troops under General Dubreton, put up a fierce resistance, causing Wellington severe casualties, one of whom was Major Edward Charles Cocks, one of Wellington's favourite officers, who was killed repulsing a sortie on 8 October. Indeed, Wellington wept openly at his funeral. The final assault went in on 18 October, but this too failed badly, although the Foot Guards gave it their very best shot. On 21 October news reached Wellington that not one but three separate French armies were converging upon Madrid, forcing Wellington to abandon the siege of Burgos altogether, and on the night of 21 October, his army slipped away silently into the night.

The siege of Burgos has attracted scant coverage in the journals written by Wellington's men, mainly due to the fact that it was a disastrous operation. Also, the majority of Wellington's soldiers lay around Madrid, leaving just the 1st Division of the army to carry on the siege. Thus, the number of diarists present at Burgos is very small indeed. One of the better accounts is to be found in *For King and Country: The Letters and Diaries of John Mills, Coldstream Guards*. Mills was an ensign in the Coldstream and had been in the Peninsula since April 1811, since when he had seen action at Fuentes de Oñoro, Ciudad Rodrigo and Salamanca. The book contains both his diaries and letters, and his account of the siege of Burgos is one of the best ever published. Mills made daily entries in his journal, and the following extracts are the entries he made on the more relevant days.

October 4th. Lord Wellington has given out orders wherein he tells the two Divisions engaged in the siege that unless they work better they will not obtain the same credit that other Divisions have done, at the same time excepting the conduct of the Brigade of Guards which has been as exemplary here as all other places. Our guns re-opened in the morning upon the old breach which at two o'clock appeared to be very practicable. It was then determined that the outer wall should be stormed at daylight, the other attempts at night having failed. The 24th Regiment supported by two hundred men of the Division were to go up the old breach. The signal for the attack was to be the explosion of the mine. The 6th Division were to mount the breach which the mine was to make. At four o'clock the hill was covered with spectators. I took post in front of the breach and about half a mile from it. At half past five the mine exploded and made an excellent breach. The troops rushed forward from the place where they were concealed. A Grenadier officer of the 24th led that regiment in the most gallant style. He was first on the breach but when near the top appeared to find great difficulty in getting up, the ground slipping from under his feet. Just at this moment about ten Frenchmen appeared; they seemed quite confounded and not to know what was going on. Two or three ran to the old breach, one fired close to the officer but missed him, the men then peered over and the French ran off as fast as they could into the fort. The 24th advanced and hid themselves behind a pile of shot from whence they commenced firing. Thus far the French seemed taken quite unawares. The explosion of the mine and the storming were so instantaneous that they had not time to do anything before the men were in and then it was too late. The 6th Division got in at their breach without any sort of difficulty. The French now opened a most tremendous fire from every part of their works — musketry, shells, round shot and grape. Every musket and gun seemed to be at work. Our men returned the fire, and as it was getting dusk the sight was truly magnificent. As it got dark the fire slackened.

I reckon myself fortunate in having had so good an opportunity of seeing it — it is a chance if ever I may have another. As soon as it was dark the working commenced, and in the course of the night a trench was dug parallel to the breach, to afford cover to the men. At twelve o'clock the garrison made a sally but were repulsed. At first they drove our men back, but the tables were soon turned. It was accompanied by a very heavy firing and loud and repeated cheers.

October 7th. It rained incessantly during the day and night. They dismounted another eighteen pounder this morning so that there is now but one left and yet the siege is continued though the chance of success must be very remote. At three in the morning the garrison made another sortie. They advanced under favour of a very heavy rain and got up to the breach without being perceived, and drove our men from every part of the wall. The Germans were on the covering party. After some time the Germans succeeded in regaining the wall after a most obstinate defensive, being so closely engaged that they knocked each other about with their butt ends. Major Cocks, of the 79th, the Field Officer in the trenches, was killed at the beginning of the business. His loss is irreparable. He was of the greatest promise and during the three years he had been in the country had greatly distinguished himself. Every officer present was either killed or wounded, and the loss in men is about a hundred and fifty. They levelled all our works and buried some of the sappers alive. Two officers and 50 men were in my post behind the shot. They [the French] got into their rear — the officers were killed and hardly a man escaped. I cannot help thinking myself very fortunate in having escaped.

October 8th. The disasters of last night have depressed everyone. We are just where we were three days ago and whenever the garrison chooses the sortie they can drive us out. The weather too conspires against us, and our resources so inadequate at first, and since so much reduced, give us no hopes of success — it must end in a blockade. The French stole out so quietly last night that they came upon the trench before the men at work had the least idea of their approach. The first intimation was finding the earth shovelled down upon their heads. One of the sappers finding it impossible to escape allowed himself to be buried, and came out when they retired. Another followed his example but was struck twice with a pick-axe, at which he said he would be damned if he stood that and ran off. The man who was buried said that a French officer of Engineers who stood over his men directing them, was shot. The rain continues.

October 15th. Our regiment formed the covering party and I went on at half past one in the morning and remained on till five. My post was to observe the gate of the Castle and I had forty men. At twelve o'clock our batteries made another attempt but they no sooner opened than twelve guns were brought to bear upon our three. In half an hour the battery was knocked to pieces and the men driven from the guns. I take this to be our last dying speech. They throw during the day a vast number of shells and as the day was dark I could see them in the air which I never remember to have done before. The splinters came back into their own works and troubled us as though under cover we were not more than twenty yards from the Castle wall. A man sitting round the fire was hit. Two Frenchmen jumped out from behind a bank and shot two sentries who were posted in advance. Upon this two officers went out to see whether there was any better place to post them and whilst looking another Frenchman jumped out from the same place, levelled and pulled at them but luckily his piece missed fire. The French army advanced a little, but did not drive in our outposts. Rain in the evening.

October 18th. The Coldstream formed the covering party in the morning. Harvey was killed whilst visiting his party. The battery continued firing upon the breach and succeeded in making it very good. At three o'clock it was communicated to us that the place was to be stormed at 4 o'clock. The signal was the explosion of the mine, on which a flag was to be held up on the hill. The mine exploded — the explosion was attended with so little noise that though we were anxiously expecting it, we could hear no noise. The earth shook a little, we looked to the hill and saw the flag. The 300 Germans stormed the breach and got well up it. They then attempted the third line, by a place in the wall which was broken down. It ended in their being beat out of the whole with the loss of 7 officers and a great many men. Our party was to escalade the wall in front. Burgess ran forward with 30 men, Walpole and myself followed with fifty each and ladders. Burgess got up without much difficulty, Walpole and myself followed. The place we stood on was a ledge in the wall about three feet from the top. A most tremendous fire opened upon us from every part which took us in front and rear. They poured down fresh men and ours kept falling down into the ditch, dragging and knocking down others. We were so close that they fairly put their muskets into our faces, and we pulled one of their men through an embrasure. Burgess was killed and Walpole severely wounded. We had hardly any men left on the top and at last we gave way. How we got over the palisades I know not. They increased their fire as we retreated, and we came off with the loss of more than half our party and all the badly wounded were left in the ditch. Burgess behaved nobly — he was the first up the ladder and waved his hat on the top. I found him lying there wounded. He begged me to get my men up and in the act of speaking a stone hit him, he fell on the ledge and was shot dead. The time we were on the wall was not more than six minutes. The fire was tremendous, shot, shells, grape, musketry, large stones, hand grenades and every missile weapon was used against us. I reckon my escape particularly fortunate. A party of sixty men attempted to escalade on our right. They were met by a very superior force and were immediately driven back but with very little loss. The mine destroyed a small church on the right. Colonel Brown with some Portuguese got possession of it. It completes our possession of the whole of the first line which was before incomplete. The failure of this is to be ascribed entirely to our want of men. Had we but double the number we could have maintained ourselves but they dropped off so fast and none coming to supply their place, we failed from sheer weakness. Crofton was slightly wounded in the arm whilst waiting with the support. Walpole had his arm shattered with a grape shot, which struck him likewise in the side, but the shot most providentially glanced, striking and tearing 'Ninon de l'Enclos,' which he happened to have in a side pocket at the time, otherwise it must have killed him. Thus finished this trying day. I was slightly wounded in the arm by a stone, but not the least hurt.

Mills survived the storming attempt, of course, but became increasingly disillusioned with the operation. Indeed, when he returned to Lisbon in December 1812 he did so fearing that the war in the Peninsula itself was lost. He also had some sharp criticisms to make of Wellington and his conduct throughout the siege and during the retreat that followed, which make interesting contemporary reading in the light of Wellington's later reputation. Indeed, they provide an illuminating insight into contemporary thinking amongst Wellington's officers, something which is rare in itself, given the mass of post-Napoleonic literature, which quite naturally has nothing but praise for the great man.

The abandonment of the siege was only the beginning of Wellington's troubles, however, for he soon found himself being pursued back towards Valladolid and then Salamanca, the troops from Madrid joining him en route. By now, the army was deep in the midst of one of its great breakdowns in discipline. George Murray, the Quartermaster General, was back in England, and his replacement, Willoughby Gordon, was simply not up to the job. There was a complete breakdown in the supply system and when the bad weather set in the army degenerated into a rabble, with only the better regiments retaining a semblance of order. The troops had been in a bad state from the outset. As early as 24 October the men discovered a vast store of wine at Torquemada, which was quickly gorged leaving hundreds of drunken British troops to be captured the following day by French cavalry.

The retreat took the army all the way back to Ciudad Rodrigo and the Portuguese border, and although the French gave up the pursuit close to Salamanca the retreat was no less a trial. It cost Wellington over 3,000 men who either died of sickness and exhaustion or were taken by the French. Amongst the latter was none other than General Sir Edward

Paget, one of the heroes of the crossing of the Douro in May 1809. Paget, who had lost an arm there, was attacked by three French dragoons during the retreat, close to the village of San Muñoz. He had come out to Spain ostensibly to act as Wellington's second-in-command, and had arrived in the Peninsula barely two weeks earlier.

One of the rarest and earliest accounts of the retreat from Burgos is *A Narrative of the Retreat of The British Army from Burgos*, written by George Frederick Burroughs, assistant surgeon of the 1st Royal Dragoons, and published in London in 1814. Burroughs' account takes the form of a series of letters, which follow an introduction dealing with the campaign of 1812 up to Burgos. The letters begin with the retreat from Burgos, following the abortive siege, and end with the army back on the Portuguese border, from whence it had begun the year back in January.

I had scarcely reposed an hour in my tent, and it was eleven o'clock at night, when my servant came to inform me the regiment was ordered to march. I arose hastily and dressed myself, the thunders of the artillery of the castle vibrating in my ears. My tent was instantly struck, and the baggage thrown upon the mule. The night was fine, the moon shone with that unvarying light an unclouded sky affords, and the neighbouring naked mountains, gilded by her beams, materially added to the solemnity of the scene. The distant sounds of the artillery rattling on the roads, the buzzing murmurs of the passing soldiery, and the angry lightning from the cannon of the besieged castle, could not fail of inspiring sublimity even in the most vacant mind.

Having mounted my horse, I directed my way to Villa Toro, a very small and insignificant village, about two miles from Burgos, where the headquarters of the army had been established during the siege. As the narrow road, (which from the late rains, was rendered heavy) led through the mountains, and lay out of the range of the shot of the castle; the spare artillery and hospital waggons, commissariat mules, and baggage of the army, proceeded by it. The throng presently became so great, that the cargoes of the mules were overturned, and in proportion to the opposition, did the desire of pushing forward increase. Every thing was at a stand and in disorder. In one place were two or three sick soldiers bolstered up by their comrades' knapsacks lying on a bullock car, and surrounded by some less sick companions; in another, bags of biscuit trodden under feet, and casks of rum stove in; here an artillery waggon had sunk axle-tree high in mud, the leading horses of which, having exhausted their strength to drag it out, were lying prostrate and panting in the road, so that it was with much difficulty I could proceed, and then

169

only by striking out a path over the mountain.

Having entered Villa Toro, which presented one scene of bustle, I found the flying artillery of the Spanish army passing, and the streets so narrow and dirty, and so blocked up with beasts of burden of every sort, that the officers' servants, of headquarters, were unable to load their mules with baggage, and the commissaries were in a like situation with regard to their supplies. Some considerable time elapsed before I got clear of this village, and had scarcely done so, when I overtook one of the eighteen-pounders, which had been employed on the horn-work of Saint Michael against the castle of Burgos. An ex-traordinary number of horses were endeavouring to drag the carriage through the muddy ground, but the resistance offered was so great, that it was ordered to be spiked and left behind. After marching the distance of about three miles, the Estrado Real, or Royal Road, presented itself, leading from Valladolid to Bayonne.

Once clear of Burgos, the retreat proper can be said to have begun. Already the road to Valladolid was becoming blocked with traffic and with straggling soldiers. Wellington's men thought the situation bad at this stage of the retreat, but they had no idea just how appalling things were to become within a few short days. Burroughs again:

The moon went down at one o'clock, when I became involved in so much darkness, that I could scarcely discover the road. The night was cold, all martial sounds had ceased; and save the distant roar of the cannon of Burgos, a gloomy stillness hung around me. I had left behind my companions, who often beguiled the tediousness of a march, or relieved the oppression of care, by the narration of a facetious story, to listen to the complaints of the Portuguese boys, of whom there was a considerable number, employed as servants in our army. These, were lamenting the famished state of their own stomachs, as well as of those excellent beasts of burden, the mules, whose unerring steps they were measuring by my side. As the word FOME, [a Portuguese word, signifying hunger] pronounced with an emphasis, too well conveying the feelings which urged it, frequently reached my ears, I began to consider that I had but once participated in its calls, and then I found wild turnips and the hawthorn berry, not the most despicable substitute for food of better kind. From these reflections, I was, however, awakened by a restive mule, who, had precipitated its burden, and entangled its legs among the cords; it was fastened to others, and had disordered the economy of the baggage of each.

Here, one limping from disease arrested my progress; there another, labouring under an unmerciful load, threatened by hoarse sighs at every step, to give up the ghost.

I had now approached a village, and feeling an ague coming on, dismounted from my horse, at the door of a house which was open. On entering, quantities of burnt straw lay on the floor, with some wood, which seemed recently to have supplied a fire. Having ordered my baggage to be unloaded, and a fire to be kindled, I wrapped myself up in my cloak, and laid down, prepared to encounter the paroxysm. This hovel, which from its exterior, looked as decent as any in the place, was entirely divested of every thing in the shape of furniture. The slender partitions which separated the upper rooms with the flooring, was removed, and only the central beam, that from its size had resisted every attempt, was remaining. Stores of all, kinds and baggage continued to pass by, and the Portuguese soldiers were frequently entering my quarters to light their paper segars. As soon as break of day, I arose, and almost the first object that presented itself, was the 5th division and Spanish army, marching over the mountains which run northward through Old Castile, and which are a continuation of those forming the northern boundary to the kingdom of Leon.

A party of German hussars marching by, informed me the whole of the infantry had passed the skirts of the village, and that the cavalry would arrive presently. Having re-mounted, and marched about three miles, I overtook the 6th division, and proceeded with it to Celada del Camino, where the headquarters of our second in command, the Honourable Sir Edward Paget, was established; and, at some little distance, the column was encamped. These troops had arrived here about two hours before, and were cooking their dinners. I had but just come to my regiment, when the route was announced. The column was soon under arms, and proceeded to Vallefena, which after several halts we did not reach until dark. Vallefena is a small village, distant eight leagues from Burgos; and is situated on the Pisuerga river, over which a good stone bridge is thrown. There is much inconvenience suffered in coming to a bivouac at night, particularly in the present instance, as it was upon vineyard grounds, so that at every step we sunk deep in the soft ground surrounding the trunk of the vines, or else were thrown down by their long branches curling round our limbs. The tents were pitched, and the camp soon began to blaze with our fires. Our horses felt this night the want of straw; indeed, what little could be obtained, was always allotted to the cavalry and artillery horses; and where there was a sufficiency, it was issued to all who were entitled, by the general orders of the commander of the forces.

About half-past four o'clock on the morning of the 23rd of October, an aide-de-camp of Sir Edward Paget's, came to our around, and ordered the tents to be struck, and the baggage to be sent off; but it was six o'clock before the column was in motion and clear of the village. We continued our march, without interruption for several hours, along a very fine and level road, which seemed to lengthen, as we advanced. The 7th division, under the command of the Earl of Dalhousie, with the cavalry, formed the rear of the army; and as these troops approached the village of Torquemada, the French cavalry, chiefly composed of the Gendarmerie of Paris, began to display themselves. The Spanish army, under General Castanos, was retiring by Palencia, with the Spanish cavalry, under that meritorious officer, Don Julian de la Sanchez; but these cavalry were unequal, both from the size of their horses, and the paucity of their numbers compared to that of the enemy, either to make a charge, or to resist one. And the French having encountered and put them into disorder, they came flying upon the British cavalry, mixed with the enemy, in pursuit. Here the difference of language, with the similarity of the Spanish to the French uniform, created much confusion; and our light dragoons, under Sir Stapleton Cotton, (now Lord Combermere) having done every thing bravery could effect, were overpowered by numbers, and obliged to retire. At this critical moment, the 7th division, composed for the most part of Foreign soldiers, was halted, and formed a square. In this square, the commander of the forces with his staff; was observed: when the enemy endeavouring to charge the square, was foiled in the attempt, and kept at a respectable distance afterwards.

In this rencontre, our loss was somewhat considerable, particularly of the 16th dragoons; whose lieutenant-colonel, (Pelly) being wounded, was taken prisoner.

The village, in whose vicinity we had last encamped, contained a great quantity of new-made wine; and as many of the inhabitants had left their houses, our soldiers drank of it to excess. The effects of which we found in this day's march; for it was with great difficulty the men who had thus indulged themselves could keep up with their regiments. This circumstance did not pass unobserved by General Paget, who, when the column halted for the evening, formed it into brigades, and addressed it. He began by expressing his regret, at the scene he had witnessed that day; which cast a severe reflection on our character as soldiers; whose particular province it was to observe discipline. He professed himself anxious to further the comforts of the private, as of the officer, but it was more especially incumbent on the officer to look after his men; and Sir Edward concluded, by avowing his determination to inflict exemplary punishment, should a similar outrage occur. As he spoke, the evening breeze blew aside his cloak, and exposed the arm which had suffered amputation in the passage of the Douro, at Oporto, in 1809; and this, with the peculiar expression of his countenance, rendered the address doubly impressive.

The retreat continued towards Madrid, where the rest of Wellington's army joined those coming from Burgos. Madrid was evacuated, and then Salamanca, where Wellington drew up once more in his old position of 22 July. How fate had turned on him in the four months since his great victory there. The march from Salamanca to the Portuguese border was considered by all to have been the most harrowing part of the retreat, with rain falling in torrents and with the commissariat suffering a total breakdown. Burroughs account continues:

On the 16th of November, the army continued its march, and the enemy followed with the whole of his cavalry, probably consisting of ten thousand, and a considerable body of light infantry. The weather was severe and the ground so heavy, that the horses at every step sunk to the fetlock, and the men to their ankles. The former suffered much last evening, not having any provender; whilst the bark of trees, and sprigs of wild briar, afforded but an indifferent substitute: indeed, we felt for these invaluable animals, and well we might, for their existence was essentially necessary to our own. Their toils had lessened many of our fatigues, which otherwise we must have shared in common with the private; and the contrast afforded comfort, though at the expense of compassion. We are more charitably disposed with our feelings on some occasions, than on others, and an object that has once awakened sympathy, may at another time pass with indifference; it was even so with ourselves, and we were oftener tempted to betray displeasure at a worn-out and limping soldier, than administer consolation.

The enemy did not press upon our rear, but contented himself with picking up those men who from fatigue or indisposition, had fallen out from their regiments. Some baggage that had strayed or lost itself in the wood, we were marching through, likewise fell into their hands; and what between the weather and the empty state of our stomachs, a gloom was thrown over our march, which rendered us very indifferent companions for one another. Providence, by affording us a supply of acorns, had not altogether abandoned us to despair, and in alighting to fill the haversack with those that had fallen from the trees, our horses were now and then enabled to pick up a little grass. At five o'clock in the evening, the army came to its bivouac, in a wood about two leagues distance from Tamames, the ground being in many places covered with water. The rain had discontinued, and the evening promised to be fine; but what was infinitely more consolatory, arose from an allowance of biscuit issued to the troops.

On the 17th, at six o'clock in the morning the army which was well concentrated, left its encampment. Our brows lowered with the clouds, and occasionally heavy showers, drenching as they fell, rendered us no less penitent, than desirous of fair weather. Ploughed lands lay before us, with an extensive wood; it was with difficulty we could march, the column halting every four or five minutes. We passed the commander of the forces here, who appeared anxious the troops should push on, and his aide-de-camps were much on the alert.

The enemy closely followed our rear; and as the weather was misty accompanied with rain, so that objects were rendered indistinct even at a little distance, the light companies of regiments were ordered to extend them-selves through the wood, to protect our flanks and cover our baggage. We could not, however, prevent the great force of the enemy's cavalry from being felt, and they took every advantage to annoy us, which numbers and the state of the weather, afforded them. At this time, the baggage of the Earl of Dalhousie was reported to be taken, though it proceeded at the head of his division; and Sir Edward Paget having gone to the rear, to ascertain the cause of the interval or space between the 5th and 7lth divisions, occasioned by the badness of the ground, was made prisoner. Sir Edward was unattended, but his rank of general officer, was known by the *chapeau plume*.

We were descending the heights near San Muñoz, the wind blowing strong and it raining fast. A body of British cavalry that had been lying in the village, advanced upon the hills on our left, to cover our rear by showing front. They formed two open lines, and their long red and blue cloaks waving to the wind, had a very enlivening effect.

The little village of San Muñoz lies in a valley at the extremity of two ranges of hills, which are covered with oak trees; along this valley, the river Huebra runs and empties itself into the Douro. The divisions as they forded this river, marched to the opposite hills, where they were formed in open columns of brigade, and halted. The difficulty of the ascent as well as descent into the valley, with the deepness and rapid current of the river rendered this place very troublesome for troops followed by an enemy. The army continued fording the river, and was regularly formed upon the hills. A thick fog came on about two o'clock in the afternoon, and the enemy availed himself of this circumstance to gain possession of a hill upon the right of our line, which was separated from those we were already upon, by a ravine, scarcely one quarter of a mile broad. Upon it the French brought up some mountain guns, and commenced a heavy fire upon the light division, commanded by Major-General Charles Alten, on its fording the river. The guns of Major Macdonald's troop of horse artillery commenced a successful fire upon them, but unfortunately, during the cannonade, the Major was severely wounded. The division had no sooner crossed, than the French cavalry followed, and began to hem them in, and though our troops formed the square, yet the enemy succeeded in charging them on the way to the heights, and occasioning some loss.

Now the army was formed for battle, and every one forgot his fatigues in the anticipation of victory. The meagre soldier in our ranks, whose furrowed cheeks bespoke an age of service, felt the fire of youth kindling in his veins, as the roar of the cannon played upon his ears; while the youth, who chiefly composed the strength of our battalions, had their memories too recently impressed with the brilliant achievements of Rodrigo, Badajoz, and Salamanca, to have been readily forgotten. In the narration of these monuments of glory and human valour, did our soldiers beguile the time, previous to the battle? The spirit of enthusiasm was however raised to the highest pitch, by the electric effect of the words, "Here he comes," which spread from mouth to mouth, with the rapidity of lightning. The noble commander passed our columns in review, as usual, unaccompanied with any mark of distinction or splendour; his long horse cloak, concealed his under garments; his cocked hat soaked and disfigured with the rain.

We now offered the enemy battle, and though so greatly superior in every species of force, they refused, and the cannonade was continued on both sides, until the close of the day. We were much disappointed in their refusing battle; and the pleasure of vanquishing them, was more than equalled by the thought of feeding on their supplies.

The troops reposed on their arms, upon wet ground, and the trees which at the season of the year, had dropped their leaves, afforded but a pitiful cover from the winds. We were pretty well aware of the enemy's intention to get possession of Spain, without hazarding a battle; and concluded, that the following day's march by bringing us to the confines of Portugal, would put an end to the retreat. We were, therefore, as anxious to commence the march, as we were to satisfy the cravings of hunger, and though this sensation, perhaps, was not equally felt by all, it was by too many. Some were fortunate enough to purchase, from the Spanish troops a little pork, so fresh and warm, that we still might have imagined the pig reeking in the slaughter-house and weltering in its blood; but it was not on that account the less unsavoury. This meat being toasted before our fires, was eat with all the avidity, (notwithstanding the want of bread and savour of salt) hunger imposes.

The moon rose early, and between the light clouds that passed in rapid succession, diffused her splendid radiance over the wistful camp; the stillness of which was only interrupted by the passing watch-word of sentries, and hoarse murmurs of our cattle. As we slumbered over the fires, our cloaks and blankets soaking with the wet, the orderlies about one o'clock, began to pass about with the general order to march; and between three and four o'clock, on the morning of the 18th we moved from the bivouac, and after proceeding half a mile, forded a large branch of the river Huebra, which detained the army a considerable time. The country before us was covered with gumcistus and the dwarf oak, and the road in many places, so narrow and dirty; the men could only pass by files.

The enemy followed us this day only with their cavalry, and to keep them in check, some companies of the 60th regiment were disposed in the woods, who occasioned them much loss. The army having gained the high road, (which in summer is fine and level) we found it inundated with water; and in many places presented a formidable picture of destruction; numbers of dead cattle, broken waggons and cars; stores and tents, being thrown away for want of carriage to bring them on.

We continued our march without interruption, and the distant view of the spires of Ciudad Rodrigo, was hailed by our troops with a proportionate degree of enthusiasm, to that which the Greeks under Xenophon, exhibited in the almost miraculous retreat through Asia, when from the Colchian Mountains they beheld the Black Sea.

On the 19th and 20th of November, the army crossed the Agueda, the course of which river may be considered as marking the north-east boundary of Portugal from Spain.

A more gripping account of the retreat from Burgos was published in Sergeant Joseph Donaldson's *Recollections of the Eventful Life of a Soldier*, the first edition of which was published in London in 1825. Donaldson served in the 94th (Scotch Brigade), one of the regiments that served in the 'Fighting' 3rd Division under Sir Thomas Picton. Donaldson saw his fair share of fighting in the Peninsula, as you would expect from a soldier in the 3rd Division. However, even he found the trials of the retreat hard to bear, as he recalled in his memoir.

About the 14th of October, we marched from Madrid to Pinto, a distance of about three leagues; in consequence of the enemy advancing in great force in that direction. Here we remained until the 30th, when we were ordered to retreat upon Madrid, and passed our pontoons burning on the roadside, having been set on fire to prevent them falling into the hands of the enemy.

We supposed at first that we would again occupy Madrid, but when we came in sight of it the Retiro was in flames, and we could hear the report of cannon, which proceeded from the brass guns in the fort being turned on each other for the purpose of rendering them useless to the enemy; the stores of provision and clothing which we had previously taken were also burned, and every preparation made for evacuating the place. The staff officers were galloping about giving directions to the different divisions concerning their route; the inhabitants whom we met on the road were in evident consternation, and every thing indicated an unexpected and hurried retreat: instead, therefore, of entering the city, we passed to the left of it. The enemy's cavalry by this time being close on our rear, and before ours had evacuated the town on the one side, the French had entered it on the other. We marched about a league past Madrid, when we encamped for the night; but next morning we proceeded on our retreat, nor halted until we reached Salamanca, having the enemy encamped close on our rear every night.

The French having taken up nearly the same position they had occupied on the 22nd of July, on the afternoon of the 15th November we turned out of the town, and forming on nearly our old ground, expected an immediate engagement. We had been so much harassed in retreating from Madrid in the severe weather, that we felt much more inclination to fight than to go farther, but we were disappointed; and after performing some evolutions, we filed off on the road leading to Rodrigo, and commenced retreating as night was setting in. I never saw the troops in such a bad humour.

Retreating before the enemy at any time was a grievous business, but in such weather it was doubly so; the rain, now pouring down in torrents, drenched us to the skin, and the road, composed of a clay soil, stuck to our shoes so fast, that they were torn off our feet. The night was dismally dark, the cold wind blew in heavy gusts, and the roads became gradually worse. After marching in this state far several hours, we halted in a field on the road side, and having piled our arms, were allowed to dispose ourselves to rest as we best could. The moon was now up, and wading through the dense masses of clouds, she sometimes threw a momentary gleam on the miserable beings

177

who were huddled together in every variety of posture, endeavouring to rest or screen themselves from the cold. Some were lying stretched on the wet ground rolled in still wetter blankets, more having placed their knapsack on a stone, or their wooden canteen, had seated themselves on it with their blankets wrapped about them, their head reclining on their knees, and their teeth chattering with cold; while others more resolute and wise, were walking briskly about. Few words were spoken, and as if ashamed to complain of the hardships we suffered, execrating the retreat, and blaming Lord Wellington for not having sufficient confidence in us to hazard a battle with the enemy, under any circumstances, were the only topics discussed.

A considerable time before day light we were again ordered to fall in, and proceeded on our retreat. The rain still continued to fall, and the roads were knee deep. Many men got fatigued and unable to proceed. Some spring waggons were kept in the rear to bring them up, but the number increased so fast that there was soon no conveyance for them; and as we formed the rear guard, they soon fell into the hands of the French cavalry, who hung on our rear during the whole retreat. When we came to our halting ground, the same accommodation awaited us as on the preceding evening. By some mismanagement the commissary stores had been sent on with the rest of the baggage to Rodrigo, and we were without food. The feeling of hunger was very severe. Some beef that had remained with the division was served out to us, but our attempts to kindle fires with wet wood was quite abortive. Sometimes, indeed, we managed to raise a smoke, and numbers gathered round, in the vain hope of getting themselves warmed, but the fire would extinguish in spite of all their efforts. Our situation was truly distressing: tormented by hunger, wet to the skin, and fatigued in the extreme, our reflections were bitter; the comfortable homes and firesides which we had left were now recalled to mind, and contrasted with our present miserable situation; and during that night many a tear of repentance and regret fell from eyes "unused to the melting mood."

About the same hour as on the preceding morning, we again fell in and marched off, but the effects of hunger and fatigue were now more visible. A savage sort of desperation had taken possession of our minds, and those who had lived on the most friendly terms in happier times, now quarrelled with each other, using the most frightful imprecations on the slightest offence. All former feeling of friendship was stifled, and a misanthropic spirit took possession of every bosom. The streams which fell from the hills were swelled into rivers, which we had to wade, and vast numbers fell out, among whom were officers, who, having been subject to the same privation, were reduced to the most abject misery. It was piteous to see some of the men, who had dragged their limbs after them with determined spirit until their strength failed, fall down amongst the mud, unable to proceed farther; and as they were sure of being taken prisoners, if they escaped being trampled to death by the enemy's cavalry, the despairing farewell look that the poor fellows gave us when they saw us pass on would have pierced our Hearts at any other time; but our feelings were steeled, and so helpless had we become, that we had no power to assist, even had we felt the inclination to do so. Among the rest, one instance was so distressing, that no one could behold it unmoved. The wife of a young man, who had endeavoured to be present with her husband on every occasion, if possible, having kept up with us amidst all our sufferings from Salamanca, was at length so overcome by fatigue and want, that she could go no farther. For some distance, with the assistance of Her husband's arm, she had managed to drag her weary limbs along, but at length she became so exhausted, that she stood still unable to move. Her husband was allowed to fall out with her, for the purpose of getting her into one of the spring waggons, but when they came up, they were already loaded in such a manner that she could not be admitted, and numbers in the same predicament were left lying on the road side. The poor fellow was now in a dreadful dilemma, being necessitated either to leave her to the mercy of the French soldiers, or by remaining with her to be taken prisoner, and even then perhaps be unable to protect her. The alternative either way was heart-rending; but there was no time to lose, — the French cavalry were close upon them. In despairing accents she begged him not to leave her, and at one time he had taken the resolution to remain; but the fear of being considered as a deserter urged him to proceed, and with feelings easier imagined than described, he left her to her fate, and never saw her again; but many a time afterwards did he deprecate his conduct on that occasion, and the recollection of it embittered his life.

On this night the rain had somewhat abated, but the cold was excessive, and numbers who had resisted the effects of the hunger and fatigue with a hardy spirit, were now obliged to give way to its overpowering influence, and sunk to the ground praying for death to relieve them from their misery; and some prayed not in vain, for next morning before daylight, in passing from our halting ground to the road, we stumbled over several who had died during the night. Inadvertently I set my foot on one of them, and stooped down to ascertain whether the individual was really dead, and I shall never forget the sickening thrill that went to my heart, when my hand came in contact with his cold and clammy face. On this day our hearts seemed to have wholly failed us: to speak was a burden, and the most helpless weakness pervaded every individual; we had now arrived at that pitch of misery which levels all distinction of rank, and I believe no order would have been obeyed unless that which was prompted by regard to the common safety.

Dennis, round whom there used to be gathered a host of his comrades, listening to his witticisms or quaint remarks, and whose spirits I had never known to fail, was now crest-fallen, and moved along with the greatest difficulty. Nothing but death, however, could altogether keep down his buoyant spirits; for if we got a minute's halt during the march, he made such ludicrous remarks on the woebegone coun-tenances of himself or his companions, that, although the effort was distressing, they were obliged to smile in spite of their misery.

This day we halted sooner than usual, and the weather being clearer, we got fires kindled, — still no rations; but we were encamped among oak trees, and greedily devoured the acorn which grew upon them, although nauseous in the extreme, the officer commanding the brigade and our colonel joining in the repast. In many respects the officers were in a worse situation than the men, not having any thing to change themselves, as their baggage had been sent on before us.

If anything could have given us comfort in our miserable situation it was having a kind and sympathising commanding officer: he made many of the weakly men throw away their knapsacks, and by every means in his power he endeavoured to infuse comfort and courage into their sinking hearts, braving every difficulty in common with the meanest individual, and even rejected the superior accommodation which his rank afforded, while he saw the men suffering. It was in a situation like this where true greatness of mind could be displayed; and there must have been something innately great and noble in the mind which could thus rise superior even to nature. In my opinion, a much greater degree of real courage was necessary to brave the horrors of this retreat, than to face the fire of a battery.

During the night our situation was worse than in the day, for there was nothing to divert our attention from our wretched state; and although we despaired of ever seeing it, we felt that indescribable longing after home, which every one must have felt in the same situation. It will be needless to detail our next day's sufferings, — they were of the same nature as the preceding, only more aggravated.

We were now drawing near Rodrigo, where our baggage had been ordered; each day our hopes had been kept alive in the expectation that we would find provision at our halting place, but we were deceived. Now, however, these expectations were more likely to be realised. About dusk we took up our ground on the face of a hill near Rodrigo, and the weather changing to a severe frost, was intensely cold. We had not been long halted when the well-known summons of "Turn out for biscuit," rung in our ears. The whole camp was soon in a bustle, and some of the strongest having gone for it, they received two days' rations for each man. It was customary to divide it, but on this night it was dispensed with, and each eagerly seizing on what he could get, endeavoured to allay the dreadful gnawing which had tormented us during four days of unexampled cold and fatigue. In a short time, two rations more were delivered, and the inordinate eating that ensued threatened to do more mischief than the former want. We went into quarters next day, and many who had borne up during the retreat now fell sick, and were sent to the hospital.

From this place we removed in a few days some way into Portugal, where we took up our winter quarters in a small village, called Fonte Arcada.

By 18 November Wellington's army was once again on the Portuguese border, right where it had begun the year in January. Despite his triumphs at Ciudad Rodrigo, Badajoz and Salamanca, and the entry into Madrid, the year had thus petered out unsatisfactorily for Wellington, whose mood had not been cheered by the events during the retreat. His men were severely shaken by the episode and their mood was not lightened much by Wellington who, upon reaching Ciudad Rodrigo, promptly issued his infamous 'Memorandum,' in which he laid the blame for the disorders during the retreat at the feet of the regimental officers and NCOs. Fortunately, the army would recover, and would bounce back in fine style in 1813.

CHAPTER ELEVEN

VITTORIA: THE DECISIVE CAMPAIGN

Writing of Wellington's 1813 campaign, William Napier wrote, 'his wings were spread for a long flight.' And so they were, for his great campaign of 1813 would see him march from the borders of Portugal, across Spain, over the Pyrenees and into France. It was the decisive and most successful of all Wellington's campaigns in the Peninsula.

The retreat from Burgos had been a sobering and harrowing experience for Wellington's army, and came as a great shock after their great achievements earlier in the year. But the army recovered remarkably quickly following the retreat, and by the spring of 1813 was fully prepared for the coming campaign. Reinforcements had arrived from England including the brigade of hussars, a much-needed cavalry force, which had not seen service in the Peninsula since the Corunna campaign of 1808–09. Fresh infantry battalions arrived also, and by the spring of 1813 the Anglo–Portuguese Army was ready for the great drive into Spain.

The campaign began on a poignant note, when Wellington, who had spent years campaigning in Portugal, turned in his saddle as he was entering Spain, and said, 'Farewell Portugal, for I shall never see you again.' He was to be proved right.

The outstanding aspect of the Vittoria campaign of 1813 was the great outflanking march by Wellington's army. No sooner had the campaign began than the French abandoned the capital, Madrid, and set out for Valladolid, on the great road to France, where they hoped to block Wellington's advance. In the event, he crossed the Douro at Toro and continued his march through uncharted countryside, passing Valladolid to the west and forcing the French to pull back further north. The French actually took up positions on three major rivers, the Douro, Esla and Ebro, but each time Wellington outflanked them, passing their right flank in a brilliant march north-east towards Vittoria. The two sides clashed only once during the advance, at San Millan on 18 June, when the Light Division scattered elements of the French rearguard as it pulled back towards Vittoria.

Fought on 21 June 1813, the Battle of Vittoria was the decisive battle of the Peninsular War. Any hopes the French may have harboured of success in Spain were crushed by Wellington who brought his army together to defeat the armies of the South, Centre and of Portugal, all three of which were under the nominal command of Napoleon's brother, Joseph, aided and abetted by Marshal Jourdan. Wellington's force had been divided into four, with Rowland Hill attacking along the heights of Puebla to the south, Wellington himself attacking the centre, Dalhousie and Picton the centre and Sir Thomas Graham the French right. Graham, in fact, took a great sweep around the back of the hills to the north of Vittoria to emerge to the north of the town where Spanish troops under Longa captured the village of Durana, and by so doing severed the French escape route back to France. Elsewhere, Wellington's men hit the French at successive points and after a fierce fighting drove them back from one position to the next until the French army collapsed close to the town itself. There then followed a total disintegration of Joseph's army, which only escaped when Wellington's men stopped to plunder the massive convoy of treasure that the French had accumulated over five years of occupation. And so, whilst private soldiers filled their pockets with jewels and coins, equivalent to many months' pay, and in some cases many years' pay, the French fled in the direction of Pamplona.

The first vital move by Wellington's army came along the summit of the heights of Puebla, upon which the French had anchored their left flank. The troops ordered to attack this position were from Sir Rowland Hill's division, and Morillo's Spanish division. One of Hill's units was the 1/28th Regiment, part of O'Callaghan's brigade. These veteran troops advanced along the foot of the heights whilst Cadogan's brigade swept the French from the summit. Marching with the 28th was Ensign William Thornton Keep, a 21-year-old officer who had previously seen service at Walcheren with the 77th Regiment. His letters were published in 1997 under the title *In the Service of the King*. On the morning after the battle of Vittoria he wrote a short account to his mother, but followed it up six weeks later with a fuller version, written in Vittoria itself.

A succession of bustling scenes and moving accidents by flood and field have engaged my attention since I wrote the few lines after the victory we obtained here on the 21st June. The triumph over our enemies has left some very grievous vestiges of the perils of the day. Soldiers are now crowding the vacant space before my windows, with disabled limbs in bandages, or are moving about on crutches to take the air. But when I arrived here a few days ago this square was in a tumult of preparation for a Bull fight to rejoice the natives with what one would suppose they were little inclined to be diverted with, after the more interesting and absorbing events that had occurred so recently within view of the town. As I have much to tell you yet about this famous field I must take you back to Toro, to continue my narrative. Here we made but a short halt, again descended into the plains, and passed so near Valladolid that we saw the nuns' handkerchiefs visibly waving from the high walls and windows of their convents to joyfully hail our arrival; and we then followed the French to that place of fierce contention in the previous year — the castle and fortifications of Burgos. On coming there the intentions of our enemies were not apparent, and a part of our force (with the 28th) were concentrated round it.

Our comfort and security during the night is confided to the vigilance of such of our comrades as are in turn appointed to this duty — which is called being on picquet. On this momentous occasion I was thus employed, and as the greatest uncertainty prevailed as to what the French intended to do, when I arrived at the outposts I found more importance attached to it than I had ever known before. The Brigade Major with great care pointed out the limits of our position, and moreover informed us (there being another officer detached from the lines with men under his orders for this purpose) that one of us must take the post of advanced sentinel with a Corporal in attendance.

We then (a young Baron of the German Legion, but an Ensign like myself) awaited his further directions, and alighting from his horse the Brigade Major plucked two stalks of grass from the ground and placing them in his hand told us that which ever drew the longest was to undertake this duty, and it fell to my lot. (Not a very desirable one as we should certainly have been the first sacrificed had the French advanced.) Being thus the advanced sentinel I took my post, and as night came on seated myself on a stone upon an open heath, my sword in the ground, and chin upon the hilt with the Corporal ready loaded at my back, and my eyes intent as the lynx to watch the first move of our foes, a very short distance in front.

It was a quiet starlit night, with a light wind blowing in mournful gusts, and remembering the trust reposed in me I did not relax in watchfulness but was wide awake. The hours rolled slowly on in this dreary spot, but with the first indications of dawn a terrible explosion took place. The earth shook, and a ball of smoke arose from the town and settled over it like a cloud. We

185

started forward, and our companions coming round us in a moment we soon found what the French were at, and that the works were blown up. It spread immediately like wild fire through the camp, and the picquets were withdrawn and we continued the pursuit.

On our advance we came into the neighbourhood of magnificent mountain scenery amidst the great fountains of the River Ebro, which takes its rise here. Cascades and waterfalls (descending from towering rocks overgrown with myrtles and blooming shrubs) making with their clattering sweet music; and the only sounds heard to disturb the repose of nature, on this beautiful road. Here we could have prolonged our stay with great satisfaction, but no time was allowed, except just enough to excite an admiration and regret to leave such places behind us, and again we entered the plains on our march to the north after the French.

Another week elapsed in following their steps, and then we approached Vittoria. But I must tell you that previously, on emerging from the fine mountainous scenery of the Ebro, we had the gratification of seeing most of our army on the march, concentrating towards each other on their advance to this point, and appearing in the long perspective like glittering scarlet threads, requiring the aid of telescopes to discern their numbers. One or two Divisions had already come in contact with the French army and shots had been exchanged, but on the 20th Lord Wellington commanded a general halt and reconnoitred the position they had taken up. At nine o'clock on the morning of the 21st the services of the 2nd Division were required to commence this memorable battle. We had crossed the Zadorra (a dark current of little width in that part with a small bridge) in quick march to support a Spanish Division, under General Morillo, on the heights above. They had commenced a brisk firing but not within view of us. Climbing over banks to a village on an eminence called Subijana de Alava we came within cannon shot of the French. One approach was so open to the range of their guns that we were saluted with a peal of artillery that did immediate execution upon a soldier of the 28th and cut his head completely from his shoulders leaving his body prostrate on the ground before us, unsoiled with blood. Lieut. Bridgland, our Adjutant, stopped a moment to look at him, and informed by a sergeant of his name observed that the worst man in the Regiment had been the first struck; the same shot took effect upon the shoulder of an officer of the 39th and his mild and amiable countenance was turned to us without exhibiting any symptoms of suffering, though the wound was too severe a one to hope he could long survive. As it was advisable not to remain longer than we could help thus exposed, Colonel Belson who commanded us led the Regiment for

186

present shelter behind the village church, which was on the slope of the hill, and encompassed with beautiful cornfields with the grain then nearly ready for the sickle, and divided, as I had never before seen in this country, with hedges. From this post, as we were required, each Company moved to the front, and occupied the narrow lanes and banks within musket shot of the French.

Captain Meacham, with that to which Lieut. Moore and I belonged, took in turn our places on the line of action, but from the field in our front few shots were fired, and the Frenchmen kept themselves well concealed from us. It is a saying that 'every bullet has its billet' and we had not been there five minutes before one whistled past my ear and penetrated the cap of the sergeant by the side of me. Luckily the height of it permitted its passage without going through his head; such escapes we continued to experience during this long and oft suspended action. Yet I found nothing more remarkable than the rapid flight of time. The day was the finest that ever shone from the Heavens. Towards one and two o'clock the fire so slackened that we supposed the action was over, but no change took place in our position, nor did the 28th advance until suddenly at last, when the enemy had fled, from the battle being won, on the French line being turned, by the left wing of our army. Then immediately we scampered over hedges and fields to a road, where the French had been stationed, and where the 14th Light Dragoons under Col. Hervey (a very gallant officer who had in a former battle lost his left arm) had been ordered up to follow them. The high pinnacles upon which our Division was placed during the battle gave us a decided advantage in the view it commanded of the whole field as we now moved forward and the splendid sight of it became fully displayed to us. Yet it was very tantalising, for had the treasures of a hundred palaces been turned out upon the plains, it could not have exceeded the multitude of things to be seen in all directions scattered about, and in the midst of them the whole of our cavalry force at full gallop, and all the infantry Regiments that had been engaged advancing together in line.

We were now mere spectators of the scene, the grandeur of which was lost in the contemplation of the spoils. Sir Rowland as he galloped off after surveying it cried out "Never mind 28th, you shall have your share of it yet," but the 6th Division which had just arrived after a long day's march, and hadn't fired a shot, came into the field quite at the nick of time for the good things. We moved only a few miles further that night in the pursuit; in the morning Alexander came to seek his quarters in the camp upon a fine horse laden with all manner of things picked up. He had been struck in the hip, but the ball fortunately intercepted by his sash, the wound was less serious than might have been expected, and he came to join us once again.

Some of our drummers made a rich harvest, and one little fellow entered the camp (who was only big enough to play upon the triangle) mounted on a French General's charger with holsters and bags of valuable commodities. The spirit that prevailed in this battle between the French and English was of the most chivalric kind, and admitted of mutual good feelings when it was over.

The Frenchmen we found wounded were carefully removed into the high roads where they might be soonest found by our Surgeons. After a brief suspension of exertion we followed Jordan's routed Army and arrived in a few days within sight of Pamplona. Defiling down the sides of a mountain, this fortified city presented a most formidable appearance, in the centre of a plain; and here we expected many broken heads, but Lord Wellington escaped this necessity by the French not having left supplies in it, and he determined to blockade it (that is, encompass them with troops to starve them out). And for this purpose employed a part of the Spanish Army, and we pursued our route to the Pyrenees, the French whilst retiring before us, showing the bitterness of their wrath against the Spaniards after their late defeat — houses being left in ashes, and their blackened walls indicating the utter ruin of villages and places they passed through. Without much further resistance we had now the satisfaction to drive them into their own territories, and took up a position at Roncesvalles, a pass of these mountains where we halted.

John Cooke's account of the Battle of Vittoria recalls the part played by the Light Division, and in particular his own regiment, the 43rd, for it was this regiment that made the daring dash across the Zadorra at the bridge of Tres Puentes, which had been left unguarded by the French, and were thus the first Allied troops to establish themselves on the French-held side of the river. His account was published in his *Memoirs of the Late War*, published in 1831.

On the 21st, we stood to our arms, and moved forward in darkness, some time before daybreak. A heavy shower of rain fell; but; as morning dawned, the clouds dispersed, and the sun arose with fiery splendour. A towering and steep ridge of mountains rose abruptly from the valley on our right, which the Spaniards climbed early in the morning, at first unopposed; the ascent was so steep, that, while moving up it, they looked as if they were lying on their faces, or crawling. They were supported, and soon followed across the river Zadorra, and through the town of Puebla de Arlanzon, by part of the second division, for the purpose of attacking the left of the enemy, who were posted on the heights above Puebla de Arlanzon and Subijana de Alava, where the contest, at the former place, began at nine o'clock, amongst deep ravines, rocks and precipices. The second division becoming heavily engaged with the enemy, under all these disadvantages it could only maintain the ground already won, and the firing seemed to die away in that quarter. Our right centre, composed of the light and fourth divisions, continued to advance, as also the great bulk of our cavalry.

At about ten o'clock, on ascending a rising ground, we observed the French army drawn out in order of battle, in two lines, their right centre resting on a round hill, their left centre occupying a gentle ascent, and their left hid from view on the heights of Puebla; the river Zadorra ran at the foot of this formidable position, and then took a sudden turn, embracing and running parallel to their right flank, towards Vittoria.

El Rey Joseph, surrounded by a numerous staff, was stationary on the hill, overlooking his own right and centre. The French army was unmasked, without a bush to prevent the sweeping of their artillery, the charging of their cavalry, or the fire of their musketry from acting with full effect on those who should attempt to pass the bridges in their front, and which it was absolutely necessary to carry before we could begin the action in the centre. When within a short distance of the river, five of the French light horse advanced on the main road to look out, and were overtaken by an equal number of our dragoons, when they wheeled about and attempted to make off, without effect; they were assailed on the near side; when three instantly fell from their saddles, covered with sabre wounds, and their affrighted horses galloped at random.

The light division left the road when within one mile of the river, and drew up in contiguous close columns behind some shelving rocks near Olabarre, with the hussar brigade dismounted on the left; the fourth division made a corresponding movement, by branching off to the right, and took post opposite their intended point of attack; the greater part of our heavy cavalry and dragoons remained in reserve, to succour the central divisions, in case the enemy should advance before the third and seventh divisions should have taken up their ground on the enemy's right flank. The first and fifth divisions, with two brigades of Portuguese, a Spanish division, and two brigades of dragoons, were making a detour from Murguia, to place themselves on the line of the enemy's retreat, towards St. Sebastian; the sixth division remained

189

some leagues in the rear of our army to guard the stores at Medina. Gen. Clausel's division was manoeuvring on our right, but not sufficiently near on this day to give much cause of apprehension.

All the movements of our army required the nicest calculations, both for the attack and defence; for at this time the four great columns advancing were separated by difficult rocks and a rugged country, interspersed with deep gulleys, narrow roads, and scattered hamlets. The enemy were again under the painful necessity, for the third time in one month, of manoeuvring on two sides of a square; and the first cannon fired by General Graham, at Abechuco and Gamarra Major, must have been to Joseph and Marshal Jourdan, (his Major-General,) like a shock of electricity: all in an instant was riot and confusion in Vittoria; the baggage stuck fast, blocking up all the roads, and even the fields.

At half past eleven o'clock the Marquis of Wellington led the way by a hollow road, followed by the light division, which he placed unobserved amongst some trees, exactly opposite the enemy's right centre, and within two hundred yards of the bridge of Villodas, which we understood was to be carried at the point of the bayonet. I felt anxious to obtain a view, and, leisurely walking between the trees, I found myself at the edge of the wood, and within a very short distance of the enemy's cannon, planted with lighted matches ready to apply to them. Had the attack begun here, the French never could have stood to their guns so near the thicket; or at least the riflemen would have annihilated them. The General-in-chief was now most anxiously looking out for the third and seventh divisions to make their appearance. We had remained some time in the wood, when a Spanish peasant told the Marquis of Wellington that the enemy had left one of the bridges across the Zadorra unprotected, and offered his services to lead us over it. Our right brigade instantly moved to its left by threes, at a rapid pace, along a very uneven and circuitous path, (which was concealed from the observation of the French by high rocks,) and reached the narrow bridge which crossed the river to Iruna. The 1st rifles led the way, and the whole brigade following, passed at a run, with firelocks and rifles ready cocked, and ascended a steep road of fifty yards, at the top of which was an old chapel, which we had no sooner cleared, than we observed a heavy column of French on the principal hill, and commanding a bird's-eye view of us. However, fortunately, a convex bank formed a sort of tete de pont, behind which the regiments formed at full speed, without any word of command. Two round shots came amongst us; the second severed the head from the body of our bold guide, the Spanish peasant. The soldiers were so well concealed, that the enemy ceased firing.

Our post was most extraordinary, as we were at the elbow of the French position, and isolated from the rest of the army, within one hundred yards of the enemy's advance, and absolutely occupying part of their position on the left of the river, without any attempt being made by them to dislodge us; scarcely the sound of a shot, from any direction, struck on the ear, and we were in momentary expectation of being immolated; and, as I looked over the bank, I could see *El Rey Joseph*, surrounded by at least five thousand men, within eight hundred yards of us. The reason he did not attack is inexplicable, and, I think, cannot be accounted for by the most ingenious narrator.

Gen. Sir James Kempt expressed much wonder at our critical position, and our not being molested, and sent his aide-de-camp at speed across the river for the 15th Hussars, who came forward singly, and at a gallop, up the steep path, and dismounted in rear of our centre. The French dragoons coolly, and at a very slow pace, came within fifty yards to examine, if possible, the strength of our force, when a few shots from the rifles induced them to decamp. I observed three bridles within a quarter of a mile of each other, at the elbow of the enemy's position. We had crossed the centre one, while the other two, right and left, were still occupied by the French artillery; at the latter, the enemy had thrown up an earth entrenchment.

We continued in this awkward state of suspense for half an hour, when we observed the centre of the enemy drawing off by degrees towards Vittoria, and also the head of the third division rapidly debouching from some rocks on our left near the hamlet of Mendoza, when the battery at Tres Puentes opened upon them, which was answered by two guns from the horse artillery on the right of the river. Some companies of the rifle corps sprang from the ground, where they lay concealed, and darted forward, opening a galling fire on the left flank of the enemy's gunners, at great risk to themselves of being driven into the water, as the river ran on their immediate left, while the French cavalry hovered on their right; however, so well did this gallant band apply their loose balls, that the enemy limbered up their guns, and hastily retired; and the third division, at a run, crossed the bridge of Tres Puentes cheering, but unopposed.

The enemy withdrew the artillery from the bridges in their centre at two o'clock p.m. and were forming across the high road to Vittoria. The third division had no sooner closed up in contiguous columns, than General Picton led them forward in very handsome style, in column, by a flank movement, so as to place them exactly opposite the French centre. The fourth division, directly after crossed the river by the bridge of Nanclares, and were hurrying forward to support the right flank of the third division; the seventh division also

191

crossed the bridge of Tres Puentes, supported by the second brigade of the light division, and faced the small village of Margarita. Our heavy horse and dragoons had deployed into line, on the other side of the river, so as to communicate with the rear of the second division, (in the event of their being driven back from the mountains,) or to support the centre of the army, in case of any disaster. They made a brilliant display of golden helmets and sparkling swords, glittering in the rays of the sun.

Three divisions being in motion, the centre and left supported by the light division and the hussar brigade, the battle began by a terrible discharge on the third division, while they were deploying into line. We closed up to them, behind a bank; when, with loud huzzas, they rushed from behind it, into the village of Arinez, with fixed bayonets, amidst flashing small arms and rolling artillery, and, after a bloody struggle, carried it. The enemy's artillery was within two hundred yards of us, ploughing up the ground in our rear: fortunately, the bank nearly covered us, during the time it was necessary to remain inactive, to support the front attack, if needful. A Portuguese regiment, attached to our brigade, had been detached for a short time, and rejoined, in close column; but, just before they reached the cover, some round shot tore open their centre, and knocked over many men; and such was the alarm of a Portuguese officer, at the whizzing of balls and bursting of field shells, that he fell into an officer's arms, weeping bitterly. For ten minutes at this point, what with dust and smoke, it was impossible to distinguish any objects in front, save the shadows of the French artillerymen serving the guns, and the shouts of troops while forcing their way into the village. The smoke had no sooner cleared away, than we came on the bodies of many dead and gasping soldiers, stretched in the dust. The sharp fire of musketry and artillery in the centre, announced it to be the point of contest. The "advance" of the second division had been severely handled on the mountains to our right, but they were now getting on as speedily as the nature of the ground would admit, it being composed of deep ravines, and such natural obstacles, as almost to delay their progress unopposed.

The first and fifth divisions were engaged at Gamarra Major and Abechuco, in front of the bridges over the Zadorra. These villages were carried after a smart action, by which a position was gained threatening the enemy's line of retreat by the high road to France, running N.E. some distance close on the left of the river. The bridge was attempted, but was found to be impracticable, until our centre had forced the enemy to give up Vittoria. The different divisions in the centre were exposed to a desultory fire, while passing the villages of Gomecha and Zuazo de Alava, and over broken ground, forming lines, columns, or threading the windings of difficult paths, according to the nature of the country, or: the opposition of the enemy. The fourth division pushed back the left centre of the French, and were fighting successfully, and performing prodigies of valour, among crags and broken ground. The seventh division now came in contact with the enemy's right centre, which resisted so desperately, and galled them from a wood and the windows of houses with such showers of bullets, that victory for a short time was doubtful; however, the second brigade of the light division coming up fresh and with closed ranks, assisted by the seventh division, broke through all opposition at a run, and routed the enemy at the point of the bayonet. The four divisions of the centre continued to gain ground, shooting forward alternately, leaving the killed and wounded scattered over a great extent of country. At six o'clock in the evening, by a sort of running fight, with hard contests at certain points, the centre of the army had gained five miles in this amphitheatre; for General Hill's corps was on the mountains, and General Graham was still on the right of the Zadorra.

The Marquis of Wellington was in the middle of the battle, vigorously driving the enemy, to finish that which the wings had so well begun. First, General Hill's movement in the morning had caused the enemy to weaken his left centre; then General Graham's attack induced him to give up the front line of the Zadorra, without a shot (hardly) being fired.

At half past six we were within one mile of the city of Vittoria, the capital of Alava, situated in, a fruitful valley; but the French army now drew up, and showed such an imposing array in front of the town, that our left centre facing Ali was completely kept at bay, owing to the blazing of one hundred pieces of cannon vomiting forth death and destruction to all who advanced against them. This roaring of artillery continued for more than an hour on both sides, with unabated vigour: the smoke rolled up in such clouds, that we could no longer distinguish the white town of Vittoria; the liquid fire marked the activity of the French gunners. During this momentous struggle, the left centre of the French covered a bare hill, and continued for a considerable time immovable; while, pouring their musketry into the now-thinned ranks of the third division, it was doubtful whether the latter would be able to keep their ground, under such a deadly fire from very superior numbers: however, they maintained this dangerous post with heroic firmness, having led the van throughout the thick of the battle.

At this period of the action, it was absolutely necessary to strain every nerve to win it before night-fall. The fourth division, on our right, shot forward against a sugar-loaf hill, and broke a French division, who retired up it, in a confused mass, firing over each other's heads without danger to themselves, owing to the steepness of its ascent. I was laughing at this novel method of throwing bullets, when one struck me on the sash, and fell at my feet, thereby cooling my ardour for a short time: however, when a little recovered from the pain, I picked it up, and put the precious bit of lead into my pocket.

The scene that now presented itself was magnificently grand: the valley resounded with confused sounds like those of a volcanic eruption, and was crowded with red bodies of infantry and the smoking artillery, while the cavalry eagerly looked for an opening to gallop into the town, on one side of the field rose majestically the spiral and purple-capped mountains, rearing their pinnacles on high; on the other ran the glassy waters of the Zadorra: and the departing sun threw his last beams to light up the efforts of those struggling in dangerous strife for the deliverance of Spain. The enemy sacrificed all their cannon, with the exception of eight pieces, while withdrawing the right of their army behind the left wing, under cover of this tremendous cannonade, which was the only chance yet left them to quit the field in a compact body. This movement being executed in strange confusion in and about Vittoria, their left wing retired by echelon of divisions and brigades from the right, while delivering their fire; and finally, their last division quitted the field with nearly empty cartridge boxes, and taking the road towards Pamplona. The greater portion of our army then brought up its left shoulder, or rather wheeled the quarter circle to its right; which movement brought us on the road to Pamplona. The French managed to drag the eight pieces of artillery across the fields for nearly a league; but, coming to marshy ground, they stuck fast, and three of them rolled into a ditch, with mules struggling to disentangle themselves from their harness. Two pieces the enemy carried clear out of the action, leaving their numerous cannon behind them; owing to the roads being so blocked up with waggons.

The dark shades of evening had already veiled the distant objects from our view, and nothing of the battle remained, save the lightning flashes of the enemy's small arms on our cavalry, who continued to hover and threaten their rear guard. The road to Pamplona was choked up with many carriages, filled with imploring ladies, waggons loaded with specie, powder and ball, and wounded soldiers, intermixed with droves of oxen, sheep, goats, mules, asses, *filles de chambre*, and officers. In fact, such a jumble surely never was witnessed before; it seemed as if all the domestic animals in the world had been brought to this spot with all the utensils of husbandry, and all the finery of palaces, mixed up in one heterogeneous mass.

Our brigade marched past this strange scene (I may well assert) of domestic strife, in close column, nor did I see a soldier attempt to quit the ranks, or show the most distant wish to do so; our second brigade had not yet joined us, when we bivouacked a league from Vittoria, on the road towards Pamplona. The half-famished soldiers had no sooner disencumbered themselves of their knapsacks, than they went to forage; for even here the sheep and goats were running about in all directions, and large bags of flour lay by the side of the road: in fact, for miles round the town, the great wreck of military stores was scattered in every direction.

Night put an end to the contest: the growling of artillery ceased, the enemy were flying in disorder, the British army bivouacked round Vittoria, large fires were kindled and blazed up, and illumined the country, over which were strewed the dead and suffering officers and soldiers: strange sounds continued throughout the night, and passing lights might be seen on the highest mountains and distant valleys.

Twenty-year-old Scot, William Hay, was an officer with the 12th Light Dragoons. He had begun the Peninsular War with the 52nd Light Infantry, before joining the cavalry. The nature of the ground at Vittoria precluded any effective use of cavalry on 21 June 1813 but Hay's account of the battle, which was published in his *Reminiscences under Wellington*, published in 1901, is worth including here. The 12th Light Dragoons formed part of George Anson's light cavalry brigade, which advanced upon Vittoria with Sir Thomas Graham's column, attacking Gamarra Mayor from the north.

Next day was the memorable June 21, 1813. Then I saw a truly grand and noble sight, and a most exciting, for any man. But first I must tell you an anecdote, to show you what a fine, noble, unselfish fellow our colonel was.

That morning early, as we were waiting orders to move, he wished me to go with him to the front. We proceeded about five miles in advance, and after reconnoitring the enemy, he said very quietly to me: "Hay, I am very ill, this is my ague day and I feel it coming on"; leading at the same time into some thick underwood by the roadside. "I must lie down here till the fit is over; take my orderly with you and keep a sharp look out, and if, from any movement of the enemy, we are to have anything to do, send me word immediately; but do not tell any one I am unwell."

It may have been about 10 a.m. when the regiment came from the camping

195

ground to where I was waiting the recovery of my colonel; and he had to resume his work. We were then formed into a brigade consisting of the 11th, 12th, and 16th Light Dragoons. As we proceeded on our march over some rather rough uneven ground, keeping within sight of the river Zadorra; which is a deep, sluggish stream, with broken banks and not a ford anywhere; we could plainly see the divisions under General Hill, which formed our extreme right, commencing their operations.

I must, in speaking of the battle of Vittoria, deviate, in a small degree, from my purpose of writing only an account of my personal proceedings, and give a short description of the day's work in which so many of my fellow soldiers were actively engaged, for this reason.

In all former battles or affairs in which I had the honour to be engaged, no opportunity was afforded me of looking on for any time inactively; and in my opinion it is the greatest presumption for any subaltern, who has the slightest pretence to say he has done his duty, to offer to the public a description of a battle in which he has taken part. If indeed a battle is to be described, it can only be done by those staff officers immediately employed by the commander-in-chief to reconnoitre the ground for the position, and who, during the battle, have sufficient leisure to observe the movements of the different divisions or corps destined to occupy the ground, with which they are already acquainted.

For my own part, I have been in my share of engagements and feel certain that my time and attention were fully occupied by the movements of my own regiment and those troops near and connected with it. But the battle of Vittoria was an exception as, from the nature of the ground allotted our brigade to move over and take up our position, we were enabled to see for miles, while we ourselves were unable to take part in whatever was going on.

From our route Vittoria seemed to stand like a large town in the midst of an even plain with high wooded hills, or mountains, in the background; but that in reality is not the case, as before reaching the plain from where we were posted, there lies (unobserved by us) a space of ground broken by deep wooded ravines.

We were from time to time the mark for a salvo of artillery; but the attention of the batteries was directed principally against the moving columns of infantry, either contending for the passage of the river, or directed to clear the ravines of the French troops in possession; hence we were not much molested and had fair time for observation. Nothing could exceed the magnificent sight or the excitement with which one viewed the progress of our gallant men.

We saw distinctly the troops, on the hills above the town, hotly engaged disputing every inch of ground as the enemy gradually gave way; on our left flank we heard the constant roar of artillery, mingled with small arms, where Sir Thomas was attacking and driving the French over the high broken ground, where infantry only could act.

Close to our front were the troops contending for the bridge over the Zadorra, leading by the main road to Vittoria. Thus, watching others and ourselves moving very slowly, the forenoon was passed.

Towards afternoon it seemed, from where we stood, as if the whole forces we had seen fighting at a distance had got close together and were contending hand to hand. Still the firing on our left continued till about 6 p.m., it was succeeded by a cheer from our troops, the bridge was carried, and a free passage opened for our brigade and the horse artillery.

To this point we directed our march, crossed the bridge, and formed on the opposite bank in brigade of squadrons: the one to which I was attached was in the rear of all, in fact I commanded the left half squadron of nine squadrons moving right in front.

In this order we advanced, first at a trot then at a canter, and soon came in sight of the French cavalry. On seeing our advance, advantage was taken of some broken ground at the extreme end of the plain over which we were advancing towards them, to halt and form for our reception.

As we drew closer this appeared madness, as their numbers did not exceed half ours. Our trumpet sounded "The Charge," when, on coming up to what seemed a regiment of dragoons awaiting their doom, their flanks were thrown back and there stood, formed in squares, about three thousand infantry. These opened such a close and well directed fire on our advance squadrons, that not only were we brought to a standstill, but the ranks were broken and the leading squadrons went about, and order was not restored till a troop of horse artillery arrived on our flank and, within about a hundred yards, opened such a fire of grape shot on the French infantry, that at the first round I saw the men fall like a pack of cards.

That was sufficient and off they went, and our regiments were reformed. Night was now setting in and we went no further.

So ended the battle of June 21, 1813. Certainly the very grandest sight I had as yet seen in my travels as a soldier.

The nature of the ground and the fine day gave it truly the appearance of one of those pictures of a battle drawn from fancy.

Our brigade bivouacked for the night nearly on the ground on which we were brought up by the French squares. It took some little time next morning to get things in order for our moving, and it was there a sergeant's party brought into our headquarters a small military chest of dollars they had hit on while on night duty; most justly, the general-in-command took upon himself to distribute the prize among the officers and men according to their rank in the service, I recollect my share came to thirty-three dollars.

Finding I had time on hand, I thought I might take a ride over the field of battle, so started towards the town of Vittoria, and certainly I saw a sight which astonished me. I was well prepared, from having on a former occasion gone over the fields of hard contested fights, to see heaps of dead and dying, but I was not prepared for the number of guns, gun-carriages, ammunition-waggons, carriages; some of them actually still containing ladies; baggage of every description, horses, and mules literally covering the ground. I hated the idea of plundering; consequently, did not appropriate to myself any single thing, though I am sure I might have done so with impunity as several others were doing, I was satisfied to look with surprise at what had been achieved by our victory.

Fighting with his regiment in front of Hay was Sergeant James Hale, of the 9th (East Norfolk) Regiment. Part of Robinson's brigade, the 9th took part in the attack on Gamarra Mayor, where the heaviest fighting of the day took place. Hale had been in the army for ten years, and was no stranger to battle having been in the Peninsula since August 1808. Hale's memoir was published in Cirencester in 1826 under the title *The Journal of James Hale, late Sergeant in the Ninth Regiment of Foot.*

Vittoria was fought. The night previous to the battle, we formed our camp about two leagues from Vittoria, on a sort of wilderness place, among brambles, thorns, &c. and to my thinking, almost all sorts of vermin; but nevertheless, in the evening, after we had got our bit of meat and cooked it, which was not long about, for most of us broiled it on some fire coals, having nothing to eat with it, we laid ourselves down two or three in a place, where it was most convenient; but hearing such music with the vermin crawling and running about among the leaves, and sometimes running over us, caused our rest to be but middling that night.

About one hour before day-light, we stood to our arms in the usual manner, as we always did when convenient to the enemy, as before mentioned, and remained till broad day-light: during which time our commissary arrived with half a pound of bread for each man, but nothing else; but however, that with a drop of good water was very acceptable, for we had then been three days without bread. We were several times, on this long advance, short of provisions, the reason why is this: when the army was advancing in pursuit of the enemy, we frequently marched double stages, in consequence of which the cattle that carried our provisions were not able to come up with the army according to the time appointed; therefore by that means, we were obliged to do without it till it did come, let the time be long or short.

Now having got that half pound of bread, we advanced, about five o'clock in the morning, towards Vittoria, knowing the enemy were there waiting to receive us. We had then about two leagues to go, as before mentioned; and between nine and ten o'clock, we arrived on the hill about one mile from Vittoria, where we had a fine view of the greater part of the French army; for they had formed all ready for combat along the river for three or four miles each way. On one side of Vittoria is a plain or a sort of marsh, on which place they were like a swarm of bees; for the whole of their baggage, together with three waggon-loads of money, (which they had got to pay the army), were all formed up regular, in readiness to follow our army; for they thought to drive us down the country again, in about the same manner as they did from Burgos; or at least, they told the inhabitants of Vittoria, that such was their intention; and so it plainly appeared, for we hardly ever knew them to exert themselves as they did at this place; but notwithstanding all their exertions they could not accomplish their design.

In a few minutes after our arrival on the hill, our division received orders to proceed to Gamarra, a village about three miles to the left of Vittoria, at which village the enemy were very numerous, with a large column placed at the bridge, and also a quantity of riflemen placed along the river. We advanced to the village in open column of companies; the light companies formed the advance, about one hundred yards in front; and when we came near, the first thing that the enemy saluted us with was a few cannon shot, for they had guns placed in all directions; but as soon as we got within gun-shot distance, we advanced to the village in double quick time, and gave them a grand charge, by which we got full possession of the village in a few minutes, and the light companies were immediately extended along, very convenient to the river, just opposite their skirmishing party, with an order not to expose ourselves more than we could help, nor advance one inch without an order: therefore we formed ourselves under cover of a bit of bank that was about knee high, and in this position we continued skirmishing for more than two hours — the remaining part of the division kept possession of the village.

The enemy made several bold attacks to force the bridge, in order to regain the village, but were repulsed every time with great loss; it was a very narrow street that led to the bridge, which was a great disadvantage to us, and their guns continued roaring tremendously; it was much in comparison to continual thunder, for they never ceased throwing shots and shells into the village during the action, by which most of the houses were very much damaged.

It plainly appeared this day, that the enemy had formed a sort of determination not to be beat, for we never saw them stand so vigorous before; but not withstanding all that, between four and five o'clock in the afternoon, we gave them another grand charge at the bridge, in consequence of which there was a great slaughter on both sides, but in a few minutes the enemy gave way, upon which we pushed on more vigorous, and got full possession of the bridge; and all of a sudden the whole French army retreated, leaving one hundred and eighty pieces of cannon, about four hundred ammunition waggons, the whole of their baggage, provisions, and cattle, together with three waggon-loads of money, and many carriages that belonged to their generals and other officers of high rank, (several with their ladies and families in them); and among the crowd was Joseph Bonaparte's carriage and lady. The whole fell into our hands, and also many prisoners; but however, we did not stand worshipping that, for we pursued the enemy about one league as close as possible, by which more prisoners were taken; but before our guns could pass over the bridge, some men were obliged to move the dead bodies, for they lay in heaps most melancholy to behold. Notwithstanding, our regiment got off rather favourably in this engagement, for I believe not more than one hundred were killed and wounded, but some regiments suffered very much.

So now having formed our camp, we fortunately beheld a field of beans very convenient to us, and just fit for use, and although we were rather fatigued, the field was swarming with soldiers in a few minutes, and before dark, there was hardly a bean to be found in the field. While some were gathering the beans, others were looking out for something to eat with them; for at this place we were not refused of getting something to eat if we could find any, although we had never been favoured with such a liberty before; and as some of our regiment were searching about a village that was little more than half a mile from our camp, they had the good fortune to find a great quantity of good flour, which they happily loaded themselves with, and brought it into the camp: so we all got as much flour as supplied our wants that night, and some to carry with us for another time. No bread could be found, but having plenty of flour and green beans with our meat, we all made a most noble supper: but still there was one thing that most of us were short of, that was salt to season our supper.

Now after we had filled our bellies, we sat and amused ourselves over what had passed during the day; in the mean time our commissary arrived with a pint of wine for each man, which occasioned our conversation to continue a little longer; and in the course of this evening I was promoted to the rank of a sergeant. So now night having approached, we laid ourselves down on the turf, under the branches of the trees, as comfortable as all the birds in the wood; for the enemy continued retreating nearly all the fore part of the night.

The Allied haul after the battle included no fewer than 151 guns and 2,000 prisoners. Total casualties for the French, in fact, exceeded 8,000 men, Wellington losing just over 5,000 men. King Joseph himself was lucky not to have been taken prisoner when he leapt out of one side of his carriage at the very moment that some British hussars rode up to the other. Marshal Jourdan's baton, meanwhile, was taken by a corporal of the 18th Hussars and presented to Wellington. The Allied commander promptly sent it to a delighted Prince Regent who immediately conferred upon Wellington the newly-created rank of Field Marshal. It was this new title that Wellington was to carry over the Pyrenees and into France, which was his next objective.

CHAPTER TWELVE

THE BATTLE OF THE PYRENEES

Following the Battle of Vittoria the French retreated through the Pyrenees, leaving behind only the armies of Marshal Suchet fighting on the east coast of Spain. The only other French troops were the garrisons of Pamplona and San Sebastian. It was to the latter fortress that Wellington now turned his attention.

The strategic importance of San Sebastian lay in the fact that it commanded the main road from Spain into France, which ran along the Atlantic coast. There still remained the passes at Maya and Roncesvalles, which ran between the two countries, but the main route lay along the coast. Furthermore, Wellington had shifted his supply base from Lisbon to Passages, an important deep-water port, which lay just a short distance to the east of San Sebastian.

It was at this point that Wellington divided his force, part of it settling down to lay siege to San Sebastian and the other guarding the two aforementioned passes at Maya and Roncesvalles. The French, meanwhile, had their own plans, which were designed to relieve the fortress of Pamplona, and with the fortress being situated just a few miles to the south of the passes it was inevitable that Marshal Soult, now commanding the French Army, would attempt it. Thus, the scene was set for the series of actions that were fought between 25 July and 2 August 1813 that collectively would become known as the Battle of the Pyrenees.

The 25 July 1813 was a day crammed full of action, with the first assault on San Sebastian, which failed, and the French counter-offensive in the Pyrenees. As disappointing as it was, the failure of the assault on San Sebastian by Wellington's 5th Division and Oswald's Portuguese probably came as no great surprise to Wellington. With the town being situated upon an isthmus, San Sebastian represented yet another stiff test for the Allies, and it would not be until the last day of August that the town fell into Wellington's grateful hands. What did come as a surprise, however, was Soult's offensive in the Pyrenees.

It was a Sunday, and the majority of British troops were still at church parade when the French attacked at Maya and Roncesvalles. The first of these two passes, which was defended by Pringle's brigade of the 2nd Division, was attacked by two French divisions who came on in overwhelming strength. The British piquets on the Aratesque hill were overrun whilst the defenders on the ridge below were driven slowly back. It fell to just 400 men of the 92nd Highlanders to stem the tide with a display of tremendous bravery, holding back the French for some time until they were forced to pull back themselves. The camps were overrun, the pass taken and it was only the intervention of Barnes' brigade of the 7th Division that prevented the French from pushing down into the valley of the Baztan, which lay beyond the pass.

Moyle Sherer, of the 34th Regiment, was on piquet duty on the Aratesque hill on that fateful morning of 25 July. He would end the day as a prisoner of the French, having been taken during the day's fighting. In his *Recollections of the Peninsula*, he described the day's events.

My regiment and the brigade now lay bivouacked, for some time, in rear of the Maya heights; and a steep and toilsome ascent of two miles and a half separated us from that part of the heights, with the defence of which we were charged, and, on which, we daily mounted a picquet of eighty men. About one mile in rear of the picquet post lay the light companies of the brigade, as a post of communication and a support.

On the 25th of July, the enemy attacked and carried the pass of Maya with an overwhelming force.

It was a day of brave confusion. It was a surprise, and it was not a surprise. It was one, because the nature of the country favoured the neat approach and concealed advance of large bodies of the enemy; and the troops who were destined to defend the right of these heights were two miles and a half distant, and had not time to arrive and form. Only one regiment, in fact, arriving at all in sufficient time to fight on the important ground, and this corps, breathless with exertion, and engaging by groups, as they came up. Again, it was not a surprise, because no affair was ever more regularly opened and contested by the picquet and light companies, than that of the 25th of July. It was not a day to be easily forgotten by me; for it threw me into the hands of the enemy, and disappointed me of the honour of marching under British colours, fearlessly, nay, triumphantly, displayed into some of the finest provinces of southern France. Such a day my life I shall give as one of strange recollections.

It was a pleasant arbour on the banks of a mountain stream, that I breakfasted on that very morning (aye, and I well remember, with a volume of the Rambler for a companion). At seven o'clock, I relieved the picquet on the Maya Heights, and learned from the captain of it, that he had seen a group of horse and a column of troops, pass along the face of a distant hill, at dawn, and disappear. I requested him to make a special report of this when he reached the camp, which he did. A deputy quartermaster-general came up soon after; rode a little in front, said, that there was, indeed, a small column discernible about three miles off in a vale, but that it was only a change of bivouac, or some trifling movement of no consequence.

I thought otherwise, and the event proved I was not mistaken. The light companies were, indeed, ordered up by this officer, as a measure of precaution; how very weak and insufficient a one, will be seen. In less than two hours, my picquet and the light companies were heavily engaged with the enemy's advance, which was composed entirely of voltigeur companies, unencumbered by knapsacks, and led by a chosen officer. These fellows fought with ardour, but we disputed our ground with them handsomely, and caused them severe loss; nor had we lost the position itself, though driven from the advances of it, when joined by the hastily arriving groups of the right corps of our brigade, (my own regiment).

The enemy's numbers now, however, increased every moment; they covered the country immediately in front of, and around, us. The sinuosities of the mountains, the ravines, the watercourses, were filled with their advancing and overwhelming force.

The contest now, if contest it could be called, was very unequal, and, of course, short and bloody. I saw two-thirds of my picquet, and numbers, both of the light companies and my own regiment; destroyed. Among other brave victims, our captain of grenadiers nobly fell, covered with wounds; our colonel desperately wounded; and many others; and surviving this carnage, was myself made prisoner. I owe the preservation of a life, about which I felt, in that irritating moment, regardless, to the interference of a French officer, who beat up the muskets of his leading section, already levelled for my destruction; which must, (for I was within six or seven paces of them,) have annihilated me: This noble fellow, with some speech about "un Francois sait respecter les braves," embraced me, and bade an orderly conduct me to Count d'Erlon.

The column by which I was taken was composed of the 8th and 75th regiments of the French line. Good God! How sudden a change! A minute before I had been uttering, and listening to the cry of "forward;" now I heard all around me "en avant," "en avant," "vive Napoleon," "vive l'Empereur." I was in the midst of these men; they passed me hurried, and roughly. None insulted, none attempted to plunder me. But in a ravine, full of rascally skulking stragglers, who are always the cowards and plunderers of an army, I was robbed by the very fellow, who, willing to leave the fight, had volunteered to conduct me. The appearance of some slightly-wounded men returning from the front, and of a sergeant-major, caused him to run off with his booty, and by the sergeant-major I was conducted to Count d'Erlon, who was on horseback, on a commanding height near, surrounded by a large group of staff officers. "Un capitaine Anglais, general," said my conductor. The count took off his hat instantly, and spoke to me in a manner the most delicate, and the most flattering, asking no questions, but complimenting highly the brave resistance which had been offered to him.

It was a strange scene — French faces and uniforms all around me; and two columns of his reserve halted just behind him. They were not here disarmed, ragged, looking spiritless, our affecting misplaced gaiety. Their clothing was nearly new, their appointments excellent, and their whole appearance clean, steady, and soldier-like.

One of the officers of the count's staff dismounted, and offered me "la goutte" from his leather bottle, which I declined. The enemy suffered severely; slightly-wounded men were passing every minute, and on the face of the heights lay very many of the killed and severely wounded: Small parties of the English prisoners; too, might be seen bringing in from the left of the Maya Heights; and from the rear, where they still contended in a brave, disjointed manner without support. The count soon dismissed me, saying he had no horse to offer me, but that the town whither he had ordered the prisoners was not very distant; and, turning to the sergeant-major, he bade him conduct himself towards the English officers taken, (for two Others were brought up while I was with him) as he would ten Frenchmen of the same rank.

In the rear of the column of reserve, all the English taken were collected; and here I met a brother officer, a lieutenant of our light company; who had much distinguished himself throughout the day, and was taken in another part of the field; and not many minutes after my capture. He was my most intimate and valued friend, and meeting him under such circumstances overcame me. I shed tears. "Regardez donc," said a vulgar-looking French officer, who was observing us, "regardez comme ils sont des enfans ces Anglois; ils pleurent." "Ah, mon ami," said his companion, "vous ne connoissez pas les Anglois: ces ne sont pas les larmes de l'enfance qu'ils versent."

Our party now set forward, conducted and followed by but few; for as

206

there was no possibility of escape, we were guided rather than escorted. There were 140 English in all, but not more than 40 of any one regiment, and only four officers. As we passed along, we met more French troops coming up along the narrow mountain road. None of the soldiers offered to insult us; many of the officers indeed saluted us, though here and there a decorated officer smoothed his mustachios as he looked upon us, with an air of impatient brusquerie. It was quite amusing to see the rapidity with which a lie had been framed, and passed down their files. Myself, and one of the officers taken as battalion officers, wore epaulettes of bullion. As the leading sections of this French brigade passed us, we heard them say, "deux chefs de bataillon prisonniers;" but, as the rear came up, they were crying out "en avant," "l'affaire va bien" — "deux bataillons prises aux ennemis." It was in vain I said "Je ne suis que capitaine;" still the cry ran, "vive Napoleon," "deux bataillons prises aux ennemis." "Battre une fois ces Anglois ce seroit un plaisir," muttered an elderly-looking, hard-featured colonel, as he passed us, bowing gravely, unconscious, no doubt, that we understood this negative acknowledgement of our past and repeated successes.

While Sherer and the survivors of the piquet were marched off towards St Jean Pied de Port, the battle continued along the main ridge. Here, elements of the 50th, 71st and 92nd Regiments fought desperately to stem the French tide, allowing Pringle's breathless brigade to gain the summit and engage the French left. One of Pringle's battalions was the 1/28th, amongst which was William Thornton Keep, who has left us by far the best account by any officer in the brigade, Keep and his comrades had made the exhausting march from the bottom of the valley of the Baztan to the summit, and arrived just after Sherer's piquet had been overrun. His account of the desperate fight comes from *In the Service of the King: The Letters of William Thornton Keep, 1808–1814*.

Three large minute guns were fired (according to preconcerted arrangement) and we toiled in haste to the top, expecting an attack from the enemy, but when we arrived it proved a false alarm. Exactly that very day week however, on Sunday the 25th July, at about eleven o'clock, when we had formed a square for Divine Service, the guns from above in three heavy admonitory peals apprised us once more of their real approach.

You must remember that we were left quite to ourselves, with no hope of immediate aid, at the force of the French, be what it might. Every man therefore was put into the ranks that we could muster, and yet our whole strength amounted to only two Brigades. With all the speed we could use we ascended again these steep hills upon hills to the summit, where we found the 92nd Highlanders had struck their tents, and were seated on the mountain brow, until their services were wanted in front. A brisk firing had commenced, and was becoming more sharp and continued, and we advanced with increased alacrity, leaving the 92nd where they were, and took up, under the command of Col. Belson, a position well secured on one side from approach. It was a level piece of ground extending like a promontory, and covered with short grass, without any trees or bushes, but having here and there pinnacles of rock rising to the height of 12 or 14 feet.

The peculiarity of it was, that it did not admit of our line being formed except at a right angle from the true front, so that only as the French advanced on a platform on the other side, the ravine dividing us, could we come into action with them. There was no means of changing this position, awkward as it was, and we had therefore no alternative but to keep our eyes right (as men in the houses on one side of a narrow street might be supposed to do, expecting an enemy to enter at the end of it).

Though the firing from small arms was increased, and approaching very close, we were left for about a quarter of an hour without a single object in sight. The depths of the ravines of these mountains is often very great, though as frequently very narrow; this was so, and a somewhat wider platform, but level like our own, was opposite us, and at the extremity of it a small hill, which shut out every thing beyond it from our view. For the few minutes therefore of that quarter of an hour, we remained in anxious expectation of what might occur, but quite alone, and within a stone's throw of that little hill I have mentioned, to which all eyes were now directed.

Our consternation you may imagine, when we perceived heads suddenly rising above it from the other side — and the 34th Regiment retreating most rapidly. At this juncture the 92nd was advancing on the platform to which the 34th descended. They ran for shelter to the Highlanders who could only form in separate wings from want of room. As soon as the French appeared following them, our fire opened, though at first in a very slanting direction and with difficulty, friends and foes were so mingled. The 92nd, a very fine strong Regiment, who would no doubt have come to the charge had the ground permitted, and for a time would certainly have repulsed the Frenchmen — who now found they had only two Regiments to oppose them and knew they had a dozen at least coming forward in their rear. In this confined space in which we were all enclosed a woeful tragedy directly ensued. Poor Lieut. Day of the

208

34th (our Duke in the Honey Moon) was killed while rallying his men in sight of us, but the volleys of the 92nd strewed the smooth green turf of that little hill with the French that fell before them. To fire with greater precision some of our men had descended to a ledge running along the edge of the ravine. Here I stood at the station of the company I belonged to, and with Col. Belson and the Honble. Major Mullins by the side of me in a state of inactivity, and merely looking on. Captain Meacham was wounded, having been firing from the ledge (very few officers make use of the musket) and having actively retreated between our legs to the rear. At this moment Mr Bridgland's voice called for me to the Colours, and I proceeded directly there and found that poor Delmar had been shot through the heart.

In the confusion of the moment a mistake had been made, and Mr Hill, being junior to me, should have been called. This the Adjutant discovered, and I returned to my company. But I had not been long there when a second call was made for me, and I found that Hill had been struck in the breast similar to Delmar, and carried away. (Luckily in the hurry of his movements, Hill had thrust his handkerchief in the bosom of his coat, and this repulsed the ball and saved his life.) I now took the fatal Colour, and entered into conversation with Ensign Tatlow, bearing the other.

The description he gave me of what had happened to our friends was whilst the action was going on, for these battles are slowly performed. I had leisure even to think of Delmar's watch, and requested Alexander to enquire for it, that it might be preserved for his family at home. The loud greetings that saluted my ears between our busy combatants now attracted my attention, and my eyes were turned to the fierce contention going on (which nothing impeded, for the smoke rolled away immediately over head). Many shouts were sent across this narrow ravine in mutual support of each other, such as 'Well done, 28th, Bravo 92nd' etc. The French were checked in their progress at the foot of the hill, and several Highlanders were unfolding their blankets to convey away wounded comrades without any hurry being shown. But as the numbers of the enemy increased, they made another effort to advance. A very gallant French officer was leading them, but he was struck to the ground where he was still waving his cocked hat. I became very much interested in the result and my attention so absorbed in it that I did not observe what was passing behind me.

The enemy had been busy surrounding us, and the Regiment had been forced instantly to flight and had left me there. A young French conscript levelled his piece at me within 20 paces, with a smiling countenance, intimating that I must surrender. A violent zeal seized me to preserve the Colours, not caring for my life, and I turned immediately and pitched myself headlong down the ravine, grasping most tightly the staff. Through bushes and briars I rolled, and scrambled, hearing shots after me. The exertion was such as under other circumstances would have been impossible. Rough stones rattled down with me, and it was some time before I put my feet to the ground, and then I set off again in the right direction. After a rapid race I was relieved from my anxiety by the shouts of a Sergeant of the 28th who waved his arm to guide my steps, and I had at last the satisfaction to join the Regiment then in close column, and preparing to move off.

Col. Belson and the officers were highly rejoiced to see the Colours again, which they feared were lost, and I fell into the ranks to bear them away on our retreat. So far Marshal Soult's object in the relief of Pamplona was achieved. He had with overwhelming numbers forced the pass of Maya, but the fortress he was proceeding to was still a long distance in front. To increase his difficulties probably we chose the most mountainous road to retreat by.

Night was approaching when we set out, and by the time we reached the first town on the route it was quite dark. The news of our disaster and the threatened arrival of the French added to the number of fugitives, many of all ranks, and some natives, being forced to pack up and accompany us. For you have no conception how many followers are indispensable to an army in the field.

Nineteen-year-old George Bell was present at Maya with the 34th Regiment, which had also had a breathless march to the ridge. Bell had been commissioned in the regiment on March 1811 and had seen service at Badajoz, Salamanca and Vittoria. His reminiscences were published in 1867 under the title *Rough Notes by an Old Soldier during Fifty Years' Service*. His description of the fight on the ridge at Maya is memorable for the way he described the famous stand of the 92nd Highlanders.

On Sunday morning, the 25th, at dawn of day, the picket and outposts were suddenly attacked by an advance of sharpshooters. The signal-gun was fired, when we got away up hill as fast as we could (the men never went on a parade at any time but in heavy marching order, just as if they were never to return to the same spot). But the pass up was narrow, steep, and tiresome, the loads heavy, and the men blown. We laboured on, but all too late — a forlorn hope; our comrades were all killed, wounded, or prisoners. The enemy had

210

full possession of the ground. Some 10,000 men were there, nearly all with their arms piled, enough of them arranged along the brow to keep us back. It was death to go on against such a host; but it was the order, and on we went to destruction; marching up a narrow path in file, with men pumped out and breathless, we had no chance. The Colonel is always a good mark, being mounted and foremost. He was first knocked over, very badly wounded. The Captain of Grenadiers (Wyatt), a very fine handsome man, being next in advance, was shot through the head. He never spoke again. My little messmate, Phillips, was also killed. I thought at the time, what a sin to kill such a poor boy. Seven more of the officers were wounded, the Adjutant, severely hit, tumbled off his horse and was left for dead (more about him hereafter). We persevered, pushed on, and made a footing notwithstanding our disadvantage, for the men were desperately enraged and renewed all their exertions to be at them with the bayonet, but in vain. We kept our ground until we were minus, in killed and wounded, some 300 men and 9 officers; some slight wounds were never returned. We did not think it very warlike to notice every skelp one got when little harm was done. But this little point of modesty was a mistake, found out too late, for at the conclusion of the war every officer who had been returned as wounded, was compensated from a great fund raised by the usual liberality of the English people, and many were well recompensed for the loss of a little claret or broken bone.

Different regiments scrambled up the hills to our relief as fast as they could. The old half-hundred and 39th got a severe mauling. Then came a wing of the 92nd and opened a flank fire on the enemy, while we moved over to another hill, got our men left, and commenced a cross fire. The 92nd were in line pitching into the French like blazes, and tossing them over. They stood there like a stone wall overmatched by twenty to one, until half their blue bonnets lay beside those brave northern warriors. When they retired, their dead bodies lay as a barrier to the advancing foe. O! but they did fight well that day. I can see the line now of the killed and wounded stretched upon the heather, as the living retired, closing to the centre. Every regiment that came up lost its quota, and the French increased as the battle went on. We had two six-pounder guns up here for signal, to give warning. Richardson, self, and two other lads made an effort to turn them to salute the French, but a few rifle-shots stopped our play, so, for fear they should go over to the other side, we wheeled them round and at the word 'Let go' away they went rattling down the mountain with great velocity, perhaps never to be seen again. We 34th for the last hour had been amusing ourselves in comparative safety, picking off our friends in the distance when a very large column came down upon us to stop our play. There was but one escape for us now — to run away, or be rid-dled to death with French lead. The officer commanding, a brave man, saw how useless it was to contend against such a multitude, gave the word to retire at the double, and away we went down hill at a tearing pace. I never ran so fast in my life! Here the French had another advantage, rather a cow-ardly one. They kept firing after us for pastime. Every now and then some poor fellow was hit and tumbled over, and many a one carried weight over the course, i.e. a bullet or two in the back of his knapsack.

We were now broken and dispersed. Our bugles sounded, few heard them — some too far way! The old corps was severely handled. We hoisted a flag at the bottom of the hill, Freeman blew his well-known blast, and all that heard the sound rallied here. Up another hill we scrambled, and passed the night among the heather. Hungry, cheerless, and thirsty, I would have given a dollar for a drink of water. Lieutenant Simmons had his horn full of brandy slung on his back going into action, and was about to rejoice over it just now, but alas, the bottle was empty. A musket-ball played one of those practical tricks one hears of after a big fight. One passed through the horn during the row, and let off the brandy without any notice. Simmons knew that he had been slightly wounded in the side, little knowing it was a cow's horn saved him! Our sergeant-major found his arm very stiff about the crook, as he said; no blood nor mark of a shot-hole. He pulled off his jacket and found a ball lodged in his elbow-joint, which had run up his sleeve in this playful way. A young officer was shot through the nose, which as he jocosely said, made him sneeze a bit! Every part of the human frame in one or other was riddled with shot, and many wonderful escapes were talked of that night — were there any thank-offerings?

The French success at Maya was accompanied by a similar one at Roncesvalles, although their success there was mainly due to the weather. The brigades of Byng and Ross fought a desperate action high up in the mountains above the pass of Roncesvalles, holding back a massive attack by over 40,000 French troops. It was just as well that the narrow frontage prevented the French from deploying the mass of their troops, otherwise the Allied troops would almost certainly have been destroyed. As it was, a thick fog descended, and Lowry Cole, in overall command, fearing an outflanking move by the French, pulled his men off of the mountains and began a withdrawal south. Thus, both passes were in the hands of the French.

Wellington was not unduly concerned at the loss of the passes for he knew there were suitable defensive positions along the road to Pamplona, which he expected Cole and Picton, who had now joined in the retreat, to take up. Unfortunately, the two generals continued their retreat until sight of Pamplona itself, and it was an annoyed Wellington who joined his men on 27 July on the heights above the village of Sorauren, the last real defensible position before Pamplona.

There were, in fact, two battles fought at Sorauren, the first on 28 July and the second two days later. On 28 July a series of French assaults on Wellington's position were driven back at bayonet point until a stalemate position was reached. Then, on 30 July, and with Wellington having been reinforced, he launched a counter-attack, which threw the French back over the French border. Sergeant John Spencer Cooper, of the 7th (Royal Fusiliers), fought at Sorauren where his regiment had formed part of Ross's brigade of the 4th Division. He recalled the battle in his *Rough Notes of Seven Campaigns*.

Early in the morning of July 28th, we were under arms. The French covered the opposite heights, waiting orders to rush through the opening on our left. First, they sent forward a few cavalry with a trumpeter, along the opposite mountain side to reconnoitre. We watched their progress till they came to a corner of the road, when suddenly they came scampering back. A few minutes afterwards a column of the enemy moved down on our left along the high road to Pamplona. To prevent their passing we descended, and attacked them in flank. At the same time other heavy bodies were launched against our right and centre, and the firing became heavier and closer. The leading column of the enemy succeeded in passing us, and marched boldly, forward to the brow of a hill 300 yards beyond our flank, when, to their surprise, a concealed division of ours rose up, and rushing upon them, poured a storm of fire into the loose mass which sent, them back in disorder. Our fire was now redoubled, and was no doubt destructive. A Portuguese company of cacadores that was joined to us hearing the French crying out. "Espanhola! Espanhola!" to make us believe they were friends, cried out "No Espanhola! Mais fuego! mais fiego!" ("More fire! more fire!") We all did so, and men fell fast on both sides. While I was kneeling and firing, a drill-sergeant named Brooks, who afterwards got a commission, came and helped to get my cartridges out more quickly. We got on bravely until a ball knocked off his cap. He, perhaps thinking the place too hot, left me to help myself.

All our officers were at this time wounded. I helped one of them whose leg was broken out of the fray a few yards. A brother sergeant, a morose fellow, and no friend of mine, I helped upon the adjutant's horse. He was shot in the loins or spine. I think he died. Why he was my enemy I never knew.

In the midst of all this, I was very ill; the fever and ague had returned most furiously. Parched with thirst, and pained all over, I could hardly drag my limbs along.

Major Crowder, who commanded the left wing of our regiment, now came, and seeing that our officers were *hors-de-combat*, ordered me to go and tell the colonel our case. In doing this, I had to pass through a cross fire. I found the colonel on foot close to the enemy. While speaking to him, the senior major's horse was killed close by the colonel, and some men were wounded just behind me. Without giving any answer to my request for officers, the colonel (Edward Blakeney) put his hands on my shoulders and said, "Sergeant Cooper, go up the hill and tell the brigade-major to send down ammunition immediately, or we must retire." This was necessary, as our men were taking cartridges out of the wounded men's pouches.

I scrambled up the steep, and performed my duty with difficulty, as my legs would hardly obey me. I then dragged a Spaniard with his mule laden with ball cartridge down to my company. The poor fellow was terribly frightened at the whizzing of the balls about him, and kept exclaiming "Jesus, Marea! Jesus, Marea!" However, I pushed him forward to my former station. Having unladen his beast, he disappeared in an instant.

Throwing off my knapsack, I smashed the casks, and served out the cartridges as fast as possible, while my comrades blazed away. Close by me, a sergeant named Tom Simpson sat, pale as death, on his pack, holding his breast. "Tom," said I, "are you wounded?" Tom spoke not. He had just received a shot in his left side.

Hardly had I served out the ammunition and thrown on my knapsack, before a swarm of the enemy suddenly rushed over the brow of the hill, and swept our much reduced company down the craggy steep behind. Some of them seized the captain of the 9th company, and attempted to pull of his epaulets, but he resented this by a blow of his left fist. However, he was led off a prisoner.

By jumping down among the rocks my dress cap fell off, having my forage cap in it, and thus I was left bareheaded under a blazing sun. However, whatever number of balls followed me, they all missed, and I had the pleasure of seeing a fresh body of red jackets coming in haste to our relief; and by them the enemy were swept off the hill in their turn.

With great difficulty I gained the hilltop, and found the company and the rest of the regiment. After repeated attacks, and as many repulses, the enemy gave up the contest, and retired up the slopes.

On calling the roll I found my company had lost twenty men. One of these, named Malony, that I had returned as missing, soon after made his appearance. I said, "Malony, where have you been?" "Fighting, sure," said Pat. "You have been skulking." "Have I! Look there!" said he, ripping open his jacket and showing his blackened breast. A ball had struck his breast plate. I could say no more; but I felt sorry for being so hasty. Our regimental loss this day was about 200.

During the night there was a panic: all started up in an instant and seized their arms; but no enemy appeared. What caused the stir no one knew; but these panics frequently occurred.

Little was done on the 29th besides burying the dead; but on the 30th the game of war began again by our cannonading the masses that attempted to break through our line in two places. Both these attacks failed, and we had the pleasure of seeing them driven down the steeps in glorious confusion by our brave Light Division. Immediately after this repulse, of which we were only spectators, Lord Wellington ordered a general advance on the enemy's position, as they were observed retreating hastily towards France, and leaving the garrison of Pamplona to its fate. That place soon after surrendered. Unfortunately, I was not able to move, being in a hot fit of ague. The doctor came to me as I was lying on the ground shaded by a bush and blanket. "What ails you, Sergeant Cooper?" "It's my old complaint, sir." "Well," said he, pointing to the retiring columns of the enemy, "the French are off yonder; we cannot leave any one with you. When the fit goes off, go down to that village below, and report yourself to the first doctor you see." Thus I was left alone on a mountain in a blazing sun, without water.

When a little recovered, I slung my knapsack and fusee, and tottered down the steep to the village of Sorauren, and threw myself down in a stable among some straw Looking about, I saw a surgeon that formerly belonged our regiment. I told him my case, and was directed to go to a large house close by and take charge of a captain and a lieutenant who were both mortally wounded. "They are your own officers, and both will die," said he. "See that their servants do not rob them." I went accordingly. The captain was wounded in the left side, and so was the lieutenant, but the shot had gone quite through the lieutenant's body.

Lieutenant Frazer died on the second or third day after the battle; Captain Wemyss on the fourth or fifth. There was something very affecting in the case of the captain's death. He had a brother who was an aide-de-camp in General Hill's division, and who had been wounded some days before in a skirmish.

215

He hearing that his brother was mortally wounded, rode off in search of him; but for some days fruitlessly. At last he ascertained where his brother was lying, and hastened to the place. A short time before he came to the door, the dying captain asked his servant if he could read. He said he could. "Then," said the captain, "take that Prayer Book, and read to me." The servant did so. Soon after, there was a loud knocking at the street door, and then a well known voice in the stairs. The dying man sprang from his bed, flew to the door, and fell dead into his brother's arms. His parents lived on Southsea Common in 1815, to whom I took a letter from our colonel, but did not make myself known. A coffin was made of some old furniture, and the captain was buried in a garden beside the lieutenant.

While here, I heard that one of my oldest comrades was lying wounded in the next house. Soon as possible I set off to see him, carrying some tea, etc. I found him in a large room that was full of wounded — all bad cases. His thigh was broken near the hip. I saw that my attention, and his own condition, affected him. I think there was a starting tear in the poor fellow's eyes. He might probably recollect his bad behaviour to me on two occasions. His wound proved mortal. Next to him, sitting on his bed, was a comrade sergeant named Bishop, sadly disfigured with blood and bandages. A ball had passed quite through his head. I did not know him at the first look; but he knew me and moved. Whether he lived or died I never ascertained. In Clonmel, Sergeant Bishop married a young Irishwoman, who had just before been married to a drummer belonging to a regiment ordered on foreign service. She accompanied Bishop for three or four years in the Peninsula. Being one day caught stealing, the provost-marshal flogged her on the breech. After this she left poor Bishop, and went to live with Colonel E., of the regiment. In a corner close by lay a man that I knew very well, breathing hard, and quite insensible. He died, and was buried. But where? In a horse-dunghill!

Here for several days I had an ague fit every afternoon. While in one, Major Crowder, who was wounded in the late battle, called to see the two officers that I had in charge. He gave me a few words also which were encouraging. However, thank God, by taking a few doses of Peruvian bark, I got rid of my disorder for a short time.

The last action of the Battle of the Pyrenees came on 2 August and was little more than a very minor skirmish involving an attack uphill by the 6th Foot against a French force at the village of Echellar. Pamplona, meanwhile, was to hold out until late October when the garrison surrendered, leaving only San Sebastian in French hands.

CHAPTER THIRTEEN

THE INVASION OF FRANCE

San Sebastian fell to Wellington, or rather Sir Thomas Graham, who was overseeing the siege operations, on 31 August 1813. The capture of the town was followed by the usual outbreak of disorder, plundering and pillaging, which was made all the worse by a fire which completely engulfed the town. The garrison itself retreated to the fortress that was situated on a hill above the town. Completely cut off, they held out for a further seven days before surrendering on 7 September.

Colonel Augustus Frazer, of the Royal Horse Artillery, celebrated his 37th birthday at San Sebastian, five days after the town had been stormed. Frazer had arrived in the Peninsula in December 1812 and had seen his first action at Vittoria, on 21 June 1813. His letters, titled simply *The Letters of Colonel Augustus Frazer*, were published in London in 1859. They are extremely detailed letters, which are valuable inasmuch as they were written literally as the events about which Frazer was writing were unfolding almost before his very eyes. Frazer also had the foresight to time the letters, as well as date them. Thus, we know that the letter that follows here, concerning the aftermath of the storming of San Sebastian, was written at 7 a.m. on 3 September 1813, with the postscript timed at 11 a.m.

Nothing very new; but I learn that the dispatches are not made up. There are difficulties in making out the numbers of killed and wounded. Ours are 1500, of whom half are killed!!

I have been in the town, and over that part of it which the flames or the enemy will permit to be visited. The scene is dreadful: no words can convey half the horrors which strike the eye at every step. Nothing, I think, can prevent the almost total destruction of the unhappy town. Heaps of dead in every corner; English, French, and Portuguese, lying wounded on each other; with such resolution did one side attack and the other defend. The enemy holds the convent of which I spoke in my last, and from it pours certain destruction on any who approach particular spots under its fire. When a man falls, we are obliged to send the French prisoners to drag away the body, and they, poor fellows, manifest reluctance in performing the dangerous duty. This convent must be carried, and soon; there is no alternative, it must not be suffered to remain in the enemy's hands. The town is not plundered; it is sacked. Rapine has done her work, nothing is left. Women have been shot whilst opening their doors to admit our merciless soldiery, who were the first night so drunk, that I am assured the enemy might have retaken part, if not the whole town. The inhabitants who have come out look pale and squalid; many women, but I think few children. I had occasion, in going to General Hay, to go into several houses: some had been elegantly furnished. All was ruin; rich hangings, women's apparel, children's clothes, all scattered in utter confusion. The very few inhabitants I saw, said nothing. They were fixed in stupid horror, and seemed to gaze with indifference at all around them, hardly moving when the crash of a falling house made our men run away. The hospitals present a shocking sight: friends and enemies lying together, all equally neglected. Many assured me they had never been seen by any medical man, and all agreed they had tasted nothing since they were brought in. This I afterwards found to be generally true, and nearly unavoidable; but on mentioning the matter to General Hay, I learned that steps had been taken for the due care of the sick. I went on with Colonel Dickson: our first object was to reconnoitre the breaches, and to discover, and concert engineers, the proper spot for the erection of batteries against the Mirador and upper defences. We agreed with Burgoyne that the batteries should be made in the ditch of the curtain; the curtain itself we found too narrow for our purpose. In examining the works from within, the effects of our own guns were most striking, not above one or two of the enemy's guns remaining mounted, and all repeatedly struck and ruined by our shot; most had their muzzles carried away. In the demi-bastion lay dismounted an English $5^1/_2$-inch howitzer (No. 388). One was taken, I have heard, at Albuera. In ascending into the breach, the descent into the town looked tremendous: three joints of scaling ladders (the joints are of six feet each) were then fixed against the descent and did not reach the top. Many of our poor fellows lay dead on the adjoining houses; the roofs seemed almost to have fallen in with the number of the dead. Below the descent of the centre of the breach was an excavation, and at some feet further back, a barricade, so that men descending found themselves, as it were in a kind of pound. It would have been unavailing to have descended till the flanking fire from the crest of the right round tower took the enemy on the curtain in reverse. In standing on the ruins of this tower and looking about attentively at all around, and the flames of the burning houses at ten yards' distance, we discovered at our feet the *saucisson* (as it is called), or train of powder to fire a mine. Henry Blachley, who was with us (for he and Charles Gordon had followed us,) cut the train with his knife, and we scrambled on to the right breach of all. In a barricade between this breach and the right tower, the unfortunate enemy seems to have had no retreat. His men lay there heaped on each other. In the hornwork and low communication across the ditch, the defences of which and those of the cavalier we had not attacked till the morning of the assault, we could not but remark that the French artillery-men lay dead by their guns. The square of the town is small, but very hand-some: there is a fine piazza. The houses are of four stories, with handsome balconies: at the west end stands (or at least stood last night) the town house. The north side was in flames when I left it; and before Gordon left the town, and returned to dinner, had fallen down. I spoke to several prisoners, gener-ally good-looking and good-humoured fellows; they had always, they said, been well fed with salt meat, had plenty of water, and soft bread, by which they meant to explain they had never been reduced to eating biscuit. One who was in the hospital slightly wounded, and attending the rest, seemed more than usually intelligent. He said that the garrison originally was of 3800 men. On my expressing surprise, and seeming to doubt, he replied, "You may rest as-sured that I speak the truth, and that I know the number and strength of the regiments." "How many are now in the castle?" said I. "There are," he answered, nearly as follows:

22nd Regiment of the Line	350
72nd	200
1st	400
Chasseurs des Montagnes	200
34th Regiment of the Line	300
Artillery	200
Sappers	50
Miners	20
Pioneers	40
	1760

Nevertheless, I doubt the fact. We know from General Rey's secretary, who has been taken prisoner, that on a muster on the morning of the assault, there were, exclusive of servants and sick, 2004 effective bayonets. This secretary confirms the report that we have repeatedly heard, that General Rey is by no means disinclined to surrender: all the prisoners concur in this, and that another officer, — some say the chief of the staff, and others, the chief of the artillery, —alone prevents it. Our prisoners all say they have been treated remarkably well; the wounded, too, have been taken good care of. Jones, of the engineers, after all, is still in the castle. We now hear, and it is believed, that all the officers, who were taken in the former unsuccessful assault, were to have been sent to France on the night of the day on which the island was taken. At this moment, a false report that the castle had hoisted the white flag, sent us to the top of the house. The fact is, the French flag still flies on the castle, but a flag of truce has just been sent into the Mirador. We yesterday visited the arsenal of the artillery: very few guns, fewer carriage ; quantities of small arms in utter confusion, and an old red coach!

As you leave the arsenal gate, where there is a sentinel, you find yourself suddenly under the Mirador battery. I had stopped a moment in the surprise of suddenly looking two or three of the enemy in the face, when one of them laughed and pulled off his hat, which salute I returned, and not trusting too much to the continued attention of the gentry against whom I had not more than an hour before been sending directions to fire, walked back again. We paid a second visit to the corner of the town, under the fire from the convent of St. Therese, where a mine is preparing, about the immediate success of which we are anxious, and then came home. General Hay's aide-de-camp, with whom I spoke, in a little while afterwards incautiously exposing himself, was killed. He had peeped round the corner, and stood on some steps to no manner of purpose, and fell the certain victim. In the midst of all these scenes of horror, are the most striking and whimsical contrasts. The people of St. Sebastian are robbed and plundered; those of Ernani and Passages come with smiling faces, and purchase their neighbours' goods. Soldiers, sailors, and muleteers are to be seen dressed in women's clothes, and with every remnant of tawdry finery. How all these things are brought out is surprising. Sentries are placed at all outlets, and the plunderers forced to lay down their ill-gotten spoils; but all that can be carried about the person undiscovered, of course escapes.

In the avenue leading to the batteries, two nights ago, a regular plundering party stopped, after dark, all who passed. Gordon, who had sent his servant for his dinner, wisely sent two soldiers to guard the man on his return. The master of a transport, who had taken a walk, "good, easy man," to look about him, complained to Parker that he had been robbed of his coat, his shoes and stockings, and his money. "What shall I do?" said the disconsolate man. "Why," said Parker, "if you wish to keep your shirt, you had better return to your ship."

Tonight we are to begin to draw our guns through the river Urumea. It must be done after dark, to avoid the enemy's fire, and is only practicable at low water (if then).

Imagining that the enemy, in the confusion of a general fire, might not know how many mortars we had, we fired several salvos of shells after dark last night: this was a prelude to the flag of truce to be sent in the morning, but I do not imagine he will surrender a post yet capable of a strong and pro-tracted defence. His bravery hitherto authorises the opinion that he will defend it to the last.

One hears with regret that the enemy received almost regularly supplies of powder and stores by sea. I fear this has been the case, but shall be particular in my inquiries by and by on the subject. All is quiet in front, where we have had no loss for a day or two, except that of Mr. Larpent, the judge-advocate-general, who having (as I hope) a clearer knowledge of law than of military positions, wandered into the enemy's lines on the 31st, having mistaken them for ours. He timed his mistake well: law is silent here.

P.S. I find I have made two mistakes in my letter relative to the assault:-

First; The advanced battery of the left attack really did fire during the assault, and was of essential use; being on the opposite side of the Urumea, and not under my immediate direction, its fire had escaped me. It consisted of three guns, the fourth having been disabled by the enemy's fire. Captain Power commanded in it.

Second; The enemy's mine, which threw down the retaining wall of the glacis, did more mischief than I had supposed. In passing yesterday, I reck-oned seventeen bodies, of which parts were visible; these were of men, whom the falling of the wall had crushed.

Sept. 3, quarter-past 11 a.m.

All firing has ceased by order. Sir Thomas Graham sends word that another message is expected to be sent into the town in the course of the day. Dickson has gone into the town to meet Sir Thomas.

On 31 August, the very day that San Sebastian fell, Soult launched an attack to try and relieve the place, but it was too late. Consequently, the troops that had crossed the river Bidassoa, which effectively marked the Spanish–French border, was left with a difficult passage back. Indeed, heavy rains swelled the river and fords that had been passable in the morning were now in full flood. Most of the French troops succeeded in gaining their own side of the river but Vandermassen's division was not so fortunate. With the fords being impassable to his men, Vandermassen headed for the only bridge still standing over the Bidassoa at Vera. Unfortunately for him it was held by a company of the

95th Rifles under Captain Daniel Cadoux and in the subsequent fight both Vandermassen and Cadoux were killed. Further efforts to break through to San Sebastian at the heights of San Marcial failed also. In fact, the San Marcial battle was Soult's last battle in Spain.

With San Sebastian finally in his hands Wellington could seriously contemplate the invasion of France. Accordingly, plans were made for an invasion which took place on 7 October. The crossing of the Bidassoa was another of Wellington's masterstrokes. Soult believed that, with the Bidassoa being so wide at its mouth, and with so narrow a frontage at the coast upon which to operate, Wellington would be forced to invade France further inland. Thus the majority of the 47,000 French troops defending the 16-mile front, were massed between Ascain and Ainhoa, with the coastal sector being defended very lightly. It came as a great shock to Soult, therefore, when he learned that Wellington's main thrust was directed precisely at the point that he considered impassable, the coast. Soult, in fact, had fallen for Wellington's diversionary moves away to the east, and whilst he sat there, waiting for the expected attack, Wellington's men were pouring across the Bidassoa at its mouth. By noon, the operation was all but completed with relatively light loss. Wellington's army, after five long years of war, had finally set foot on French soil.

Edmund Wheatley, of the 5th Line Battalion KGL, was one of the first to cross, being with the 1st Division of Wellington's army. Wheatley and his comrades crossed the Bidassoa close to the burnt bridge of Behobie, where a bend in the river made for a fairly narrow crossing. The crossing was also made slightly easier than it might have been by the fact that Soult's defences here, close to the coast, were not as deep as Wellington would have expected. In fact, it was his ruse further inland — making demonstrations in the east, close to Maya, that caused Soult to mass his troops inland. Thus, the French troops defending the coastal sector of the line were relatively thin on the ground. Wheatley's story appeared in *The Wheatley Diary*, published in London in 1964.

At one o'clock this morning the dead silence of the camp was suddenly changed to a scene of hurry and commotion. A passe-parole ordered the companies instantly under arms; and the rattling of artillery passing soon shook off every drowsy sensation. All was conjecture and expectation. We supposed the forcing of the river to be the object.

We remained till daybreak in a field to the left — the Guards in our rear on the right. The morning was cloudy with a sharp hoar-frost.

About seven o'clock the cry was "Fall in!" We ran to the river side and dashed into it, up to our armpits in water, through a shower of musketry from the French. On reaching the opposite shore, my Company and the 2nd ran to cover the riflemen…The Bidassoa is very rapid at the place where I crossed and so very strong was the current that we were constrained to take each other by the arm, holding our swords and muskets in the air, the water being up to the arm pits and knee deep in mud. The French were stationed in the houses opposite, behind the hedges and in the ditches keeping up a regular fire upon us as we struggled through the cold river. Many fell wounded and were drowned through the rapidity of the element. The balls splashed around us like a shower of rain. But the water was so excessively cold and strong that I was insensible to the splashing of the musketry around my chest and I struggled through mechanically, without even reflecting that I was walking to fight a few thousand devils before breakfast.

On reaching the opposite shore we cleared the houses of the French and recovered breath for a few minutes. My company and the 1st under Major Gerber then sallied out. We dived into a wood on the slope of a hill behind every tree of which stood a Frenchman, distraction in his eye and death in his hand, popping from the ditches, between the thickets, and among the bushes.

And now I first heard that hissing and plaintive whistling from the balls around me. The hiss is caused by the wind but when a ball passes close to you a strong shrill whistle tells you of your escape. I felt no tremor or cold sensation whatever. I walked without thought or reflection.

We soon gained the outside of the wood, the French scampering like rabbits in a warren. On ascending higher up the hill a 9 lb. shot from our own artillery across the river fell short and nearly cut off half of us. We jumped down a ditch to escape its range and, creeping along a hedge, we gained a field which we had to cross to take a small farmhouse.

On the edge of the field we became exposed to an elevated battery. A heavy shot fell two yards to my left and covered me with mud and slime. The noise was so great and the splash into the earth so violent that I mechanically jumped against a tall Polack who, good-naturedly smiling, pushed me back saying, 'Don't flinch, Ensign.' Little hump-backed Bacmeister behind me also said 'Vall, Veatley, how you like dat?'

'Not good for the kidneys,' I said.

That very moment another volley came and cut a fellow to pieces before my face.

I looked up at the battery and fancied every mouth pointed at me alone,

223

and I moved on expecting my two legs off every moment. The idea of flight never entered my mind but the hotter the fire the stronger I felt myself urged to advance. And in spite of the cannon shot, we gained the farmhouse with the loss of one killed and two wounded.

We remained in this house until that accursed battery destroyed it about our ears, and after some consultation we resolved to rush up and endeavour to storm it. This was the hottest part of the action for it was literally rushing into the cannon's mouth. The balls dashed the earth into my eyes. The wind of the shot was sensibly felt. But we panted up the hill, jumped into the ditch, climbed the mud walls. Away ran the French, and thus fell the battery into our hands containing the 10-pounders, plenty of onions, rotten biscuit and hay.

Thank God for this escape, for my pantaloons were simply torn at the right knee, and the flesh blackened by the wind of the ball.

I cannot refrain noticing one circumstance which occurred during this my first battle. While standing in a ditch with my men, popping through the hedges at the enemy as they ran from field to field, the fellow who stood on my left set up a most lamentable roar and, on turning, I found his cheek swelled up like a currant pudding from a ball which, passing downwards, had shattered his jaw and had lodged in his throat. I, like a novice, took out my handkerchief and endeavoured to staunch the blood. But my bullying Captain Notting bellowed out, 'Wheatley! Mind your duty and leave the man alone!'

Experience afterwards convinced me how unwise was the action, but the sudden impulse of human feeling in the breast of a young soldier was the only answer I could return to the jokes and merriment afterwards practiced upon me.

Colonel Ompteda with the rest of the regiment stormed the other battery at the same time; and the army on our right and left were equally successful excepting the 95th Regiment which did not succeed until the whole day's fighting enabled them to gain their point.

Thus we entered the French Empire, October the 7th, 1813, about seven o'clock in the morning; and after fighting until four in the afternoon we encamped on the hills where I now write this.

Must not forget to write to Henry tomorrow. I've just returned from burying the dead. How it rains! Poor fellows! No more colds for them.

Augustus Frazer, meanwhile, forded the Bidassoa with his artillery not far from Wheatley. His account of the crossing was related in one of his letters, published in 1859.

We left Oyarzun at midnight of the 6th. The columns which moved by the direct road to Irun (and it was not possible to advance by another) completely filled it. The night was at first stormy; thunder and lightning, and some rain. It afterwards was so sultry as to be the subject of every one's remark; the little wind there was like the breath of an oven. The road was so blocked up, that though the distance is but two leagues from Oyarzun to Irun, it was daylight before we reached the latter. All seemed quiet in the enemy's position. On reaching Irun, Ramsay's troop inclined to the right, leaving the high road. I here learned that Mitchell's battery (late Parker's) was to join me when it came up, which it soon did: and we found 400 infantry waiting to pull the guns over the mountain to the places previously intended. Bull's horses never want assistance; they were soon posted on a height with some Spanish horse artillery. The affair began at 8; a column of our infantry having crossed previously at Fuenterrabia, opposite to which place they forded the Bidassoa. Another column crossed by fording just below the burnt bridge at Irun, followed close by Webber Smith's troop. Another column, at the same time, about a mile higher up; and the Spaniards, as if impatient, rushed down the mountains, a little to the right of the enemy's village of Biriatu, and in spite of every opposition forded the river, and carried the mountain called (even in orders) the "Montagne de Louis XIV." During this time, our guns and those of the Spanish horse artillery played on the enemy; but he made a very feeble resistance, and, at 9 o'clock, the burning of the huts of the mountain posts showed that he had abandoned them. Finding that the affair was losing all appearance of becoming serious on our right, I quitted Ramsay's. and Mitchell's batteries, sending them orders to cross at the burnt bridge at Irun, and crossed myself the river at this point, which is close to the high Bayonne road, and leaves to its left the Isle de la Conference, where Louis XIV, and Charles IV of Spain had the conference from which the little isle takes its name. The moment after I had crossed, I saw the Marquis approaching the ford, and rode up to report to Dickson what I had done. I had also previously ordered Ross to leave the mountains and to cross. This last was left to my discretion, but I had no instructions relative to the other two batteries, and though clear in my mind that they should advance, I was not so that it would be approved, since at times his lordship allows no troops to be moved, but in obedience to his own orders. Dickson thought my having moved them hazardous, and I sent Bell off again to stop them where he might find them, but with orders that they should be ready to move rapidly forward when ordered, which they afterwards were. Indeed, Ramsay having found out a new ford, had already crossed the Bidassoa, and had gained the road communicating with the main one to Bayonne. At this time, the enemy had retired from the river at all points, and had fallen back on what I presumed to be his second line, from a redoubt in which he opened a fire of a few guns, having previously fired three or four 24-pounders only from a battery a little below Andaya, which battery had been immediately taken by our troops, who crossed near Fuenterrabia. The redoubt was also immediately taken, and on our ascending the height we found the troops formed somewhat in advance of it. An instantaneous hurrah burst from the line on seeing Lord Wellington, who rode on a little towards the left, where the enemy yet showed a feeble line but disputed some woody ground. In the front was the village of Urugne, which our advanced troops were then entering. On a height, not above 1400 yards beyond it, were two French divisions, drawn out before their encampment, which was partly entrenched and had an apparently strong redoubt which they strengthened with fresh troops. About a mile to their left, before the encampment, were two field-pieces, the first they had shown. From these, they cannonaded the village and our troops then entering, which were the German and other light troops of the first division. On looking attentively at the village, the inhabitants appeared in a body in a field adjoining the road. There were women and children among them. This was before the field-pieces played much on the village. The inhabitants disappeared, I know not how but suddenly, for on turning round, after looking for a little at what was doing on the left, they were gone. The enemy's fire from the two guns became more rapid, and the village was obviously on fire. Whether this may have been from the enemy's shells (if they fired any), or from our troops setting fire to the houses, I do not at this moment know, but I know that the troops who first entered got drunk, and that many were laden with plunder. I shall make more particular inquiry, since it was distressing to see the first French village (or little town, for it is of some size) on fire. I imagine, too, that had the enemy shown more enterprise he might have easily taken the troops who entered the village. It soon became necessary to withdraw them, and the affair ended about half past 12 (one hour after Urugne was on fire) by our assuming a position a little retired, and nearly the same one on which the second line of the enemy had rested in the morning. On questioning the prisoners, they agree that some battalions and many guns had marched that morning for Bayonne, that Soult was at last really gone, and they believed to Germany: and that Suchet had slept the night before at Bayonne, and was come to take the command. It is certain that they made a very feeble resistance, being as it were taken by surprise, or at least, without preparation. The guns taken in the redoubt are old iron ship guns, on sea carriages. They showed no field guns but the two near Urugne, during the firing of which their tents were struck and sent off. Their redoubt beyond their encampment and to the left of it apparently commanded the approaches from the Pass of Vera. No attack seemed to have been made through this Pass, but more to our right there was much smoke. I am not yet aware of what has been done on our right. Little can be seen in these mountainous regions beyond the next mountain, and the fatigue and difficulty of communication are beyond what could be imagined. Few lives were lost yesterday, I know not how many, but as the action was fought over much ground, many fell in detail. I saw several Spanish bodies in the nooks of the river. The Spaniards behaved nobly. — Adieu; I must quit my pen for the saddle.

Our final eyewitness of the crossing of the Bidassoa is a subaltern in the 85th Light Infantry, George Gleig, whose book *The Subaltern* has since become one of the most famous of Peninsular War memoirs. Gleig's most enjoyable memoir was published in London in 1825 and recounts his services in the Peninsula from his arrival, just prior to the storming of San Sebastian, until the end of the war. Gleig was also responsible for 'ghosting' and writing several other memoirs, including those of George Farmer, of the 11th Light Dragoons, featured earlier in this book. Gleig's regiment took no part in the crossing of the Bidassoa itself, but Gleig was obviously well-placed to take note in great detail of the operation.

It was, as nearly as I can now recollect, about four o'clock next morning, when I was aroused from my slumber by the orderly sergeant of my company. By this time the storm had completely passed away, and the stars were shining in a sky completely cloudless. The moon had, however, gone down, nor was there any other light except what they afforded, to aid the red glare from the decaying fires, which, for want of fuel, were fast dying out. The effect of this dull light, as it fell upon the soldiers, mustering in solemn silence, was exceedingly fine. You could not distinguish either the uniform or the features of the men; you saw only groups collecting together, with arms in their hands; and it was impossible not to associate in your own mind the idea of banditti, rather than of regular troops, with the wild forest scenery around. Of course, I started to my feet at the first summons; and having buckled on my sabre, stowed away some cold meat, biscuit, and rum, in a haver-sack, and placed it, with my cloak, across the back of my horse, and swal-lowed a cup or two of coffee, I felt myself ready and willing for any kind of service whatever.

In little more than a quarter of an hour, the corps was under arms, and each man in his place. We had already been joined by two other battalions, form-ing a brigade of about fifteen hundred men; and about an hour before sun-rise, just as the first streaks of dawn were appearing in the east, the word was given to march. Our tents were not, on this occasion, struck. They were left standing, with the baggage and mules, under the protection of a guard, for the purpose of deceiving the enemy's piquets, in whose view they were exposed, into the belief that nothing was going forward. This measure was rendered necessary, because the state of the tide promised not to admit of our fording the river till past seven o'clock, long before which hour broad day-light would set in; and hence, the whole object of our early movement was to gain, unobserved, a sort of hollow, close to the banks of the Bidassoa, from which, as soon as the stream should be passable, we might emerge.

As we moved in profound silence, we reached our place of ambuscade without creating the smallest alarm; where we laid ourselves down upon the ground, for the double purpose of more effectually avoiding a display, and of taking as much rest as possible. Whilst lying here, we listened, with eager curiosity, to the distant tread of feet, which marked the coming up of other divisions, and to the lumbering sound of artillery, as it rolled along the high road. The latter increased upon us every moment, till at length three ponder-ous eighteen-pounders reached the hollow, and began to ascend the rising ground immediately in front of us. These were placed in battery, so as to com-mand the ford, across which a stone bridge, now in ruins, was thrown; and by which we knew, from the position which we now occupied, that we were destined to proceed. By what infatuation it arose, that all those preparations excited no suspicion among the enemy, whose sentinels were scarcely half musket-shot distant, I know not; but the event proved, that they expected this morning anything rather than an attack.

Before I proceed to describe the circumstances of the battle, I must endeav-our to convey to the minds of my non-military readers something like a clear notion of the nature of the position occupied by the right of the French army. I have already said, that its extreme flank rested upon the sea. Its more cen-tral brigades occupied a chain of heights, not, indeed, deserving of the name of mountains, but still sufficiently steep to check the progress of an advanc-ing force, and full of natural inequalities, well adapted to cover the defenders

228

from the fire of the assailants. Along the face of these heights is built the straggling village of Andaye; and immediately in front of them runs the frith or mouth of the Bidassoa, fordable only in two points, one opposite to Fontarabia, and the other in the direction of the main road. Close to the French bank of the river, is a grove, or strip of willows, with several vineyards, and other enclosures, admirably calculated for skirmishers; whilst the ford beside the ruined bridge, the only one by which artillery could pass, was completely commanded by a fortified house, or tete-du-pont, filled with infantry. The main road, again, on the French side of the river, winds among over-hanging precipices, not, indeed, so rugged as those in the pass of Irun, but sufficiently bold to place troops which might occupy them in comparative security, and to render one hundred resolute men more than a match for a thousand who might attack them. Yet these were the most assailable points in the whole position, all beyond the road being little else than perpendicular cliffs, shaggy with pine and ash trees.

Such was the nature of the ground which we were commanded to carry. As day dawned, I could distinctly see that the old town of Fontarabia was filled with British soldiers. The fifth division, which had borne the brunt of the late siege, and which, since the issue of their labours, had been permitted to rest somewhat in the rear, had been moved up on the preceding evening; and reaching Fontarabia a little before midnight, had spent some hours in the streets. Immediately in rear of ourselves, again, and in the streets of Irun, about eight thousand of the Guards and of the German Legion were reposing; whilst a brigade of cavalry just showed its leading files, at a turning in the main road, and a couple of nine-pounders stood close beside them. It was altogether a beautiful and an animating sight, not fewer than fifteen or twenty thousand British and Portuguese troops being distinguishable at a single glance.

Away to our right, and on the tops of San Marcial, the Spanish divisions took their stations; nor could I avoid drawing something like an invidious comparison between them and their gallant allies. Half clothed, and badly fed, though sufficiently armed, their appearance certainly promised no more than their actions, for the most part, verified. Not that the Spanish peasantry are deficient in personal courage, (and their soldiers were, generally speaking, no other than peasants with muskets in their hands,) but their corps were so miserably officered, and their commissariat so miserably supplied, that the chief matter of surprise is, how they came to fight at all. Even at this period of the war, when their country might be said to be completely freed from the invader, the principal subsistence of the Spanish army consisted in the heads

229

of Indian corn, which they gathered for themselves in the fields, and cooked by roasting them over their fires.

It will readily be imagined, that we watched the gradual fall of the river with intense anxiety, turning our glasses ever and anon towards the French lines, throughout which all remained most unaccountably quiet. At length a movement could be distinguished among the troops which occupied Fontarabia. Their skirmishers began to emerge from under cover of the houses, and to approach the river, when instantly the three eighteen-pounders opened from the heights above us. This was the signal for a general advance. Our column, likewise, threw out its skirmishers, which, hastening towards the ford, were saluted by a sharp fire of musketry from the enemy's piquets, and from the garrison of the tete-du-pont. But the latter was speed-ily abandoned as our people pressed through the stream, and our artillery kept up an incessant discharge of round and grape shot upon it.

The Fench piquets were driven in, and our troops established on the oppo-site bank, with hardly any loss on our part, though those who crossed by Fontarabia were obliged to hold their firelocks and cartouch-boxes over their heads, to keep them dry; and the water reached considerably above the knees beside the bridge. The alarm had, however, been communicated to the columns in rear, which hastily formed upon the heights, and endeavoured, but in vain, to keep possession of Andaye. That village was carried in gallant style by a brigade of the fifth division, whilst the first, moving steadily along the road, dislodged from their post the garrison of the hills which com-manded it, and crowned the heights almost without opposition: A general panic seemed to have seized the enemy. Instead of boldly charging us, as we moved forward in column, they fired their pieces, and fled without pausing to reload them, nor was anything like a determined stand attempted, till all their works had fallen into our hands, and much of their artillery was taken. It was one of the most perfect and yet extraordinary surprises, which I ever beheld.

There were not, however, wanting many brave fellows among the French officers, who exerted themselves strenuously to rally their terrified com-rades, and to restore the battle. Among these I remarked one in particular. He was on horseback; and, riding among a flying battalion; he used every means which threat and entreaty could produce, to stop them; and he succeeded. The battalion paused, its example was followed by others, and in five min-utes a well-formed line occupied what looked like the last of a range of green hills, on the other side of a valley which we were descending. This sudden movement on the part of the enemy was met by a corresponding formation on ours; we wheeled into line and advanced. Not a word was spoken, nor a shot fired, till our troops had reached nearly half way across the little hollow, when the French, raising one of their discordant yells, — a sort of shout, in which every man halloos for himself, without regard to the tone or time of those about him, — fired a volley. It was well directed, and did considerable execution; but it checked not our approach for a moment. Our men replied to it with a hearty British cheer, and giving them back their fire, rushed on to the charge.

In this they were met with great spirit by the enemy. I remarked the same individual, who had first stopped their flight, ride along the front of his men, and animate them to their duty, nor was it without very considerable difficulty, and after having exchanged several discharges of musketry, that we succeeded in getting within charging distance. Then, indeed, another cheer was given, and the French, without waiting for the rush, once more broke their ranks and fled. Their leader was still as active as before. He rode among the men, reproached, exhorted, and even struck those near him with his sword, and he was once more about to restore order, when he fell. In an instant, however, he rose again and mounted another horse, but he had hardly done so when a ball took effect in his neck, and he dropped dead. The fall of this one man decided the day upon the heights of Andaye. The French troops lost all order and all discipline, and making their way to the rear, each by himself as he best could, they left us in undisputed possession of the field.

On the right of our army, however, and on the extreme left of the enemy, a much more determined opposition was offered. There Soult had added to the natural strength of his position, by throwing up redoubts and batteries upon every commanding point, and hence, it was not without suffering a very considerable loss, that the light division succeeded in turning it. All attempts, indeed, to carry the Hermitage, failed, though they were renewed with the most daring resolution, till a late hour in the night. But of the operations of the army in these quarters, I could see nothing, and therefore I will not attempt to describe them.

The day was far spent when our troops, wearied as much with the pursuit as with fighting, were commanded to halt, and to lie down in brigades and divisions along the heights which the enemy had abandoned. With us all was now perfectly quiet; but the roar of musketry, and the thunder of the cannon, still sounded on our right. As the darkness set in, too, the flashes became every moment more and more conspicuous, and produced, on account of the great unevenness of the ground; a remarkably beautiful effect. Repeated assaults being still made upon the Hermitage rock, the whole side of that con-

231

ical hill seemed in a blaze, whilst every valley and eminence around it sparkled from time to time like the hills and valleys of a tropical climate, when the fire-flies are out in millions. Nor were other and stronger lights wanting. Our troops, in the hurry of the battle, had set fire to the huts of the French soldiers, which now burst forth, and cast a strong glare over the entire extent of the field. On the whole it was a glorious scene, and tended much to keep up the degree of excitement which had pervaded our minds during the day.

Our loss, I mean the loss of the corps to which I was attached, chanced to be trifling. No particular companion, or intimate acquaintance of mine at least, had fallen, consequently there was nothing to destroy the feeling of pure delight, which the meanest individual in an army experiences when that army has triumphed; nor do I recollect many happier moments of my life, than when I stretched myself this evening beside a fire, near my friend Gray, to chat over the occurrences of the day. The Quarter-master coming up soon after with a supply of provisions and rum, added, indeed; not a little to my satisfaction, for the stock which I had provided in the morning was long ago disposed of among those who had been less provident; and my meal was followed by a sleep, such as kings might envy, though the heavens were my canopy, and the green turf was my bed.

Gleig was just one of many British soldiers who laid down to sleep on French soil on the momentous night of 7 October 1813. The British army's journey had been a long and often painful one, beginning in August 1808 at Lisbon and continuing back and forth across Spain. Now, after literally thousands of miles of marching and counter-marching, they had finally set foot on the so-called 'sacred soil' of France. What a poignant moment it must have been for those men who had been present throughout the war. But the crossing of the Bidassoa was only the first phase of Wellington's plan to drive deeper into France. After all, it represented only a foothold on enemy territory. The following month Wellington would call upon his men to fight yet again, taking the war deeper into 1813, with winter just around the corner. The resulting battle would be one of Wellington's finest achievements; the Battle of the Nivelle.

CHAPTER FOURTEEN

ΓHE NIVELLE AND THE NIVE

On 10 November 1813, just over four weeks after the crossing of the Bidassoa, Wellington achieved what he himself considered to be one of his greatest victories, the Battle of the Nivelle. With the Allies firmly on French soil, Soult retreated to a position on some heights along the river Nivelle, heights that boasted a series of forts and redoubts, some of which were armed with guns. The French line was divided into three, with the coastal sector being the most heavily defended. After all, Wellington had attacked along the coast the previous month. Surely he would repeat the exercise? Well, of course he didn't. On 10 November, Wellington attacked the French position in overwhelming strength along both the centre and left of Soult's line, leaving Sir John Hope to demonstrate against the coastal sector. Soult was paralysed with inactivity and lost all control of the battle. When darkness fell on the late afternoon of 10 November, Soult's men had been driven from their positions along the entire length of their line, losing over 4,000 men. Wellington himself lost around 2,450 men. It was a crushing victory which moved Napier to comment that Wellington had brushed aside Soult's iron barrier, 'as if it were a screen of reeds.'

George Gleig, of the 85th Light Infantry, was part of the force attacking and demonstrating against the coastal sector of the French line. His regiment's effort was directed against the town of Urugne, which the French had barricaded with huge casks, filled with stones. In his book, *The Subaltern*, Gleig paints a wonderful picture of the fighting along the coast road on the morning of 10 November 1813.

The column being formed, and the tents and baggage so disposed, as that, in case of a repulse, they might be carried to the rear without confusion or delay, the word was given to march. As our route lay over ground extremely uneven, we moved forward for a while slowly, and with caution till, having gained the high road, we were enabled to quicken our pace. We proceeded by it, perhaps a mile, till the watch-fire of a German piquet was seen; when the order to halt being passed quietly from rank to rank, we grounded our arms, and sat down upon the green banks by the road side. Here we were directed to remain, till a gun on our left should sound the signal of attack, and objects should be distinctly visible.

Men are very differently affected at different times, even though the situations in which they may be cast bear a strong affinity to one another. On the present occasion, for example, I perfectly recollect, that hardly any feeling of seriousness pervaded my own mind, nor, if I might judge from appearances, the minds of those around me. Much conversation, on the contrary, passed among us in whispers, but it was all of as light a character, as if the business in which we were about to engage was mere amusement, and not that kind of play in which men stake their lives. Anxiety and restlessness, indeed, universally prevailed. We looked to the east, and watched the gradual approach of dawn with eager interest; but it was with that degree of interest which sportsmen feel on the morning of the twelfth of August, or rather, perhaps, like that of a child in a box at Covent-Garden, when it expects every moment to see the stage-curtain lifted. We were exceedingly anxious to begin the fray, but we were quite confident of success.

In the meanwhile, such dispositions were made as the circumstances of the case appeared to require. Three companies, consisting of about one hundred and fifty men, were detached, under the command of a field-officer, a little to the right and left of the road, for the purpose of surprising, if possible, two of the enemy's piquets, which were there posted. The remaining seven, forming again into column, as day broke, extended their front so as to cover the whole breadth of the road. and made ready to rush at once, in what is called double quick time; upon the village. That it was strongly barricaded, and filled with French infantry, we were quite aware; but, by making our first attack a rapid one, we calculated on reaching the barricade before the enemy should be fully aware of the movement.

We stood perhaps half an hour, after these dispositions were effected, before the signal was given, the dawn gradually brightening over the whole of the sky. Now we could observe that we had diverged in some degree from the main road, and occupied with our, little column a lane, hemmed in on both sides by high hedges. Presently we were able to remark that the lane again united itself with the road about a hundred yards in front of us; then the church and houses of the village began to show through the darkness, like rocks, or mounds; by and by the stubble fields immediately around could be distinguished from green meadows; then the hedge-rows which separated one field from another became visible. And now the signal-gun was fired. It was immediately repeated by a couple of nine-pounders, which were stationed in a field adjoining to the lane where we stood; and the battle began.

The three detached companies did their best to surprise the French piquets, but without success, the French troops being far too watchful to be easily taken. They drove them in, however, in gallant style, whilst the little column, according to the preconcerted plan, pressed forward. In the meantime, the houses and barricade of Urugne were thronged with defenders, who saluted us as we approached with a sharp discharge of musketry, which, however, was more harmless than might have been expected. A few men and one officer fell, the latter being shot through the heart. He uttered but a single word — the name of his favourite comrade, and expired. On our part, we had no time for firing, but rushed on to the charge; whilst the nine-pounders, already alluded to, cleared the barricade with grape and cannister. In two minutes we had reached its base; in an instant more we were on the top of it; when the enemy, panic-struck at the celerity of our movements, abandoned their defences and fled. We followed them through the street of the place, as far as its extremity, but, having been previously commanded to proceed no farther, we halted here, and they escaped to the high grounds beyond.

The position now attacked was that famous one in front of St Jean de Luz, than which, Lord Wellington himself has said that he never beheld any more formidable. It extended for about three miles, along the ridge of a rising ground, the ascent of which was, for the most part, covered with thick wood, and intersected by deep ditches. In addition to these natural defences, it was fortified with the utmost care, Marshal Soult having begun to throw up upon it redoubts and breastworks, even before our army had crossed the Bidassoa, and having devoted the whole of that month which we had spent above Andaye, in completing his older works and erecting new. Towards our left, indeed, that is, towards the right of the enemy, and in the direction of the village which we had just carried, these works presented so commanding an appearance, that our gallant leader deemed it unwise to attempt any serious impression upon them; and hence, having possessed ourselves of Urugne, we were directed to attempt nothing farther, but to keep it at all hazards, and to make from time to time a demonstration of advancing. This was done, in order to deter Soult from detaching any of his corps to the assistance of his left, which it was the object of Lord Wellington to turn, and which, after twelve hours' severe fighting, he succeeding in turning.

As soon as we had cleared the place of its defenders, we set about entrenching ourselves, in case any attempt should be made to retake the village. For this purpose, we tore up the barricade erected by the French, consisting of

235

casks filled with earth, manure, and rubbish, and rolling them down to the opposite end of the town, we soon threw up a parapet for our own defence. The enemy, in the meanwhile, began to collect a dense mass of infantry upon the brow of the hill opposite, and, turning a battery of three pieces of cannon upon us, they swept the street with round shot. These, whizzing along, soon caused the walls and roofs of the houses to crumble into ruins; but neither they, nor the shells which from time to time burst about us, did any considerable execution. By avoiding conspicuous places, indeed, we managed to keep well out of reach; and hence the chief injury done by the cannonade was that which befell the proprietors of houses.

We found in the village a good store of brown bread, and several casks of brandy. The latter of these were instantly knocked on the head, and the spirits poured out into the street, as the only means of hindering our men from getting drunk, and saving ourselves from a defeat; but the former was divided amongst them; and even the black bread, allowed to the French soldiers, was a treat to us, because we had tasted nothing except biscuits, and these none of the most fresh, for the last three months. We were not, however, allowed much time to regale ourselves.

It was now about eleven o'clock, and the enemy had as yet made no attack upon us. We could perceive, indeed, from the glancing of bayonets through the wood in front, that troops were there mustering; and as the country was well adapted for skirmishing, being a good deal intersected with ditches, hedges, and hollow ways, it was deemed prudent to send out three or four companies to watch their movements. Among the companies thus sent out was that to which I belonged. We took a direction to the left of the village, and being noticed by the enemy's artillery, were immediately saluted with a shower of round shot and shells. Just at this moment a tumbril or ammunition-waggon coming up, a shell from a French mortar fell upon it; it exploded, and two unfortunate artillery-drivers, who chanced to be sitting upon it, were hurled into the air. I looked at them for a moment after they fell. One was quite dead, and dreadfully mangled; the other was as black as a coal, but he was alive, and groaned heavily. He lifted his head as we passed, and wished us success. What became of him afterwards I know not, but there appeared little chance of his recovery.

Having gained a hollow road, somewhat in advance of the village, we found ourselves in connection with a line of skirmishers thrown out by Colonel Halkett from his corps of light Germans, and in some degree sheltered from the cannonade. But our repose was not of long continuance. The enemy having collected a large force of tirailleurs, advanced, with loud shouts and every show of determination. To remain where we were, was to expose ourselves to the risk of being cut to pieces in a hollow way, the banks of which were higher than our heads, and perfectly perpendicular ; the question therefore was, should we retire or advance: Of course, the former idea was not entertained for a moment. We clambered up the face of the bank with some difficulty; and, replying to the shouts of the French with a similar species of music, we pressed on.

When I looked to my right and to my left at this moment, I was delighted with the spectacle which that glance presented. For the benefit of my more peaceable readers, I may as well mention, that troops sent out to skirmish, advance or retire in files; each file, or pair of men, keeping about ten yards from the files on both sides of them. On the present occasion, I beheld a line of skirmishers, extending nearly a mile in both directions, all keeping in a sort of irregular order; and all firing, independently of one another, as the opportunity of a good aim prompted each of them. On the side of the French, again, all was apparent confusion; but the French tirailleurs are by no means in disorder when they appear so. They are admirable skirmishers; and they gave our people; this day, a good deal of employment, before they again betook themselves to the heights. They did not, however, succeed, as I suspect was their design, in drawing us so far from the village as to expose us to the fire of their masked batteries; but having followed them across a few fields only, we once more retired to our hollow road.

It was quite evident, from the numerous solid bodies of troops, which kept their ground along the enemy's line, that the plan of Lord Wellington had been perfectly successful; and that no force had been sent from the right of Soult's army to the assistance of his left. The continual roar of musketry and of cannon, which was kept up in that direction, proved, at the same time, that a more serious struggle was going on there than any to which we were exposed. It was no rapid, but intermitting rattle, like that which we and our opponents from time to time produced; but an unceasing volley, as if men were able to fire without loading, or took no time to load. At length Soult appeared to have ...scovered that he had little to dread upon his right. About three o'clock, we could, accordingly, observe a heavy column, of perhaps ten or twelve thousand men, beginning its march to the left; and at the same instant, as if to cover the movement, the enemy's skirmishers again advanced. Again we met them, as we had done before, and again drove them in; when, instead of falling back to the hollow way, we lay down behind a hedge, half way between the village and the base of their position. From this they made several attempts to dislodge us, but without effect, and here we

237

remained till the approach of darkness put an end to the battle.

The sun had set about an hour, when the troops in advance were every-where recalled; and I and my companions returned to the village. Upon it we found that the enemy still kept up an occasional fire of cannon; and hence, that the houses, which were extremely thin, furnished no sufficient shelter for the troops. It was accordingly determined to canton the corps, for the night, in the church, the walls of that building being of more solid materials, and proof against the violence of at least field artillery. Thither, therefore, we all repaired, and here I had the satisfaction to find that our Portuguese follower had arrived before us, so that a comfortable meal was prepared. Provisions and grog were likewise issued out to the men, and all was now jollity and mirth.

The spectacle which the interior of the church of Urugne presented this night, was one which the pious founder of the fabric probably never calcu-lated upon its presenting. Along the two side aisles, the arms of the battalion were piled, whilst the men themselves occupied the centre aisle. In the pulpit was placed the large drum and other musical instruments, whilst a party of officers took possession of a gallery erected at the lower extremity of the building. For our own parts, Gray and myself asserted a claim to the space around the altar, which, in an English church, is generally railed in, but which, in foreign churches, is distinguished from the rest of the chancel only by its elevation. Here we spread out our cold salt beef, our brown bread, our cheese, and our grog; and here we eat and drank, in that state of excited feel-ing which attends every man who has gone safely through the perils of such a day.

Nor was the wild nature of the spectacle around us diminished by the gloomy and wavering light, which thirty or forty small rosin tapers cast over it. Of these, two or three stood beside us, upon the altar, whilst the rest were scattered about, by ones and twos, in different places, leaving every interval in a sort of shade, which gave a wider scope to the imagination than to the senses, The buzz of conversation, too, the frequent laugh and joke, and, by and by, the song, as the grog began to circulate, all these combined to produce a scene too striking to be soon forgotten.

As time passed on, all these sounds became gradually more and more faint. The soldiers, wearied with their day's work, dropped asleep, one after another, and I, having watched them for a while, stretched out like so many corpses upon the paved floor of the church, wrapped my cloak round me, and prepared to follow their example. I laid myself at the foot of the altar, and though the marble was not more soft than marble usually is, I slept as soundly upon it as if it had been a bed of down.

One of the toughest tasks facing any of Wellington's troops was allotted to the Light Division, whose job it was to storm the French forts high up on the top of the Rhune mountain. Once this had been accomplished, the division was to descend the mountain and attack the strongly-held Signal Redoubt, which commanded the French position above Sare. Captain John Cooke, of the 43rd Light Infantry, was in the thick of the action, and he left a vivid account of the battle in his superb *Memoirs of the Late War*.

On the evening of the 9th of November, the division received orders to move during the night, for the purpose of taking up its ground previously to the attack on the enemy's position in France, on the following morning. The whole of the ample store of ready-cut wood, (a portion of which had been split up by the officers to keep themselves in exercise,) was piled up, and a monstrous fire kindled, which soon burst into a tremendous blaze, throwing a bright glare on the distant objects moving between the trees of the forest. At the usual hour, the owl began to utter her notes, and continued her cries longer than heretofore; all which was construed into something ominous by Lieut. Baillie, a sinewy young Highlander, who, with an eagle's wings held on each shoulder, which he had shot with a single ball a few days before, recited those tragic lines sung by the witches in Macbeth, as we all joined hands and danced around the crackling faggots, and sang in chorus, which at intervals was intermingled with the screeches of the aforesaid owl. The flickering and livid glare of the flames, glancing on the scarlet uniforms, the red sparks flying over the forest, and the soldiers packing and beating their knapsacks, gave an unusual wildness to our midnight orgies.

Before striking our tent, we partook of a comfortable breakfast, after which we each secured a biscuit, of American manufacture; they were of a peculiar hardness (nearly an inch thick), so much so, that it required the stamp of an iron heel, or some hard substance, to break them. An officer jocularly remarked, while placing one of them under the breast of his jacket, that it might turn a ball, which actually occurred.

During the darkness we got under arms, and moved silently under the north-west side of la Rhune, by a narrow pathway, which had been cut at that point to facilitate the passage of the troops to the destined point of attack, within a few hundred yards of the enemy's outposts. We had scarcely taken up our ground, when we perceived the flash of a cannon, fired by the enemy on the high road to Saint Jean de Luz, and immediately followed by five others from the same spot. The conclusion was, that these discharges were fired as a signal; for, soon after, we heard the martial sounds of the French drums beating to arms, over a great extent of country, *au petit point du jour*; our eyes anxiously glanced towards the spot, where we expected to see the second brigade of the division already formed. But nothing seemed to be under the rough side of the mountain of Siboure, except slabs of rock, when, all of a sudden, as if by magic, the whole of the fancied rocks were in motion; and as the haze gradually cleared away, we could see the soldiers packing the blankets with which they had covered themselves, having taken up their ground long before us, as they had had a greater distance to march.

The rising of the sun above the horizon was to be the signal for the battle of the Nivelle to begin; or, if the weather proved cloudy, the heavy artillery (which had been dragged with great difficulty through the pass of Echalar,) were to open on the French occupying a fort, which had been constructed to block up the break of the ridge of the Pyrenees leading towards the village of Sare, in France. The sky was free from clouds, and a sharp cold wind whistled through the barren and cheerless rocks, whilst all eyes were directed towards the east, watching the inflamed orb of the sun as he rose to view. Our regiment, under Major W. Napier, then fixed bayonets, and rapidly moved forward in column to the assault of the three stone forts on the top of la Petite la Rhune; two companies rushed forward to skirmish; four formed into line, and four supported in column. The heavy guns opened at the puerta de Echalar; part of our brigade moved further to the right; the second brigade scrambled over the rocks, precipices, and ravines, to take the enemy in reverse; and the mountain guns fired into the forts from a ledge of ragged grey rocks.

In a few minutes we reached the summit of the small mountain by a green slope (not unlike a large breach) within twenty yards of the walls of the first fort. The soldiers and officers gasped for breath: many of the former, from the weight of their knapsacks and accoutrements, staggered and fell, and, before they could recover their limbs, were pierced with bullets to rise no more; the officers led on in a group and carried the first fort. The second was then attacked hand to hand, the French using their bayonets and the butt ends of their pieces; one of our officers gallantly jumped into the second fort, and a French soldier thrust a bayonet through his neckhandkerchief, transfixed him to the wall, and then fired his piece which blew away the officer's collar who jumped up unhurt. Another officer, while clambering up the wall, received a

240

most tremendous blow on the fingers with the butt-end of a firelock, which made him glad to drop his hold; and we were so hard pressed, that one or two of the officers seized the dead soldiers' firelocks and fought with them. Among others, Sir Andrew Barnard of the rifle corps joined in this hard fight.

As the enemy rushed out of the second fort, a little athletic man with red hair eagerly followed a French officer; the Frenchman parried two of his thrusts, but finding his men giving way, he turned suddenly round and made off, and the, soldier, fearing his prey might escape, hurled his firelock at him; the bayonet flew through the back, of his body, and he fell heavily on his face with the weight of the musket and the bayonet still sticking in him. Another French officer, who had shewn a noble example of heroism, stood on the top of the wall with both his eyes hanging on his cheeks, with his short cloak flapping in the wind, and not daring to move from his perilous position, lest he should tumble headlong down the steep precipice of many hundred feet in depth.

The forts being now carried, I seized the hand of an officer to congratulate him on his escape; the next instant he was down with a horrible wound, and a ball grazed my left cheek.

Thus, in ten minutes, six companies assaulted a tremendous post, and carried three forts at the point of the bayonet. It was one of the beat contested fights I ever saw; but ten officers were killed and wounded, and nearly a hundred men. General Sir James Kempt, and his gallant aide-de-camp, the Honourable C. Gore; had urged their horses up the rocks with hats off, and were cheering us on while carrying the third fort; when the General was wounded in the wrist of the right arm.

The four companies in support had moved forward at a moderate pace and in good order, to succour us in case of need; but finding there was nothing more to be done at this point, and seeing a line of the enemy in front of a star fort, a few hundred yards distant; they became wild with impatience to share in the combat, and simultaneously burst into a run; and it was only by Sir James Kempt's galloping ahead of them that he could restrain their ardour. He was well aware the movement of the second brigade would entirely dispossess the enemy of La Petite la Rhune without further bloodshed.

From this post we had an admirable view of the fourth and seventh divisions, who had succeeded in capturing the fort opposite St. Barbe, and were now debouching on the rugged ground, and bringing up their right shoulders in succession to form a line of battle in front of the ridge of Sare. The second, third, and sixth divisions formed the right, coming down the pass of Maya.

The enemy's main position convexed in the centre, and extended about twelve miles, as the bird flew; but a greater distance to march, owing to the windings of roads, rivulets, and the steep and barren country lying towards their centre and left. Their right was posted in front of Saint Jean de Luz, amid fortified chateaux, farm-houses, villages, woods, and orchards, converted into formidable abattis, and partly defended by an inundation, and fifty pieces of heavy artillery. Their centre rested on the rocky heights of La Petite la Rhune, the ridge of Sare, and adjacent eminencies which were crowned with redoubts. Their left was stationed on the heights of Ainhoa on the right bank of the Nivelle, which was also strongly entrenched.

The extreme left of our army consisted of the first and fifth divisions, Lord Alymer's brigade, a corps of Spaniards, with artillery and two brigades of cavalry under General Hope to demonstrate and to guard the high road to Spain, while the centre and left of the army were employed in more active operations.

The firing and rolling of musketry were now vehement to our right towards the village of Sare. On the first retreat of the enemy, they had set fire to some hundreds of huts built of fern and wicker work, near the rocks of St. Antoine, but soon returned with drums beating the pas de charge, to endeavour to retake them from the Spaniards. The smoke, however, was so dense, owing to the wind blowing direct in their faces, that they were forced from the contest, more from the heat of the flames and downright suffocation than the good management of their antagonists, who, as usual, plied them with long shots.

As soon as the fourth and seventh divisions were well engaged with the enemy under General Beresford, aided by the third division moving to its left, who were combating and driving the enemy up the heights east of Sare, our division descended from La Petite la Rhune, left in front for the purpose of attacking the great redoubt in the centre, on the bare mountain of Esnau, near Ascain. It was defended on all sides by clouds of skirmishers, engaged with the Cacadores and rifles of our division. Here Sir Andrew Barnard fell pierced through the body with a musket-ball amongst the light troops. The rattling of small arms was incessant and very destructive on the 52nd regiment, under Sir John Colborne, which suffered a most severe loss while moving round, and to the rear of the large square redoubt. After some parleying, nearly six hundred of the 88th French, finding themselves forsaken by their main body, surrendered prisoners of war; but their commander gave way to the most bitter invectives.

After night-fall, the flashes of the fire-arms of General Hill's corps still brightly sparkled, while driving onwards and making their last efforts and discharges to decide the victory, and turn the left flank of the enemy, which obliged them during the night to evacuate St. Jean de Luz, and retire to Bayonne, leaving fifty pieces of cannon in their formidable lines in front of the former place. Field-marshal Wellington directed the attack of the right of our army against the left of the French.

At night some companies of our division were pushed into a valley on pic-quet; and at nine we observed the heather of the camp had caught fire, illu-minating the country for miles around, while the men and animals were seen gliding about, representing a sort of phantasmagoria. By degrees the fire reached the base of the hill and ignited a small forest; around two hours after midnight we were encompassed with a sheet of flames crackling and whizzing with terrific violence; and the heat was so overpowering that we were glad to cross a rivulet, to save ourselves from being consumed by this conflagration. To add to our night's misery, my companion was groaning from excessive pain caused by the rap over the knuckles given him while we were storming the forts.

At ten o'clock on the following day our division edged off to the right and crossed the Nivelle by a small stone bridge near St. Pe. The whole army moved forward in three columns, the right marching upon Souraide and Espelette and taking post on the left bank of the Nive, at Cambo, Ustaritz, and the vicinity, to watch the enemy on the right bank of that river; the centre on Arrauntz and Arbonne, and the left crossing the Nivelle at the town and vicinity of Saint Jean de Luz, and advancing through Guethary on Bidart, eight miles from Bayonne. In the afternoon it came on to rain, while we were marching through *le bois de St. Pe*. The roads were very deep, and we passed the night shivering and wallowing in the grass and mud of a saturated plan-tation.

The head quarters of the general-in-chief were now established at Saint Jean de Luz, an old town situated on the right bank of the river Nivelle, and within a few hundred yards of the sea coast. Through this town the high road runs from Spain to Bayonne, the latter place being strongly fortified and sit-uated at the junction of the Nive with the Adour. The enemy occupied the farmhouses and villas three miles in front of the fortress. A morass, which was only passable at two places covered an entrenched camp which was within cannon shot of the ramparts of Bayonne. The left of our army fronted the enemy, forming a line amidst chateaux, farmhouses, woods, heaths, plan-tations, hedges, swamps and ditches, as far as the sea-coast, the right being thrown back towards Ustaritz and Cambo, facing the French who lined the right bank of the Nive, as far as St. Jean Pied de Port. With the sea therefore on our left, the river Adour and Bayonne in our front, the river Nive on our right, and the lofty mountains of the Pyrenees at our backs — it may fairly be said that the army were in a cul de sac. The great strength of this frontier seems, particularly during the winter, hardly to be understood; for beyond the river Nive many rapid rivers cut across, and intersect the muddy country and clayey roads, so as to make offensive operations very difficult.

The advanced posts of our first brigade were in a church behind the village of Arcangues, at a chateau two hundred yards east of it, and at a cottage half a mile further to the right, situated close to a lake, on the other side of which was the chateau of Chenie, on a rising ground, and enclosed by the small plantation of Berriots, through which a road runs towards Ustaritz. The second brigade prolonged their line towards a deep valley which separated them from the fifth division, holding the plateau, in the neighbourhood of a chateau on the high road to Bayonne, six or seven miles in front of St. Jean de Luz.

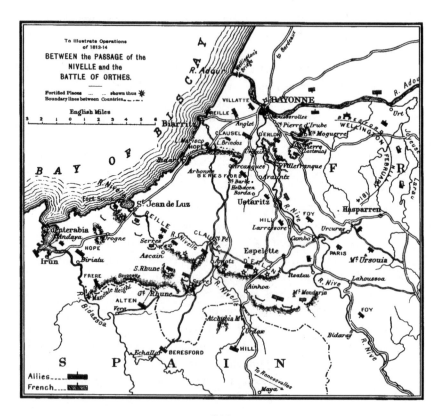

Fighting alongside Cooke was Lieutenant John McLean. Commissioned in the 43rd Light Infantry in March 1810, MacLean sailed to the Peninsula in 1812 and had seen action at Vittoria, and during the crossing of the Bidassoa. He described the Battle of the Nivelle in a letter, written on 12 December 1813, which was printed in Sir Richard Levinge's *Historical Records of the Forty-Third Regiment*, published in London in 1868.

On the night of the 9th we received orders to hold ourselves ready to march at an early hour the following morning, to assault the position of the enemy on La petite la Rhune. Breakfast was ordered by 2 a.m. which we managed to eat most heartily; and having some remarkably thick American biscuits, Madden observed that their thickness would turn a bullet aside, at the same time putting one into the breast of his jacket. Never was prediction more completely verified, for early in the day the biscuit was shattered to pieces, turning the direction of the bullet from as gallant and true a heart as ever beat under a British uniform. Another bullet passed through Madden's left arm immediately afterwards.

The regiment having moved off about 3 o'clock, ascended the side of the mountain, halting within a short distance of La Petite la Rhune, and close to our left we saw and passed the Rifles, lying down in close column, covered by their white blankets, in the faint light resembling a flock of sheep much more than grim warriors prepared for the strife. The most perfect silence had been enjoined, and the 43rd were directed to lie down in close column to await the signal of attack — the firing of a third gun from the right.

We heard the French drums beating to arms, and even could distinguish voices, although not in sight of them; for being on the slope of a hill, we had no idea we were so near or about to attack. Sir James Kempt, who commanded the 1st Brigade of the Light Division, ordered that two companies of the regiment should lead in skirmishing order, followed by a support of four in line under Lieut. Colonel Napier, and a reserve of three companies under Lieut. Colonel Duffy. Major Brock's and Captain Murchison's companies were to lead the advance in extended order.

The sunrise in those regions is most sudden, for darkness is dispelled by a burst of glowing light as the sun clears the head of a high mountain, and startles the beholder with its glorious brightness. Such was its appearance as it glanced on the recumbent troops, and sparkled from their bayonets along the arms piled by companies that eventful morning. The next moment the sound of a gun followed by others was heard, and every ear was on the alert to count each shot. The men were on their feet in an instant, and the words "Stand to your arms" being given, each soldier seized his Brown Bess. The Rifles folded their blankets and moved off to their left. General Kempt mounted his horse, and said, "Now, 43rd, let me see what you will do this morning;" and pointing to an entrenchment on a rising ground in front to the left of the regiment lined with French infantry; gave the order to advance and carry it; and then await the arrival of the support before an attempt was to be made on the stone redoubts on the ridge of rocks on the top of La Petite la Rhune.

The companies then extending and bringing their right shoulders forward, were at once in fire, and after descending a short distance and crossing a piece of marshy ground, made a rush for the breastwork, which was quickly evacuated by the enemy; but not before they had by their sharp practice dropped a few of their assailants, who had scarcely returned their fire, so intent were they on rushing at the entrenchment. On clearing the breastwork, we brought our left shoulders forward to face redoubt No. 1, and as we were directed to wait for the four companies, we took such shelter as some scattered rocks afforded at about fifty or sixty yards from the first redoubt. The enemy made our quarters pretty hot, as they when firing were well covered, which our men perceiving were endeavouring to check by aiming at their heads when opportunities offered; but, to avoid exposing themselves, they preferred firing at the support and reserve, although not so close, for thus they had a far better chance of killing and not being hit lay our men, and consequently could fire coolly. The redoubts were built of rough stones, but had no cannon.

Captain Murchison and myself got alongside of a flat piece of rock within about forty yards of the redoubt, and as they could see part of us, they made the rock smoke with their shots. Captain Murchison raised his head to look over, and instantly his face assumed a lucid appearance as if choking. I inquired what was the matter, when he with difficulty said, "he was struck in the neck and must see a doctor !" but in the meantime, should the support arrive, he desired me to take on the company. Shortly after the surgeon examined him, and found that the bullet had got entangled in his neckcloth and had run round his neck. A sergeant pointed out better cover about twenty-five yards nearer the redoubt, to which we both went; and I borrowed his fusee and fired several shots at the heads of the French, the sergeant loading for me. While so employed, Colonel Napier and the support came sweeping up behind us, on which I gave the order to advance, and we all dashed forward with a cheer. Napier, boiling with courage, and being withal very active, attempted to scale the walls without observing the bayonet points

246

over his head; and, being rather short-sighted, would certainly have been very roughly handled had not James Considine and myself laid hold of the skirts of his jacket and pulled him back, for which we received anything but thanks. We of course apologised to Colonel Napier for the liberty we had taken, for he was very wrath at the time. We then pointed out an easier ascent for him, and assisted each other over the wall. To show the danger he was in at the moment, I was even under the necessity of striking a bayonet up with my sword, though they were giving way, as a hint that we were coming over in spite of them. The hint was taken, and a free passage left.

On getting inside I saw a French officer kneeling with his arm raised begging for quarter, and his head and face covered with blood. I told one of the men to take care of him, and proceeded through the gate at the rear, following the retiring enemy towards the second redoubt on the ridge of rocks, similarly constructed to the one we had just taken. I then met Cooke and Considine, and we consulted what was best to be done, as we had not a sufficient number of men with us to assault the second redoubt, most of them having joined the regiment below the rocks. We were then about 100 yards from it, and exposed to its fire. I proposed to Considine to follow a path leading along the face of the ridge of rock, which I expected would lead to the redoubt, and if I found it practicable would not return. I had judged correctly as to the direction of the path, for it led direct on the redoubt in question; but although the enemy must have seen me distinctly they did not fire in my direction: I suppose from seeing me alone, and being occupied by the others who were gathering for a rush. I quickly discovered they were about to quit the redoubt by the gate behind, for some were taking that direction, and before I could get close up they were off.

On reaching the top of the ridge again, I found that I was on the flank of a long trench, filled with a regiment of French infantry, but high above it. The entrenchment was cut across a nearly level green, approaching which I perceived a portion of the 43rd advancing in column under General Kempt, and the French having fired a volley, I observed he had been wounded, and his A.D.C. Captain Gore (now Honourable General Sir Charles Gore), K.C.B., binding a handkerchief quickly round his arm.

The order to charge was then given, a British cheer followed; a line of levelled steel showed what the enemy might expect. I saw them waver, then spring out of the entrenchment and retire down the hill at a rapid pace.

This had no sooner taken place than I observed on the other side, and also below me, a French officer waving his sword and encouraging his men to advance and retake the redoubt, but he could not induce them to follow. One of the 43rd skirmishers rushed at him with his bayonet at the charge, and in spite of his attempts to defend himself with his sword ran him through, and then returned to the level ground behind the trench the regiment had carried in such gallant style.

Gore then rode up to me with orders from the General to stop the pursuit on which the men were eagerly bent; and it was with considerable difficulty that their ardour was checked and the men halted, for they were rushing after the enemy like greyhounds, so excited were they.

The French, finding that they were no longer pressed, retired more tranquilly but still in confusion, our men firing on them as they descended the hill to some huts forming an old bivouac. I observed an officer on the way separate himself from the mob of fugitives, which removed him from our line of fire, and walk quietly along: on which a short stout soldier asked my permission to follow and take him prisoner. I consented, provided no one accompanied him; and although his musket had been discharged he would not wait to reload, but ran forward. He had not gone above 300 or 400 yards, when he overtook the officer and called on him to surrender. The Frenchman presented a pistol on turning round, which the 43rd man observing, and being then very near, poised his musket over his head, and pitched it with such precision that the bayonet penetrated his thigh and brought him to the ground, where he lay at the mercy of his adversary, who merely took possession of the pistol, and, what he considered of greater value, a flask of brandy. On rejoining his company, after offering it to me, he gratified his heated comrades with a sip as far as the supply would go. Both these French officers, who fell under our bayonets, were removed to Vera, and I was told were doing well.

I now learned that Considine had his thigh broken by a bullet, and that Murchison, shortly after the doctor had examined him, was struck by another musket ball, which carried him off in twenty-four hours.

After about a quarter of an hour's halt the Division moved on, the Rifles and 52nd leading: and some of the former were sent down the hill to drive the French from the bivouac to which they had returned. This was quickly done, but the French being reinforced again advanced; the drummers beating the *pas de charge* to retake the huts. The Rifles, however, were too wily, for, perceiving that the wind blew in the enemy's faces, they fired the huts, which with the straw therein blazed and smoked to such a degree that the French were obliged to relinquish their intention.

The sight at this moment was truly grand: we looked from our vantage ground over an extent of about twenty miles occupied by two gallant armies, of which the Light Division composed the centre of the British. To the right the pass of Maya and St. Jean de Pied de Port, to the left St. Jean de Luz, and from each extremity could be distinctly traced, by the flashes of fire and rising smoke, the advance of our troops and the gradual retreat of the French, offering an obstinate resistance at every favourable spot. But the British were not to be denied, and went in to win; and in short carried everything before them, notwithstanding the gallant resistance they met with.

While looking around, William Freer came up and inquired anxiously for his brother Edward. Seeing that something was amiss, he turned round, saying, "I see how it is," and started off to the rear, where his worst fears were too soon confirmed: his brother having been shot through the head. Both brothers were fine courageous fellows, much liked in the regiment; each had been wounded, the elder had lost an arm at Badajoz. The younger frequently told me had a presentiment he would be killed in the attack of La Petite la Rhune. He happened also to be in the last company that went into action that day, when his presentiment was fulfilled, to the great sorrow of all his brother officers and the entire regiment.

The Division then crossing a narrow valley ascended the nearest hill, driving in the French skirmishers, and at the top came upon a fine star-fort of earth, surrounded by a deep ditch containing about 700 men; and although the 52nd attacked it with their accustomed determination, they were repulsed with loss. The Commandant was then called upon to surrender, which he at first refused to do; but seeing that he could not defend the work for any length of time, he agreed: provided he was not to be marched to the rear by Spanish or Portuguese troops. This being accepted, the redoubt was given up and the French disarmed.

This may be said to have ended the day's fighting.

Twenty-two-year-old Surgeon Walter Henry joined the army in 1811 and sailed to Portugal that same year. By the time of the Battle of the Nivelle Henry had seen action at Badajoz, Vittoria and in the Pyrenees. The grisly cases which Henry dealt with as a young army surgeon can best be imagined, but he nevertheless recorded his experiences in his 2-volume journal, *Events of a Military Life*, published in London in 1843. At the Battle of the Nivelle, Henry's regiment, the 66th, took part in the attack on the French left, on the heights behind the river to the west of Ainhoa.

A full hour before daylight, on the 10th of November, did we wait for the firing of a gun on the extreme left, which was a signal for our advance, whilst high feelings were working in many bosoms. After the lapse of three centuries, the banner of St. George was once more to be unfurled in Gascony.

As soon as the long expected echoes rolled amongst the mountains, the column was set in motion and crossed the frontier, whilst a heavy firing was going on to our left. We marched about two leagues, until within cannon shot of the fortified heights above the small stream of the Nivelle, which had the honour of giving its name to the battle. Here we halted in front of a very strong part of the fortified mountain, which was allotted to our Division to storm; and as soon as the Sixth Division, immediately on our left, had done their work, and driven the enemy from a large redoubt, General Byng's Brigade pushed up the steep abbatied height at one place, whilst the Light Companies of the Division and the two other British Brigades assailed it at other points. When the leading regiment of Byng's Brigade reached the plateau on the top, they looked such a handful, that a French column opposed to them deployed into line and prepared to charge; but though I saw their officers cheering them on gallantly, they would not advance, but kept up an irregular fire; which, being badly aimed, did less mischief than it ought to have done. When more force came up, and the Brigade, most gallantly led by Byng, formed and advanced in line, the enemy's line wavered — not metaphorically, but as I myself witnessed — visibly and materially; and after two or three strange oscillations they broke and ran.

There still remained a field redoubt, with two guns, in possession of the enemy on the extreme left of the position; these were large ship carronades, and being loaded with double charges of grape, did much execution among our people. Lieut-Colonel Leith, 31st Regiment, Lieut-Colonel Nicol, 66th, and Ensign Dunn of the same Corps, at the head of a few men, charged this work and carried it in good style. Indeed the three officers took it themselves; for they cleared the ditch with a running leap, and dropped down amongst the garrison before a man could enter to assist them. As they leaped in, the Artillery officer and most of his men jumped out, but not with impunity; for Leith, a Hercules in figure and strength, knocked the red-headed officer down with a brickbat, but his cap saved his skull, and he managed to scramble up and get away. His Sergeant, a formidable looking person, "bearded like the pard," was not so lucky — he dislocated his shoulder in the leap, was taken prisoner, and I set his arm to rights immediately afterwards.

This extensive position was an enormous entrenched camp, on the plateau at the top of which were several lines of clean and regular huts. As soon as our different columns succeeded in penetrating to the top, they set the huts on fire, as did some of the French troops on quitting them. Thus we had a splendid blaze along the summit, to the extent of two or three miles, as a bonfire of triumph, kindled by our enemies' own hands.

We lost a good many people in storming this mountain. The Light Companies of the Division, who were up first, suffered severely — every officer was hit, and Major Ackland, 57th, who commanded them, was killed. The death of his pretty spaniel that had during the action amused itself by barking at the dust the balls raised as they struck the ground preceded its master's fall only by a few minutes.

Our time was occupied professionally till late in the evening when we had done, and were in quest of some refreshment, a well-dressed woman accosted us, apparently in a state of the greatest distress and distraction. She told us she lived in the village of Espelette, immediately under us, at the bottom of the hill; that Morillo's Spaniards had entered the place, and were beginning to burn and plunder, and her husband had run away and left his family, from dread of the Spaniards; and that she had come up the hill alone, trusting in English generosity, to beg for protection. She implored us, therefore, to accompany her home, as our presence would save her helpless family from the Spaniards. This poor woman appeared so distressed, and was so importunate, that we asked for permission, and accompanied her to her house. The town was in the greatest alarm and confusion, and part of it on fire; but, when this was known, a regiment was sent down from camp to extinguish the fire and turn out the Spaniards. A party of plunderers visited our residence, but instantly decamped when they found it in possession of British officers.

Poor Madame Dupre's family was also labouring under distress of a peculiarly severe nature, from another cause; and in meeting accidentally with two English surgeons, good lady was piously pleased to consider the circumstance as a special ordination of Providence. By a most unlucky fatality, Jacqueline, one of her daughters, during the action on the hill, happened to be looking out of the window listening to the firing, when a grape-shot from a gun in the redoubt last taken, which was turned on the enemy as they ran down to the town, miserably fractured her elbow joint. It was represented to the mother that amputation was inevitable to save the poor girl's life, and the sooner the better. After a sad scene, and not without great difficulty, the patient gave her consent, and I took off the arm the same evening, and am happy to add that she soon recovered.

It would be a graceful finale to state that Mademoiselle Jacqueline was very beautiful. Truth forbids this; but she was amiable and grateful, and after she had recovered the first dreadful shock of such a loss, she presented me with a handsome purse of her own netting, as a fee, adding affectingly, "C'est le dernier ouvrage de ma pauvre main !"

Commanding the 2nd Provisional Battalion was George Ridout Bingham, of the 2/53rd. Part of the 4th Division, Bingham's battalion took part in the attack on the very centre of the French line at Sare. One week after the battle, he wrote to his father from the village of Ascain, which by then had been ravaged by Spanish troops, keen to avenge the outrages perpetuated by French troops in their own country. His letter covers the Battle of the Nivelle itself and his movements during the following few days.

We have been so much occupied the last few days, that I have not time to write to any one, but now being comfortably established I hope for the winter in the Cure's house in this village, I will try to give you an account of all that happened to us after we broke up from our mountain bivouac on the 10th. which we were not sorry to do, the lateness of the season together with the cold and the wet, making it anything but agreeable. Before daybreak then, on that day, we started, it having been determined to force Soult's strong line of entrenchments on the Nivelle, and to establish ourselves on the plain; this movement was of an extended nature from the sea on our left nearly to St. Jean Pied de Port on our right, which was to be the point of attack, our left being only a feint, but as this movement was of so extended a nature, I shall not attempt to give you any account beyond what actually happened to us on the right of the centre, leaving you to make out from the Great Lord's despatch the position of the whole.

Two or three days enabled us to get up three Brigades of Artillery (18 pieces) to the rear of the wood where we were encamped by roads supposed to be perfectly impassable to carriages of any description. Operations were to commence at dawn by opening a fire on the redoubt of Sarre, the same at which the French had been at work strengthening since the 13th. of October, when they retook it from the Spaniards and which was to all appearance very strong. As soon as the fire of the artillery had made an adequate impression the Battalion which I commanded was to carry it by storm. Accordingly leaving our packs behind and carrying bags filled with leaves to facilitate our descent into the ditch, we moved off, and, suffering but little from the fire of the work, established ourselves under cover of the hill within thirty paces of it. There was another redoubt to our right within four pounder range which part of the 7th., Division were to carry, and before their attack began we had the fire on us; to save our people from this teasing fire before the artillery had made any impression on the redoubt, we jumped up and dashed at the gorge of it, but found the French had been too quick for us. We were only in time to secure a few prisoners who were making their escape. Thus this work which had appeared so formidable was taken with a very trifling loss within half an hour after the commencement of the action. The next point to be attacked was the village beyond which was a height, defended by two large redoubts, with an abbatis at the foot of the hill. Sarre was soon in our possession, and being exposed to a cannonade from the heights I got my Battalion in column behind the largest house in the place waiting further operations; in this house had assembled all the better description of women of the village, and whilst the cannonade was destroying the back part of the building and offices in the rear, we were chattering with the ladies in the front, whose tongues ran faster than the roll of musketry on every side of us. We were not delayed long but soon moved out from our cover to assist in the attack on the abbatis which the 27th carried in great style. I had forgot to mention that I left an officer in the great house at Sarre, to protect its inmates, who justly dreaded the followers more than the Army itself. I heard afterwards they were very thankful for my protection. As for ourselves we continued to push on not meeting with that firm resistance we had reason to expect from the nature of the ground and the strength of the defences. The redoubt immediately behind Sarre having been evacuated, we pushed on beyond it cutting off from their own Army a Battalion of the 88th., who had stoutly defended a redoubt on the left from several attacks of the Light division following the enemy close; our Light company took from them, a light six pounder and about this time Fehrszen whose conduct through the day had been most conspicuous was struck down by a spent musket ball. For a short time we lamented him as dead, until looking to the front I discovered him as active and as gay as ever, leading his company on in gallant style. About mid day we brought up on a height from which we had a splendid though distant view of the position of both Armies; being almost in the rear of the French right, and apparently as near if not nearer St. Jean de Luz than they were. The battle raged furiously on our right and several of these redoubts defied the efforts of our old friends the 6th., Division to take them. In our front and just below us was a bridge over the Nivelle, which the French had not destroyed, and we remained wondering why we were not ordered to force this pass which would have brought us in rear of the right wing of the French. Probably the protracted resistance on our right prevented our making this movement, which would indeed have been decisive.

We had three divisions besides Spaniards at the point, mustering strong, notwithstanding the casualties of the morning. The loss in our Battalion amounted to one sergeant, four rank and file killed, three officers forty-one rank and file wounded. Towards evening the 6th and 2nd Divisions obtained possession of the left of the enemy's position and the firing ceased all along the line. Some time after dark, when I had laid myself down comfortably amongst the heather for the night, I was roused by an aide-de-camp to tell me to take possession of the village of St. Pe at the foot of our hill and rather to the right; so grumbling at the disturbance and the darkness of the night off we set to find the place. It was eleven o'clock before we got there and having as well as we could, found out the avenues to the place and posted picquets Fehrszen and myself took up our quarters at a large farm house and threw ourselves down on the sweetest quarters at a large farm house and threw ourselves down on the sweetest cock of hay I ever remember to have met with; it perfumed our cloaks for a week after. The inhabitants had absconded and there was nothing to be had in an empty house. About two in the morning we heard some cocks crowing under a tub. We soon had them in the pot; and excellent chicken broth we had for breakfast. Before the day dawned we got under arms and began to look over our quarters, which were very good. We found also a surgeon who had been at St. Domingo and who spoke English very well. Soult had ordered the inhabitants to retire but this order had been but partially obeyed, and of the absentees, after daylight many began to return. From these we heard the French had retired to their entrenched camp near Bayonne. Here we stayed lounging about till about noon, when off we set to join the remainder of the Division on the route towards Bayonne. About sunset we fell in with the enemy and were ordered to drive back their pic-quets, which we did without loss, and we took up our ground in the Bois de St. Pe, where as the night was cold our people suffered severely. The tents had not come up and our men had taken off their packs the more easily to carry the redoubts the day before, and we were without blankets. The fuel fortu-nately was abundant. The 12th we halted; a fine day, quite warm. We got up our packs and blankets with a firm resolve on my part, never to part with them again under any of the exigencies of the service. Our tents too came and we were happy fellows.

The left of the Army pushed on towards Bayonne, from which we were not far distant. The night was dreadful, such a storm of wind, rain, thunder, and lightening we had not experienced for some time. I had placed my tent on a very tempting spot of the green sward, on a flat surface which made me overlook the circumstance of it's being in the run of the Valley; in a moment the flood rushed down, and tent and bed and self were washed away. The remainder of the night was passed in collecting my floating goods and chattels. The next day (14th) afforded no opportunity of drying our soaked articles. It was wet and we sat shivering and shaking and hoping and wishing for cantonments and speculating on what our next movement would be; looking like fowls on a rail, in a wet day, cold and miserable. The 15th was only showery, and in a fair interval I got as far as the General's who had a sort of a house. The Portuguese Brigade having gone into cantonments gave us great hopes we should soon follow. Do not wonder we wished for the shelter of a house, the Bois de St. Pe in the middle of a wet November held out no great inducement for the most sanguine to long to keep the field. The night was again dreadful with torrents of rain and a heavy gale of wind. I had got clear of my smooth valley and although on rough ground stood the night out well. Fortunately we were well off in eatables and drinkables which was a great consolation; and I contrived to entertain three officers at dinner under circumstances far from uncomfortable. On the 17th the joyful news of cantonments arrived, and starting at eight, through a road up to the knees in mud, we arrived at this place at three in the afternoon, but our baggage did not get here till after dark; and now snugly settled at the Cure's comfortable house, we hope all our fatigue and toil is at an end till better weather will enable us to enjoy taking the field again, and we speculate the beating Soult got in the last affair, and the advance of the Allies in the north may keep him on the defensive till the weather will enable us to open the campaign under more auspicious circumstances; that is to say as far as individual comfort is concerned, for I think in England you will say we have done our duty in this instance and be satisfied for some short time to come. Adieu.

But the fighting in 1813 was not done yet, for the year closed with yet another victory for Wellington, albeit a hard-fought one. The Battle of the Nive, fought over three days from 10 to 12 December, came as a result of Soult's counter-attack, his men sallying forth from their positions around the strongly-defended town of Bayonne to surprise Wellington's blockading troops. The French were thrown back only after some severe and confused fighting across a wide front. On 13 December Soult attacked once again, this time choosing the 14,000-strong force under Rowland Hill that had become isolated on the right bank of the river Nive following the sweeping away of the pontoon bridge that connected his force with the main Allied army on the left bank. Successive attacks by Soult almost succeeded, and Hill was forced to use up all his reserves. In a very close-fought battle, Hill succeeded in throwing back the French just as Wellington arrived on the scene, the pontoon bridge having been restored. Seventeen-hundred Allied casualties were sustained during the battle, which has become known as the Battle of St Pierre after the village that lay at the northern end of Hill's position.

On the left of Hill's position at the Battle of St Pierre was Pringle's brigade, amongst which was the 1/28th. William Thornton Keep, who had saved one of the regiment's colours at Maya, was with the regiment that day and was badly wounded in the action. In a letter written to his mother on 28 December 1813, published in *In the Service of the King*, he described the fighting and how he came to be wounded.

This information had a most surprising effect upon the men, who turned out with the greatest steadiness, and fell into their ranks, so that when I marched them up to the Regiment they were in perfect order. The artillery was reverberating around us, and we were moved forward directly, under the direction of an Aide de Camp, for as the light increased, and day advanced, it became evident the French had commenced an attack upon us.

Captain Carol being ordered away, I was the only officer going into action with the Company, and when the Regiment had halted for a few minutes our Adjutant passing down the ranks told Col. Belson in a loud voice there was no officer but myself with it, to which the Colonel replied in the same loud tone "Then let Mr Keep command the Company". This was complimentary, and I felt the importance of it, but unluckily discovered I had left my sword at my billet, and sent Robert directly to request Alexander would send me one, which he did; and then we advanced again forward; and here Col. Ross and General Pringle, both on horseback, were quite close to me, the Colonel having a sore throat with flannel bandages round it, and the General in loud conversation with him about the picquets. We came then upon an open space with a bank formed by the side of this wood, where we halted a long time; and I never was more surprised to find whilst we were seated here, and the men eating what they had about them for a breakfast, that random shots were flying among us, one of which a soldier by the side of me took from amidst the brushes in his pack. Looking over this bank into the wood, I perceived men skirmishing from behind the trees, but the Regiment were acting so completely under orders that no one thought of interfering in what was going on, and as if it was no business of ours to notice it.

256

Presently however Sir Rowland's Aide de Camp, Captain Egerton, prick-ing his steed gently forward over rough ground, intimated that we were to advance. In a moment the whole Regiment entered the wood under Col. Belson's command, and here beneath trees scattered at distances about, with fallen leaves up to our ankles, we moved forward in a very good line, the skirmishers of the enemy retreating very slowly, and turning their backs most unconcerned to us.

We came at last to the extremity of this wood, where the Regiment stopped, as there was a somewhat steep descent in front, and open fields, with a wood on higher ground opposite to us, occupied by the French with artillery. The other companies of the Regiment were partially concealed and sheltered by some of these trees growing on the edge of this bank, but only one or two were near the left of my Company, and of course we were immediately exposed to view, and a cannon shot struck the breast of my left hand man, and the breath of life was wrested from him with a dismal shriek. The rank closed up, and our firing directly opened upon the numerous skirmishers crossing this field. In the centre of it was a small house, having only one win-dow over the door, and here the most dreadful hand to hand fighting was going on between the French and some Portuguese; and such as was terrible to behold. In the meanwhile we did not interfere, but encompassed this small field on three sides of it, a French close column being in our front, and Captain Hartman with a company of the 28th on the right hand side of this square with the distant open country opposite to him in front. Nor did the French skirmishers run there to give any assistance, but were the bravest men I ever saw, for they retreated most leisurely, though now receiving the fire of our whole line, returning it as they retired, to the column opposite, across this little field. Many of my men were killed or wounded in a short time, and Ensign Waring was for a few minutes by the side of me before he was struck, and Nelson on my left, firing like Robinson Crusoe from a tree, with men loading the muskets for him, as he is an excellent shot, but he was soon wounded, and then came my turn from the enemy as I suppose on the oppo-site height, and more distant, though the French column there I did not see deploy (or form into line) but it could not have come from the skirmishers, for they being below me, the shot would not have descended to my neck. The bullet struck me down, and covered me with the crimson fluid, spurting like a fountain from my mouth, whilst I was laying on my back. The blow was severe, it was like a cart wheel passing over my head, but this was instanta-neous only, for all pain ceased, and I was left in full possession of my senses, with the warm drops falling upon my face. After a minute or two I got again upon my legs and went only a few paces to the rear before I saw our Assistant Surgeon under a tree, attending some soldiers there. He directly examined the wounds I had received, and cut the ball from my neck, and told me I was safe, but he had scarcely uttered the words when a cannon shot struck the top of the tree, reminding us both that we were still in the way of them, so that at once we moved further into the wood, where his attention was called to others, and I left him to proceed, but had not gone far before I came to a farm house in the large kitchen of which the wounded had come before me, and one or two young women ran directly to assist me, which they had a very good opportunity of doing, for there was a large boiler on the fire, with jugs of warm water and several dishes, into the latter I was surprised at the quantity of blood that flowed from my mouth, and it was some time before I could remove it effectually from my face and hair and eyes, for my cap had fallen off and rolled away, and at the moment I got up I couldn't find it, and the shots were flying too quickly to look for it.

The wounded in this kitchen were seated against the walls, and none apparently requiring such aid as myself. When I had cleansed my face I left the farm house, and proceeded to a small collection of cottages very near me. Descending a small declivity in front of this village, I perceived women assembled at the doors, and here I met my hostess of the previous day, that poor distressed creature, who I had been up all night with to protect from our soldiers, who had got drunk and staved her wine casks. She lifted up her hands in malediction upon the author of all these calamities at the sight of me, covered as I was with blood still flowing over my clothes and hands, and without a hat, and in a fit of distraction punning upon his name and calling him no Bonaparte mais malaparte, with many Jesu Maries! in commiseration of my misfortune. This procured me immediate reception into a comfortable but small dwelling with some kind young women, where I was followed by Dr Dakers who came very anxiously to see me, and carefully looked to my wounds, advising me to get to bed. In such a scene of confusion, I was glad enough to do so, you may be sure, as night was now approaching. The place was so crowded that the front room of this cottage was immediately filled with very boisterous artillerymen, and the females were glad to shut themselves up with me in the adjoining back room, where however there was only one comfortable bed and bedstead. These three young women therefore spread some clothes upon the ground at the foot of it for themselves and insisted upon my occupying it. They were in some uneasiness at being discovered, bolted the door and placed chairs against it. This I found they had good reason for, as the artillerymen carousing began to talk very loud, and as

I lay I heard such things related by them as fully assured me it was no more than a necessary precaution. At night these good females came in turns to my bedside to attend upon me, as the blood at intervals bubbled forth so fast it threatened to choke me. I was quite speechless with the swelling, not knowing what was the extent of the injury, and my mouth in that state that I didn't dare to move my tongue, even to ascertain it, except by degrees.

In the morning Robert came to me, with his arm in a bandage, having been wounded, but not dangerously (Officers' servants are always with their masters when in action) and he procured me a forage cap, and by the authorities I was furnished with a horse and left my good angels behind me, to meet again with kind people here, where Wolfe and I are now residing. Thus my dear Mother you may fancy all the rest that has occurred to me, in the endeavour to swallow food to strengthen me, and give good hopes of my speedy restoration. As I cannot talk, Wolfe does his utmost to amuse me, and has a book of anecdotes to refer to, but some of his own are equally entertaining, and we have newspapers from England occasionally, where I read of nothing but rejoicings for victories. When the public mind is thus occupied they little think of the mangled heaps that are stretched upon the field of battle. I am told that in which we contributed to the late glorious achievement was so covered with the French and Portuguese slain that it was a grievous task to bury them, and exceeding anything before witnessed.

How strange it appears that all these horrors should arise from the ambition of an individual, when he himself might his "quietus make with a bare bodkin", an acre of ground suffice to maintain him, and a few feet of it to hide his remains from the world. The French officers on the banks of the Nive were kept in great ignorance of passing events. To enlighten them a little we threw over the papers containing patches of Bonaparte's defeats. The French here certainly show no signs of attachment to him, and without that how unenviable must the condition of such potentates be.

I can add nothing more at present my dear Mother, but to request you will make your mind perfectly easy about me, and to express a hope of getting home soon, as I am now, with the loss of baggage and in my present state, quite hors de Combat and only fit to return to the 2nd Battalion and Old England again. The Spanish Officers here invited us last night to a Ball, but of course we couldn't accept it, and besides had nothing gay to sport in, as we could wish as British officers.

We have no news from the Army. Everything quite in status quo. Marshal Soult is not recovered yet from his late defeat. We hope to see a good account of our gallant Division, but shan't I suppose receive the Dispatch for some time.

William Keep survived the wound but played no further part in the war. Despite his wound, he lived to the ripe old age of 92.

The year of 1813 saw more fighting than any other year in the Peninsula. It was also the most successful. After having started in May on the Portuguese border, Wellington had defeated the French at Vittoria, driven them back over the Pyrenees, had invaded France and had successfully bottled up the French in the fortress of Bayonne, leaving Soult with little option but to continue his retreat deeper into France.

CHAPTER FIFTEEN

THE FINAL BATTLES: ORTHES AND TOULOUSE

On the morning of 23 February 1814 British troops crossed the Adour river west of Bayonne to begin their encirclement of the town. The operation was yet another daring one, with small groups of soldiers being ferried across the river under cover of rockets, which for once proved very effective weapons. Indeed, one rocket landed slap bang in the middle of a French column that was marching along the sand dunes to attack the small British force that had crossed to the far side of the river. The town was the blockaded north and south by Wellington's men.

Marshal Soult and the main French field army had already left Bayonne, however, leaving behind a garrison of around 14,000 men under General Thouvenot. The town was too strong to be taken by regular siege, and in any case there was little point in besieging the place as Soult's army had already gone east. It was the French Army itself that had to be dealt with, and so, while the 1st and 5th Divisions settled down to blockade Bayonne, the main Allied field army marched east in pursuit of Soult.

There followed a series of small actions as the French turned to dispute the crossings at several rivers that lay in their path. The Bidouze, Saison, Joyeuse and Pau, were all crossed after initial French resistance. The sharpest fight came at Garris where Wellington famously ordered his men to 'take the hill before dark.'

Wellington finally caught up with Soult at Orthes, a small town on the Gave de Pau. Soult positioned his 36,000 men along the top of a ridge that ran along the Dax–Orthes road, and in the town of Orthes itself. The position was marked by a series of spurs that jutted out from the main ridge. It was this ridge that Wellington's men attacked on the cold and frosty morning of 27 February.

The battle involved Wellington's infantry in a series of bloody attacks on the main French position, which Soult's men defended with great tenacity. After all, they were now fighting on home soil. Nevertheless, Wellington's men were not to be denied and eventually the 3rd and

Light Divisions managed to establish themselves on the main road, a move which threatened to cut the French Army in two. In fact, those defending the French right, fearing they would be cut off from the rest of the army, broke and fled to the north, leaving Wellington with another victory. The price of victory was not cheap, however, to which a further 2,100 casualties testified.

The French right flank was anchored upon the small village of St Boes, against which Wellington directed the 4th Division. The fighting here was as fierce as any other point on the battlefield, and indeed, the Allied attacks were continually repulsed by a determined enemy. Sergeant John Spencer Cooper, of the 7th (Royal) Fusiliers, was amongst those engaged with the French at very close quarters. Indeed, the Battle of Orthes featured genuine hand-to-hand fighting amongst the streets and houses of St Boes. Cooper described his day in his book *Rough Notes of Seven Campaigns*.

It was surprising that General Soult did not try to prevent our passage of the last mentioned river. Perhaps he wished us to get entangled among those streams, and then he would have a chance of giving us a thrashing; but Wellington was more cautious in all that he undertook than to risk the lives of his men without a prospect of victory.

The artillery having dashed past, our regiment was ordered to move to the left, in order to flank the enemy's right, and drive in the outposts. We directly surprised a piquet behind a farmhouse. They were busy cooking; but their bugler roused them, and they fell back firing briskly. In the flat below, the contest was sharp between the French skirmishers and ours. The main body of the enemy occupied a steep ridge with numerous artillery, which blazed away while we were massing and closing on them. Our company was posted behind a large building, and commenced firing in rapid bopeep fashion. Some of our men in the meantime broke into the house, and finding a store of wine, handed it out copiously to the combatants, so that the game was "Drink and fire, fire and drink." Others were engaged in stoning and bagging the wandering astonished poultry.

Tired of inaction, Sergeant Simpson, who was wounded, as before mentioned, on the heights of Pamplona, shouted, "Come, let us charge these fellows!" Away he and most of the company went double quick, and drove the enemy from their hiding places: but poor Simpson received a shot which laid him dead. Receiving a reinforcement, the enemy drove our men back, and stripped our wounded of their knapsacks, etc. It was here that wicked man fell with both his legs broken who in my hearing several years before said, "I don't care a d—m for Jesus Christ." He died of his wounds at Orthes.

From behind the house I was sent with a party to make a circuit farther to the left, in search of French skirmishers that might be skulking behind hedges, etc. In our round we came to a deserted farmhouse. My companions would enter for plunder. I warned them of their danger, and moved on. While they were rummaging the house, Lord Wellington and his Staff passed; but he being occupied with things of greater moment, did not notice us. We joined our company where two roads met, and had hardly taken breath before some of the enemy rushed up one of the lanes and opened fire upon us. Our captain turning round said sharply, "Give those rascals a charge." In an instant a few of us jumped over a hedge and at them. But they cut like rabbits, and we after them headlong. During the chase my bayonet flew off: I stopped not to pick it up, but plunged into a wood, firing as fast as I could, till my trigger finger was swollen as to be nearly useless.

Again and again the enemy rallied; but were as often repulsed. Now a pause ensued, which generally indicated a coming storm. Presently on came a long line of red jackets at quick step, a little to our right, and when within eighty or a hundred yards of the enemy, poured a terrible and prolonged fire upon them. This was answered by the French until the combatants were completely enshrouded in smoke.

The scattering of the powder cloud showed the British closing on the foe; but they avoided the shock by going to the right about in great haste.

The right wing of our army was equally successful; and the enemy hurried from the field in order to gain the great high road. Our cavalry pursued them hotly for several miles, so that many of the enemy in their hurry threw away their arms.

Though sadly fatigued with this day's work, we moved on to Sault-de-Navailles.

Some equally hard fighting took place away to Cooper's right, where the 3rd Division, under Sir Thomas Picton, met with stiff resistance whilst attacking the French position. Twenty-five-year-old Private William Brown was with the 45th Regiment at Orthes. He had been with his regiment at many of its great battles in the Peninsula, such as the stormings of Ciudad Rodrigo and Badajoz, and Salamanca. Orthes was no less a trial for both his regiment and his division. His journal, *The Autobiography of Narrative of a Soldier*, was published in Kilmarnock in 1829. We pick up his narrative just before the battle.

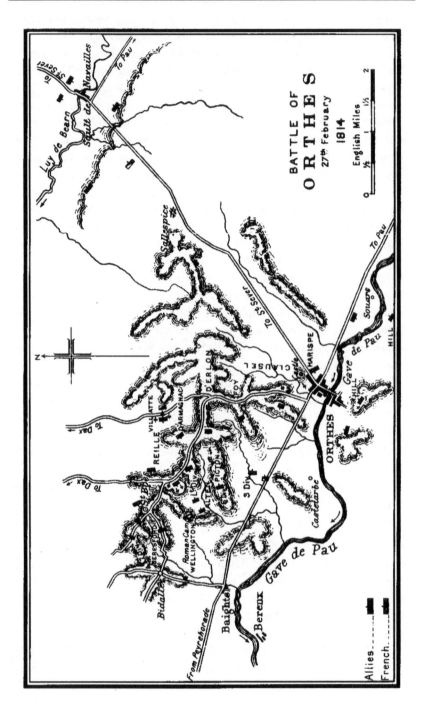

By the 24th, the Gave de Oleron, and Gave de Pau rivers, were passed by our army. The enemy then fell back upon Orthes, where they assembled their army, determined to try the fate of a general engagement, and took up a strong position in the neighbourhood of that town, on which their left rested, while their right extended to the heights on the road to Aix, and occupied the village of St. Boes. Owing to the course of the heights, their centre was considerably retired, forming their line into a kind of semicircle, which, with the strength of their position, rendered them very formidable.

On the morning of the 27th, part of our light troops advanced, and commenced skirmishing with the enemy's advanced corps, while the bristling columns on both sides were drawn up in dread array, to decide the fortune of the day. In a short time orders were given to advance, when the whole like lions rushed to the combat. By a simultaneous movement of the divisions composing our army, the enemy were attacked from right to left. General Hill, upon our right, attacked and threatened to turn their left, white their right encountered the shock of the fourth and seventh divisions, supported by a strong body of cavalry. The centre and left were attacked by the third and sixth divisions, under General Picton, supported by Lord Edward Somerset's brigade of cavalry. When advancing, our brigade passed along a narrow lane directly in front of the enemy's centre, from which they kept up a heavy cannonade, by which we were sorely annoyed, and had a number kilted and wounded. We dashed forward, however, at double quick time, and soon got under cover of the heights on which the enemy were placed. Being thus secured from the destructive fire of their cannon, our General halted, and after drawing us up in close columns by regiments, he seemed to get into a kind of quandary, and appeared not to know well what to do. In the meantime the enemy advanced to the brow of the hill, and continued to pour volleys of musketry upon us, until the Adjutant General, who was a most gallant officer, came galloping from the left, exclaiming, "Good God! General B—e, what stand you there for, like an old woman, while the brigade gets cut off? form line, and send out the 45th a skirmishing." Two companies being left with the colours, the remaining eight ascended the hill, but were received in such a manner as I had seldom before experienced. We were but a mere handful of men, a skirmishing party, opposed to a dense column of infantry, supported by artillery and cavalry the bullets flew as thick as hail, and literally tore up the ground from under our feet. Thirteen men of our company alone fell within a few yards of each other, on the brow of the hill; notwithstanding, our men continued to press on the enemy, who, after a dreadful conflict and carnage, gave way, when we got possession of a ditch, which we kept until the brigade advanced in line. Our party having been reinforced by several light companies from the division, now advanced at double quick, and giving three cheers, charged the enemy's light troops, and drove them from a ditch, in a parallel line with the one we had just left. In turning round the angle of the ditch, one of our company, before he had time to front the enemy, received a shot in the hip, and fell on the bank, exclaiming, "Blast my limbs! I would not have cared a d—n if I had got it any where else, but now people will say I was running away, and got shot in the —!" Having repeatedly charged and been charged in turn, our party got on a height, from which we had a com-plete view of the dark masses of the enemy in column, one of which was advancing to the point we were on, while their officers, with hat in hand and loud huzzas, encouraged their men to advance. By this time our party was greatly diminished in number, nearly the one-half having been killed or wounded, and would in all probability have been obliged to give way; but a staff-officer came up at the critical moment and encouraged us to stand our ground, as we would be relieved in a few minutes by the troops that were advancing. Accordingly, two brigades of the light division, which had hitherto been kept in reserve, formed immediately in our rear, when we retired, filing through their line, which advanced and encountered the enemy on the summit of the height, where a most desperate and sanguinary conflict ensued. Our troops when at the distance of a very few yards, fired a volley and instantly charged, pushing with the bayonet their adversaries down hill, who fled in the greatest haste and consternation.

The enemy, being driven from all their positions, commenced a retreat, which was for some time conducted in good order, but General Hill having passed the Gave de Pau, attacked and threatened to turn their left, which threw their whole army into confusion. Their retreat was soon converted into a ruinous and disorderly flight, in which they were charged by our cavalry, making dreadful havoc amongst them. Many of their soldiers threw away their arms, and thousands were taken prisoners, besides a number of cannon: The total loss in this action was estimated at 10,000, while 3,000 was said to be that of the Allies. The pursuit was continued until night, when our division encamped in a field by the wayside.

This had been a day of great exertion by the greatest part of our regiment. We had since morning been running, and leaping hedges and ditches; and for my own part, I had fired two hundred and fifty rounds of ball cartridge, by which my shoulder at night was as black as coal. The consequence was, the men were so fatigued, that when encamped, they either could not, or would not pitch the tents, but threw themselves on the ground exhausted. We were, however, ordered to set them up for our own welfare, which was at last, with manifest reluctance, complied with, for few entered them, but sat or lay round the fires, although it was a keen frost. Notwithstanding the toil and peril we had been exposed to during the day, there was no bread for us at night; we were therefore obliged to put up with the carrion that was served to us for beef, which we frizzled over the smoky fire, and having swallowed it, composed ourselves to sleep on the cold frozen ground.

Retrospect of a Military Life During the Most Eventful Periods of the Last War is the rather lengthy title of the military life of James Anton, Quartermaster-Sergeant of the 42nd Highlanders. Published in Edinburgh in 1841, the book follows Anton from his enlistment in the militia, through his experiences in the Peninsula from 1813 to 1814, to the Waterloo campaign of 1815, and through the rest of his career, which took him to Gibraltar, Malta and Ireland. At Orthes, the 42nd Highlanders were part of Denis Pack's brigade, which in turn was part of Clinton's 6th Division. In fact, the 6th Division made a telling contribution to the battle, supporting the 3rd Division at a crucial time when Picton's men were taking a real hammering from the tenacious French defenders. James Anton's story begins on the cold, frosty morning of 27 February 1814.

Early on the morning of Sunday the 27th, we marched down the left bank of the Pau, passed on a pontoon bridge, and directed our course upon the main road up the valley towards Orthes. Two divisions of the army were already on the road before us. The heights on our left appeared to be in the possession of the enemy, and as our movements were plainly to attack his centre or his left, which was posted in and above the town, corresponding movements became necessary on his part, and his ranks were seen advancing along the ridge parallel with ours. As the mountain approaches that place where the road St. Severe passes over it from Orthes, there is a downward bend of about a mile; it rises, however, to a considerable height on the east side of that road, and commands the town and its approaches. On our coming near this bending, our brigade was ordered to move to its left; several enclosures were in our way, but this was no time to respect them, as the enemy was welcoming us with round shot and shell. The gardens and nurseries were trodden down in an instant, and a forest of bayonets glittered round a small farmhouse that overlooked a wooded ravine on the north side.

The light companies, which had preceded the brigade, were keeping up a sharp fire upon the enemy's skirmishers, and our grenadier company was ordered to take post along the bank overlooking the ravine, and commanding a narrow road below. No place seemed less practicable for cavalry to act, but the enemy were determined to make every effort to re-establish their lines on the heights from which they had been driven by the light troops, and some of their squadrons were seen approaching to drive back our advance, which by this time was reinforced by the grenadiers; but the more effectually to repel an attack, two additional companies were dispatched to reinforce those already sent, and these had scarcely been formed when the charge of cavalry was announced: it was met and repulsed; men and horses were tumbled over the steep bank on the narrow road below, skirting the ravine. The gallant young officer who led that charge, passed through the ranks like a lion pouncing on his prey, and was made prisoner by McNamara of the grenadier company. This man, if my memory serve me well, gave the horse and sword to one of our captains, who was afterwards appointed brevet-major; but poor McNamara, who was more of a soldier than a courtier, rose not to corporal; he is yet to he seen, not like the Sidonian whom the messengers of Alexander found weeding his garden when they sought him to be king, nor like the Roman cultivating his little field, when he was requested to take the charge of an army, but employed in the humbler avocation of making wooden dishes, and occasionally selling them on the market street of Newry.

After this repulse of the cavalry, we passed through the ravine, and moved towards the road that passes over the bending of the hill. The light-infantry companies of the brigade, under the command of Major Cowel (afterwards brevet lieutenant-colonel), were skirmishing in front. The major was severely wounded and carried to the rear.

The hill rises rather abruptly on the east side of the road, and slopes gradually towards the north side, to which our advance was directed, in order to turn the enemy's right, which had fallen back as we advanced. The main road now defined the direct line between both armies; the enemy's left at Orthes, his centre on the south ascent to the summit of the hill, and his right from the summit descending to the fields on the north side. There is a small village consisting of one street on that brow of the hill towards the north, upon which the enemy was driven back, and from this kept up a destructive fire of musketry from garden walls, windows, and loopholes. Our regiment was ordered to drive him from that annoying post, which I may say had now become the right of his position. The bearer of this order was Lieutenant Innes, who was then acting brigade-major to Sir D. Pack; he preceded the regiment, and may be said to have led it on. The word of command to advance at the charge, was received with loud animating cheers.

No movement in the field is made with greater confidence of success than that of the charge; it affords little time for thinking, while it creates a fearless excitement, and tends to give a fresh impulse to the blood of the advancing soldier, rouses his courage, strengthens every nerve, and drowns every fear of danger or of death; thus emboldened amidst the deafening shouts that anticipate victory, he rushes on and mingles with the flying foe.

In an instant the village was in our possession, and the fugitives were partly intercepted by the advance of the second division of the army, under Lord Hill, which had passed the Pau above Orthes, and was now approaching round the east end of the heights.

The enemy, thus dispossessed of his last position of any importance, commenced a hasty retreat through some enclosed fields and young plantations, through which his columns directed their course, until impeded by intersecting ditches which induced them to take the main road; there the ranks were broken, confusion ensued, and a complete route was the consequence.

Fortunately for them the sun was nearly set, and although the pursuit continued for several miles, they succeeded in keeping the lead; and having reassembled during the night, continued their retreat towards the Adour.

The loss of the regiment in this battle was four officers, six sergeants, and eighty-eight rank-and-file.

I have already mentioned that Lieutenant Innes (our adjutant) was doing the duty of brigade-major. It was near the close of this day's contest that he carried the orders of the general for the regiment to drive the enemy from the village situated on the north brow of the hill; he might have retired after delivering the orders, without throwing a blot on his good name, but his heart was with the regiment, and he advanced to the charge in person; not with a fearful heart or a half-shut eye, to watch the distant motions, but spurring forward his steed in the blazing front of battle, led the way to victory. It was amidst the animating shouts which arose around him, that the last hostile and fatal bullet pierced his brain, and laid him in the dust. He fell amidst our foremost ranks, and breathed his last between the saddle and the ground.

We left behind us our dead, our dying, and our wounded; the former careless who shut those eyes that looked up to heaven from their gory bed, or who should consign their naked limbs to a grave in the field of a strange land. But our dying are sometimes left to the mercy of strangers. Shall some good Samaritan bind up their wounds and afford them protection under some hospitable roof, in the country which their invading feet have trod, and while their hands are still reeking with the blood of its harvest defenders? Or shall some sanguinary wretch put an end to their life and pain at once? Perhaps this might be the most welcome to the toil-worn soldier; But, alas! a harder fate awaits many. The midnight plunderer shuts his ears to mercy's call, strips the helpless, bleeding, dying sufferer, and leaves him naked to breath his last beneath the frosty sky, on the field saturated with his blood.

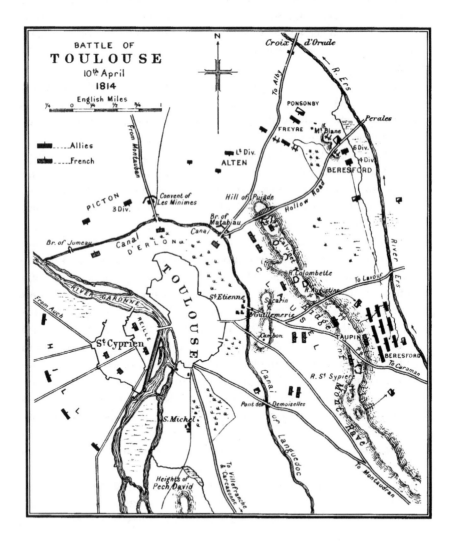

270

Orthes was the last great battle fought in the open by Wellington's army in the Peninsula. Although there were some sharp actions still to come, such as Aire and Tarbes, there would be no more Salamancas or Vittorias. Instead, Soult continued to retreat east until he reached Toulouse on 24 March 1814. This would prove to be the last battle of the war. It would also be one of the hardest and bloodiest.

The assault on Toulouse was, in some ways, a strange affair, for although the town was surrounded by a wall the main French defences lay outside the town on the Calvinet Ridge, upon which the French had constructed a series of strong redoubts. These would bear the brunt of Wellington's attacks for the other sides of the town were covered by the river Garonne to the west, by the royal canal to the north and by impassable muddy ground to the south.

The battle began at 5 a.m. on 10 April with diversionary attacks by Picton at the Ponts de Jumeux and by Hill against the suburb of St Cyprien. Picton, in fact, exceeded his orders and instead of simply confining himself to a demonstration launched a full-blooded attack on the canal, suffering severe casualties in the attack. Meanwhile, the main Allied assault floundered with heavy loss, particularly to Wellington's Spanish troops. Beresford's attacks on the redoubts turned into a real battle of attrition, with some of the redoubts changing hands several times until by around 5 p.m. the French abandoned them altogether and retreated to the relative safety of the town.

The hardest fighting by any British division, and consequently the heaviest casualties sustained, was by Clinton's 6th Division. In fact, Clinton's men suffered more casualties than the rest of Wellington's British divisions put together. Only the Spanish troops suffered more at Toulouse, suffering just over 2,000 casualties, compared with a British loss of 1,900. The two British brigades of the 6th Division, Pack's and Lambert's, attacked the French redoubts at the southern end of the Calvinet Ridge, and received a real battering from the French, who even emerged from the redoubts to attack their British assailants. Three of the best and most vivid accounts of the Battle of Toulouse have, consequently, been left to us by men of the 42nd Highlanders, who sustained heavier casualties than any other British regiment. This first extract comes again from James Anton's *Retrospect of a Military Life During the Most Eventful Periods of the Last War*. We have already read of his experiences at Orthes. Here, he describes events at Toulouse.

The sun arose over the hills that stretch along the eastern banks of the Ers, and shone forth on forty thousand bayonets that glistened round the heights of Toulouse, where Marshal Soult stood, determined to oppose our advance.

General Pack's brigade was formed in continuous columns of regiments to the left of the road leading to Toulouse. At this time the Spaniards, who were in advance and ascending the heights, were attacked with such fury that they gave way in all directions. It was apprehended that the enemy would have borne down upon us in the impetuosity of the movement, and we deployed into lines. The 79th regiment was at this time in front of the 42nd, and General Pack, anticipating a charge from the enemy's victorious and elated infantry, after thus scattering the Spaniards, gave orders to the 79th to receive them with a volley, immediately form four deep, face about, and pass through the ranks of the 42nd. The latter received orders to form four deep, as soon as the former had given its fire; let the line pass through, then form up, give a volley, and charge.

This was providing against what might have taken place, but did not, for the enemy was recalled, and the Spaniards were afterwards rallied.

We now moved off to our left, along a green embankment, a small lake or large pond on our left, and a wet ditch and marshy meadow on the right. The shot and shell were flying over our heads into the lake, but the range was too elevated to hurt us, and we ran along the bank until we came to a place where we could leap the ditch and form on the swampy ground beyond it. We had scarcely formed, when a strong column of the enemy, with drums beating a march, descended the hill in our front, and thinking from the nature of the ground that we should be neither able to advance or retreat, rushed down confident of success. For us to retire would have been scarcely practicable; the bank from which we had leaped down and over the ditch was too high in several places for us to leap back, from such uncertain footing; for we were sinking to the ankles, and sometimes deeper at every step; to advance was the only alternative, and it was taken.

The light companies of the division were by this time in our front, and without any hesitation dashed forward; we followed fast, and the opposing column re-ascended the hill and left us the undisputed masters of the valley.

We now ascended at double quick time, and the whole of the division crowned the eastern summit of the heights. Here we were exposed to a destructive fire of round shot, shell, grape, and musketry, while we had not as yet got up one gun, owing to the numerous obstructions that lay in the way. The ground we occupied sloped towards one of the main roads that runs over the hill to the city, and the fields on the opposite side of the road were in possession of the enemy, and extremely broken and intersected by deep crossroads, breast-works, and redoubts; but could, from our present position, have been commanded by artillery, had it been practicable to bring a few guns forward; but this required some time, and indefatigable labour.

The light companies of the division advanced beyond the road, and maintained a very unequal skirmish with the enemy, who lay securely posted behind their breast-works and batteries, and in their redoubts, from all of which they took the most deadly aim. The 61st regiment was ordered forward to support the skirmishers, and became the marked object of the enemy's batteries, from which incessant showers of grape cut down that corps by sections, while Soult was perhaps not losing a man, being so safely sheltered from our musketry; it was therefore seen necessary to withdraw the skeleton of that regiment to the road on which we had taken post after its advance; it was now warmly welcomed back, for its retreat was no defeat, and its loss was scarcely equalled by any corps in the field. Not a subaltern left the field without a wound, and the honour of the colours was assigned to sergeants.

The enemy, emboldened by this momentary success on his part, began to advance towards the road, and our regiment was ordered to advance by wings and storm one of the redoubts.

Our colonel was a brave man, but there are moments when a well-timed manoeuvre is of more advantage than courage. The regiment stood on the road with its front exactly to the enemy, and if the left wing had been ordered forward, it could have sprung up the bank in line and dashed forward on the enemy at once. Instead of this, the colonel faced the right wing to its right, countermanded in rear of the left, and when the leading rank cleared the left flank it was made to file up the bank, and as soon as it made its appearance the shot, shell, and musketry poured in with deadly destruction; and in this exposed position we had to make a second countermarch, on purpose to bring our front to the enemy. These movements consumed much time, and by this unnecessary exposure exasperated the men to madness. The word "Forward — double quick!" dispelled the gloom, and forward we drove, in the face of apparent destruction. The field had been lately rough ploughed or under fallow, and when a man fell he tripped the one behind, thus the ranks were opening as we approached the point whence all this hostile vengeance proceeded; but the rush forward had received an impulse from desperation, the spring of the men's patience had been strained until ready to snap, and when left to the freedom of its own extension, ceased not to act until the point to which it was directed was attained. In a minute every obstacle was surmounted; the enemy fled as we leaped over the trenches and mounds like a pack of noisy hounds in pursuit, frightening them more by our wild hurrahs than actually hurting them by ball or bayonet.

The redoubt, thus obtained, consisted of an old country farm-cottage, the lower part of its walls stone, the upper part mud or clay. It stood in the corner of what had been a garden, having one door to a road or broad lane and another to the garden; the whole forming a square which had been lately fortified on three sides by a deep but dry trench, from which the earth had been cast inwards, and formed a considerable bank, sloping inwards, but presenting a perpendicular face of layers of green turf outwards. The cottage served as a temporary magazine, and the mound or embankment as a cover to the enemy from the fire of our troops; and from this place our men had been dreadfully cut down.

It cannot be for an instant supposed that all this could have been effected without very much deranging our ranks, and as the enemy had still a powerful force, and other works commanding this, time would not permit of particularity, and a brisk independent fire as kept up with more noise than good effect by our small groups upon our not yet defeated enemy. Our muskets were getting useless by the frequent discharges, and several of the men were having recourse to the French pieces that lay scattered about, but they had been as freely used as our own, and were equally unserviceable. Our number of effective hands was also decreasing, and that of the again approaching foe irresistible. Two officers (Captain Campbell and Lieutenant Young) and about sixty of inferior rank were all that now remained without a wound of the right wing of the regiment that entered the field in the morning. The flag was hanging in tatters, and stained with the blood of those who had fallen over it. The standard, cut in two, had been successively placed in the hands of three officers, who fell as we advanced; it was now borne by a sergeant, while the few remaining soldiers who rallied around it, defiled with mire, sweat, smoke, and blood, stood ready to oppose with the bayonet the advancing column, the front files of which were pouring in destructive showers of musketry among our confused ranks. To have disputed the post with such over-whelming numbers, would have been the hazarding the loss of our colours, and could serve no general interest to our army, as we stood between the front of our advancing support and the enemy; we were therefore ordered to retire. The greater number passed through the cottage, now filled with wounded and dying, and leaped from the door that was over the road into the trench of the redoubt, among the killed and wounded.

We were now between two fires of musketry, the enemy to our left and rear, the 79th and left wing of our own regiment in our front. Fortunately the intermediate space did not exceed a hundred paces, and our safe retreat depended

274

upon the speed with which we could perform it. We rushed along like a crowd of boys pursuing the bounding ball to its distant limit, and in an instant plunged into a trench that had been cut across the road: the balls were whistling amongst us and over us; while those in front were struggling to get out, those behind were holding them fast for assistance, and we became firmly wedged together, until a horse without a rider came plunging down on the heads and bayonets of those in his way; they on whom he fell were drowned or smothered, and the gap thus made gave way for the rest to get out.

The right wing of the regiment, thus broken down and in disorder, was rallied by Captain Campbell (afterwards brevet lieutenant-colonel) and the adjutant (Lieutenant Young) on a narrow road, the steep banks of which served as a cover from the showers of grape that swept over our heads.

In this contest, besides our colonel, who was wounded as he gave the word of command, "Forward," the regiment lost, in killed and wounded, twenty officers, one sergeant-major, and four hundred and thirty-six of inferior rank.

Meantime the Portuguese brigade was ordered to take possession of the evacuated redoubt, which was accomplished with little loss, for the enemy had been backward of entering, lest we might have been drawing them into an ambush, or had an intention of blowing up the cottage, in which a considerable quantity of loose cartridges had been left near a large fire, by themselves when they were driven out, and most likely intended for that purpose, but we had removed the whole to a place of less danger.

Thus far the left flank of our army was secured; the Spaniards, further to the right, were making good their advances, our artillery was about getting posted on commanding eminences, while only one battery remained on the western summit in the enemy's possession, and before sunset it was also stormed, and all the heights overlooking Toulouse remained in our possession.

Considering the punishment sustained by the 42nd Highlanders, Anton can consider himself fortunate to emerge relatively unscathed. Not so our next two correspondents. The following extract comes from the diary of a private soldier of the 42nd, who took a French musket ball in his arm. His account of his experiences in the Peninsula and at Walcheren was published in 1821, seven years after the battle, under the title *The Personal Narrative of a Private Soldier in the 42nd Highlanders*.

Lord Wellington having got the army in readiness again, and the pontoons prepared for laying on the Garonne, we received orders, on the 5th of April, to march that night at eleven o'clock, so we bade adieu to the remainder of the fifty pipes of wine, and by daylight next morning we were arrived at the pontoon bridge; but it was not finished. This bridge was throwing over about three leagues below Toulouse. None of the enemy appeared to oppose the operations of the bridge party, as the plan of throwing it across so far below the city must have deceived them; and General Hill was left in front of the town, at the bridge which the French occupied. Hill remained there during all our operations, and even while the battle was fought: his presence detained a very strong force to defend the bridge.

In the course of two hours the bridge was thrown over upwards of twenty boats broad. The rifle brigade, and part of the cavalry, with a few guns of flying artillery, crossed first; then the sixth division. We marched about a league, the day being very wet. The most of us got into quarters that night; the rest were in camp. The next day we moved close upon Toulouse, where we took up our camp ground in fields. All the houses near us had been deserted: the inhabitants had all fled into the city.

On the night of the ninth our orders came to march; three hours before day we were under arms.

I had charge of the left-hand tent of the company. Eighteen men of us struck the tent that morning merrily; and little did we think there would not be one to pitch it at night. Our regiment's strength in marching from this camp was about 500, rank and file; all good soldiers as ever belonged to the 42nd — the most self conceited regiment in the army — a regiment that thought and said there was no regiment under the crown like them — men that would not take a word, when drinking in tap-rooms, from any soldier, but in an instant up and box him — men that reckoned it their pride to conquer or die — and this was the day that was to try them.

After daylight we were halted: the third division had by this time begun the bloody fight about Toulouse, driving in the enemy's piquets; but the strong position that they had was about a mile from the town, and almost surrounded by canals. When we halted, the general of brigade called all the officers, and told them that he had received orders fur the Highland brigade to attack the enemy's breast-works and redoubts, on the right, saying, at the same time, "The gallant 42nd will lead and attack, and be supported by the 79th and the 91st."

We were then formed into square, and told by our commanding officer what we had to do. The division then moved, and in the course of half an

276

hour we were right under the enemy's position; a canal on one side of us, and the enemy on the other.

We marched in columns of companies past their position, till we had fairly got beyond their works: but it was not a march; we were running all the time; and the enemy had opened upon us a tremendous fire; still we went on undauntedly, although our men fell in heaps, resolved, when we got up to the French, to show them British play.

As soon as we had run past their works, we were halted, and in the course of a very few minutes there were two very strong columns of the enemy's infantry and one of cavalry appeared on the height in front of the Highland brigade. At this time the canal was about 100 yards in rear of us, and the enemy about 300 yards in front; so, what would the consequence have been, if we did not both fight and conquer on this position? In an instant the enemy's columns marched down upon us, cheering and beating their drums, as if they had been going to scare crows from a cornfield, by their shouts and the hammering of sheepskins. Their officers too were in front of their men, waving their swords, and swaggering like Showmen at a fair. I dare say they thought we would surrender without resistance, or that they would easily thrash us, and drive us into the canal.

We were busy forming line, and they took advantage of this to pour in upon us a brisk fire of musketry. As soon, however, as our line was formed, and it was complete, in a thought, we gave them a volley, and advanced with three cheers to meet the foe, keeping up a very brisk fire on them.

The 79th formed square on the right, as the cavalry had begun to attempt our right flank. The ground we were on was ploughed, and extremely soft, on account of so much rain a few days before this; and it was with a great deal of difficulty we could get our feet lifted without leaving our shoes behind; and many a hardy soldier left his brogues and came on barefooted.

As soon as we got out of the field we mounted the height, where we had good footing on firm ground. We then came to the charge with three cheers, the enemy about forty yards in front of us. Not being able to stand the Highlander's rage in the charge, the French went to the right about, and flew through the fields like a flock of mad geese, and made for their redoubts like cowards, there to lurk and annoy us with their recreant shots. When we got to the top of the height there was a tremendous fire opened upon us from the enemy's redoubts and breastworks.

As soon as we got within 200 yards of their works we were halted in a road that had been cut out between two heights. Here we had a very fine cover. We remained here about an hour. Our loss was very great before we got into this road; and hard was that part of the day, but harder still was the remainder of it to be, for the bloody fight had not begun with the 42nd: all yet was in the ordinary way of battle; what followed, was more deadly than Burgos.

The redoubts on the left were to be attacked by the Spanish army; and the attack of the works on the right was to he delayed till those on the left were carried. This was a wise measure; though some of us thought we ought to have gone pell-mell to work with the whole, and complete their conquest at one and the same time.

The Spanish army then made the attack on the left of the enemy's works, but were beat back with an immense loss before they reached the redoubts.

I heard it often said that my Lord Wellington, when he saw the Spaniards get such a beating, sent part of his staff amongst them to encourage them. They then attacked again with amazing boldness, and with double spirit, when they knew that they had English officers leading them on. I have heard it said that when they got into the works, they were so savage that they put every man to the bayonet, and took no prisoners. This was cruel, but revenge is sweet; and though the Spaniards are not vindictive people, the remembrance of their wrongs never lost an opportunity of retaliation.

General Pack came up to our commanding officer, Colonel Macara, as soon as we were to attack, and ordered him to form the regiment by wings, or half battalions, in a ploughed field on the side of this road. We were to march by wings on the works. Whenever we were formed, our orders were to charge the breastworks and the redoubt in front of us. Colonel Macara then gave us orders to file by companies up the face of the side of the road; but it was on our hands and feet.

As soon as the enemy observed us forming our line, in a moment they opened upon us a most tremendous fire of grape, shells, and small shot, that mowed down our ranks as we formed them. It was shocking to see the carnage that was made on this spot. Macara could hardly get the right wing formed; it was mostly all cut off before the men got to the works, although the distance was only 200 yards. I belonged to the right wing: it was, for all the world, like a target to the enemy; for we received their first fire; and it raged most dreadfully. The smoke and fire obscured the sky; the cannon and musketry roared like thunder; and many a hero fell to rise no more.

As soon as the wing was about formed, the colonel went off at the charge with us, cheering all the way, and the left wing followed in the same gallant style. All the troops who saw us start cheered us, and "Bravo, forty-second,' could be heard above all the noise of guns. "Hurra! Hurra! Hurra!" sounded on all sides of us, from the division, Portuguese, and Spaniards: all saw the work of death we were going on; all saw our men fall like the fruit off an apple tree, when shook by the boisterous blast of the sky. I had escaped hitherto in all the actions I had been in, but I had no hope now of leaving the field alive. The shot was whizzing past us like hail; most of the right wing that were killed and wounded received two, three, and some several shots at once. The man on my right hand received six grape shots in his body, and fell like a log; and his brother, on his other side, was wounded at the same time. When about fifty yards from the redoubt, I received a shot through my right arm, and was obliged to halt; but I was almost sure of receiving another before I could get under cover. I went to the rear a few yards, (my arm hung motionless by my side) and lay down in the furrow of two rigs, thinking this might afford me some cover. I had hardly stretched myself on the wet ground when a round shot from a cannon covered me almost wholly over with earth; then I started to my feet again, and made for the road we had marched from, knowing that I would have good cover there. My wound bled very much. I could not get it bound up. I had about half a mile to walk to the ground the surgeons were on; but I was obliged to halt by the way, I became so weak from the stream of blood flowing down my arm. I was several times so dizzy I could with difficulty stand and look round me; then I would become sick and languid. I was parched up with thirst; but no water could I get.

At this moment our artillery were passing me, making for the position we had taken up: one of them dismounted from his horse, seeing the state I was in, and gave me a draught of wine out of his canteen. I bade God bless him. "You deserve it," said he, "if it was gold you could drink, for you have fought hard: away with you to the doctors; there are crowds of the 42nd about them, down at those houses which we passed." Again I thanked this brave artilleryman: he clapped spurs to his horse, and was off after the guns.

I revived very much after I had swallowed the wine, and made the best of my way for the houses he pointed to. It was full two hours before the surgeons could look at my arm; they were amputating legs and arms so fast, and so many, it was very lamentable to be two hours the spectator of this sight.

I must now go to the regiment, and, as I received my information of what befell the 42nd on that memorable day, the 10th of April, from one of the men who was in the action till the last of it, give you such details as may keep the regiment in your view till I again joined it.

The redoubts and breast-works were taken at the point of the bayonet, but the 42nd were not long in possession of them till the enemy, greatly reinforced, seeing the handful of men that was left of the 42nd, and no other support with them in the works, they attacked the works again, and overpowered the few brave men who were left.

Dreadful was the havoc that was made in the redoubt before the 42nd were put out of it. I have heard it said, over and over again, that they could get out of the redoubt at any place, as the ditch that surrounded it was filled with the dead and wounded.

The general then sent the 79th to support the 42nd, and make another attack. The two regiments then charged the redoubt again, and beat the enemy out of it with great slaughter. The 79th fought like lions. I was told the enemy were then beaten from their strong position, and retreated into the city of Toulouse. The British did not follow, as the canal was between them and the town. Next morning the enemy retreated from Toulouse, and the British followed.

The loss of the 42nd on this memorable day, was 414 private men and 27 officers, in killed and wounded. Of the company to which I belonged there were only five men left. We had 1 captain, 1 subaltern officer, 3 sergeants, 47 rank and file, killed and wounded; 1 subaltern officer, 1 corporal, and 4 privates, left: but a good many men joined the regiment in a few days that received slight wounds.

As soon as I got my wound dressed, I felt easy, but I was excessively weak from the loss of blood. The bullet hit my right arm between the elbow and wrist; and as I pulled off my jacket, a half ball dropped out of the sleeve: it had passed directly through between the two bones in the lower branch of the arm. In fourteen days after this the other half of the ball oozed out, after causing me immense pain, and a consultation of the doctors, as to whether they should dock me by the elbow. If they had I should have been minus an arm, which I now use as well as ever I used it in my life.

As soon as I got my wound dressed, I and six more of the company I belonged to, went about a mile to some houses, that we might rest ourselves. There was no hospital for the army. All the surrounding houses without the town were taken possession of by the wounded. The inhabitants had all fled into Toulouse. There were three featherbeds in the house to which my party went, for the six men looked upon me as their corporal. There was a guard belonging to the commissariat in this house: their noise would have kept a fatigued man awake, but I was kept so by the pain of my wound, which now smarted more than ever. Next day I was feverish, and could hardly walk to the door: the guard that were in the house behaved kindly to us; they brought us wine from the cellar, water from a well, and a sheep from some snug quarter; and here for three days they nursed us before any one else came to see us.

On the third day the head surgeon came and looked at our wounds, and told us hospitals were getting ready for us in Toulouse, and that peace had been made before the battle was fought. I cannot tell how this news affected me; I was sick and wounded; and I thought on the thousands who had fallen a few days before. My period of service was up, and I cast my eyes on my native land: but all was dark and disheartening. Ten years, the best of my life, had been spent among the lowest of the army; my habits were fixed, I thought, and a soldier I must continue! I had, in that time, lost all my family but one brother: still he was my brother, affectionate and kind; and my country was dear to me even in this poor and miserable plight I now lay in. Darkness fell upon me, as a thousand schemes engaged my thoughts: at length sleep stole my senses, and I had some dozing, dreaming naps; the visions of by-gone days, battles, places, home, my wound, poor, friendless, and maimed, perhaps for life:—these were my dreams.

Our third account of the Battle of Toulouse comes from the pen of an officer of the 42nd Highlanders, Lieutenant John Malcolm. Like our previous correspondent, Malcolm was also badly wounded, and had the misfortune to be carried off the field a prisoner by the French. His account of the battle was printed in 1828 in Constable's *Memorials of the Late War* under the title, 'Reminiscences of a Campaign in the Pyrenees and South of France in 1814.'

Early on Sunday morning, the 10th April, our tents were struck, and we moved along with the other regiments of the 6th division, towards the neighbourhood of Toulouse, until ordered to halt on a level ground, from whence we had a distinct view of the enemy's position on the ridge of hills already mentioned. At the same time, we saw Lord Wellington, accompanied by his Staff, riding back from the front at a hard trot. He was easily known, even at a considerable distance, by the peculiarly erect carriage of his head, and the white cravat which he always wore. Some of the men called out, "There goes Wellington, my lads; we shall have some hot work presently." At that moment General Pack, who commanded our brigade, came up, and, calling its officers and non-commissioned officers around him, addressed them in words to the following effect: — "We are this day to attack the enemy. Your business will be to take possession of these fortified heights, which you see towards the front. I have only to warn you to be prepared to form close column, in case of a charge of cavalry, and to restrain the impetuosity of the men, and prevent them from wasting their ammunition." The drum then beat to arms, and we received orders to move on towards the enemy's position.

Marshal Beresford crossed the Ers, at the bridge of Croix d'Orade; and, with the fourth division, carried the village of Mont Blanc; and the Spanish General Don Manuel Freyre, proceeding along the left of the Ers, formed his corps on a height in front of the enemy's left; moved on to the attack under a heavy fire of musketry and artillery, and lodged his troops beneath some banks, immediately under the enemy's entrenchments; but, in attempting to turn their left flank, the Spaniards were repulsed, and the French, rushing out upon them from the entrenchments, drove them down the hill in great confusion. They suffered considerably in retiring; but rallied again, upon seeing the light division come up to their assistance.

Meantime, our division (the 6th) approached the foot of the ridge of heights, on the enemy's right, and moved in a direction parallel to them, until we should reach the point of attack. We advanced along the foot of the ridge, under a heavy cannonade from some redoubts on the heights. At one part of the ground over which we passed, many of the shot took effect; and a soldier, immediately before me, was struck: by a cannon-ball, about the middle of the body, and fell a frightful and shapeless mass, scarcely retaining a trace of humanity. We arrived, at last, immediately in front of a redoubt, which protected the right of the enemy's position, where we were formed in two lines, — the first consisting of some Portuguese regiments, and the reserve, at this point, of the Highland brigade. Darkening the whole hill, flanked by clouds of cavalry, and covered by the fire of their redoubt, the enemy came down upon us like a torrent their generals and field-officers riding in front, and waving their hats amidst shouts of the multitude, resembling the roar of an ocean. Our Highlanders, as if actuated by one instinctive impulse, took off their bonnets, and, waving them in the air, returned their greeting with three cheers. A deathlike silence ensued for some moments, and we could observe a visible pause in the advance of the enemy. At that moment, the light company of the 42nd regiment, by a well-directed fire, brought down some of the French officers of distinction, as they rode in front of their respective corps. The enemy immediately fired a volley into our lines, and advanced upon us amidst a deafening roar of musketry and artillery. Our troops answered their fire only once, and, unappalled by their furious onset, advanced up the hill, and met them at the charge. Our bayonets, however, pierced nothing but wreaths of smoke; for, our foes having suddenly changed their minds, were charging in the opposite direction: and just such a glimpse did we obtain of them, vanishing over the ridge of the hill, as did Geoffrey Crayon of "the stout gentlemen." Upon reaching the summit of the ridge of heights, the redoubt which had covered their advance fell into our possession ; but they still retained four others, with their connecting lines of entrenchments, upon the level of the same height on which we were now established, and into which they had retired.

Meantime, our troops were drawn up along a road, which passed over the hill, and which, having a high bank at each side, protected us in some measure from the general fire of their last line of redoubts.

Here our brigade remained a considerable time, until Marshal Beresford's artillery, which, in consequence of the badness of the roads, had been left in the village of Mont Blanc, could be brought up, and until the Spaniards under Don Manuel Freyre could be re-formed, and brought back to the attack.

During this pause, we were ordered to sit down along the sides of the road, the embankments of which afforded us protection from the point-blank shot of the redoubt and fortified houses into which the enemy had retired, but not from their shells, which they threw among us with great precision, and by which we lost a good many men; and latterly they moved round some guns to a position, from which the line of the road was completely raked by their fire. During this period of the battle, General Pack sat on horseback in the middle of the road, showing an example of the most undaunted bravery to the troops. I think I see him now, as he then appeared, perfectly calm and unmoved, and with a placid smile upon his face amidst a perfect storm of shot and shells. His aide-de-camp, Le Strange, who was afterwards killed at Waterloo, had his horse shot under him, and both came down together. A few minutes afterwards, I observed General Pack suddenly turn pale, and seem as if going to faint. This was occasioned by a ball which had passed through his leg. He rode slowly to the rear, where he had his wound dressed, and in a few minutes returned again.

Marshal Beresford's artillery having at length arrived, and the Spanish troops being once more brought forward, General Pack rode up in front of our brigade, and made the following announcement: "I have just now been with General Clinton, and he has been pleased to grant my request, that in the charge which we are now to make upon the enemy's redoubts, the 42nd regiment shall have the honour of leading on the attack: — the 42nd will advance." The order was immediately passed along the troops, and I could hear the last words dying away in the distance along our lines.

We immediately began to form for the charge upon the redoubts, which were about two or three hundred yards distant, and to which we had to pass over some ploughed fields. The grenadiers of the 42nd regiment, followed by the other companies, led the way, and began to ascend from the road; but no sooner were the feathers of their bonnets seen rising over the embankment, than such a tremendous fire was opened from the redoubts and entrench-ments, as in a very short time would have annihilated them. The right wing, therefore, hastily formed into line, and, without waiting for the left, which was ascending by companies from the road, rushed upon the batteries, which vomited forth a storm of fire, grape-shot, and musketry, the most incessant, furious and terrific, I ever witnessed.

Amidst the clouds of smoke in which they were curtained, the whole line of redoubts would every now and then start into view amidst the wild and frightful blaze, and then vanish again into utter darkness. Our men were mown down by sections. I saw six of the company to which I belonged fall together, as if swept away by the discharge of one gun; and the whole ground over which we rushed, was covered with the dead. The redoubts were erected along the side of a road, and defended by broad ditches filled with water. Just before our troops reached the obstruction, however, the enemy deserted them, and fled in all directions, leaving their last line of strongholds in our possession; but they still possessed two fortified houses close by, from which they kept up a galling and destructive fire.

I was then standing at the side of one of the batteries, which we had just taken, along with some of the regiment, and a young officer, one of the tallest and finest looking men I ever beheld. This was the first time he had ever been under fire; but he behaved like a hero, and had snatched up a musket belong-ing to some soldier who had fallen, with which he was firing away upon the enemy like the most practised veteran. I happened to turn about my head for a moment, and when I looked back again, he was lying stretched on his back, the blood welling from his breast, and his feet quivering in the last convul-sions of expiring nature. He had arrived from England only a short time before; and in his march from Passages through France to join his regiment, had been taken prisoner by a marauding party of French in our rear. He had escaped from his guard during a dark night, and concealed himself in a wood for a day or two until they were gone. When almost famished with hunger, he proceeded on his march, and luckily met with a British officer of rank, who supplied him with the means of reaching his regiment. He had joined us only two or three days previous to the battle, and was standing close beside me in the flush of youth, and health, and hope — in the very moment of victory — the proudest one of life: His eye but twinkled once, and he lay a corpse at my feet!

While I was yet gazing upon him in a kind of stupor, I received a blow, as if from a huge club on the elbow. A musket-ball had passed through the upper part of my arm, and splintered the bone. I felt stunned, and, in a few moments, became faint, and dizzy, and fell. The first sensation which I was conscious of after my fall, was that of a burning thirst, universally felt after gunshot wounds. I observed our men still falling around me, in consequence of the fire from the two fortified houses, but at last the firing suddenly ceased, and a dead silence ensued. My faintness now beginning to wear off, I raised my head; and through the clouds of smoke which were clearing away, I observed that the road was covered with troops in blue uniform. At first I supposed them to be Spaniards, but was soon undeceived, and discovered them to be French. Out of about 500 men, which the 42nd regiment brought into action, scarcely 90 reached the fatal redoubt from which the enemy had fled.

As soon as the smoke began to clear away, they discovered how matters stood, and advanced in great force in order to regain their strongholds. The 42nd regiment immediately fell back upon the 79th and some other corps, now moving up to their support. Of these circumstances at the time, however, I was quite ignorant; and as escape was impossible, I lay quietly where I was on the roadside, hoping to avoid notice among the wounded and the dead.

The enemy marched past me in great force, keeping up a tremendous fire, and having drums beating in the rear. The main body had passed without taking any notice of me, when I was seized upon by two stragglers who had loitered behind. They immediately began to rifle my pockets, and one of them was in the act of tearing off my epaulet, when an officer came up, sword in hand, and drove them off, to my great relief. My situation, however, became extremely uncomfortable, as I was exposed to the fire of our own troops, who were advancing upon the French to retake the batteries. Believing that the enemy would soon be driven back, and fearing that they might carry me off along with them; I got up, as soon as they were fairly past, and, supporting my wounded arm with the other, began to make the best of my way over the ploughed fields, in order to gain some place of safety; but I had not proceeded far, when I felt myself seized from behind by two French soldiers, who had been loitering in the rear, and also most unceremoniously marched off with me towards Toulouse.

The issue of this last attempt of the enemy to retake their redoubts, is well known; they were a second time repulsed with great loss, and their whole army driven into Toulouse: But I proceed with my personal narrative.

As soon as my conductors and I were out of range of the fire from the British, they allowed me to rest a little, and one of them only remained with me. He presented me with his canteen of wine, and asked me if the French were not a very brave people; which leading question I thought proper to answer in the way he wished. As we proceeded along the road, we met a tall, grim-looking soldier, who eyed me with a ferocious look, and threw a bundle of ball-cartridges at me, by which I received a severe blow on the head. My attendant was abundantly wroth, and, after abusing the ruffian, proceeded with me towards the town.

It was a bright, beautiful evening, as we approached Toulouse. About a hundred yards from the entrance into the town, upon the high road, sat Marshal Soult and his staff on horseback. He was looking earnestly towards the heights, from which he saw his troops beaten back in all directions. I passed close by the Marshal and his generals, who eyed me with a look of grave curiosity.

At last I arrived in the town, which exhibited such a scene of confusion as I never witnessed. Almost the whole French army occupied the streets: the house-tops were covered with crowds, and the windows seemed bursting with the population. All was terror and excitement; for Soult seemed determined to make a stand even in the town, and Wellington commanded a position from which he could reduce it to ashes. I had no sooner entered the streets, than I became so faint and exhausted from fatigue and loss of blood, that I sunk down upon the ground. In a few minutes a French surgeon made his appearance and examined my wound, which he laid open with the knife at both orifices; but so much was my arm deadened by the ball, that I scarcely felt the operation. As soon as it was over, I was escorted by a file of *gens d'armes* to an hospital, prepared for the reception of the wounded. As we passed along the streets, crowds of ladies rushed out from their houses, and presented me with wines and cordials; and being much exhausted and parched with thirst, I drank largely of every thing they offered me.

Upon arriving at the hospital, I was ushered into an immense room, which was crowded from end to end with the wounded and dying officers of the French army. I was then given in charge to two fat rosy sick nurses, who, without any coy delays, or the slightest attempt at a blush, stripped off my clothes and put me to bed. In a short time afterwards I received a visit from an English physician, who had been long resident in Toulouse. He informed me that the French army would be obliged to retire, and that the inhabitants of Toulouse were well affected towards the English. I expressed a fear, that, in the event of the French army retiring, they might carry me along with them; but he set my mind at ease by informing me, that he had sufficient interest with the medical department to prevent anything of that sort; and, after promising to repeat his visit, he took his leave.

Towards night I began to fall into a slumber, but was every now and then startled out of it by the cries of the wounded especially of such as were undergoing amputations.

In the bed next to mine lay an English officer, who had been wounded and taken prisoner; but he was then speechless, and died during the night. On my other side lay a German, an officer in the French service, whose skull had been fractured. He sung and conversed to himself in the wildest manner imaginable; and, about midnight, started out of bed, and marched up and down the room in a state of delirium, quite alarming to the rest of us. He also died in a short time.

Sleep came upon me at last; but it was a sleep of horrors. The various scenes of the preceding day, mixed up with the phantoms of imagination, passed in dire review before me. My friends seemed falling around me; — the thunders of battle were in my ears, and we seemed retreating and closely pursued by the enemy's cavalry. From these imaginary horrors, a return to real pain was a relief. I awoke towards morning with a burning thirst, and the taste of sulphur in my throat, in consequence of the smoke which I had breathed the preceding day. I was amply supplied with lemonade; but my fair attendant allowed me scarce any thing to eat, for fear, as they informed me, of fever.

About ten o'clock at night, I observed several officers enter the hospital, and bid adieu to their wounded companions, by which I guessed the French army were about to evacuate Toulouse. Shortly afterwards, there were symptoms of commotion without — the movement of a great army, infantry, cavalry, and artillery, through the narrow streets, with the confusion attending such a scene, produced a great noise, like the roar of the sea after a storm. I listened to the wild sound for hours, till at last it began to wax faint, and die away through the night, when I again sunk into a slumber. On awakening in the morning, I observed a number of priests in the act of administering extreme unction to the dying men by whom I was surrounded; and the moment any of them expired, he was carried out, to make room for some other wounded man, by whom his bed was immediately occupied.

Yet, even in that house of mourning, there occurred one circumstance, which I still think of with peculiar pleasure. About midday, a young lady entered the hospital, probably to see some friend or acquaintance among the wounded. In proceeding along the room, she paused opposite to the place where I was lying, and, being informed by one of the sick-nurses in attendance that I was an Englishman, she stepped up to my bedside, and gazing on me with a look, in which curiosity was mingled with pity — all at once, yielding to the impulse of her feelings, she bent over me, and, throwing her arms around my neck, pressed her cheek to mine. It was a burst of nature, and but the action of a moment; for she raised herself hastily, glided away, and I never saw her again. Yet, trivial as this circumstance may seem, it remains fair and fresh in my recollection, while weightier matters have been long forgotten; and there are times, even yet, when, in the silence of the night, and far away amidst the dreaming land, my couch seems spread in the hospital of Toulouse; and when, amidst that scene of suffering, my ear is tortured with shrieks of agony, and my sealed eye blasted with heart-rending sights — then, too, smiling away these horrors, the vision of the young French girl breaks upon my dreams, and in all the vividness of reality do I behold her, like a ministering angel, bending over my couch, till once more I feel her dark tresses clustering over my brow, and the pressure of her soft warm cheek to mine. But to return:—-

It was not till the mists had cleared away, on the morning of the 12th, that the British army discovered the retreat of the enemy, and began to feel their way towards Toulouse, which they entered very quietly; and it was only by hearing their bands of music that I was made aware of their approach. About noon I was visited by some of my brother officers, who gave me an account of the termination of the battle, and the names of those who had fallen. Though I was no longer a prisoner, the state of my health was such as to prevent my removal from the hospital, where I remained for ten days.

The Battle of Toulouse was not one of Wellington's most successful actions. It cost him over 4,500 casualties, Soult losing just over 3,200. Indeed, if we judged the success by casualties alone Toulouse would be marked down as a French victory, which some historians claim anyway. Although Wellington forced Soult to abandon his defences, he was unable to enter the town until two days later, by which time Soult had fled, leading his army out of Toulouse and marching towards Carcassone to the south. Therefore, even Wellington's strategic aims were not entirely achieved.

Toulouse had no bearing on the war's outcome, for on 6 April, four days before the battle, Napoleon had abdicated. When Wellington received the news, two days after the battle of Toulouse, he immediately despatched couriers to Soult, informing him that the Peninsular War was finally at an end. Although Wellington's main field army had fought its last battle, there was still one final tragic act to be played out at Bayonne: the garrison had yet to hear news of Napoleon's abdication.

CHAPTER SIXTEEN

THE SORTIE FROM BAYONNE

With four days having passed since the Battle of Toulouse, and eight days since Napoleon had abdicated, Wellington's men can be forgiven for thinking that their fighting days in the Iberian Peninsula had finally come to an end. There was, however, one final sting in the tail, for on 14 April 1814 Governor Thouvenot, commanding the garrison at Bayonne, decided to launch a sortie that would cost over 1,500 French and Allied casualties.

The besieging force consisted of the 1st and 5th Divisions, who together blockaded Bayonne on both north and south banks of the river Adour, upon which the town stands. In fact, the bulk of the town stood on the south bank, with only the powerful citadel and the suburb of St Esprit standing on the north bank facing the Allied siege line. The British troops to the north of Bayonne, occupying positions from the Adour, east to a position directly north of the citadel, were mainly from the 1st Division, nicknamed 'The Gentlemen's Sons,' as it consisted of the two brigades of Foot Guards. A brigade of the 5th Division and a further brigade of infantry of the King's German Legion were in position on the left of the line, close to the suburb of St Etienne. The blockading troops occupied a series of wrecked houses, in addition to the siege lines, although these were not of the sort employed at the sieges at Ciudad Rodrigo and Badajoz, for example.

The governor of Bayonne, Thouvenot, planned the sortie for dawn on 14 April. Whether it was through sheer malice, knowing that this would be the last opportunity he would have of striking out at his emperor's enemies, or whether he genuinely did not know of the armistice is not clear. Whatever the reason, the sortie was planned with great precision, and carried out with determination by the French.

Three French columns emerged from the citadel on the north bank of the Adour at around 3 a.m., one attacking the left of the British line, one the centre and one the right. The attack was initially a great success and caught the British troops completely unawares. A French deserter had, apparently, informed the British of the coming attack but the officer in charge, Major General Hay, could not speak French and so passed him on to Major General Hinuber, of the King's German Legion. Hinuber at least had the foresight to get his men under arms and inform the over-all commander, General Sir John Hope, of the attack. The information came too late, however, and the Foot Guards occupying the siege lines were overrun everywhere.

There followed a tremendous fight in the darkness, with confusion reigning in the British ranks. Trenches were filled in, works destroyed and severe casualties inflicted by the French. Hay himself was killed when the French overran the suburb of St Etienne, while Hope was captured when he rode straight into the middle of French infantry. To add insult to injury, Hope was wounded in the foot by an English musket ball.

The situation was eventually restored, largely through the efforts of Hinuber and the King's German Legion, who threw the French out of St Etienne and stabilised the left-hand end of the British line. Maitland's Foot Guards came up also, having repulsed the French on the right. With the line having been restored and with Maitland leading a counter-attack, Thouvenot decided that his men had done enough damage and the recall was sounded.

Daylight revealed the true extent of the disaster to the British, and a disaster it was too. Over 800 British and German troops had been either killed or wounded, with a further 230 taken prisoner. The French did not get off lightly either, losing over 900 men in what had been a totally futile gesture on the part of Thouvenot. In fact, it was to be another twelve days before he finally accepted that the war was over.

Robert Batty, of the 1st Foot Guards, was commissioned as an ensign in the regiment on 14 January 1813 and sailed to Spain later that year. He saw service throughout the remainder of the Peninsular War and recorded his experiences in his superb book, *The Campaign of the Left Wing of the Allied Army in the Western Pyrenees and South of France*, published in London in 1823. The book provides a wonderful account of the fighting from the Pyrenees onwards but is more renowned for the series of very accurate drawings that are included. Batty was a draughtsman and was well qualified to draw the various scenes that appear in the book. Although it has since appeared in facsimile form, the first edition is highly sought after, not only by military historians but also by collectors of travel books. Serving with the 1st Foot Guards placed him in an ideal — if unenviable — situation to record the events on the tragic night of 14 April 1814.

On the night of the 13th, two deserters came over to the outposts, and gave information that the whole of the garrison was under arms, and prepared to make a sortie early on the following morning. At the early hour of three in the morning the first division was ordered to arms, and in a few minutes afterwards the enemy commenced his movements by a feint attack upon the troops guarding the outposts in front of Anglet. The night was extremely dark, and the view of their onset was very singular from the heights near the citadel; but it was evident, from the little vigour displayed in this feint, that the enemy's chief efforts would not be made on that side. The troops around the citadel did not remain long in suspense, for parties of the French crawled up the side of the hill on which the allied picquets were stationed, and came upon them almost by surprise. Some of the sentinels being instantly put to death, two columns of the French rushed forward with loud cheers of *En avant, En avant*; and, by their overpowering numbers, broke through the line of picquets between St. Etienne and St. Bernard. Another very strong column advanced direct upon the village of St. Etienne, and, in a few moments a most furious contest ensued along the greater part of the line of picquets on the right bank of the Adour.

The cross road which has been already described, marking the line of outposts through the village of St. Etienne, and along the height towards Boucaut, is worn in places to a deep hollow way; or, as the French term it, is a *chemin encaisse*, and the banks at the sides are so steep that it is no easy matter to get out of the road, excepting at long intervals, where gaps were broken down for the passage of the troops; in many places too, it is bounded by high garden walls; and thus, when the French columns broke through the line in different places, part of the picquets were completely cut off from all communication with their supports, and retreat was impossible; in these places the soldiers fought with desperation, and heaps of the slain, both French and English, were afterwards found on the points of attack; most of them had been killed with the bayonet. It was supposed that the enemy would make his principal efforts against the bridge of vessels; and to be in readiness for the approach on that side, Lord Saltoun barricaded every entrance to the old Convent of St. Bernard; this post he had strongly entrenched, and with great ability had converted it into a respectable little fortress. The French gunboats descended the river opposite to the limits of the entrenched camp, and opened a heavy flanking cannonade against the first division, which now

291

moved forward to support the picquets upon the right flank of the line. Major-General Hay, whose division had crossed the Adour some time before, and encamped near Boucaut, was the General in command of the outposts for the night; and, whilst giving directions for the defence of some of the most important buildings in the village of St. Etienne, was unfortunately killed, and the enemy gained possession of nearly the whole of them.

In the early part of the attack, Sir John Hope, accompanied by all his staff, went forward to ascertain the enemy's movements against St. Etienne; and wishing to arrive there by the shortest way, entered the cross road, or lane, before described, not aware that a great part of it was in the enemy's possession, and that the picquets of the right flank had fallen back when the French columns pierced the line of outposts. He had not proceeded far, before he discovered, by a faint glimmer in the horizon, that he was upon the point of riding into the enemy's line, and immediately ordered his staff to face about and get out of the hollow road. The general, with his aide-de-camp Lieutenant Moore, and Captain Herries of the Quarter-Master General's Department, were in front, and consequently the last in retiring; however, before they could get out of the road, the French infantry came up to about twelve yards' distance, and began firing. Sir John Hope's horse received three balls and instantly fell dead, bringing him to the ground, and entangling his foot under its side. Lieutenant Moore and Captain Herries immediately dismounted to his assistance, and were in the act of attempting to raise the General and disengage his foot, when the latter officer fell severely wounded; and, as ill-luck would have it, the instant after a ball struck Lieutenant Moore and shattered his right arm. The General himself received a slight wound in the arm, and the French soldiers instantly came up and made them all prisoners. It appeared that they were only able to extricate Sir John Hope by drawing his leg out of the boot, which was afterwards found under the horse's side. As the French were conducting the General along the road towards Bayonne, he was again struck by a ball, supposed to be fired from our own picquets, which wounded him severely in the foot.

The enemy having thus far completely succeeded in his attack, lost no time in filling up the entrenchments made by the Allies on the line of outposts. They had taken many prisoners, and amongst them was the Honourable Colonel Townshend, commanding the picquets of the first brigade of Guards. Nearly seventy pieces of their artillery had been constantly firing to support their attack; shells were continually flying through the air, describing beautiful curves of light as they fell; and the flashes from the cannon were almost incessant, rendering darkness doubly obscure at any momentary pause.

In this state of the action, Major-General Howard directed Colonel Maitland to support the right flank with the first brigade of Guards; and Major-General Stopford, with the second brigade of Guards, to co-operate in recovering the ground between the right flank and St. Etienne. Major-General Stopford was soon after wounded, leaving the command of the second brigade to General Guise. As it was supposed that the enemy would push on in the direction of Boucaut, with a view to destroy the bridge of vessels, Colonel Maitland formed his brigade on the heights above the old convent of St. Bernard, to be in readiness to charge the enemy in flank, should he advance towards the bridge; but, when it was found that the attack was wholly directed against the centre of the semicircular countervallation opposite to the citadel, he advanced with the third battalion of the First Foot-Guards, under the Honourable Lieutenant-Colonel Stuart, to attack the French in the hollow road, and in the fields in its rear, of which they had gained possession.

On arriving near the French line, which, from the extreme obscurity of the night, we could still only distinguish by the firing of their musketry from behind the hedges and walls, the whole battalion was ordered to lie down on the ground, and await a signal to rush forward and charge; whilst orders were communicated to the Coldstream Guards, under Lieutenant-Colonel Woodford, to make a simultaneous attack for the recovery of the old position in the hollow road. During this interval, a hot fire was kept up by the skirmishers, and several officers and soldiers, in both brigades, were wounded. The third battalion, under Lieutenant-Colonel Stuart, was obliged to keep close to the ground, on a little eminence, which was so exposed to the fire of artillery from the citadel, that, had they stood up for a few moments, they must soon have been nearly annihilated. At length, the signal was given to charge; and the battalion, rising in mass, rushed forward with an appalling shout; the Coldstream battalion, under Lieutenant-Colonel Woodford, charging the enemy in the opposite flank at the same moment. This well-combined attack decided, immediately, the contest on this part of the line; for the French, fearing to have their retreat upon the citadel cut off, ran with all speed to scramble through the difficult hollow lane, which, in a few moments after, was again in possession of the Guards. A most destructive fire was instantly commenced by both battalions against the French, in their retreat over the glacis of the citadel within the covered way.

On the side of St. Etienne, the contest was extremely obstinate; but the enemy in vain endeavoured to take possession of a house occupied by Captain Foster of the Thirty-eighth regiment, who bravely maintained his post, although the greater part of his men were killed and wounded, till the brigade of the King's German Legion, commanded by Major-General Hinuber, retook the village, and rescued this brave officer and his intrepid little garrison. When the enemy was driven out of St. Etienne, a field-piece was brought to bear on the retreating columns, and no less than thirteen rounds of grape and canister shot were fired with effect at them, as they retreated down the great road into St. Esprit: the slaughter at this point was terrific.

Towards the close of the action, the moon had risen, and, as dawn broke over the scene of battle, we began to discern the dreadful havoc that had been made; the French and English soldiers and officers were lying on all sides, either killed or wounded; and so intermixed were they that there appeared to have been no distinct line belonging to either party.

It would be almost impossible to convey an idea of the effect produced by the numerous flashes from the cannon and the sparkling light from the musketry, or of the confused noise from the roar of cannon. the bursting of shells, and the cheers of the soldiers, inter-mingled with the piercing shrieks and groans of the dying and wounded. At times the darkness was in part dispelled by the bright blue light of fire-balls thrown from the citadel, to show the assailants where to direct their guns; which they effectually did, by the great brilliancy with which they burned. Some of these fire-balls and shells fell in the midst of the depot of fascines, which instantly caught fire and burnt with great fierceness; so as to require constant exertions before they could be extinguished. Several houses caught fire, and two in particular burnt for a time with great violence, casting a lurid light under the vaulted clouds of smoke which rose to the skies. It seemed as if the elements of destruction had all burst forth together over this deep ensanguined scene of two contending armies.

The loss, as may well be imagined, was severe, during so hard a conflict on a narrowly circumscribed space. It amounted, of the Allies, to nearly eight hundred men, of whom about three hundred were prisoners. The loss of the French was much more severe; besides a general of brigade and a great number of officers killed, their ascertained loss in killed, wounded, and prisoners, was nine hundred and thirteen, but of these there were barely twenty prisoners. Independent of the mortification caused by the capture of their General-in-Chief, the left wing had to lament the loss of many brave officers. In the brigades of Guards, Lieutenant-Colonel Sir Henry Sullivan, and Captain Crofton of the Coldstream Regiment, were killed, and about twelve officers of the three regiments received severe wounds, and unhappily most of these proved fatal.

After the engagement was over, a momentary truce took place on the out-posts, and the officers of both armies conversed together. On our expressing the deep regret we felt at the useless sacrifice that had been made of so many brave men, it was quite disgusting to observe the nonchalance affected by these gentlemen, and the light manner in which they pretended to treat it, remarking that, after all, it was nothing more than a petite promenade mili-taire. But it would be difficult to convey an idea of their astonishment, when we informed them of the events which had recently occurred in Paris, and they would not believe it possible that their idol Napoleon had abdicated the throne.

But notwithstanding they could now no longer be ignorant of the termina-tion of the war, the French still manifested the same jealousy of the Allies, and continued occasionally firing from the citadel and works. Major-General Colville succeeded Sir John Hope in the command of the left wing, and unremitting vigilance was observed on the outposts till the cessation of hos-tilities.

Ensign Edmund Wheatley, of the 5th Line Battalion, King's German Legion, found himself in the thick of this confused action. The KGL, in fact, played a major part in holding the line and thrusting the French back. Wheatley's account of the fight is to be found in his journal, *The Wheatley Diary*.

Last night the 47th and two other Regiments relieved our brigade in order to give us three nights' rest, our physical strength being so much reduced. Nothing and self slept together in the same tent.

The whole Battalion went to bed very early. I undressed for the first time in seven weeks and had sank into a sound repose. About two o'clock this morn-ing Captain Notting cried out, 'Wheatley, Wheatley, don't you hear?' I lis-tened and said, 'Only the outposts skirmishing,' and fell asleep instantly. Nothing again awoke me with, 'I'm sure the French are coming out. Hark!' I heard a pop, then another. All was silent again, and I was on the point of again falling off, when more than five hundred reports burst upon our ears, a thunder of cannon followed, and loud cries of 'Fall in!' 'Fall in!' echoed over the hills and heaths.

The repeated flashes of the cannon from Bayonne and the shells in the air enabled us to find our clothes and in five minutes the whole Brigade was on its way. Nothing could equal the beauty of the scene. The stillness of night doubled the report of the ordnance. The air filled with stars and shells like a Vauxhall exhibition; and the very earth appeared like a mirror reflecting the lights of the atmosphere, for every bush and hedge was spangled with flashing stars from the musketry, and the fields covered with blue lights shot from Bayonne to show the men on the ramparts when our troops passed where to direct their guns.

An immense bomb hovered over our heads and in the act of falling scattered our battalion over a large field. But men are like sheep. A common danger attracts them; and they soon returned to a body, the Officers being the nucleus of attraction.

The little I have read of gunnery has informed me never to avoid a shell in the air and I cannot persuade my brother Officers to imitate me. Llewellyn and myself on this occasion put it into practice; for I ran to meet it, by which means you avoid it as is generally the case in all apparent danger. On getting into the heat of the fight I found the warfare an unpleasant one, as not a soul could be seen. Now and then a voice in the hedge would say 'Francais ou Anglais?' and a thrust through the bush was an answer. Our Brigade Major, Dreschel, lost his life that way. The same question was put to him and instead of jumping into it, he proudly answered, 'A German,' when a ball in his groin convinced him how much the snake in the bush respected his nativity. Giesmann and Buhse seized the Frenchman and sent him in the rear, an honourable prisoner. Lord Ellenborough would have acted otherwise. What incongruity!

Our Battalion now drew up in a small garden. The French were around us and it was impossible to distinguish Friends from foes. The French had seized the Windmill in our rear and we began to fear for our Camp and baggage. The batteries played increasingly, and the wounded lay very numerous around. It was impossible to send them in the rear as no hospital had been appointed. By the flashes of light I saw something wrapped in a boat cloak on the other side of the hedge.

Impelled by curiosity as well as humanity, I broke through and on turning it up I washed away the blood and gore from the features with the skirt of the wrapper and discovered the countenance of Lieutenant Kohler of my Regiment. My promotion instantly suggested itself and thoughts of my own danger. I walked up to Captain Bacmeister and, bowing, said in the midst of the shot, 'Allow me to introduce Lieutenant E. Wheatley to your notice.' And I actually received his congratulation. Can there be any thirst for glory when actions like these take place on the fields of havoc? Ambition's made of sterner stuff. Interest is the impulse in these our modern wars. Paulus Emilius threw his spoils into the public treasury. I throw mine into my private pocket.

Nothing could be more harassing than our occupation till daybreak — firing at hazard, the men dropping, killed by an invisible adversary.

In the warmth of a volley of small arms a ball came through the hedge, tore off the fourth button on my right breast, went through Notting's arm and severely wounded Bacmeister in the knee. He fell. Notting, in his fear, begged of me to keep from him as no luck ensued where I was, and I'm sure no good results from his society. Nor do I know who ever is benefited by it.

As soon as daylight appeared, a little amusement began. We drove the French back with the bayonet, scoured the fields, gave three huzzas and stood behind the stone walls from the cannon shot. While engaged firing over these places, I was surprised by something heavily falling in the earth without noise. So watching the next fall, I went up to the spot and turning up the earth with my sword discovered a cannon ball within. Astonished, I fancied the very clouds were firing upon us; so, telling Llewellyn, we watched and at last discovered that the French, to save shells, fired their shot perpendicularly in order to catch us in our hiding places.

About eight o'clock the French ceased firing and looking into the Town I discovered the three coloured flag down and the white hoisted.

A solemn pause of half an hour ensued and then a sudden order to bury the dead came round. The French poured out from the town, unarmed, and a singular scene ensued — they picking up their dead, and we ours. I went under the French batteries and had a long chat with some French Officers who gave me some snuff. And as the French soldiers passed us with their dead comrades, we reflected on the miserable trade of war.

Suddenly a blank shot was fired from the Citadel. We hastily shook hands and in five minutes I was as eager to shoot them as they had been to present their *râpé* to me.

About half past nine we returned to camp, triumphantly playing our Regimental march in spite of their shot, and I now write this next the tent wherein lie Meyer and Kohler smashed and lacerated. Last night they rejoiced over the social bowl. Tonight the voice of mirth and jollity is still to them forever. Had we all the spirit of divination the prospect of inevitable destruction open to our view would embitter every worldly joy. The goodness of God is manifest in this point, and evidently testifies his omniscience as well as the beneficence of his dealings towards us in suffering our future happenings to depend upon our own gratitude and actions towards him.

The sortie from Bayonne was a total waste of life. It achieved nothing

297

whatsoever, other than to stoke up ill-feeling between victors and vanquished. Indeed, it was with great sorrow that the officers of the two brigades of Foot Guards buried their dead afterwards, including the last of hundreds of British soldiers, killed during the war. We know the name of the first British officer to be killed in the Peninsula; Lieutenant Ralph Bunbury of the 95th Rifles. But what of the last casualty? Laying good claim to that dubious distinction is Captain John Dobbs, of the 52nd Light Infantry, but serving with the 5th Caçadores at the time of his wound. Dobbs, who had lost his brother, Joseph, at the storming of Ciudad Rodrigo, was wounded by the last shot fired during the last action, at Bayonne. He also wrote what is perhaps the rarest of Peninsular War memoirs, *Recollections of an Old 52nd Man*, published in Waterford in 1863. The book has eluded even the most thorough bibliographies and does not appear in any of the great works on the campaign. Dobbs served in Sweden with Sir John Moore, before taking part in the Peninsular War, serving with distinction throughout the entire campaign. Our last short extract, written by a veteran of Wellington's army, comes, therefore, from its last casualty, John Dobbs.

With the exception of a shot from the fortress, (when they could get an object to fire at), nothing particular occurred till the 14th of April, when the enemy made a sortie on our advanced posts at St. Etienne, and succeeded in forcing their way through our troops, killed General Hay, and taking General Hope and Colonel Townsend prisoners. General Hay's wife and daughters had joined him from England a few days before the sortie. General Hinuber with his Germans succeeded in stopping the enemy; in this engagement the 6th Caçadores took an active part.

We occupied a gentleman's country house in rear of the outposts, and having heard the night before of the Peace having been concluded at Paris, the Governor of Bayonne having likewise been informed of it, we retired to rest under the impression that the last shot had been fired — what was our astonishment to be awakened a little before daylight by the enemy's balls flying through our windows. A few minutes found us under arms, and on the left of the Germans, with whom we advanced to the relief of the troops engaged, driving the French into their fortress. Being in command of a wing of the Caçadores, I had them in column in front of the citadel, waiting to see if any further attack would take place, when a ball from the walls wounded one of my men, on which I moved the column behind a house on my left, remaining myself on the look out. Suddenly I felt a blow on the shin, and on looking down found that a ball had entered between the two bones, carrying in a piece of the trousers, which I believe was the last shot fired.

On returning to my quarters I found it occupied as a hospital. General Hay lay dead in the room I had slept in, and General Bradford was under the hands of a surgeon. On seeing me General Bradford ordered the surgeon to stop, and attend to my wound before he finished his dressing.

Bayonne was subsequently declared out of bounds to British troops who were required to have passes before entering the town. The men then marched north to Bordeaux where they joined Wellington's main field army. From here the infantry and supporting arms sailed home to England whilst the cavalry marched in three great columns back through France for the channel ports from where they sailed home to England.

The Peninsular War was Britain's main military effort during the Napoleonic Wars, and saw the emergence of one of the finest armies ever to fight for Britain. The battles featured in this book are now enshrined in British regimental history, but the great army that flushed Soult from his position on the Nivelle, which thrashed the French at Salamanca and Vittoria, and which stormed the fiery breaches of Badajoz, was destined not to play a part in the final act of the wars, for the ink was barely dry upon Napoleon's letter of abdication than the British government set in motion plans for the dispersal of Wellington's victorious army. Thus, when the Corsican ogre escaped from exile on the island of Elba, in February 1815, Wellington was forced to rely upon an 'infamous army,' one which was a pale shadow of that which had fought in the Peninsula. We will never know how that all-conquering army would have fared at Waterloo, but it is a safe bet that the outcome of the battle on 18 June 1815 would have been much less of a close run thing had the Connaught Rangers, The Buffs or The Die Hards, for example, been present. But it was not to be. Instead, we must satisfy ourselves with reflecting upon the great battles and sieges that took place between 1808 and 1814, which have been the subject of this book.

The extracts thus far in this book have all come from the officers and men of Wellington's army, who formed part of one of the finest armies Britain has ever sent to war. But what of its great chief, Wellington himself? Well, his *Despatches* appeared in 1832, edited by John Gurwood, who had served with the 52nd Light Infantry. These twelve volumes remain a prime source for anybody researching the Peninsular War,

299

and, indeed, any of Wellington's battles. In addition to these volumes, there are literally scores of books written by friends and associates who appear to have been hanging on every word the great man said. Indeed, it appears that it was not possible for Wellington to sneeze without somebody making a note of it! Fortunately, this has provided us with quote after quote from him, not only referring to his military campaigns but his views on all manner of subjects.

It is, perhaps, fitting to leave the last word with Wellington, who summed up his part in the Peninsular War with typical understatement. Speaking in 1846, he said, 'I went abroad and took command of the Army, and never returned, or even quitted the field, till the nations of the Peninsula...were delivered from the French armies; till I had invaded France, won the battle of Toulouse; established the British Army within French territory; of which I governed several departments; till the general peace was signed at Paris; and the British cavalry, sent by sea to Portugal, Spain and the south of France, marched home across France, and embarked for England in the ports of France in the English Channel!'

BIBLIOGRAPHY

Anon. *The Personal narrative of a Private Soldier who served in the 42nd Highlanders for twelve years during the late war.* (London, 1821.)

Anon. *Memoirs of a Sergeant late in the Forty-Third Light Infantry Regiment, previously to and during the Peninsular War.* (London, 1835.)

Anton, James. *Retrospect of a Military Life, During the Most Eventful Periods of the Last War.* (Edinburgh, 1841.)

Batty, Captain Robert. *Campaign of the Left Wing of the Allied Army in the Western Pyrenees and South of France in the years 1813–1814, under Field Marshal the Marquess of Wellington.* (London, 1823.)

Bell, Sir George. *Rough Notes of an Old Soldier during Fifty Years' Service, by Major General Sir George Bell.* Edited by B. Stuart. (London, 1867.)

Bingham, Lt. Col. George Ridout. Typescript of MSS Letters, written between 1809 and 1814.

Blakeney, Robert. *A Boy in the Peninsular War; the Services, Adventures and Experiences of Robert Blakeney, subaltern in the 28th Regiment.* Edited by J. Sturgis. (London, 1899.)

Brooke, Major William. 'A Prisoner of Albuera.' In *Studies in the Napoleonic Wars.* (London, 1929).

Brown, William. *The Autobiography or Narrative of a Soldier.* (Kilmarnock, 1829.)

Burroughs, George Frederick. *A Narrative of the Retreat of the British Army from Burgos, in a series of letters.* (Bristol, 1814.)

Clarke, S.L. *The Life of the Most Noble Arthur, Marquis and Earl of Wellington.* (London, 1812.)

Cooke, Captain John. *Memoirs of the Late War, comprising the personal narrative of Captain Cooke of the 43rd Regiment of Infantry.* (London, 1831.)

Cooper, John Spencer. *Rough Notes of Seven Campaigns in Portugal, Spain, France and America, during the years 1809, 10, 11, 12, 13, 14, 15.* (Carlisle, 1869).

Costello, Edward. *The Adventures of a Soldier, or memoirs of Edward Costello, formerly a non-commissioned officer in the Rifle Brigade and late captain in the British Legion, comprising narratives of the campaigns in the Peninsula.* (London, 1841)

Dobbs, Captain John. *Recollections of an Old 52nd Man.* (Waterford, 1863.)

Donaldson, Joseph. *Recollections of the Eventful Life of a Soldier.* (Edinburgh, 1845.)

Eadie, Robert. *Recollections of Robert Eadie, private of His Majesty's 79th Regiment of Infantry, giving a concise account of his campaigns in Ireland, Denmark, Walcheren and the Peninsula.* (Kincardine, 1829.)

Frazer, Augustus. *Letters of Colonel Sir Augustus Frazer, KCB, commanding the Royal Horse Artillery in the army under the Duke of Wellington, written during the Peninsular and Waterloo Campaigns.* Edited by Major General Edward Sabine. (London, 1859.)

Gleig, G. *The Subaltern.* (London, 1825.)

Good, Surgeon Samuel. Quoted in *The History of the Scots Guards, 1642–1914.* By Major General Sir F. Maurice. (London, 1934.)

Gordon, Captain. *A Cavalry Officer in the Corunna Campaign, 1808–1809.* Edited by Col. H. C. Wylly. (London, 1847.)

Grattan, William. *Adventures with the Connaught Rangers, 1809–1814.* Edited by Charles Oman. (London, 1902.)

Green, John. *The Vicissitudes of a Soldiers's Life, or a series of occurrences from 1806 50 1815.* (Louth, 1827.)

Hale, James. *Journal of James Hale, late Sergeant 9th Foot.* (Cirencester, 1826.)

Hay, Captain William. *Reminiscences under Wellington, 1809–1815.* Edited by Mrs S. Wood. (London, 1901.)

Henry, Walter. *Events of a Military Life: Being recollections after service in the Peninsular War, the invasion of France, the East Indies, Saint Helena, Canada and elsewhere.* (London, 1843.)

Hopkins, Lieutenant John. Quoted in *Historical Records of the Forty-Third Regiment, Monmouthshire Light Infantry.* By Sir Richard Levinge. (London, 1868.)

Keep, William Thornton. *In the Service of the King: The Letters of William Thornton Keep, at Home, Walcheren, and in the Peninsula, 1808–1814.* Edited by Ian Fletcher. (Staplehurst, 1997.)

Landsheit, Norbert. *The Hussar: The Story of Norbert Landsheit, Sergeant in the York Hussars and the 20th Light Dragoons.* Edited by G. R. Gleig. (London, 1837.)

Lawrence, William. *Autobiography of Sergeant William Lawrence, a hero of the Peninsular and Waterloo Campaigns.* Edited by G. N. Bankes. (London, 1886.)

Malcolm, John. 'Reminiscences of the Campaign in the Pyrenees and the South of France in 1813–14.' In *Constable's Memorials of the Late War.* (Edinburgh, 1828.)

McLean, Lieutenant John. Quoted in *Historical Records of the Forty-Third Regiment, Monmouthshire Light Infantry.* By Sir Richard Levinge. (London, 1868.)

Mills, John. *For King and Country: The Letters and Diaries of John Mills, Coldstream Guards, 1811–1814*. Edited by Ian Fletcher. (Staplehurst, 1995.)

Morley, Stephen. *Memoirs of a Sergeant of the 5th Regiment of Foot, containing an account of his service in Hanover, South America and the Peninsula*. (Ashford, 1842).

Napier, General Sir George T. *Passages in the Early Military Life of General Sir George T. Napier*. Edited by his son, General W. C. E. Napier. (London, 1884.)

Patterson, Captain John. *The Adventures of Captain John Patterson, with notices of the 50th or the Queen's Reginment from 1807 to 1821*. (London, 1837.)

Schaumann, Augustus. *On the Road with Wellington: The Diary of a War Commissary in the Peninsular Campaigns*. Edited by A. M. Ludovici. (London, 1924.)

Sherer, Moyle. *Recollections of the Peninsula*. (London, 1824.)

Simmons, Major George. *A British Rifle Man: The Journals and Correspondence of Major George Simmons, Rifle Brigade, During the Peninsular War and Campaign of Waterloo*. Edited by Lt. Col. W. Verner. (London, 1899.)

Wheatley, Edmund. *The Wheatley Diary: A Journal and Sketchbook kept during the Peninsular War and the Waterloo Campaign*. Edited by Christopher Hibbert. (London, 1964.)

Wheeler, William. *Letters of Private Wheeler, 1809–1828*. Edited by Basil Liddell Hart. (London, 1951.)